Lecture Notes in Computer Science   15351

Founding Editors

Gerhard Goos
Juris Hartmanis

Editorial Board Members

The series Lecture Notes in Computer Science (LNCS), including its subseries Lecture Notes in Artificial Intelligence (LNAI) and Lecture Notes in Bioinformatics (LNBI), has established itself as a medium for the publication of new developments in computer science and information technology research, teaching, and education.

LNCS enjoys close cooperation with the computer science R & D community, the series counts many renowned academics among its volume editors and paper authors, and collaborates with prestigious societies. Its mission is to serve this international community by providing an invaluable service, mainly focused on the publication of conference and workshop proceedings and postproceedings. LNCS commenced publication in 1973.

Johann Knechtel · Urbi Chatterjee ·
Domenic Forte

Editors

Security, Privacy, and Applied Cryptography Engineering

14th International Conference, SPACE 2024
Kottayam, India, December 14–17, 2024
Proceedings

 Springer

Editors
Johann Knechtel
New York University Abu Dhabi
Abu Dhabi, Abu Dhabi, United Arab
Emirates

Urbi Chatterjee
Indian Institute of Technology Kanpur
Kanpur, Uttar Pradesh, India

Domenic Forte
University of Florida
Gainesville, FL, USA

ISSN 0302-9743   ISSN 1611-3349 (electronic)
Lecture Notes in Computer Science
ISBN 978-3-031-80407-6   ISBN 978-3-031-80408-3 (eBook)
https://doi.org/10.1007/978-3-031-80408-3

Preface

The 14th International Conference on Security, Privacy and Applied Cryptographic Engineering (SPACE 2024) was held from December 14–17, 2024 at the Indian Institute of Information Technology Kottayam, Kerala, India. This annual conference serves as a vital platform for researchers and practitioners to delve into the latest advancements and challenges in security, privacy, applied cryptography, and cryptographic engineering. This interdisciplinary field demands a unique blend of expertise, drawing from areas such as mathematics, computer science, and electrical engineering.

This year, SPACE 2024 received 43 submissions from a diverse range of authors representing India, Singapore, Vietnam, Australia, Italy, Switzerland, UAE, USA, and Austria. These submissions underwent a rigorous double-blind review process, each with three meticulously prepared reviews by 50 TPC members from India, UAE, USA, Germany, Belgium, Singapore, Canada, China, Israel, and the Netherlands. Notably, India and UAE each contributed 14 TPC members, highlighting the collaborative spirit and research ties between these two nations. Ultimately, 8 submissions were accepted as regular full papers, resulting in a competitive acceptance rate of approximately 19%, upholding SPACE's strong commitment to quality and selectivity.

In a new development for SPACE, this year's conference introduced two additional paper categories: work-in-progress papers and extended abstracts. Work-in-progress papers, while demonstrating promising novelty and merit, were not yet mature enough to be accepted as full papers. By still accepting these submissions and providing authors with a platform for short presentations, SPACE aims to nurture innovative ideas and foster early-stage research within the community. A total of six such work-in-progress papers were accepted, bringing the overall acceptance rate to around 33%, aligning with the inclusive level of previous SPACE conferences.

Four extended abstracts, which are exclusively linked to poster submissions, were carefully selected for acceptance by the poster chairs. This process put particular emphasis on how effectively the core ideas and findings of the posters would be communicated to the broader audience through the form of such extended abstracts.

A common thread running through the various works presented at SPACE 2024 was the integration of machine learning techniques, reflecting the growing prominence of this approach in contemporary research on security and cryptography. Furthermore, the conference showcased a strong focus on hardware security, the exploration of post-quantum cryptography, and the development of efficient implementations for emerging cryptographic primitives.

Beyond the proceedings, SPACE 2024 featured a rich program that included four insightful keynote talks by distinguished speakers such as Navid Asadi (UFL), David Johnston (Independent, previously with Intel), and Ulrich Rührmair (TU Berlin and UConn). The conference also hosted seven workshops and tutorials covering a wide array of topics including Oblivious RAM, Secure Multi-party Computation, Hardware Security, Fault Attacks, Post-Quantum Cryptography, Counterfeit Electronics Detection, and Hardware Design for Cryptographic Accelerators. These sessions were led by experts like Adithya Vadapalli (IIT Kanpur), Utsav Banerjee (IISc Bangalore), Sayandeep Saha (IIT Bombay), Sarani Bhattacharya (IIT Kharagpur), Domenic Forte (UFL), Johann Knechtel (NYUAD), and Debapriya Basu Roy (IIT Kanpur). Furthermore, SPACE 2024 fostered industry engagement through dedicated talks and a liaison session with representatives from Vehere, IBM Research, and Texas Instruments, bridging the gap between academic research and real-world applications.

The success of SPACE 2024 would not have been possible without the dedication and contributions of numerous individuals. We extend our sincere gratitude to the General Chairs, Anupam Chattopadhyay (Nanyang Technological University, Singapore) and Chester Rebeiro (Indian Institute of Technology Madras), for their leadership and guidance. We also thank the Organizing Chair, Panchami V. (Indian Institute of Information Technology Kottayam), and all local colleagues, for their meticulous planning and execution of the event. Our appreciation goes to the Poster Chairs, Chandan Karfa (IIT Guwahati) and Sayandeep Saha (IIT Bombay), for their careful selection of poster presentations. We acknowledge the efforts of the Web Chair, Debapriya Basu Roy (IIT Kanpur), for ensuring a seamless online experience. We thank the Steering Committee, comprising Debdeep Mukhopadhyay (Indian Institute of Technology Kharagpur), Chester Rebeiro (Indian Institute of Technology Madras), Veezhinathan Kamakoti (Indian Institute of Technology Madras), and Ulrich Rührmair (Technical University Berlin and University of Connecticut), for their valuable insights and strategic direction.

We also thank the team behind EasyChair, which enabled a smooth handling of all the review and proceedings tasks, despite some hardware glitches for their third-party webhosting. We thank our publisher Springer for agreeing to continue to publish the SPACE proceedings as a volume in the Lecture Notes in Computer Science (LNCS) series. Finally, we gratefully acknowledge the support of the cybersecurity company Vehere for their sponsorship contribution to the conference.

October 2024

Johann Knechtel
Urbi Chatterjee
Domenic Forte

Organization

Program Committee

Lilas Alrahis	Khalifa University, UAE
N. Nalla Anandakumar	Continental Automotive, Singapore
Victor Arribas	Rambus, The Netherlands
Arnab Bag	Indian Institute of Technology Kharagpur, India
Utsav Banerjee	Indian Institute of Science, India
Debapriya Basu Roy	IIT Kanpur, India
Jitendra Bhandari	New York University, USA
Shivam Bhasin	Temasek Labs@NTU, Singapore
Sarani Bhattacharya	Indian Institute of Technology Kharagpur, India
Alessandro Budroni	Technology Innovation Institute, UAE
Isaac Canales	Technology Innovation Institute, UAE
Rajat Subhra Chakraborty	IIT Kharagpur, India
Durba Chatterjee	Radboud University, The Netherlands
Urbi Chatterjee	Indian Institute of Technology Kanpur, India
Andre Esser	Technology Innovation Institute, UAE
Domenic Forte	University of Florida, USA
Wei Hu	Northwestern Polytechnical University, China
Paul Huynh	Technology Innovation Institute, UAE
Vincent Immler	Oregon State University, USA
Ramya Jayaram Masti	Ampere Computing, USA
Kyle Juretus	Villanova University, USA
Angshuman Karmakar	Katholieke Universiteit Leuven, Belgium
Rupesh Raj Karn	New York University Abu Dhabi, UAE
Elif Bilge Kavun	University of Passau, Germany
Johann Knechtel	New York University, USA
Mukul Kulkarni	Technology Innovation Institute, UAE
Itamar Levi	UCL, Belgium
Nimisha Limaye	Synopsys, USA
R. Sumesh Manjunath	New York University, USA
Likhitha Mankali	New York University, USA
Victor Mateu	Technology Innovation Institute, UAE
Robert Merget	Technology Innovation Institute, UAE
Mainack Mondal	Indian Institute of Technology, Kharagpur, India
Thorben Moos	Université catholique de Louvain, Belgium
Colin O'Flynn	NewAE Technology Inc., Canada

Rogerio Paludo	Technology Innovation Institute, UAE
Satwik Patnaik	University of Delaware, USA
Sikhar Patranabis	IBM Research India, India
Michael Pehl	Technical University of Munich, Germany
Rajesh Pillai	Government of India, India
Raghvendra Rohit	Technology Innovation Institute, UAE
Kala S.	IIIT Kottayam, India
Somitra Sanadhya	IIT Jodhpur, India
Pascal Sasdrich	Ruhr-University Bochum, Germany
Patrick Schaumont	Worcester Polytechnic Institute, USA
Dean Sullivan	University of New Hampshire, USA
Mohammed Nabeel Thari Moopan	New York University, USA
Adithya Vadapalli	IIT Kanpur, India
Ricardo Luis Villanueva Polanco	Technology Innovation Institute, UAE
Keita Xagawa	Technology Innovation Institute, UAE

Additional Reviewers

Bohra, Dixit
Buschkowski, Fabian
Chaturvedi, Bhuvnesh
Ghosh, Bishakh Chandra
Gupta, Sanchit
Sadhukhan, Rajat
Schinkel, Armand
Stelzer, Tobias
Varshney, Nitin
Yap, Trevor
Zweydinger, Floyd

Contents

Attacks and Countermeasures for Digital Microfluidic Biochips
Extended Abstract

Navajit Singh Baban[1(✉)], Prithwish Basu Roy[2], Pauline John[1], Azhar Zam[1,2], Sukanta Bhattacharjee[3], Yong-Ak Song[1,2], Ramesh Karri[2], and Krishnendu Chakrabarty[4]

[1] Division of Engineering, New York University Abu Dhabi, Abu Dhabi, United Arab Emirates
{nsb359,pj2266,az2832,rafael.song}@nyu.edu
[2] Tandon School of Engineering, New York University, New York, USA
{pb2718,rkarri}@nyu.edu
[3] Department of Computer Science and Engineering, Indian Institute of Technology Guwahati, Guwahati, India
sukantab@iitg.ac.in
[4] School of Electrical, Computer and Energy Engineering, Arizona State University, Tempe, USA
krishnendu.chakrabarty@asu.edu

Abstract. Digital Microfluidic Biochips (DMFBs) precisely control droplets on an electrode array, making them vital for healthcare. However, they are vulnerable to numerous security threats, including structural modifications during the design phase, material vulnerabilities in manufacturing, and code-level cyber-physical attacks. These risks encompass microstructural changes, chemical tampering, and manipulation of bioprotocols. This study experimentally demonstrates these attacks on a commercial DMFB and proposes using the optical coherence tomography (OCT) technique as a countermeasure to detect structural and material anomalies, along with hash-based techniques for code-level defense.

Keywords: Digital Microfluidic Biochips · Cyber-physical Security · Optical Coherence Tomography · Plasma · Hash · Droplet

1 Introduction

Digital Microfluidic Biochips (DMFBs) use electrowetting-on-dielectric (EWOD) technology for precise droplet control, enabling bioprotocols-automated sequences of chemical or biological tasks designed for precise and efficient biochemical analyses [1]. However, DMFBs face security threats across various stages, including stealthy structural modifications during design, such as micro-level alterations to electrode or dielectric thickness [2]; material vulnerabilities like chemical degradation during manufacturing [3]; and bioprotocol code alterations, which can lead to faulty diagnostics and denial of service (DoS) [4]. Using

J. Knechtel et al. (Eds.): SPACE 2024, LNCS 15351, pp. 1–5, 2025.
https://doi.org/10.1007/978-3-031-80408-3_1

benchtop techniques, we demonstrate material-level plasma-induced surface wettability attacks and code-level electric arc attacks caused by droplets engulfing high-voltage lines. As countermeasures, we propose OCT-based techniques for detecting structural and material threats, along with hash function-based code-level security measures to safeguard DMFBs.

2   Background and Threat Model

The complex supply chain of DMFBs, combined with high market demand, creates opportunities for cyber-physical attacks to jeopardize patient safety [2]. Attackers may include disgruntled employees, industrial saboteurs, third-party insiders, or opportunistic actors, motivated by personal grievances or illicit monetary gains [3]. Figure 1 presents a threat model outlining potential attack stages across the DMFB supply chain, from design to customer delivery [3]. In the design phase, attackers may stealthily modify structural aspects, like electrode thickness or dielectric layers, which evade detection in standard quality checks [4]. During manufacturing, attackers may introduce harmful chemicals into critical material components or alter machine parameters, compromising the reliability of DMFBs [3]. After quality control, tampering with components or modifying bioprotocol can cause system failures, inaccurate diagnostics, or denial of service (DoS).

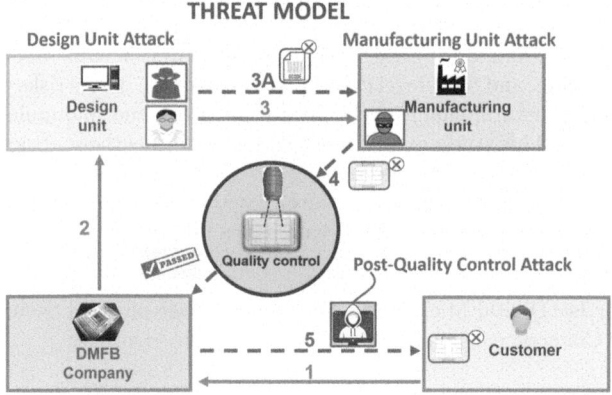

Fig. 1. Threat model for DMFBs.

3   Methodology

This work demonstrates two attack vectors: plasma attacks at the material level, altering wettability and disrupting droplet behavior, and code-level electric arc attacks, triggering deliberate short circuits.

3.1   Plasma Attacks

Employing benchtop techniques, we performed a plasma attack on a commercial DMFB by directing oxygen plasma from a plasma gun (Fig. 2a) onto a 4 mm^2 region of the DMFB's top plate for 5 s. This treatment effectively etched the superhydrophobic layer, compromising surface wettability and subsequently altering droplet shape and dynamics.

3.2   Electric Arc Attacks

Open-source DMFB code allows attackers to modify the user interface (UI), keeping the device at a hardcoded high voltage even when a lower voltage is selected [5]. We executed this by setting one electrode to a lower voltage and another to a higher one, causing the droplet to move toward the high-voltage electrode, resulting in an electric arc.

4   Results

Figure 2 illustrates material-level plasma attacks and code-level-induced electric arc attacks on DMFBs, along with proposed OCT-based countermeasures. Plasma attacks (Fig. 2b) alter surface wettability, impacting droplet shape and movement, while electric arc attacks (Fig. 2c and Fig. 2d) use high voltage to force and engulf droplets into adjacent lines, resulting in short circuits. Plasma attacks can be introduced both during manufacturing and after quality control, subtly altering surface properties and disrupting droplet manipulation. In

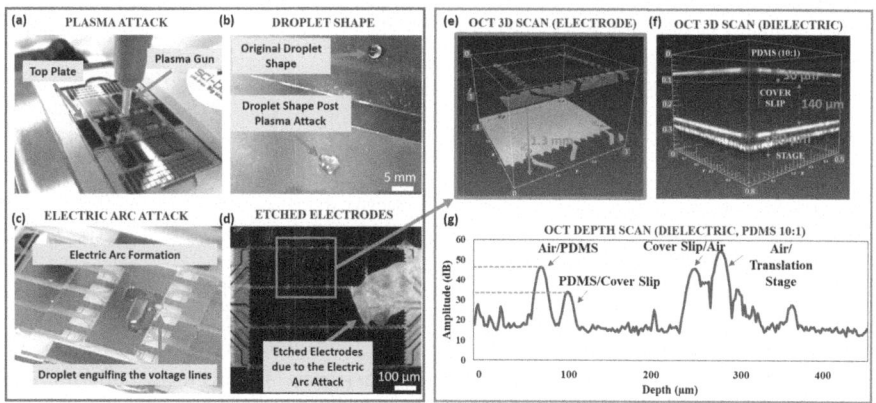

Fig. 2. Attacks and countermeasures for DMFBs: Plasma attacks (a, b) and electric arc attacks (c, d) on DMFBs (red border), alongside OCT-based countermeasures for microstructural (e, f) and material-level (g) detection (green border), highlighting its noninvasive, layer-by-layer detection capability with high resolution down to a few micrometers. (Color figure online)

contrast, electric arc attacks can be launched by malicious code modifications that display an intended voltage on the user interface, while a higher voltage is applied at the physical level, causing droplets to engulf high-voltage lines and induce short circuits.

5   Countermeasures

To prevent code-level cyber-physical attacks on DMFBs, we propose verifying each execution by comparing the hash of a trusted reference executable with that of the current version upon each execution [5]. DMFBs face numerous threats, especially from structural and material levels [6]. To counter them, we propose OCT-based measures that use low-coherence light source to capture interference signals, creating high-resolution 3D images [7]. We conducted an OCT scan on the commercial DMFB, precisely identifying subsurface thicknesses (Fig. 2e: combined dielectric and electrode thickness, 1.3 mm) and (Fig. 2f: poly-dimethylsiloxane (PDMS) thickness, 30 μm). Moreover, using PDMS (10:1 curing ratio), we demonstrate that material irregularities can be detected through depth-specific signal variations, including peak locations and distances between them (Fig. 2g). We conducted an OCT test on PDMS samples with a 30:1 curing ratio, revealing signals that were significantly different from those of the 10:1 standard. A similar approach could be adopted to detecting material anomalies in DMFBs.

6   Conclusion

We demonstrated plasma and electric arc attacks on DMFBs and proposed OCT- and hash-based countermeasures to address structural, material, and code-level vulnerabilities, enhancing DMFB security.

References

1. Baban, N., et al.: Biotrojans: viscoelastic microvalve-based attacks in flow-based microfluidic biochips and their countermeasures. Sci. Rep. **14** (2024). https://doi.org/10.1038/s41598-024-70703-0
2. Baban, N.S., et al.: Physically unclonable fingerprints for authentication. In: International Conference on Applied Cryptography and Network Security, pp. 235–239. Springer, Heidelberg (2024). https://doi.org/10.1007/978-3-031-61489-7_21
3. Baban, N.S., et al.: Material-level countermeasures for securing microfluidic biochips. Lab Chip **23**, 4213–4231 (2023). https://doi.org/10.1039/D3LC00335C
4. Baban, N.S., et al.: Structural attacks and defenses for flow-based microfluidic biochips. IEEE Trans. Biomed. Circuits Syst. **16**(6), 1261–1275 (2022). https://doi.org/10.1109/TBCAS.2022.3220758
5. Belikovetsky, S., Yampolskiy, M., Toh, J., Gatlin, J., Elovici, Y.: dr0wned-cyber-physical attack with additive manufacturing. In: USENIX Workshop on Offensive Technologies (WOOT) (2017)

6. Mohammed, S., Bhattacharjee, S., Song, Y.A., Chakrabarty, K., Karri, R.: Security of Biochip Cyberphysical Systems. Springer, Heidelberg (2022)
7. Zam, A., et al.: Feasibility of correlation mapping optical coherence tomography (cmoct) for anti-spoof sub-surface fingerprinting. J. Biophotonics **6**(9), 663–667 (2013). https://doi.org/10.1002/jbio.201200231. Sep

SideLink: Exposing NVLink to Covert and Side-Channel Attacks Official Work-in-Progress Paper

Issa Baddour[✉][iD], Dip Sankar Banerjee[iD], and Somitra Kumar Sanadhya[iD]

Indian Institute of Technology, Jodhpur, Jodhpur 342030, Rajasthan, India
{baddour.1,dipsankarb,somitra}@iitj.ac.in

Abstract. For the past decades, covert and side channels have posed significant threats to user privacy in computing systems, targeting almost every component. In this paper, we present SideLink, a novel attack that exploits the NVLink bus for covert communication and information leakage. NVLink is a recent bus in the NVIDIA GPU systems known for its high bandwidth, which became a necessity for AI applications in data centers. Despite the extremely high bandwidth, we investigated its contention characteristics and built the first contention-based covert channel, and observed the presence of a side channel on the NVLink interconnect bus for the first time. We evaluated SideLink against NVIDIA DGX A100, a widely used system in data centers and cloud environments nowadays. The covert channel reached a bandwidth of 8.8 Kbps with a negligible error rate. Moreover, we demonstrated the side channel through an application fingerprinting attack using a deep learning FCN model, achieving an accuracy of 93.1%, which involved collecting the first dataset consisting of latency traces of the NVLink bus from applications running on dual-GPU systems.

Keywords: Side channel · Covert channel · Interconnect buses · NVLink

1 Introduction

In modern computer security, covert- and side-channel attacks on GPUs represent a critical challenge. These stealthy methods of unauthorized information transfer go unnoticed by traditional security mechanisms, exploiting unintended communication paths to facilitate secretive data exchange between processes or entities within a computing environment. Covert and side channels are born out of the complex interactions between different elements of the system, often utilizing low-level resources such as caches [3,5,6,10,11,16], interconnect buses [3,4,7,9,14,17], processing units [15], or shared memory [15]. These channels are typically characterized by their capacity to bypass security boundaries, aiming to compromise the confidentiality and integrity of sensitive data. As GPUs have become increasingly the building blocks of AI training data centers, safeguarding sensitive information on GPU-equipped systems from such threats

J. Knechtel et al. (Eds.): SPACE 2024, LNCS 15351, pp. 6–15, 2025.
https://doi.org/10.1007/978-3-031-80408-3_2

has become essential, as well as a constant battle against innovative attack techniques. Interconnect buses provide an ideal conduit for covert communication and information leakage, whether physical connections, network protocols, or communication interfaces. In this paper, we delve deeper into the vulnerabilities of a specific interconnect bus, NVLink [1], developed by NVIDIA, which plays an essential role in modern computing architecture. Its high-speed connections are designed to enhance data transfer rates between GPUs, as well as between GPUs and CPUs, significantly boosting the performance of parallel computing tasks. However, the unique characteristics of NVLink also render it susceptible to covert communication and information leakage. To address these vulnerabilities, we present SideLink, a novel attack that examines the inherent threats by exposing this bus to covert- and side-channel attacks. Previous approaches cannot detect or mitigate SideLink. These approaches have primarily focused on isolating GPU internal resources [18–20], introducing obfuscation/randomization to memory access [8,12,13], or limiting access to hardware profiling counters [16]. However, these measures do not prevent our attacks, as they lack any form of isolation or division for the NVLink bus.

The CUDA programming model enables developers to leverage the parallel processing capabilities of modern GPUs by dividing tasks into smaller threads that run concurrently. Two key features utilized in this work are CUDA streams and CUDA events. CUDA streams manage task execution on GPUs, with asynchronous streams allowing overlapping communication and computation, which helps create contention on the NVLink interconnect to explore latency patterns. CUDA events, using functions like `cudaEventRecord` and `cudaEventElapsedTime`, provide precise timing and synchronization, making them essential for measuring latencies and analyzing contention behavior on NVLink. With the introduction of NVIDIA's multi-instance GPU (MIG) feature in the A100 and H100 GPUs, resource partitioning across memory, streaming multiprocessors (SMs), and cache has significantly improved, providing better isolation in virtualized environments. However, despite these advancements in GPU partitioning, the NVLink interconnect bus remains shared across users in such environments, posing potential risks of information leakage due to the lack of isolation on this shared resource. This shared NVLink, combined with asynchronous CUDA streams and precise event timing, allows the observation of contention patterns and the potential exploitation of side channels for information leakage.

Our Contributions

The key contributions of our work are as follows.

1. We create the first contention-based covert channel that exploits the NVLink interconnect bus. The channel reaches a bandwidth of 8.8 Kbps with a negligible error rate.
2. We demonstrate the first side-channel in multi-GPU systems that exploits the NVLink interconnect bus, showcasing information leakage through an

application fingerprinting attack using a deep learning Fully Convolutional Network (FCN) model, achieving an accuracy of 93.1%.

3. To demonstrate the side channel, we collect the first dataset comprising latency traces on the NVLink interconnect bus for applications running on dual-GPU systems.

4. We investigate the contention characteristics of the NVLink interconnect bus to optimize our attacks. By identifying the precise threshold at which detectable contention occurs, we minimize unnecessary overhead. This optimization enables us to achieve a covert channel with high bandwidth and efficiently collect latency traces for side-channel analysis.

The rest of the paper is organized as follows. In Sect. 2, we explore NVLink contention characteristics essential to perform the attacks and show the details of developing our contention-based covert channel. Section 3 shows the details of exploiting side-channel vulnerability through an application fingerprinting attack. Finally, concluding remarks and future works are presented in Sect. 4.

2   Contention-Based Covert Channel

In this section, we inspect the contention characteristics of the NVLink bus, state our threat model for the covert channel, and explain the details of implementing our contention-based covert channel.

2.1   Contention Characteristics of NVLink Interconnect Bus

We explored the latency patterns of the NVLink interconnect, focusing on one prominent GPU model widely used in data centers, the A100. In the experiment, to utilize the NVLink bus, we transferred data from one GPU's memory to another's using `cudaMemcpyPeerAsync` function and measured the time required for every operation using `cudaEventRecord` function while increasing data size. To explore contention, we performed concurrent data transfer operations using the CUDA streams (we used CUDA 11.4 in this work). Figuer 1 shows the latencies obtained while increasing the data size from 4 Bytes to 128 MB, using 1, 2, and 4 streams, where the number of streams indicates the number of concurrent data transfer operations. We observed that a detectable additional delay caused by another concurrent operation starts at a data size of 512 KB and gets more noticeable at larger sizes. This data size marks the threshold at which a detectable contention can be obtained, which later can be exploited to efficiently perform the attacks as explained in Sects. 2.3 and 3.2.

2.2   Threat Model

In our threat model, we consider two entities: the victim and the attacker. Both entities operate within the same physical multi-GPU system using virtualization support (multiple-tenant, multiple-GPU). Specifically, the victim runs an application compromised by a Trojan (sender), while the attacker consistently runs

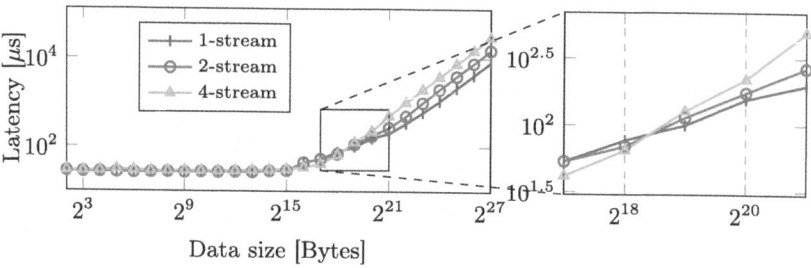

Fig. 1. Latencies of single and concurrent data transfer operations for data size from 4 Bytes to 128 MB on DGX A100 system.

Spy software (receiver). These processes cohabit within a shared virtual machine environment equipped with multiple-instance GPUs connected via the NVLink interconnect bus. The Trojan process is located on instance 1 of virtualized multi-GPU system and is responsible for covertly transferring information to an instance 2, where the Spy process is hosted. This transfer occurs through the NVLink by exploiting timing variations. The Spy process monitors the timing traces to extract information transmitted from the Trojan.

2.3 Implementation

The implementation of our covert channel is guided by the methodology outlined in Fig. 2, which provides a visual overview of the key steps involved (Steps from **A** to **D**). The process primarily entails designing and implementing a Spy and a Trojan capable of exploiting the NVLink bus in an unauthorized manner to facilitate covert communication. Algorithm 1 shows procedures of the Trojan and the Spy that exploit contention on NVLink bus between two GPUs (`GPU_src` and `GPU_dst`). The Spy and Trojan allocate 512 KB of memory on each GPU. `D[]` is a binary array containing the victim's data. The Trojan (Step **A** in Fig. 2) has direct access to the victim's data since it shares the same security domain with the victim's application. For every bit in the array `D[]`, the Trojan

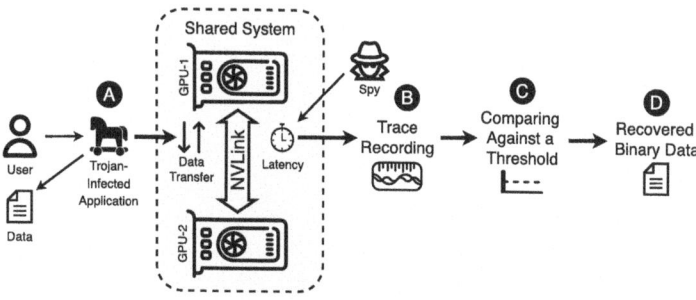

Fig. 2. Overview of the methodology of our contention-based covert channel.

either executes a data transfer operation for 512 KB (a threshold obtained as discussed in Sect. 2.1) between the two GPUs using cudaMemcpyPeerAsync (contention represents D[i]=1) or does nothing (no contention represents D[i]=0). The Spy (Step **B**), on the other hand, continuously executes a data transfer operation between the same two GPUs and measures the latency. Then, by comparing against a threshold Step **C**), the Spy decodes the changes in latency into binary data (i.e., from latencies of 95 μs and 75 μs into 1 and 0) stored in the array (R[]) representing the Trojan's recovered message (Step **D**).

2.4   Results and Discussion

The signal of 256 bits observed by the Spy requires 29 ms of transmission time. The calculated bandwidth and bit error rate for the covert channel in the experiments are 8.8 Kbps and 0.14%, respectively.

Algorithm 1. Covert Channel Using Contention Over NVLink

```
 1: procedure TROJAN(D[ ])
 2: //Input: D[] binary array of size N
 3:    Allocating 512 KB on both GPUs
 4:    for i=0 to N-1 do
 5:        switch D[i] do
 6:            case 0 NOP
 7:            case 1 MemoryCopy(GPU_dst,GPU_src)
 8:    end for
 9: end procedure
10:
11: procedure SPY(R[ ])
12: //Output: R[], binary array of size M
13: //L[]: integer array of size M
14: //T: a threshold to detect high latency
15:    Allocating 512 KB on both GPUs
16:    for i=0 to M-1 do
17:        EventRecord(start)
18:        MemoryCopy(GPU_dst,GPU_src)
19:        EventRecord(stop)
20:        ElapsedTime(L[i], start, stop)
21:        if L[i] < T then
22:            R[i]=0
23:        else
24:            R[i]=1
25:        end if
26:    end for
27: end procedure
```

---

3   Contention-Based Side Channel

In this section, we state our threat model for the side channel and explain the details of performing an application fingerprinting attack exploiting the information leakage on the NVLink interconnect bus.

3.1   Threat Model

Unlike the threat model for the covert channel attack, where a Trojan is deliberately introduced, the side-channel attack model requires no such intentional communication between the attacker and the victim. Both entities share a virtualized environment with multiple-instance GPUs connected via an NVLink interconnect bus, and cohabit the same physical GPU infrastructure. In this model, the attacker passively measures contention on the shared NVLink bus. By analyzing contention patterns, the attacker can infer the victim's running applications and computational behavior.

3.2   Application Fingerprinting Attack

The inherent characteristics of applications and the implemented algorithms on multi-GPU systems often result in distinctive and unique patterns of data transfer operations (in terms of both frequency and volume) between GPU units utilizing the NVLink bus. Figure 3 provides an overview of the methodology of our application fingerprinting attack. The diagram visually outlines the stages involved (Steps from Ⓐ to Ⓓ). In the subsequent paragraphs, we will delve into the details of the process. Algorithm 2 shows the procedure of the *Listener* that exploits contention on the NVLink bus between two GPUs (GPU_src and GPU_dst). It continuously executes a data transfer operation and measures the latencies, which are later stored in the latency array L[] (Step Ⓐ in Fig. 3).

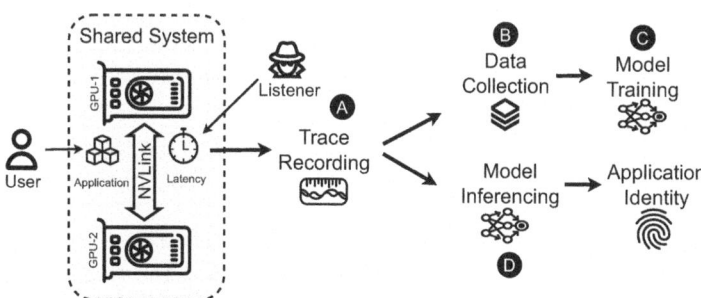

Fig. 3. Overview of the methodology of our application fingerprinting attack.

Algorithm 2. Collecting Latency Traces on NVLink

```
1: procedure LISTENER(L[ ])
2: //Output: L[] integer array of size M
3:     Allocating 512 KB on both GPUs
4:     for i=0 to M-1 do
5:         EventRecord(start)
6:         MemoryCopy(GPU_dst,GPU_src)
7:         EventRecord(stop)
8:         ElapsedTime(L[i], start, stop)
9:     end for
10: end procedure
```

Data Collection (Step ❸). While executing the *Listener* procedure alongside an application (executed from two separate user accounts), we collected latency traces from 24 applications (cryptocurrency mining, hashing, and scientific simulations), totaling 1536 traces. Each trace encompasses 5000 samples, providing a dataset for our analysis. The traces were collected by measuring the latency of data transfer operations between two GPUs of NVIDIA DGX A100 at approximately 1900 samples per second, resulting in the accumulation of 5,000 samples in around 2.6 s. Figure 4 displays the recorded latency traces for five algorithms as examples.

Model Training (Step ❹). We employed a deep learning Fully Convolutional Network (FCN) model for the classification task. FCNs have proven effective in capturing intricate patterns in data, making them particularly suitable for the dataset. The model features a simple FCN architecture, which is a customized adaptation of the model documented in the Keras documentation [2]. This architecture is commonly employed for classification tasks, particularly with sequential data such as time series or extracted features from time series, and it was used in similar works, such as the study by Side et al. [17].

Model Inference (Step ❺). After training the model, it can be deployed to a virtualized shared-resources environment such as the cloud. In this step, instead of training, we utilize the trained model to classify newly recorded traces and obtain the identity of the running applications.

3.3   Results and Discussion

After training the model with 400 epochs and a batch size of 16 and performing K-fold cross-validation 32 times, randomly shuffling the traces each time to ensure the robustness and generalization of our model, we achieved an overall accuracy of 93.1%. The macro-average F1-score, which provides a holistic view of the model's performance across all classes, was found to be 92.8%. The dataset used consists of only 24 applications,which may limit the generalization of the

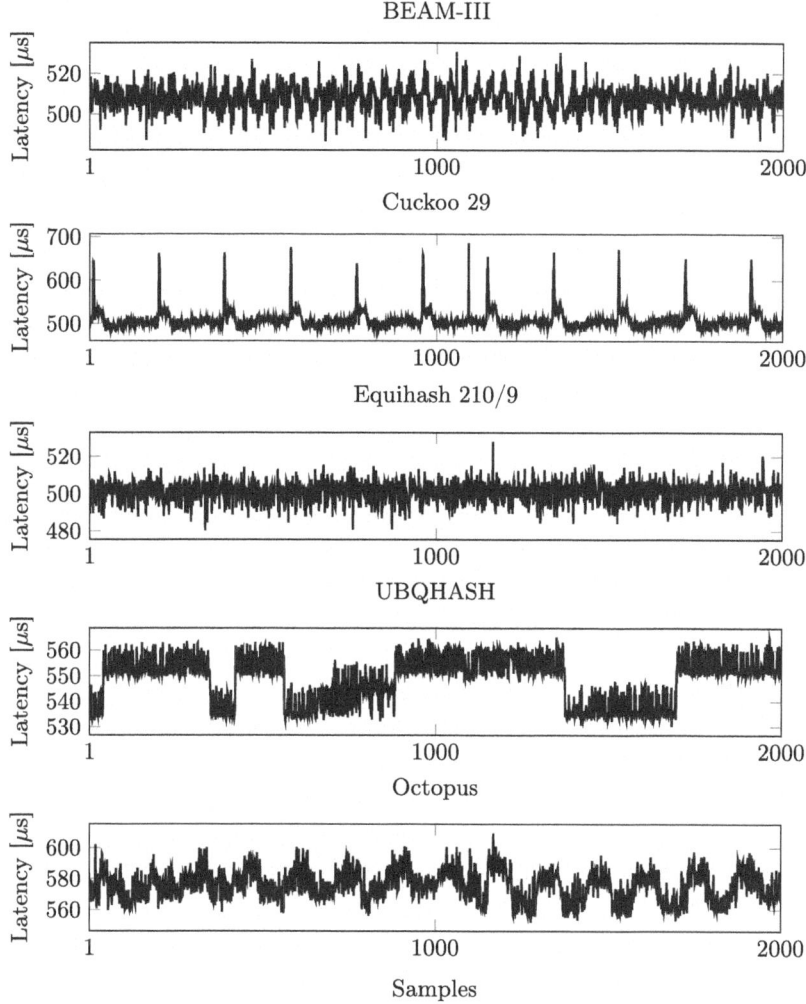

Fig. 4. Example latency traces (showing 2000 samples out of the 5000 captured) for five algorithms.

model. However, it was sufficient to validate the model's ability to fingerprint applications based on contention patterns. Future work could expand the dataset to include a more diverse set of applications for broader evaluation. Additionally, the storage overhead for the model is minimal due to the compact representation of the FCN model and can be easily accommodated within typical GPU memory limits.

4 Conclusion

In this paper, we showed the first covert-channel attack that allows attackers to exploit the NVLink bus to communicate covertly, and we demonstrated the first side channel on the NVLink bus through an application fingerprinting attack. We evaluated the attacks on DGX A100, reaching a maximum bandwidth of 8.8 Kbps with a negligible error rate and achieving the accuracy of 93.1% in the application fingerprinting attack. Although achieving an accuracy of 93.1% marks a milestone in our application fingerprinting attack, further improvements may be attainable. Factors such as dataset size, model complexity, and training parameters could have influenced the accuracy of our model. In future work, we aim to address these aspects comprehensively, considering potential refinements to enhance the performance of our model. Additionally, we plan to investigate the presence of vulnerabilities in newer generations of NVLink to ensure that defense strategies remain adaptable to evolving hardware architectures. Moreover, we aim to explore hardware-level mitigations as potential alternatives to software or hypervisor-level countermeasures. Hardware-based security mechanisms can minimize performance overhead while enhancing the overall resilience of the system against side- and covert-channel attacks.

References

1. NVLink and NVLink Switch (2024). https://www.nvidia.com/en-us/data-center/nvlink/
2. TensorFlow Tutorials, Convolutional Neural Network (CNN) (2024). https://www.tensorflow.org/tutorials/images/cnn
3. Ahn, J., et al.: Network-on-chip microarchitecture-based covert channel in GPUs. In: Proceedings of the Annual International Symposium on Microarchitecture, MICRO, pp. 565–577. IEEE Computer Society (2021). https://doi.org/10.1145/3466752.3480093
4. Das, A.: Preserving privacy of neuromorphic hardware from PCIe congestion side-channel attack. In: 2023 IEEE 47th Annual Computers, Software, and Applications Conference (COMPSAC), pp. 689–698. IEEE (2023)
5. Dutta, S.B., Naghibijouybari, H., Gupta, A., Abu-Ghazaleh, N., Marquez, A., Barker, K.: Spy in the GPU-box: covert and side channel attacks on multi-GPU systems (2022). http://arxiv.org/abs/2203.15981
6. Gao, Y., Zhou, Y., Cheng, W.: Cybersecurity Efficient electro-magnetic analysis of a GPU bitsliced AES implementation (2020). https://doi.org/s42400-020-0045-8
7. Giechaskiel, I., Tian, S., Szefer, J.: Cross-VM information leaks in FPGA-accelerated cloud environments. In: 2021 IEEE International Symposium on Hardware Oriented Security and Trust (HOST), pp. 91–101. IEEE (2021)
8. Gurunath Kadam, Danfeng Zhang, A.J.: BCoal: bucketing-based memory coalescing for efficient and secure GPUs. In: Proceedings - IEEE International Symposium on High Performance Computer Architecture, HPCA 2020, pp. 570–581. Institute of Electrical and Electronics Engineers Inc. (2020)
9. Hu, X., et al.: Deepsniffer: a DNN model extraction framework based on learning architectural hints. In: Proceedings of the Twenty-Fifth International Conference on Architectural Support for Programming Languages and Operating Systems, pp. 385–399 (2020)

10. Jiang, Z.H., Fei, Y., Kaeli, D.: A complete key recovery timing attack on a GPU. In: Proceedings - International Symposium on High-Performance Computer Architecture, vol. 2016-April, pp. 394–405. IEEE Computer Society (2016)

11. Jiang, Z.H., Fei, Y., Kaeli, D.: Exploiting bank conflict-based side-channel timing leakage of GPUs. ACM Trans. Arch. Code Optim. **16** (2019). https://doi.org/10.1145/3361870

12. Kadam, G., Zhang, D., Jog, A.: RCoal: mitigating GPU timing attack via subwarp-based randomized coalescing techniques. In: Proceedings - International Symposium on High-Performance Computer Architecture, vol. 2018-February, pp. 156–167. IEEE Computer Society (2018). https://doi.org/10.1109/HPCA.2018.00023

13. Karimi, E., Fei, Y., Kaeli, D.: Hardware/software obfuscation against timing side-channel attack on a gpu. In: 2020 IEEE International Symposium on Hardware Oriented Security and Trust (HOST), pp. 122–131. IEEE (2020)

14. Kim, H., Hur, J.: PCIe Side-channel attack on I/O device via RDMA-enabled network card. In: 2022 13th International Conference on Information and Communication Technology Convergence (ICTC), pp. 1468–1470. IEEE (2022)

15. Naghibijouybari, H., Khasawneh, K.N., Abu-Ghazaleh, N.: Constructing and characterizing covert channels on GPGPUs. In: Proceedings of the Annual International Symposium on Microarchitecture, MICRO, vol. Part F131207, pp. 354–366. IEEE Computer Society (2017). https://doi.org/10.1145/3123939.3124538

16. Naghibijouybari, H., Qian, Z., Neupane, A., Abu-Ghazaleh, N.: Rendered insecure: GPU side channel attacks are practical. In: Proceedings of the ACM Conference on Computer and Communications Security, pp. 2139–2153. Association for Computing Machinery (2018). https://doi.org/10.1145/3243734.3243831

17. Side, M., Yao, F., Zhang, Z.: LockedDown: exploiting contention on host-GPU PCIe bus for fun and profit. In: 2022 IEEE 7th European Symposium on Security and Privacy (EuroS&P), pp. 270–285. IEEE (2022)

18. Taram, M., Ren, X., Venkat, A., Tullsen, D.: SecSMT: securing SMT processors against contention-based covert channels. In: USENIX Security Symposium (2022)

19. Volos, S., Vaswani, K., Bruno, R.: Graviton: trusted execution environments on GPUs. In: 13th USENIX Symposium on Operating Systems Design and Implementation (OSDI 2018), pp. 681–696 (2018)

20. Xu, Q., Naghibijouybari, H., Wang, S., Abu-Ghazaleh, N., Annavaram, M.: GPU-Guard: mitigating contention based side and covert channel attacks on GPUs. In: Proceedings of the International Conference on Supercomputing, pp. 497–509. Association for Computing Machinery (2019). https://doi.org/10.1145/3330345.3330389

Faster and More Energy-Efficient Equation Solvers over GF(2)

Subhadeep Banik[1(✉)] and Francesco Regazzoni[1,2]

[1] Universita della Svizzera Italiana, Lugano, Switzerland
`subhadeep.banik@usi.ch`
[2] University of Amsterdam, Amsterdam, Netherlands
`f.regazzoni@uva.nl`

Abstract. In a recent paper by Banik et al. at IACR TCHES 2024, the authors have constructed hardware circuits to compute the Möbius Transform of a Boolean function using polynomial space. This core circuit is then used to solve equations over $GF(2)$ of degree d (where d is typically a small integer). In this paper we outline two improvements to the above circuit that make it faster and consume even lower energy. The first comes from an observation of the purely combinatorial part of the circuit which extracts input indices of a truth table where the entry is zero. We show that the process can be extracted using a new circuit element that has much lower critical path. We also identify that the principal circuit component that contributed to the overall latency of the solver is the **Expmob1** circuit that converts the algebraic form of a Boolean function to its truth table using a single cycle. We show that if suitably spaced pipeline stages are inserted in it, both the energy consumption and total circuit latency can be reduced. We end the paper by implementing our circuit on the **SAKURA-X** fpga device for solving quadratic equations of moderately sizes.

1 Introduction

Solving low degree equations over a finite field is an important problem in many cryptanalytic contexts. It is known that cryptanalysis of the block cipher LowMC [ARS+15] using single plaintext-ciphertext pair from an r-round instance of LowMC gives rise to a system of equations in the secret key-bits of algebraic degree $2^{r/2}$ [Din21]. The public key in the signature scheme **PICNIC v3.0**, consists of a single plaintext/ciphertext pair generated by $r = 4$ round instance of LowMC block cipher using the secret key as the block cipher key. In this case, finding the secret key requires solving a system of n Boolean equations of degree 4 in the in the n unknown bits of the key. Other than this, it is also known that forging a signature in public key signature schemes like UOV can be done by solving a set of quadratic equations over $GF(2)$ [KPG99].

The problem we target can be stated thus: given n variables $x_1, x_2, \ldots, x_n$, and m polynomials $f_i \in \mathbb{F}[x_1, x_2, \ldots, x_n]$ (for $i \in [1, m]$), where $\mathbb{F}$ is any finite field, we want to find common solutions $x^* \in \{0, 1\}^n$, such that $f_i(x^*) = 0$

J. Knechtel et al. (Eds.): SPACE 2024, LNCS 15351, pp. 16–39, 2025.
https://doi.org/10.1007/978-3-031-80408-3_3

for all i. Over any finite field $\mathbb{F}$, the problem is NP-complete already when the polynomials are quadratic. For a complete analysis of the significance of equation solvers in cryptography please see the discussion in [Bou22]. Hereafter, we will focus on the case of the Boolean field $\mathbb{F} = GF(2)$.

1.1 Previous Work

The hardware/software architectures for fast exhaustive search over $GF(2)$ were explored in [BCC+10,BCC+13]. The secret x^* is a point which all the f_i's evaluate to zero. Thus at the point x^*, the truth tables of all the Boolean functions f_i will have the constant 0. Hence, we want indices x^* at which the logical **OR** of all the truth tables of all the f_i's evaluates to 0. In [BCC+10], the Gray code technique is used to evaluate the truth table of each polynomial f_i. The space of points in the domain of the polynomials f_i is traversed in the order specified by the Gray code. Since successive codewords of the Gray code are known to differ in only one bit, it is more efficient to evaluate $f_i(g_{j+1})$ from the knowledge of $f_i(g_j)$, where g_j is the $j - th$ codeword. Note that $f_i(g_0) = f_i(\mathbf{0})$ is just the constant term of f_i, thereafter if t is the only bit-position where the successive codewords g_j and g_{j+1} differ in, then we can use a Taylor-like expansion formula for Boolean functions to compute $f_i(g_{j+1})$:

$$f_i(g_{j+1}) = f_i(g_j) \oplus \frac{\delta f_i}{\delta x_t}(g_j). \tag{1}$$

Here $\frac{\delta f_i}{\delta x_t}$ is the 1st order derivative of the function f_i at the point x_t. It is common knowledge that the derivative has algebraic degree at least one less than the original function, and so if the derivative is not a constant or a degree one function we recursively evaluate the derivative term in Equation (1) with another round of Taylor expansion. The method obviously works best if the function f_i is quadratic, but can also be applied to evaluate moderately higher degree functions if some of the derivatives are precomputed. In a follow up work [BCC+13], the same authors proposed a hardware circuit for the problem, however, for only quadratic functions (that needed negligible amount of pre-computations).

In [BR24], the authors used Möbius Transform algorithm to evaluate the truth table of the Boolean functions f_i directly from their algebraic expressions. Although a straightforward algorithm to circuit conversion of the transform takes exponential amount of circuit resources[1], the authors followed a recursive description of the algorithm used in [Din21] to construct a polynomial sized circuit for it. The authors then use this core circuit to sequentially evaluate truth tables of multiple Boolean polynomials and do the logical **OR** operation over them to extract the correct solution. The authors present many such architectures for the solver, the final of which is the most energy-efficient.

---

[1] Exponential in the number of variables n of the Boolean function.

Limitations: One of the limitations of this work is that the analysis is limited to the finite field $GF(2)$, and analogous observations can not be made for higher order fields. For solving equations over higher order fields, the method using computation of Gröbner bases is still the most effective.

1.2 Contribution and Organization

In this paper we first briefly revisit the architectures described in [BR24] to bring the reader up to speed with some mathematical preliminaries, the basic solver circuit and the related engineering issues. We then look at two improvements in the circuit elements used in design. The first is replacing the "encoder followed by decoder" circuit with an encoder and "r **OR** $r+1$" circuit. While functionally these two circuits evaluate the same operation, the latter can be constructed to have a shorted critical path in hardware. Secondly, we observe that the longest combinatorial path in the solver circuit is an exponential sized Möbius Transform circuit (exponential in the degree of the Boolean function). We observe that by placing multiple pipeline stages in this circuit we can reduce both the energy consumption and latency of the circuit.

   The rest of the paper is organized in the following manner. Section 2 presents the necessary background about the circuit architectures required to read the paper. Section 3 describes the "r **OR** $r+1$" circuit. Section 4 discusses the introduction of pipeline stages in the circuit to reduce latency and energy. Section 5 present simulation results and a comparison of our architecture with [BR24]. In Sect. 6 we present an FPGA implementation of our circuit on the **SAKURA-X** device. Section 7 concludes the paper.

2   Background

Boolean Function: An n-variable Boolean function is a map from $\{0,1\}^n \to \{0,1\}$ and it can be uniquely represented by its algebraic expression, called algebraic normal form or ANF. We can write the algebraic expression of such a function using the $(\oplus, \cdot)$ basis:

$$f(\boldsymbol{x}) = f(x_0, x_1, \ldots, x_{n-1}) = \bigoplus_{i \in \{0,1\}^n} a_i x^i$$

Here $i := i_0 i_1 \cdots i_{n-1}$ is the binary string of length n, where i_j are the individual bits and x^i is defined as $\prod x_j^{i_j}$. The ANF vector $\boldsymbol{u} = [a_0, a_1, \ldots, a_{2^n-1}]$ is defined as the 2^n-length binary string of all the a_i's.

Example 1. For example, consider the 3-variable function $f = 1 \oplus x_0 x_1 \oplus x_2 \oplus x_0 x_2$. We can write this as $x_0^0 x_1^0 x_2^0 \oplus x_0^1 x_1^1 x_2^0 \oplus x_0^0 x_1^0 x_2^1 \oplus x_0^1 x_1^0 x_2^1$. The function can be written as a length 8 bit-vector $\boldsymbol{u}$ with bits at locations given by the binary strings 000, 110, 001 and 101 i.e. 0, 6, 1 and 5 set to 1 and the rest of the bits 0, which is to say that $a_0 = a_1 = a_5 = a_6 = 1$ and the rest of the $a_i = 0$.

The **algebraic degree** of the function (provided it is not identically zero) is defined as the maximum hamming weight of the string i such that $a_i = 1$. Thus in the previous example, the algebraic degree is 2. For functions having algebraic degree d, all the coefficients a_i such that $hw(i) > d$ are naturally 0. Since there exist exactly $\binom{n}{i}$ length n strings of hamming weight i, we can see that the ANF of degree d function can be expressed using $\binom{n}{\downarrow d} := \sum_{i=0}^{d} \binom{n}{i} < n^d$ binary coefficients.

Truth Table: The vector of evaluations of a Boolean function at all its input points is called its **Truth Table** (therefore this is a binary vector of length 2^n). The truth table is another way in which a Boolean function can be uniquely represented. The ANF and the Truth table vectors of any Boolean function are related by the Möbius transform. Let $\boldsymbol{v} = [v_0, v_1, \ldots, v_{2^n-1}]$ be the truth-table of the function f, with its i-th element being the function evaluation at the binary string representation of i, i.e. $v_i = f(i_0, i_1, \ldots, i_{n-1})$. Then it is well known that $\boldsymbol{v}$, $\boldsymbol{u}$ are related as $\boldsymbol{v} = M_n \cdot \boldsymbol{u}$, where M_n is the Möbius matrix of size $2^n \times 2^n$. The i, j-th element of this matrix m_{ij} is given as

$$m_{ij} = i^j \text{ where the power operation is as defined earlier.}$$

The Möbius matrix M_n has been well studied in the literature: it is well known that the matrix is lower-triangular and involutive i.e. $M_n^{-1} = M_n$. Thus both $\boldsymbol{v} = M_n \cdot \boldsymbol{u}$ and $\boldsymbol{u} = M_n \cdot \boldsymbol{v}$ hold. We also have an alternative recursive definition of M_n in terms of tensor multiplication. If we define $M_1 = \begin{bmatrix} 1 & 0 \\ 1 & 1 \end{bmatrix}$, then for all $n > 1$, we have $M_n = M_1 \otimes M_{n-1}$, where $\otimes$ is the matrix tensor product.

Multiplication of a vector by this matrix can be efficiently performed by the butterfly-like operations shown in Fig. 1. The butterfly circuit shaded in blue is the multiplication of input 2-bit vector by the matrix M_1. The figure shows that for an n-variable function, the algorithm can be done in-place (without any additional memory) using $n \cdot 2^{n-1}$ xor operations and 2^n space.

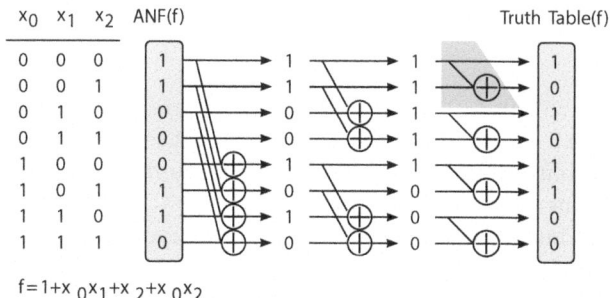

$f = 1 + x_0 x_1 + x_2 + x_0 x_2$

Fig. 1. Möbius transform on $f = 1 \oplus x_0 x_1 \oplus x_2 \oplus x_0 x_2$. The blue shaded component represents one butterfly unit. Note that the diagram is taken from [BR24]. (Color figure online)

Expmob1: The circuit obtained by arranging the butterfly layers as shown in Fig. 1 was named **Expmob1** in [BR24]. It computes the Möbius Transform in a single cycle, but it requires $n \cdot 2^{n-1}$ two-input **xor** gates and so has size exponential in n. Notice that in the first butterfly stage, the top half of the input array (call it A_{top}) undergoes no transformation at all, whereas the bottom half (call in A_{bottom}) requires one layer of xor gates. Subsequent stages can be seen as this basic operation executed on upper and lower halves of the output of the previous stage. In fact it was shown in [BR24], that the top and bottom halves of the first stage output were ANFs of the $n-1$ variable Boolean functions $f(0, x_1, \cdots)$ and $f(1, x_1, \cdots)$ respectively.

Polymob1: The recursive nature inherent in the algorithm is clear from the previous description and was formally proposed in [Din21]. The polynomial size Möbius Transform circuit was constructed according to this description which is given in Algorithm 1. In the algorithm A_0 is the input algebraic normal form of a Boolean function f of n variables and degree d having only $\binom{n}{\downarrow d}$ coefficients. To compute the transform, first an additional space of size $\binom{n-1}{\downarrow d}$ is created (for storing the ANF of an $n-1$ variable function) for the top and bottom halves of the input array, and the algorithm is called recursively on both halves. If the number of variables at the leaf stages of the recursion become equal to d then a circuit like **Expmob1** can be used to find the truth table of this smaller function in one cycle.

Algorithm 1: Recursive Möbius Transform [BR24]

---

1 Möbius (A_0, n, d)
  Input: A_0: The compressed ANF vector of a Boolean function f
  Input: n: Number of variables, d: Algebraic degree
  Output: The Truth table of f

---

2 /* Final recursion step, i.e. leaf nodes of recursion tree */
3 **if** $n=d$ **then**
4 | Use the formula $B = M_n \cdot A_0$ to output partial truth table B.
5 | /* Use **Expmob1** to do this */
6 **end**
7 **else**
8 | Declare an array T of size $\binom{n-1}{\downarrow d}$ bits.
9 | /* Compute the 2 operations of the butterfly layer */
11 | Store 1st butterfly output i.e. A_{top} in T (requires no xors).
12 | Call Möbius $(T, n-1, d)$
14 | Store 2nd butterfly output i.e. A_{bottom} in T (requires some xors).
15 | Call Möbius $(T, n-1, d)$
16 **end**

It is not difficult to see that notionally executing Algorithm 1, is equivalent to traversing the tree shown in Fig. 2a in a depth-first manner, i.e. along the orange line. In [BR24], it was shown that this could be done using the circuit shown in Fig. 2b. The total space required is given as $\sum_{i=0} \binom{n-i}{\downarrow d} \in O(n^{d+1})$, and it was shown that the total number of clock cycles required to execute the algorithm on the circuit was 2^{n-d}, i.e. one for each of the leaf nodes in Fig. 2a. In each of these cycles the circuit outputs a partial truth table, i.e. that of the function f in which the first $n - d$ variables have been set to one of the 2^{n-d} binary strings.

There is one top-level register of size $\binom{n}{\downarrow d}$ storing the initial ANF vector A_0. There is only one $\binom{n-1}{\downarrow d}$ size register to store the second level coefficients A_{top} and A_{bottom}. This means that if in the first clock cycle the 2nd register stores A_{top}, it must preserve this state till the entire left sub-tree rooted at this node is executed before it overwrites its state to A_{bottom}. Similarly there is only one $\binom{n-2}{\downarrow d}$ register to store potentially four ANF vectors (two each from the butterfly operation on A_{top} and A_{bottom}). Thus the engineering challenge was to ensure that each register at the successive levels store and preserve appropriate state vectors till it is time to overwrite them, and do this in a manner that minimizes the total number of clock cycles required to execute the algorithm. It was shown in [BR24] that this could be done by engineering the multiplexer signals $S[i]$ by using circuits of logarithmic depth.

The map $\chi_{n,d}$: The uncompressed ANF vector of an n-variable Boolean function has 2^n entries and mapping each coefficient into an array can be done canonically, i.e. for example the $x_0 x_2$ term has coefficient 1 in Example 1: since the term can be written as $x^{101} := x_0^1 \cdot x_1^0 \cdot x_2^1$, the exponent vector 101 (5 in decimal) denotes the position where a one is inserted in the array. However for functions of a small degree d, coefficients of all terms of degree larger than d are zero and so in order to accommodate the potentially $\binom{n}{\downarrow d}$ non-zero coefficients in an equal length array there has to be a map $\chi_{n,d}$ from the set of monomials (or equivalently the set of n-bit strings of hamming weight at most d) to an integer in $\left[0, \binom{n}{\downarrow d} - 1\right]$. In [BR24], the authors define $\chi_{n,d}(D) = y$ if D is the y-th largest integer whose n-bit binary representation has hamming weight less than or equal to d. It was shown that the map was easy to compute, and had the additional property that for all $n - i$ bit integers $\chi_{n-i,d} = \chi_{n,d}$ and so while traversing down the recursion tree where one needs to work with functions of lower degree becomes seamless.

2.1 Solvers

The authors in [BR24] present different architectures when the Polymob1 circuit is used to construct hardware solvers. Here we shall describe three of them.

Polysolve1: This is the simplest possible solver architecture and also the most straightforward. Given m polynomials $f_1, f_2, f_3, \ldots, f_m$ of degree d or smaller, we want to find the root $r \in \{0, 1\}^n$ which simultaneously evaluates to $f_1(r) = f_2(r) = \cdots = f_m(r) = 0$. Combining the above in a single equation we get: $\bigvee_{i=1}^{m} f_i(r) = 0$. Fig. 3a shows us the circuit architecture: there are m copies of **Polymob1** that outputs partial truth tables of the functions f_i of 2^d bits at a time. The **OR** of all the truth tables is computed to get the partial truth table

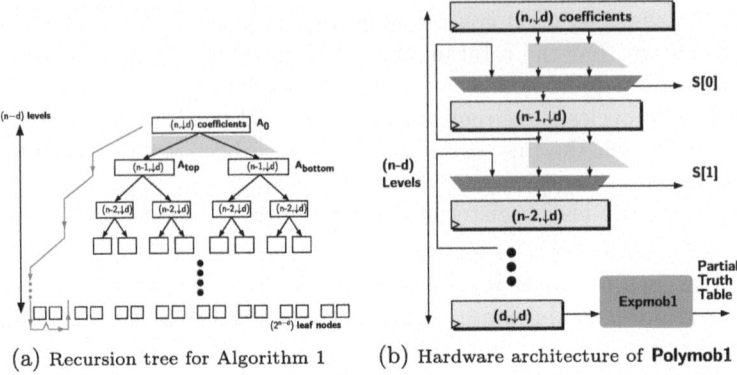

(a) Recursion tree for Algorithm 1   (b) Hardware architecture of **Polymob1**

Fig. 2. The blue shaded part roughly represents one arm of the butterfly unit. Note here $(x, \downarrow d) := \binom{x}{\downarrow d}$. Note that the diagram is taken from [BR24]. (Color figure online)

of the Boolean function $\bigvee_{i=1}^{m} f_i$. Now the task is to find indices in the table for which the corresponding entry is 0. This is found by using a priority encoder that outputs the index of the first 0 of an input string. Thus this circuit although can not find all roots of a given equation system, it can certainly tell if the underlying system has a root or not, thus serving as a decisional oracle. Note that the figure shows a large critical path of the circuit which can be reduced by putting pipeline stages before and after the **OR** network.

Polysolve3: The architecture was then modified to output every root of any equation system. After one root is extracted by the priority encoder, the root is input to a decoder circuit which is functionally the opposite of an encoder. If we **OR** the decoder output and the original encoder input, the resulting string has one less 0, which is written back on to the register before the encoder. The process is continued over as many cycles it requires for the string to be all one. [BR24] contains an example of this process which we reproduce here for clarity.

Example 2. [BR24] Let $d = 4$, and let the **OR** of the truth tables be $T_0 = $ 1011 1111 1111 0111. Then the priority encoder in the first cycle outputs 0001 which is the index of the first 0. The decoder outputs $D_0 = $ 0100 0000 0000 0000, which after **OR** with T_0 becomes $T_1 = T_0 \vee D_0 = $ 1111 1111 1111 0111, and has one less zero than T_0, and is written back to **Reg2**. In the next cycle we get the next root 1100 from the priority encoder which decodes to $D_1 = $ 0000 0000 0000 1000. Therefore we have $T_2 = T_1 \vee D_1 = $ 1111 1111 1111 1111 which is now the all one string.

It was proven that if the underlying equation system had R roots, then the architecture takes $2^{n-d} + R$ clock cycles to execute.

Polysolve4: This architecture was introduced with a view to improve energy efficiency. First of all the authors observed that having m **Polymob1** circuits results in a lot of redundant computation. For example consider the case when $n = m = 50$, and the common solution-space of the first 10 equations is only

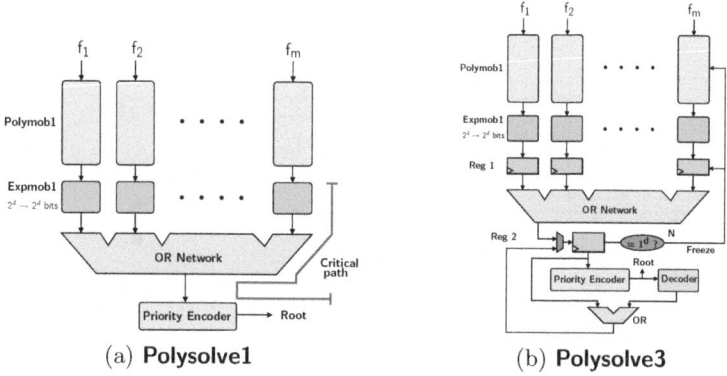

(a) **Polysolve1** (b) **Polysolve3**

Fig. 3. Circuits for solving m equations. Note that the diagram is taken from [BR24]

around 90–100 vectors in $\{0, 1\}^{50}$. In that case it makes is easier to do the following: **a)** Take each root $r \in$ the common solution-space of the first 10 equations, and **b)** evaluate $f_i(r)$ for $11 \leq i \leq 50$: if all these $f_i(r)$'s evaluate to 0 then r is a root of the equation system. Note that this essentially amounts to evaluating around 40 Boolean functions over 90–100 points. So the idea is to have only 10 Möbius Transform circuits that extract the common roots of the first 10 equations then we can do the functional evaluations of the remaining 40 equations over this common solution-space using some other method. This is much better than using the Möbius Transform circuit 50 times, which is mathematically equivalent to evaluating the remaining 40 equations over all the 2^{50} points of its input space.

The architecture for **Polysolve4** is shown in Fig. 4. As explained there are only $\mu < n$ **Polymob1** circuits, which produce the common roots of the first μ Boolean polynomials. To evaluate these roots over the remaining $m - \mu$ equations, there are two additional circuit elements introduced: (a) the Expander and (b) the Dot-product. The expander is a function from $\{0, 1\}^n \rightarrow \{0, 1\}^{\binom{n}{\downarrow d}}$, that is takes an n-bit string r and produces a $\binom{n}{\downarrow d}$-bit vector $\mathbf{r}$ that are the values of all the degree d monomials (arranged as per the map $\chi_{n,d}$) at the point r. If $\mathbf{v}_i$ is the compressed ANF vector of the function f_i then the dot-product $\mathbf{r} \cdot \mathbf{v}_i$ is actually the evaluation $f_i(r)$. It was shown in [BR24], that both circuits can be constructed in polynomial number of gates and depth. The evaluations are then forwarded to an **OR** and if all the values $f_i(r)$, for $i \in [\mu + 1, m]$ are zero then r is output as root.

Since a Boolean polynomial is on average "almost" balanced,[2] assuming that the first μ equations are independently sampled, the common solution space of the first μ equations is expected to be around $\overline{R} = 2^{n-\mu}$ in cardinality. Since

---

[2] It can be shown that $\mathbf{Pr}[|wt(f) - 2^{n-1}| \leq \sqrt{2^{n-1}}] > 0.8$ (for f sampled uniformly randomly from the set of n-variable Boolean functions), which means that Boolean functions are close to balanced with high probability.

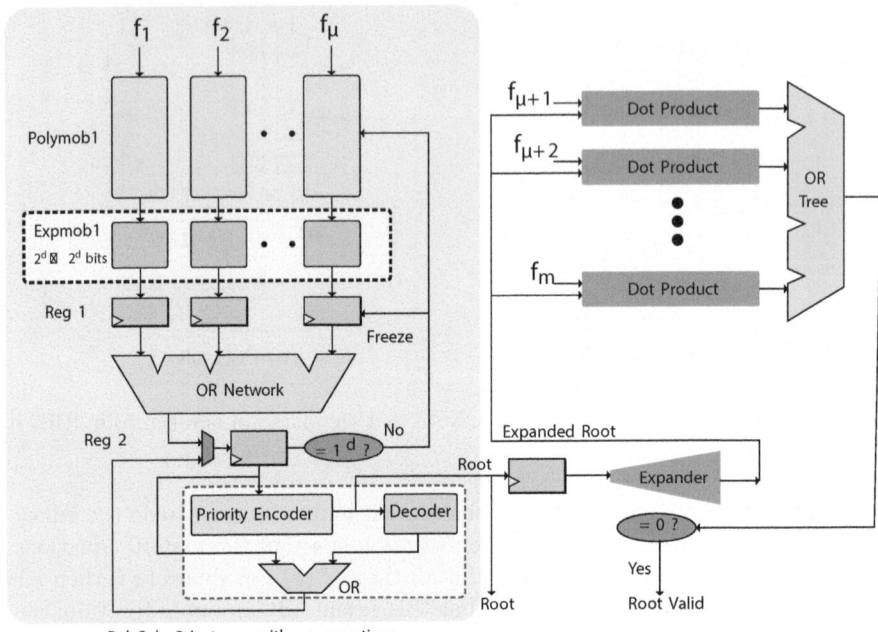

Fig. 4. Polysolve4 Architecture. Note that the diagram is modified from [BR24]. The components in the blue dashed boxes are the ones that have been modified in this work. (Color figure online)

each root of this space is evaluated in the same clock cycle as it is produced, the total number of cycles the circuit takes is $\overline{R} + 2^{n-d} = 2^{n-\mu} + 2^{n-d}$. Since the dot product circuits consume much less power than the **Polymob1** circuits, the setup is much more energy efficient than the **Polysolve3** solver.

Bounded-Depth Trees : The full-depth **Polymob1** tree has height $(n - d)$ and takes around 2^{n-d} clock cycles as seen in Fig. 2a. If instead, we bound the height of the tree to $n - h$ (i.e. by limiting the number of vertically stacked registers in the circuit in Fig. 2b to $n - h$), for some $h > d$, it follows that we obtain a new Möbius Transform circuit which completes in 2^{n-h} clock cycles, i.e. faster than the plain **Polymob1** circuit by a factor of 2^{h-d}. This would however require that the **Expmob1** circuit connected to the bottom-most register must be of h-variables instead of d-variables needed in **Polymob1**.

The total number of clock cycles is thus reduced from $2^{n-\mu} + 2^{n-d}$ to $2^{n-\mu} + 2^{n-h}$. However as explained in [BR24], increasing h arbitrarily does not result in energy/time of execution of the solver. This is because larger h ensures that the energy consumption and critical path of the **Expmob1** becomes dominant. Once this happens we can clock the circuit at lesser frequencies, which would increase the physical time of computation. Also many circuit components that follow the

Expmob1 unit, scale exponentially with h. This also ensures that scaling the value of h after a certain point is infeasible.

3   The Circuit r **OR** $r + 1$

One of the sources of large critical path in the circuit is the "encoder-decoder-or" circuit that follows the **Expmob1** circuit. Since these circuits are connected sequentially one after the other, the total latency of this circuit element is the sum of the latencies of the encoder, decoder and the **OR** gate. From the discussion in Example 2, we see that the primary use of the "encoder-decoder-or" setup is to decrease the number of zeros in the input string one at a time. We show that this can also be achieved with a "r **OR** $r + 1$" circuit. Which is to say the string r is first seen as an integer and incremented by 1, and the result is **OR**-ed with r. The following lemma is easy to prove.

Lemma 1. *Functionally the "r **OR** $r + 1$" circuit produces the same output as the "encoder-decoder-or" combination.*

Proof. The behavior of the increment operation on a binary string is well known. If the string ends with 0 (i.e. the lsb of the string is 0) then it simply flips the lsb to 1 and keeps the remaining bits unchanged. Otherwise it replaces the least significant contiguous block of 1 s in the string with a string of 0 s of equal length. Then the 0 bit just preceding this block is flipped to 1, and the remaining bits are left unchanged.

Since $1 \vee 0 = 1$, when this result is **OR**-ed with the original string r, the least significant 0 of r is flipped to 1, and so the resultant string has one less 0 than the original string r. In the language of bit-strings this can be written as

$$(\text{case 1}) \quad *0 \stackrel{\text{increment}}{\rightarrow} *1, \quad *1 \vee *0 \rightarrow *1$$
$$(\text{case 2}) \quad *01^t \stackrel{\text{increment}}{\rightarrow} *10^t, \quad *10^t \vee *01^t \rightarrow *11^t$$

This is exactly what the "encoder-decoder-or" combination aims to do.   □

Furthermore the operation of the "r **OR** $r + 1$" circuit is independent of the encoder operation, so these two circuits can be operated in parallel and not sequentially as was the case of the "encoder-decoder-or" combination. Thus the total latency of this circuit can be expressed as maximum of the two latencies, i.e. **max**[encoder, r **OR** $r+1$] which in theory should be much lower than the sum of the latencies of the encoder, decoder and **OR** gate. However there are some other factors to consider too. In the case of the parallel connection of the encoder and the "r **OR** $r + 1$" gate, the circuit elements which drive this combination (which is typically a register) sees much higher load capacitance on its output ports (due to the 2 circuits both connected to it). This implies that the register needs much higher electrical charge and effort to drive this combination which in turn increases the signal delay across the output port a little. However in our simulations we found that the parallel combination still has lower latency.

3.1 Incrementer Architecture

If $r = r_{t-1}r_{t-2}\cdots r_0$ is the input string then each i-th output bit s_i of the incrementer can be written as

$$s_0 = r_0 \oplus 1$$
$$s_1 = r_1 \oplus r_0$$
$$s_2 = r_2 \oplus r_0 r_1$$
$$\vdots$$
$$s_i = r_i \oplus r_0 r_1 r_2 \cdots r_{i-1}$$
$$\vdots$$
$$s_{t-1} = r_{t-1} \oplus r_0 r_1 r_2 \cdots r_{i-1} \cdots r_{t-2}$$

The Boolean product sequence r_0, $r_0 r_1$, $r_0 r_1 r_2$,... is commonly known as a prefix sequence. Since the Boolean **and** operation is associative, the circuit implementing the prefix sequence can be generated using the so-called Parallel Prefix architectures that are known to compute these prefix sequences in logarithmic circuit depth asymptotically. For this work we experimented with three popular Parallel Prefix architectures, namely the ones due to (1) Brent-Kung [BK82], (2) Kogge-Stone [KS73] and (3) Ladner-Fischer [LF80]. The circuit diagram for the three architectures are shown in Fig 5. The three architectures have unique features as it applies to our case. For example, as can be seen in Fig. 5, the Kogge-Stone architecture has minimum logic depth, with minimum fan-out, resulting in a fast circuit but with a large area. The Ladner-Fischer architecture also has minimum circuit depth but has a large fan-out requirement. The Brent-Kung topology has minimal area but slightly higher circuit depth.

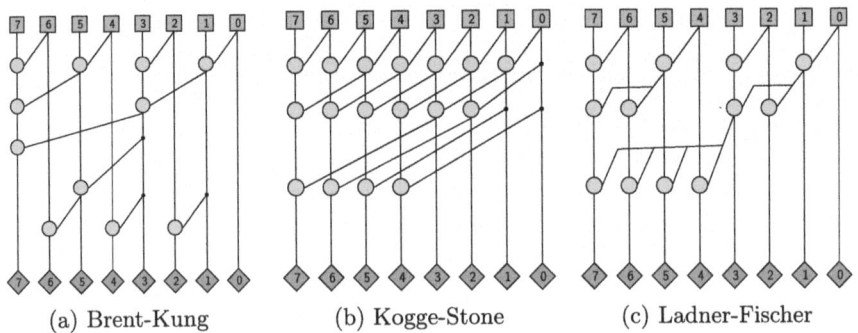

(a) Brent-Kung   (b) Kogge-Stone   (c) Ladner-Fischer

Fig. 5. Parallel Prefix architectures over 8 bits. The sky-blue nodes represent AND operations between two wires. (Color figure online)

3.2   Experimental Verification

To gain a fair understanding of which circuit architecture would provide us with lower latency and circuit area, we decided to perform an experiment in which we asked the circuit compiler to synthesize a) the "encoder-decoder-or" circuit and b) "r **OR** $r+1$" circuit on $t = 2^h$ input bits, for increasing values of h ($5 \leq h \leq 14$). The compiler used the Nangate 15nm standard cell library [MMR+15] for the synthesis and was instructed to minimize latency of the circuit. For (b), we used the three Parallel Prefix architectures to construct the incrementer circuit as outlined above. In addition we also synthesized the circuit where the synthesizer is allowed to optimize the "r **OR** $r+1$" circuit as it sees fit, i.e. the source RTL code presented to the synthesizer only mentions the functionality of the circuit without mentioning any particular architecture to optimize it. Fig. 6 shows us a comparison of the area and latencies of all the architectures. We can see that all the "r **OR** $r+1$" circuits almost guarantee better latency than the "encoder-decoder-or" circuit. The Kogge-Stone architecture gives minimal latency but its circuit area is around double than that of the other parallel prefix and synthesizer optimized circuits. The other Parallel Prefix architectures have slightly higher circuit area as compared to the encoder-decoder circuit. So in the interest of latency minimization without imposing too high a penalty on circuit area one could use any one between the Brent-Kung, Ladner-Fischer or the Synthesizer optimized circuit to construct this functionality.

4   Pipelining of the Butterfly Stages in **Expmob1**

Once we use height bound trees for some $h > d$, the **Expmob1** circuit required in the architecture has to be from $2^h \rightarrow 2^h$ bits, which requires h levels of butterfly layers as shown in Fig. 1. This combinatorial block becomes a source signal delay, which can be no longer ignored as h increases beyond a point. Since large signal delay across combinatorial blocks increases transients and glitches across the circuit, it also leads to increased power and energy consumption [BBR15] (see also [BBI+15, Figure 2]).

4.1   Adding Pipeline Stages

One way to alleviate both these issues is by inserting pipelines inside the **Expmob1** block at regular intervals as shown in Fig. 7. The pipeline not only cuts down on the latency across the block, it prevents the propagation of glitches from one register to the next. A complete **Expmob1** circuit with 2^h bit input would require h layers of butterfly circuits (see Fig. 1). To break things up, we take shorter **Expmob1** circuits with w stages (for $w < h$) and place registers in between them. We would need $\lfloor h/w \rfloor$ such register insertions. The final stage (if h is not a multiple of w) needs $h \bmod w$ stages. Since the **Polymob1** circuit continuously produces output vectors these are then in effect pushed into the pipeline, thereby increasing the total operation time by only a constant value, i.e. the number of pipeline stages $\lfloor h/w \rfloor$ that we have chosen to insert. The trade-off over here is over the value of w. A smaller value of w,

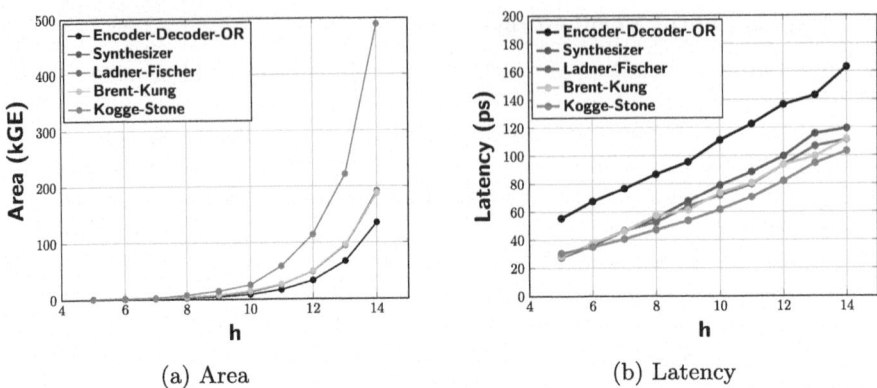

(a) Area   (b) Latency

Fig. 6. Comparing Area/Latency of "encoder-decoder-or" circuit and "r **OR** $r+1$" circuits.

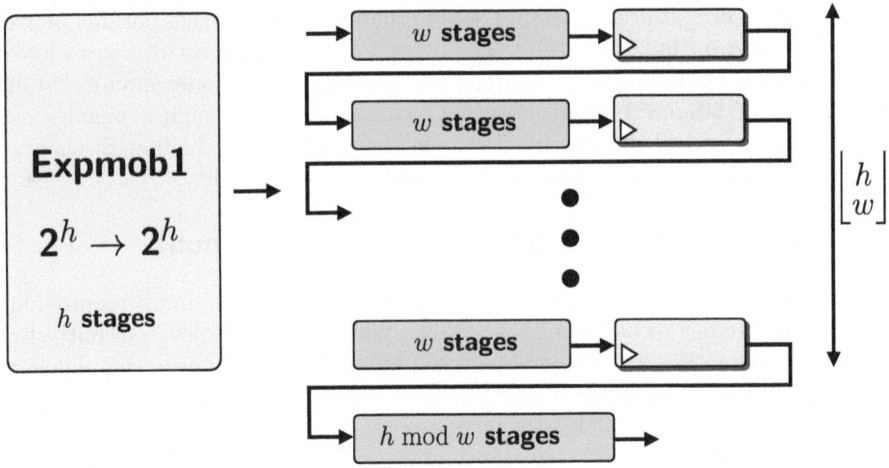

Fig. 7. Converting the fully combinatorial **Expmob1** block to a pipelined circuit

↑↑ ensures that the latency of the **Expmob1** pipeline remains bounded i.e. by w butterfly units,

↑↑ decreases the energy consumption in the combinatorial part of the circuit as we will show.

A larger value of w however

↓↓ increases the power/energy consumption in the sequential part, due to the larger number of register write operations that the circuit needs to perform inside the **Expmob1** pipeline,

↓↓ increases the circuit area, since we have to place more (i.e. $\lfloor h/w \rfloor$) registers to construct the circuit.

Even though a large value of w reduces register writes, for example, a value close to or equal to h, it increases the signal latency and glitches in the **Expmob1** circuit itself. Thus it stands to reason that there ought to be a value of w at which the power/energy consumption and the critical path of the circuit is optimized.

4.2   Energy Analysis

In [BR24, Equation 5] the authors model the energy consumption of the **Poly-solve4** solver whose height is bound by the parameter h, which solves m equations in n variables (with μ **Polymob1** and $m - \mu$ Dot product circuits) as follows:

$$E(m, \mu) = (\mu \cdot P_{mob} + \mu P_{expmob} + (m - \mu) \cdot P_{dp} + C) \cdot (2^{n-\mu} + 2^{n-h}) \cdot T_{clk}, \quad (2)$$

where

A: P_{mob} is the power consumed by the **Polymob1** circuit. The authors show that this figure is proportional to the number of flip-flops in the circuit, i.e. $P_{mob} \propto \sum_{i=1}^{n-h} \binom{n-i-1}{\downarrow d} < C_1 \cdot n^{d+1}$.

B: P_{expmob} is the power consumed by the **Expmob1** circuit. It was shown that P_{expmob} varies as $h^2 \cdot 2^h$. The reasoning provided was similar to the one followed in [BBR15]. If we assume that each xor gate in the first layer of the butterfly consumes power proportional to 1 unit (see Fig. 1), then due to the propagation of glitches from one layer to the other, each xor-gate in the second, third, fourth layers consume power proportional to $1 + \delta, 1 + 2\delta, 1 + 3\delta$ etc., where δ is some positive constant. The sum $\sum_{i=1}^{h} 1 + (i-1)\delta$ is a well known arithmetic series and is of the order $h^2 \delta$. Since there are 2^{h-1} xor gates in each layer we can conclude that the power consumption of the **Expmob1** varies as $h^2 \cdot 2^h$.

C: P_{dp} is the power consumed by the Dot-product circuit. and C is the power consumed by the other circuit components. Both these components are significantly smaller when compared to P_{mob}, P_{expmob}.

D: T_{clk} is the clock period, and we have already shown that on average the circuit requires $(2^{n-\mu} + 2^{n-h})$ clock cycles to execute.

The authors chose to run the simulations at 1 GHz as at that frequency the contribution of the static power to the total energy consumption was negligible. For $m = n$, the best way to balance out the the two components of the clock cycle count is to have $h = \mu$, from where we obtain $E(n, h) \approx (h \cdot (P_{mob} + P_{expmob}) + (n - h) \cdot P_{dp}) \cdot 2^{n-h+1} \cdot T_{clk}$. Since both $P_{mob}, P_{expmob} \gg P_{dp}$, we have the asymptotical expression as follows: $E(n, h) \approx (h \cdot C_1 \cdot n^{d+1} + h^3 \cdot C_2 \cdot 2^h) \cdot 2^{n-h+1} \cdot T_{clk}$, where C_1, C_2 are constants of proportionality. The value of h at which a minimum is achieved depends on how much C_1 is larger than C_2.

4.3   Due to Pipelined **Expmob1** Circuit

The changes introduced to the expression for $E(m, \mu)$ when the **Expmob1** circuit is pipelined will be primarily in the expression for P_{expmob}. Instead of being modeled as $C_2h^2 \cdot 2^h$, we model this as the total power consumed in the w-stage **Expmob1** circuits (there are $\lfloor h/w \rfloor$ of them) and the $\lfloor h/w \rfloor$ registers of size 2^h bits each. In addition if $h \not\equiv \mathrm{mod} w$, we need an additional $h \bmod w$ layers of butterfly.

Since there are only w slayers of butterfly the total power due to the glitches is proportional to $2^{h-1} \sum_1^w 1 + (i-1)\delta \propto w^2 \cdot 2^h$. Putting this together we can write (where C_3, C_4 are constants of proportionality)

$$P_{expmob,c} = C_3 \cdot \lfloor h/w \rfloor \cdot w^2 2^h + C_4 \cdot \lfloor h/w \rfloor \cdot 2^h = \lfloor h/w \rfloor \cdot 2^h \cdot [C_3 w^2 + C_4]$$

where $P_{expmob,c}$ is the power consumed in the combinatorial part of the circuit. However some power is also consumed in the register write operations. Each additional register is of size 2^h bits and there are a total of $\lfloor h/w \rfloor$ stages the additional power consumed due to these writes can be modeled as

$$P_{expmob,s} = C_5 \cdot \lfloor h/w \rfloor \cdot 2^h$$

Combining both the expressions, we have $P_{expmob} = P_{expmob,c} + P_{expmob,s} = \lfloor h/w \rfloor \cdot 2^h \cdot [C_3 w^2 + C_4 + C_5]$. For the energy consumed by the new circuit to be lower than that of the original **Polysolve4** circuit we need $C_2h^2 > \lfloor h/w \rfloor \cdot [C_3 w^2 + C_4 + C_5]$. The exact values of the constants C_i obviously depend on the particular standard cell library used to construct the circuits. In the following section, we simulate the energy consumption for the Nangate 15nm standard cell library.

4.4   The Solver **Polysolve5**

We now formally propose the solver family **Polysolve5**. The main changes over **Polysolve4** are the ones highlighted in yellow in blue dashed boxes in Fig. 4. More formally, the changes are outlined as follows:

1. We replace the Encoder-decoder-or circuit with the "r **OR** $r+1$" circuit. We could use any Parallel Prefix architecture for the incrementer, and although we used the Brent-Kung architecture, this particular choice is left to the discretion of the implementer.
2. We replaced the **Expmob1** circuit with a pipeline, with w butterfly stages in each pipeline.

We varied the value of h and for each value of h, tried to find the value of w that results in the optimal energy consumption. We present formally the simulation results in the following section.

5   Simulation Results

In this section we will describe the flow of simulation followed for each of the circuits reported in the paper. The design was described at the RTL level using a hardware description language and functional correctness was first verified. Thereafter the circuit was synthesized using the Nangate 15nm Open Cell Library [MMR+15] using *Synopsys Design Vision*, mainly to ensure that the results obtained can be reproduced readily. In order to ensure that equations are solved as quickly as possible, the circuit compiler was instructed to specifically optimize the total critical path of the circuit. A timing analysis is then performed on the synthesized netlist using sufficient number of randomly generated test vectors, which outputs the switching statistic of every node in the circuit. This information is used by a power compiler software to estimate the average power consumed by the circuit. Energy is computed as the product of the average power and the total physical time taken for the circuit to execute a given operation.

Figure 8 shows the comparative simulation results for the **Polysolve4** and the **Polysolve5** circuits for $n = 20$ and varying values of h. Note that we were unable to take measurements for larger values of n, h since each simulation takes close to 24 h beyond this point. For these plots, we have only used the data-point corresponding to the value of w which yields the most optimum results in energy and critical path in the **Polysolve5** circuit. For complete tabulated simulation results, for all values of $w < h$, and $w \in [3, 6]$, please see the Tables 1, 2, 3 in the Appendix B. The plots show that we are able to achieve considerable reduction in critical path (of the order of 25–30%) for each value of h we have simulated. The reduction in energy consumption, is less pronounced, but is of the order of 10–15% over all the circuits.

6   Solving Fukoka-Like Challenges on FPGA Devices

The Fukoka MQ challenge [fmq] is an online equation solving challenge. The Multivariate Quadratic polynomial (MQ) problem is the basis of security for some proposed post-quantum cryptosystems [YDH+15]. The hardness of solving MQ problem depends on a number of parameters, most importantly the number of variables, as well as the number of equations, the size of the base field, etc. The challenge basically consists of m quadratic equations over n variables in some base field $\mathbb{F}$, whose roots one is asked to find, i.e.

$$f^{(k)}(x_1, x_2, \ldots, x_n) = \sum_{1 \leq i \leq j \leq n} a_{ij}^{(k)} x_i x_j + \sum_{1 \leq i \leq n} b_i^{(k)} x_i + c^{(k)} = 0, \ \forall k \in [1, m]$$

The attacker is given all the coefficients $a_{ij}^{(k)}, b_i^{(k)}, c^{(k)}$. The goal is to find an answer $\mathbf{r} = [r_1, \ldots, r_n]$ in $\mathbb{F}^n$ of the above system. The website presents 6 different category of challenges: of which the most relevant to this work is **Type I**: where $m = 2n$ and $\mathbb{F} = GF(2)$ and **Type IV**: where $m = 1.5n$ and $\mathbb{F} = GF(2)$.

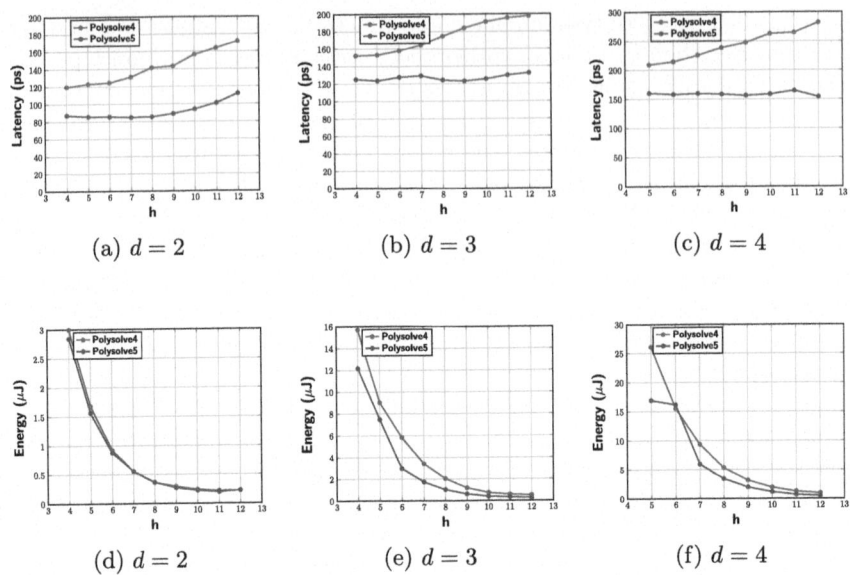

Fig. 8. Critical path and Energy results for **Polysolve4**/**Polysolve5** circuits

6.1   Type Conversion

For each k, the coefficients $a_{ij}^{(k)}, b_i^{(k)}, c^{(k)}$ are presented in a graded reverse lex order. For example, let x_1, x_2, x_3 and x_4 be the four variables of the system with $x_1 > x_2 > x_3 > x_4$. Then for a quadratic system, the order of monomials should be $x_1^2 > x_1 x_2 > x_2^2 > x_1 x_3 > x_2 x_3 > x_3^2 > x_1 x_4 > x_2 x_4 > x_3 x_4 > x_4^2 > x_1 > x_2 > x_3 > x_4 > 1$. However we know that $y^2 = y$ for any $y \in GF(2)$, and so although the challenge includes coefficients for both x_i and x_i^2 these need to be xored together before we convert it to the order given by the mapping $\chi_{n,2}$. We explain the algorithm to convert from the graded reverse lex order to our mapping in Algorithm 2 in the Appendix A.

6.2   Solving on the **SAKURA-X**

SAKURA-X is also named as **SAKURA-GIII**, was mainly designed for side-channel attack experimentation. The board has Xilinx 28-nm Kintex-7 FPGA device, which enables advanced measurement with on-the-edge technology. The board has Two Xilinx FPGAs:

(a) Control FPGA: Spartan-6 `XC6LX45-2FGG484C`, that houses the FIFO and other control signals that feed into the cryptographic core of the second FPGA, and
(b) Cryptographic FPGA: Kintex-7 `XC7K160T-1FBGC` that usually contains an implementation of the cryptographic algorithm targeted for side channel analysis.

As it has been alluded to, the board was designed for side channel experiments and not really intended for heavy calculations, and so the computational powers of the device are rather limited. For the purpose of our experiments, the control FPGA was clocked at 24 MHz and the equation solver was implemented on the cryptographic FPGA at 8 MHz.

The website [fmq] contains challenges starting at $n = 55$, however we could not solve them due to time and resource constraints given the size of the device. The largest solver circuit we could fit in the device was with $m = 83$, $n = 30$, $d = 2$ and $h = \mu = 12$. We randomly generated type **I,IV** instances of size $n = 45$. For type **I** we took the first 83 equations of the system and for type **IV** (which has around 67 equations), the remaining equations were taken as the all zero string (since any root satisfies the equation $0 = 0$).

Thereafter, we guessed the first 15 bits of the solution and converted the resultant bit string to a reduced equation system of 83 equations, in 30 variables as required. For each guess the reduced system of equations were fed to the circuit which in turn either returned no solution or one/multiple candidate solutions. Each run of 2^{15} guesses took around 4 hours to complete. Thereafter if the cardinality of the candidate system is 1, the candidate is output as the root. If not each Boolean function in the system was evaluated at the candidate points. Those which passed the system are output as roots.

7   Conclusion

In this paper we make two improvements to the **Polysolve4** circuit of [BR24] which reduced latency and energy consumption. We show that the process can be executed using a new circuit element that has much lower critical path. We also identify that the principal circuit component that contributed to the overall latency of the solver is the **Expmob1** circuit that converts the algebraic form of a Boolean function to its truth table using a single cycle. We show that if suitably spaced pipeline stages are inserted in it, both the energy consumption and total circuit latency can be reduced. We end the paper by implementing our circuit on the **SAKURA-X** FPGA device for solving quadratic equations of moderate sizes.

Acknowledgment. The authors wish to thank all the reviewers whose feedback helped improve the paper. The research presented in this paper was partially funded by the European Union, by grant No. 101135183 (MYRTUS). Views and opinions expressed are however those of the author(s) only and do not necessarily reflect those of the European Union. Neither the European Union nor the granting authority can be held responsible for them.

Appendix A: Conversion from grlevex ordering to $\chi_{n,2}$

The following algorithm converts from the graded reverse lex order to the coefficient mapping given by $\chi_{n,2}$. The initial array of coefficients of length $1 + 2n + \binom{n}{2}$ is X, i.e. if $n = 4$ by the ordering given in Sect. 6.1, X will be of length 15. For example, the polynomial $x_1^2 + x_1 x_3 + x_4 + x_1 + 1$ is expressed as $X = [1, 0, 0, 1, 0, 0, 0, 0, 0, 0, 1, 0, 0, 1, 1]$. Note due to $x^2 = x$ in $GF(2)$ the corresponding Boolean function for this polynomial is $x_1 x_3 + x_4 + 1$.

Algorithm 2: Type Conversion

---

17 **Conversion from *grlevex* ordering to $\chi_{n,2}$**

 Input: n: Number of variables, X:Input Array of length $1 + 2n + \binom{n}{2}$
 Output: Y:Output Array of length $\binom{n}{\downarrow 2}$ arranged as per $\chi_{n,2}$

---

18 $b \leftarrow 0, \quad e \leftarrow 0, \quad r \leftarrow 0, Y \leftarrow [0] * \binom{n}{\downarrow 2}$; /*Initialize Y to all 0s*/

19 **for** $r \leftarrow 0$ *to* $n + \binom{n}{2} - 1$ **do**

20   /*For the Quadratic terms*/

21   coff $\leftarrow X[r], monomial \leftarrow (1 \ll b)|(1 \ll e)$; /* "|" denotes bitwise-**OR***/

22      $Y[\chi_{n,2}(monomial)] \wedge = $ coff;

23   **if** $b == e$ **then**

24         $b \leftarrow 0, \quad e \leftarrow e + 1$;

25   **end**

26   **else**

27         $b \leftarrow b + 1$;

28   **end**

29 **end**

30 $b \leftarrow 0$;

31 **for** $r \leftarrow n + \binom{n}{2}$ *to* $2n + \binom{n}{2} - 1$ **do**

32   /*For the Linear terms*/

33   coff $\leftarrow X[r], \quad monomial \leftarrow (1 \ll b), Y[\chi_{n,2}(monomial)] \wedge = $ coff;

34      $b \leftarrow b + 1$;

35 **end**

36 /*For the Constant term*/

37 $r \leftarrow 2n + \binom{n}{2}$,   coff $\leftarrow X[r], Y[0] \leftarrow $ coff;

Appendix B: Post-synthesis simulation results for the Polysolve4 [BR24]/Polysolve5 circuits

We present tabulated results for the **Polysolve4/Polysolve5** circuits in the paper.

Table 1. Comparative results for the **Polysolve4** [BR24]/**Polysolve5** circuits for $d = 2$. Power reported at 1 GHz.

	Polysolve4						Polysolve5				
h	Area KGE	T_{cr} (ps)	T_{min} (ns)	Power (mW)	Energy (μJ)	w	Area KGE	T_{cr} (ps)	T_{min} (ns)	Power (mW)	Energy (μJ)
3	56.677	124.67	32681.49	20.177	5.2892						
4	70.332	119.63	15680.14	22.852	2.9953	3	71.848	87.16	11424.24	21.674	2.8409
5	85.475	122.94	8057.00	25.667	1.6821	3	93.917	92.11	6036.52	23.846	1.5628
						4	87.829	85.62	5611.19	25.437	1.6670
6	101.202	124.37	4075.36	28.102	0.9208	3	107.186	87.04	2852.13	28.357	0.9292
						4	105.434	86.04	2819.36	26.632	0.8727
						5	106.400	85.55	2803.30	27.078	0.8873
7	122.115	130.94	2145.32	33.520	0.5492	3	134.596	85.88	1407.06	36.923	0.6049
						4	126.904	84.82	1389.69	33.736	0.5527
						5	130.384	85.16	1395.26	34.571	0.5664
						6	132.471	86.13	1411.15	35.756	0.5858
8	153.022	141.29	1157.45	43.836	0.3591	3	172.130	85.99	704.43	48.014	0.3933
						4	179.482	87.94	720.40	51.883	0.4250
						5	163.209	85.52	700.58	44.647	0.3658
						6	168.176	85.25	698.37	46.599	0.3817
9	206.305	143.17	586.42	70.914	0.2905	3	280.905	96.83	396.62	91.668	0.3755
						4	259.777	91.37	374.25	81.078	0.3321
						5	220.002	88.91	364.18	65.446	0.2681
						6	229.775	88.82	363.81	68.853	0.2820
10	312.200	156.39	320.29	116.714	0.2390	3	447.557	96.72	198.08	152.315	0.3119
						4	395.395	98.16	201.03	129.845	0.2659
						5	429.240	97.88	200.46	147.796	0.3027
						6	342.199	94.02	192.55	108.305	0.2218
11	531.863	163.87	167.80	208.395	0.2134	3	774.851	113.87	116.60	268.379	0.2748
						4	646.017	100.80	103.22	215.541	0.2207
						5	769.716	101.21	103.64	268.503	0.2749
						6	567.352	100.38	102.79	188.983	**0.1935**
12	996.395	171.78	87.95	435.441	0.2229	3	1888.760	114.37	58.56	646.505	0.3310
						4	1613.352	119.56	61.21	560.009	0.2867
						5	1350.513	111.99	57.34	438.349	0.2244
						6	1515.018	116.04	59.41	530.501	0.2716

Table 2. Comparative results for the **Polysolve4** [BR24]/**Polysolve5** circuits for $d = 3$. Power reported at 1 GHz.

	Polysolve4						Polysolve5				
h	Area KGE	T_{cr} (ps)	T_{min} (ns)	Power (mW)	Energy (μJ)	w	Area KGE	T_{cr} (ps)	T_{min} (ns)	Power (mW)	Energy (μJ)
4	348.237	152.21	19950.47	119.732	15.6935	3	370.207	124.94	16376.14	92.800	12.1634
5	413.541	153.15	10036.84	137.641	9.0204	3	438.083	123.50	8093.70	114.114	7.4786
						4	438.056	123.50	8093.70	114.136	7.4800
6	474.366	158.04	5178.65	178.054	5.8345	3	515.884	131.11	4296.21	90.369	2.9612
						4	511.413	127.62	4181.85	141.337	4.6313
						5	511.486	127.62	4181.85	141.604	4.6401
7	543.620	164.43	2694.02	207.352	3.3973	3	596.715	129.13	2115.67	107.855	1.7671
						4	592.670	131.21	2149.74	105.712	1.7320
						5	592.458	130.34	2135.49	105.712	1.7320
						6	592.149	129.83	2127.13	105.716	1.7320
8	622.745	174.61	1430.41	249.145	2.0410	3	707.752	124.14	1016.95	129.466	1.0606
						4	707.453	125.44	1027.60	129.464	1.0606
						5	680.006	124.52	1020.07	124.643	1.0211
						6	680.004	124.52	1020.07	124.643	1.0211
9	729.193	184.04	753.83	287.649	1.1782	3	912.111	124.76	511.02	171.456	0.7023
						4	870.505	123.05	504.01	160.586	0.6578
						5	829.050	123.46	505.69	149.740	0.6133
						6	828.755	123.46	505.69	149.738	0.6133
10	899.647	191.15	391.48	355.497	0.7281	3	1270.908	125.37	256.76	236.900	0.4852
						4	1161.546	127.37	260.85	212.755	0.4357
						5	1162.636	127.19	260.49	212.766	0.4357
						6	1066.555	129.67	265.56	188.682	0.3864
11	1209.696	195.50	200.19	560.684	0.5741	3	1989.728	132.68	135.86	364.723	0.3735
						4	1763.519	133.01	136.20	311.676	0.3192
						5	1760.819	134.40	137.63	311.674	0.3192
						6	1066.555	129.67	265.56	188.682	0.3864
12	1859.154	197.57	101.16	969.071	0.4962	3	4016.560	133.51	68.36	743.956	0.3809
						4	3530.580	133.82	68.52	628.289	0.3217
						5	3044.701	132.16	67.67	512.796	**0.2626**
						6	3044.183	133.14	68.17	512.807	0.2626

Table 3. Comparative results for the **Polysolve4** [BR24]/**Polysolve5** circuits for $d = 4$. Power reported at 1 GHz.

	Polysolve4						Polysolve5				
h	Area KGE	T_{cr} (ps)	T_{min} (ns)	Power (mW)	Energy (μJ)	w	Area KGE	T_{cr} (ps)	T_{min} (ns)	Power (mW)	Energy (μJ)
5	1621.265	208.87	13688.50	398.157	26.0936	3	1594.933	160.14	10494.94	258.322	16.9294
						4	1594.831	162.53	10651.57	258.653	16.9511
6	1866.587	213.82	7006.45	474.863	15.5603	3	1868.220	157.82	5171.45	495.868	16.2486
						4	1873.258	162.73	5332.34	493.577	16.1735
						5	1873.258	162.73	5332.34	493.717	16.1781
7	2084.936	225.81	3699.67	571.070	9.3564	3	2138.182	159.43	2612.10	585.247	9.5887
						4	2130.157	163.52	2679.11	362.901	5.9458
						5	2130.157	163.52	2679.11	362.901	5.9458
						6	2130.271	163.42	2677.47	362.896	5.9457
8	2372.227	238.72	1955.59	652.621	5.3463	3	2408.222	160.82	1317.44	422.525	3.4613
						4	2409.596	158.39	1297.53	422.535	3.4614
						5	2384.429	159.69	1308.18	417.688	3.4217
						6	2383.904	155.13	1270.82	417.668	3.4215
9	2659.779	247.40	1013.35	765.022	3.1335	3	2769.321	162.33	664.90	499.352	2.0453
						4	2733.671	156.22	639.88	488.443	2.0007
						5	2697.118	157.77	646.23	477.580	1.9562
						6	2697.119	157.77	646.23	477.580	1.9562
10	2996.840	262.67	537.95	933.736	1.9123	3	3254.323	159.34	326.33	597.959	1.2246
						4	3188.238	161.57	330.90	573.866	1.1753
						5	3188.602	158.40	324.40	573.867	1.1753
						6	3088.427	158.75	325.12	549.725	1.1258
11	3677.842	264.61	270.96	1192.6	1.2212	3	4146.645	167.55	171.57	756.142	0.7743
						4	3924.798	167.25	171.26	703.132	0.7200
						5	3924.758	164.30	168.24	703.138	0.7200
						6	3694.089	166.94	170.95	650.107	0.6657
12	4908.635	281.91	144.34	1831.8	0.9378	3	6292.108	159.35	81.59	1745.4	0.8900
						4	5804.803	153.69	78.69	1618.7	0.8300
						5	5317.195	154.70	79.21	930.600	0.4765
						6	5319.151	155.43	79.58	930.630	0.4765

References

[ARS+15] Albrecht, M.R., Rechberger, C., Schneider, T., Tiessen, T., Zohner, M.: Ciphers for MPC and FHE. In: Oswald, E., Fischlin, M. (eds.) EURO-CRYPT 2015. LNCS, vol. 9056, pp. 430–454. Springer, Heidelberg (2015). https://doi.org/10.1007/978-3-662-46800-5_17

[BBI+15] Banik, S., Bogdanov, A., Isobe, T., Shibutani, K., Hiwatari, H., Akishita, T., Regazzoni, F.: Midori: a block cipher for low energy. In: Iwata, T., Cheon, J.H. (eds.) ASIACRYPT 2015. LNCS, vol. 9453, pp. 411–436. Springer, Heidelberg (2015). https://doi.org/10.1007/978-3-662-48800-3_17

[BBR15] Banik, S., Bogdanov, A., Regazzoni, F.: Exploring energy efficiency of lightweight block ciphers. In: Dunkelman, O., Keliher, L. (eds.) SAC 2015. LNCS, vol. 9566, pp. 178–194. Springer, Cham (2016). https://doi.org/10.1007/978-3-319-31301-6_10

[BCC+10] Bouillaguet, C., Chen, H.-C., Cheng, C.-M., Chou, T., Niederhagen, R., Shamir, A., Yang, B.-Y.: Fast exhaustive search for polynomial systems in $\mathbb{F}_2$. In: Mangard, S., Standaert, F.-X. (eds.) CHES 2010. LNCS, vol. 6225, pp. 203–218. Springer, Heidelberg (2010). https://doi.org/10.1007/978-3-642-15031-9_14

[BCC+13] Bouillaguet, C., Cheng, C.-M., Chou, T., Niederhagen, R., Yang, B.-Y.: Fast exhaustive search for quadratic systems in F_2 on FPGAs. In: Lange, T., Lauter, K., Lisoněk, P. (eds.) SAC 2013. LNCS, vol. 8282, pp. 205–222. Springer, Heidelberg (2014). https://doi.org/10.1007/978-3-662-43414-7_11

[BK82] Brent, R.P., Kung, H.T.: A regular layout for parallel adders. IEEE Trans. Comput. **3**, 260–264 (1982)

[Bou22] Bouillaguet, C.: Boolean polynomial evaluation for the masses. IACR Cryptol. ePrint Arch., 1412 (2022)

[BR24] Banik, S., Regazzoni, F.: Compact circuits for efficient möbius transform. IACR Trans. Cryptogr. Hardw. Embed. Syst. **2024**(2), 481–521 (2024)

[Din21] Dinur, I.: Cryptanalytic applications of the polynomial method for solving multivariate equation systems over GF(2). In: Canteaut, A., Standaert, F.-X. (eds.) EUROCRYPT 2021. LNCS, vol. 12696, pp. 374–403. Springer, Cham (2021). https://doi.org/10.1007/978-3-030-77870-5_14

[fmq] Fukoka mq challenge. https://www.mqchallenge.org/

[KPG99] Kipnis, A., Patarin, J., Goubin, L.: Unbalanced oil and vinegar signature schemes. In: Stern, J. (ed.) EUROCRYPT 1999. LNCS, vol. 1592, pp. 206–222. Springer, Heidelberg (1999). https://doi.org/10.1007/3-540-48910-X_15

[KS73] Kogge, P.M., Stone, H.S.: A parallel algorithm for the efficient solution of a general class of recurrence equations. IEEE Trans. Comput. **22**(8), 786–793 (1973)

[LF80] Ladner, R.E., Fischer, M.J.: Parallel prefix computation. J. ACM **27**(4), 831–838 (1980). Oct

[MMR+15] Martins, M., et al.: Open cell library in 15 nm freepdk technology. In: Proceedings of the 2015 Symposium on International Symposium on Physical Design, ISPD '15, New York, NY, USA, pp. 171–178. Association for Computing Machinery (2015)

[YDH+15] Yasuda, T., Dahan, X., Huang, Y.J., Takagi, T., Sakurai, K.: MQ challenge: hardness evaluation of solving multivariate quadratic problems. IACR Cryptol. ePrint Arch., 275 (2015)

Transferability of Evasion Attacks Against FHE Encrypted Inference
Official Work-in-Progress Paper

Reeshav Chowdhury[✉], Aman Kumar, Vaibhav Dashrath Mohite, and Ayantika Chatterjee

Indian Institute of Technology Kharagpur, Kharagpur, India
creeshav@gmail.com

Abstract. In the realm of modern Machine Learning and Deep Learning, ensuring data privacy is paramount. Encrypted inference holds tremendous potential in this arena and Fully Homomorphic Encryption (FHE) stands at the forefront of privacy-preserving technologies, offering a pathway to secure computation on encrypted data. While encrypted inference offers promising solutions to safeguard sensitive data, a critical question arises: Are the vulnerabilities and attacks that threaten conventional ML (Machine Learning) and DL (Deep Learning) models also applicable in the encrypted domain? This study particularly investigates this question in the context of evasion attacks. The major challenge of evasion attack in encrypted domain is that it is not possible to decide upon perturbations similar to plaintext methods. From Adversary's point of view, there are no known methods to generate adversarial examples by solving data-dependent optimization problems homomorphically over ciphertext space and it is also not possible to get attack assurance without knowledge of secret key. We present a solution where adversaries use partial training data distribution and Universal Adversarial Perturbations (UAPs), which are image-agnostic and capable of inducing misclassification across multiple images sampled from data distribution. Our research reveals that the equivalent notion of UAPs varies depending on whether a symmetric or public key FHE scheme is used, which we investigate specifically in the context of two libraries: Concrete ML and TenSEAL. While TenSEAL supports more direct attack methods, Concrete ML requires intermediate compiled representations for a successful attack in API-only setting. Additionally, Concrete ML's integer-based quantization alters targeted UAP behavior. We propose a Quantization-aware UAP generation algorithm, which preserves UAP property, ensuring consistent attack success rates in encrypted and plain classifiers.

Keywords: Fully homomorphic encryption · Evasion · Universal adversarial perturbation

J. Knechtel et al. (Eds.): SPACE 2024, LNCS 15351, pp. 40–68, 2025.
https://doi.org/10.1007/978-3-031-80408-3_4

1 Introduction

In the rapidly evolving landscape of machine learning and deep learning, there is a growing emphasis on safeguarding privacy of data while harnessing the power of data-driven insights. As machine learning applications become integral to various domains, the protection of sensitive information has become a critical concern. Homomorphic encryption (HE) [1] has emerged as a promising solution, allowing computations on encrypted data without revealing the underlying plaintext. This paradigm enables encrypted inference, where the client can offload encrypted data to the server for computation. While IND-CPA (Indistinguishability against choosen plaintext attacks) security of FHE (Fully Homomorphic Encryption) schemes effectively addresses confidentiality concerns, computing on encrypted data requires malleable ciphertexts (e.g., adding two ciphertexts results in valid ciphertext).

However, this malleability also introduces a potential integrity issue [2], as the server may not adhere to the computation requested by the client. On the other hand, there are many reported attacks that involve adding small, often imperceptible modifications to the original input to mislead the neural network into making incorrect predictions or classifications. These type of attacks are termed as evasion attack [3]. Evasion attacks can be particularly problematic for security-sensitive applications, such as medical image analysis, biometric authentication, spam detection, and autonomous driving. Therefore it is imperative to assess if the integrity issue of encrypted inference could be exploited to stage an evasion attack. Consider the case where an individual encrypts their X-ray image and sends it to a cloud-based service for medical analysis, such as detecting potential diseases like chronic inflammatory lung disease (COPD), evasion attacks in such cases can have serious consequences.

The definition of HE claims theoretically that any arbitrary plaintext operation can be translated to the encrypted domain. Hence apparently, it seems that the translation of such attacks is straightforward. However, in this work, we highlight the practical challenges of implementing evasion attacks on HE encrypted ML framework. While there are numerous evasion attacks [4] in the plaintext domain (message space), most are generated based on a specific image by solving a data-dependent optimization problem. However, once an image is encrypted, an adversary cannot determine the appropriate perturbation using these techniques. Universal adversarial perturbation (UAP) which is an image-agnostic perturbation becomes relevant in this context. UAPs are fixed perturbations that when added to any image sampled from the data distribution of images are capable of inducing misclassification. Considering the basic claim of homomorphic computation, an attacker with sufficient information to construct UAPs for the plaintext model can use homomorphic encryption to encrypt UAPs and add them to encrypted client data. Because UAPs are universal, it does not matter by definition that the client data are unknown to the attacker.

However, there are many inherent challenges in translating the attack to the encrypted domain. One prominent challenge in the encrypted domain is to perform the attack validation which means the attacker cannot directly assess whether the attack is successful or not. Though from the basic definition of HE, it can be argued that it is needless to verify this. The reason is if a high fooling rate of UAP is ensured in the plaintext domain, the same will be reflected in the encrypted domain. However, our experiment shows due to the inherent approximation or quantization involved in existing homomorphic encryption libraries these exact mapping cannot be confirmed (For example, FHE schemes like BGV [5], BFV [6], and Zama's variant of TFHE [7], which encode only integers, it is necessary to convert floating-point numbers to integers using quantization, and schemes like CKKS [8] support approximate floating-point computation), the reason is quantized UAP is not a direct equivalent perturbation for quantized floating-point input. It requires one to generate Quantization-aware perturbation while ensuring that universal property is preserved. Our exploration also shows implementation differences of different homomorphic encryption libraries posing varied challenges in actual attack implementation. We would like to highlight while it is straightforward for any adversary to add perturbation by intercepting the ciphertext in TenSEAL [9] due to the support of floating-point arithmetic and homomorphic addition through operator overloading, it becomes challenging in Concrete ML. In Concrete ML [10] it requires one to generate Quantization-aware UAP and careful selection of FHE operator to represent the equivalent notion of UAP under API-only setting. Moreover, the attack complexity varies for symmetric key and public key scenarios. Furthermore, Concrete ML does not allow the composition of circuits with different parameters, which is desirable for the adversary to perturb ciphertexts. We demonstrate how shifting to a different attack surface, referred to as MLIR (Multi-level Intermediate Representation), can be advantageous. MLIR serves as an intermediate representation with FHE operators when compiling any model defined in the Concrete ML frontend. While addressing these challenges, our contributions in this paper can be summarized as follows:

- We propose the notion of UAP in encrypted domain and provide theoretical justifications regarding the adversarial vulnerability of symmetric and public key ciphers based on the learning with errors (LWE) framework specifically in the Zama's variant of the TFHE scheme and the CKKS Scheme. This notion can be extended to any Regev ciphertext [11] similarly. While previous work focused on constructing universal adversarial perturbations for plaintext, to the best of our knowledge this is the first paper on targeted and untargeted evasion attacks in the encrypted domain.
- Secondly, we explore how the attack strategy differs while we perform white-box evasion attacks in image classifiers implemented in Concrete ML and TenSEAL. Our investigation also shows while an attack can be realized with only API-based operator utilization in TenSEAL it is not straightforward in Concrete ML. Moreover, in TenSEAL any party (Man-In-The-Middle Attacker) intercepting the ciphertext can act as an adversary while in Concrete ML only an untrusted server can act as an adversary or any Man-In-The-Middle Attacker (MITM) simulating as a server can act as an adversary.

– Since quantization plays a key role in case of successful implementation of the attack, We also propose the algorithm to generate Quantization-aware UAP for conducting attacks in symmetric key scenarios in Concrete ML. In public key implementation of CKKS Quantization-aware UAP generation is not a requirement.

2   Related Works

Evasion Attacks in Plaintext Domain

Several targeted and untargeted attack methods have been proposed in the literature, each with its unique approach and objectives. Previous studies [12–17] have extensively investigated evasion attacks in the plaintext domain, demonstrating their efficacy and potential security risks for machine learning and deep learning models. However, there remains a significant gap in understanding the transferability of these attacks in encrypted domain.

Attacks on Homomorphic Encryption Based Deep Learning

Given the growing adoption of Homomorphic Encryption (HE) for privacy-preserving machine learning, it is imperative to assess the vulnerability of encrypted models to different kinds of attacks. Although this field is gaining attention, there are currently no reported works on performing evasion attacks strictly within the encrypted domain. While there exist key recovery attacks, such as the practical full-key recovery attack on TFHE and FHEW schemes demonstrated by Chaturvedi et al. [18] and on CKKS schemes [19] by Guo et al., and attacks on the service model of HE-based deep learning systems proposed by Shin et al. [20], these methods do not address evasion attacks conducted directly within the encrypted domain. Thus, none of the existing works have performed evasion attacks specifically in the encrypted domain.

3   Preliminaries

Evasion Attacks

Evasion attacks involve adding perturbation δ to input samples x to induce misclassification by a model f. Non-targeted or untargeted attacks aim to find δ for which $f(x_{\mathrm{adv}}) \neq y_{\mathrm{true}}$, where $x_{\mathrm{adv}} = x + \delta$ and y_{true} is the true label corresponding to x. They minimize the perturbation norm $\|\delta\|$ subject to $f(x + \delta) \neq y_{\mathrm{true}}$. Targeted attacks aim to force $f(x_{\mathrm{adv}})$ to predict a specific incorrect label t. They minimize the perturbation norm $\|\delta\|$ subject to $f(x + \delta) = t$. Based on the attacker's capabilities, the attack can be categorized into two types: white-box and black-box. In a white-box approach, the attacker is assumed to have complete knowledge of the target model, including its architecture, and partial or full access to the dataset. In contrast, in a black-box approach, the attacker can only acquire restricted knowledge about the model, usually executed by observing the outputs of queries such as labels or confidence scores.

Untargeted Universal Adversarial Perturbations and Targeted Universal Adversarial Perturbations

Moosavi-Dezfooli et al. [21] introduced the concept of **Untargeted Universal Adversarial Perturbations** (UAPs). These are fixed perturbations for a given dataset capable of inducing misclassification across various images. The goal is to find v which satisfies two conditions: $\|v\|_p \leq \epsilon$, where ϵ controls the imperceptibility of v measured in terms of the p-norm with $p \in [1, \infty)$, and $\mathbb{P}_{x \sim \mu}[\hat{k}(x + v) \neq \hat{k}(x)] \geq 1 - \delta$, where δ quantifies the desired fooling rate and $\hat{k}$ is the classifier. The fooling rate is defined as the proportion of total perturbed images $(x + v)$ in a dataset for which $\hat{k}(x) \neq \hat{k}(x + v)$. Unlike imperceptible adversarial perturbations, which are tailored for individual data points, UAPs are image-agnostic and deceive classifiers uniformly. For more details, please refer to Appendix A.

Targeted Universal Adversarial Perturbations [22] are crafted to manipulate samples drawn from the image distribution so that the predicted class is the target class defined by the adversary. The proposed algorithm is an extension of the iterative approach for non-targeted UAPs, where it iteratively generates UAPs under the constraint of the adversarial sample being classified to the target class. For more details, please refer to Appendix B.

Fully Homomorphic Encryption Schemes

Fully Homomorphic Encryption (FHE) schemes [23] allow arbitrary computations to be performed on encrypted data without decryption. Proposed by Craig Gentry in 2009, FHE schemes support both addition and multiplication operations, which are sufficient to perform any arbitrary computation as these two operations constitute a functionally complete set over finite rings.

4   System Model and Threat Model

The system and threat model is described in detail for both Concrete ML [10] and TenSEAL [9] in Appendix H and Fig. 2. Additionally, for an overview of the libraries used, please refer to Appendix F.

Formalizing Equivalence of Plain and Encrypted Models

In the plaintext domain, let a classifier be represented by $f_{\mathrm{model}}(x; w)$, where $x \in \mathbb{R}^d$ is the input image and w are the model parameters. In the encrypted domain, we denote the classifier as f_{eval}, which operates on encrypted data. The plain and encrypted models are equivalent if for most $m \in \mathcal{M}$, $\mathrm{Dec}_{\mathrm{sk}}(f_{\mathrm{eval}}(\mathrm{Enc}(m))) = f_{\mathrm{model}}(m)$, ensuring that decrypted inference matches the plaintext model output. For further details (along with symbols and notation used), see Appendix C.

5   Evasion Attack Methodology in TenSEAL (CKKS) in Public Key Scenario

We consider the public key variant of CKKS scheme as implemented in TenSEAL. For more details on CCKS scheme and overview of TenSEAL please refer F D. As displayed in Fig. 1, the attack step involves homomorphically adding encrypted targeted/untargeted perturbations to the encrypted image sent by the client to the server for prediction.

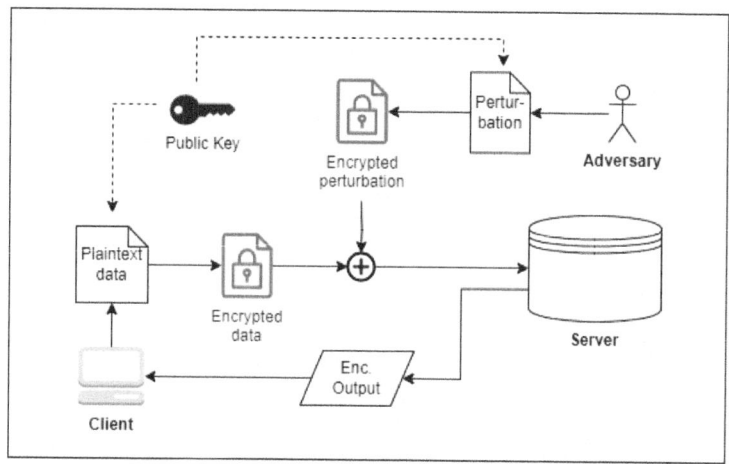

Fig. 1. General evasion attack strategy in public key encryption scheme

---

Algorithm 1. Targeted/Untargeted Attack using Encrypted Universal Adversarial Perturbation in Public Key Scenario

---

1: **Input:** Encrypted client input x_{client}, Public Key pk, Encrypted perturbation $v_{encrypted}$ (targeted/untargeted UAP encrypted w.r.t. public key of the Client)
2: **Output:** Adversarial example x_{adv}
3: $x_{adv} \leftarrow$ FHE.add($v_{encrypted}, x_{client}$)
4: **return** x_{adv}

Rationale: Algorithm 1 demonstrates a targeted or untargeted evasion attack using an encrypted Universal Adversarial Perturbation (UAP) in a public key encryption scenario. The adversary generates a UAP and encrypts it using the client's public key. The adversary, either the server or a man-in-the-middle (MITM) attacker, uses the addition operator for ciphertexts (`FHE.add`) to create an adversarial example. The rationale for why encryption of floating point perturbation w.r.t public key is a universal adversarial perturbation for the ciphertext space is discussed theoretically in Appendix G.

5.1   Experimental Setup and Results

Datasets Used: In our experimental setup, we utilize two commonly used image datasets: MNIST and Fashion-MNIST (FMNIST). For more details about the dataset, please refer Appendix I.

Table 1. The table displays the test accuracy on MNIST and FashionMNIST datasets in plaintext and encrypted domains for both targeted and untargeted attack scenarios where UAP was generated with 10% of training data. The table validates our observation that under the equivalence of plain and encrypted models, the effect of the misclassification rate of UAPs remains consistent both in plain and encrypted domains.

Inference Domain	MNIST	FashionMNIST
Plaintext		
Test Accuracy	97.99%	87.5%
Test Accuracy (after adding untargeted UAP)	1.13%	0.34%
Test Accuracy (after adding targeted UAP)	9.8%	10%
Targeted attack success rate	100%	99.99%
Encrypted		
Test Accuracy	98%	86.78%
Test Accuracy (attack using untargeted UAP)	1.14%	0.31%
Test Accuracy (attack using targeted UAP)	9.8%	10.3%
Targeted attack success rate	100%	99.99%

System Setup: All experiments were conducted using Google Colab, Kaggle Notebooks, and a local system running Ubuntu 22.04.4 LTS with an Intel i7-8700 CPU (12 cores) @ 4.6 GHz and 32 GB of memory. Please refer to Appendix I for more details on the configuration of Google Colab and Kaggle.

Parameters used for UAP Generation Using ART Library: The UAP has been generated using ART library [24,25]. The following parameters are used to do the attack, fooling rate parameter $\delta = 0.2$, perturbation magnitude bound $\epsilon = 10.0$. The maximum iteration to compute UAP is set to 20. The reason for choosing these parameters has been discussed in Appendix P.

Cryptographic Parameters: We adopt the same encryption parameters as provided by the library: Polynomial modulus degree: $N = 8192$, Security level: $\lambda = 128$. The scaling factor is set to 2^{26} and the coefficient modulus bit sizes are $[31, 26, 26, 26, 26, 26, 26, 31]$.

Model Architecture: We consider the pre-trained model with model parameters and model architecture as provided by the TenSEAL library. The details of the architecture are mentioned in Appendix I.

Results and Discussion: We evaluated the impact of adversarial attacks on plaintext and encrypted models, as described in Table 1, using the MNIST and FashionMNIST datasets. The test accuracy of the model on plaintext data was 97.99% for MNIST and 87.5% for FashionMNIST. After adding untargeted UAPs, the accuracy dropped significantly to 1.13% and 0.34%, respectively. Targeted UAPs classified 100% of the test samples into the target class (target class = 0 for MNIST and 1 for FashionMNIST), reducing the overall accuracy to 9.8%

for MNIST and 10% for FashionMNIST.

In the encrypted domain, the results were nearly identical. The test accuracy remained 98% for MNIST and 86.78% for FashionMNIST. After adding untargeted UAPs, the accuracy decreased to 1.14% and 0.31%, while targeted UAPs resulted in 100% and 99.99% targeted attack success rates with accuracies of 9.8% and 10.3% for MNIST and FashionMNIST, respectively. This consistency across domains supports our claim that the encrypted perturbation behaves as a UAP for the encrypted model.

6 How is the Attack Different in the Case of Concrete ML?

We examine the theoretical foundations of evasion attacks on Concrete ML, which implements Zama's variant of the TFHE scheme (see Appendix E). We demonstrate the adversarial vulnerability of LWE encryption in a symmetric key setting, extendable to GLWE-based encryption as implemented in Zama's variant of the encryption scheme. Notably, every LWE encryption of message $m = (a, \text{Encoding}(m))$ can be perturbed by adding $(0, \text{Encoding}(v))$, where v is the Quantization-aware UAP. For further details (along with symbols and notation used), refer to Appendix K.

Attack Challenges with Concrete ML Frontend: Concrete ML is built on top of Concrete library [26] and allows for encrypted inference with ML and DL models. While one may try to perform evasion attacks using the above methodology, Concrete's design eliminates such possibilities as the encryption returns the ciphertext as an immutable object preventing direct modification of the LWE representation.

Also, even if the adversary tries to define an adder circuit to add perturbation to the ciphertext object using Concrete-ML APIs, the cipher text obtained from the circuit class instance of the model cannot be evaluated over that adder circuit, as circuit composition [27] is only allowed for circuits having different cryptographic parameters as opposed to TenSEAL where it involves a static choice of cryptographic parameters. The reason is detailed below.

Executing any operation in Concrete ML from the Python frontend requires compiling the operation represented as a function using a representative input set to a `Circuit Class object` [28]. This class then utilizes the function call `run` for evaluation defined within the `Circuit Class` to evaluate a ciphertext over that circuit. Since the objective of the adversary is to add perturbation to the ciphertext, which is an immutable object returned after encryption, the adversary must compile an addition function to a circuit. This evaluation circuit takes ciphertext as the input and returns the addition of the ciphertext with the UAP to generate a perturbed ciphertext. However, Concrete restricts the evaluation phase of ciphertexts over circuits having different cryptographic parameters and precision requirements [27]. As evident from the parameter selection strategy by Concrete optimizer [29] which is discussed in Appendix J, the model that the server owns and the adder circuit defined by the adversary to generate perturbations will differ significantly in the number of operations and thus select different macro and micro parameter sets. Hence successful attack will not be possible in this context which requires circuit composition [27] with the same cryptographic parameters and the same precision of input and output LWE ciphertexts defined by Concrete [30].

7   Evasion Attack Methodology in Concrete ML by an Untrusted Server

We discuss the challenges and techniques for evasion attack by untrusted server in detail in Appendix L, We propose Algorithm 2 which is instrumental in realizing the attack as Concrete ML quantizes floating point values with uniform quantization [31,32] method before encoding followed by encryption. This step is necessary because currently FHE in Concrete ML can only handle integers up to 16 bits [31].

7.1   Experimental Setup and Results

Digits Dataset: In our experimental setup, we utilize an image dataset consisting of grayscale images depicting handwritten digits ranging from 0 to 9 [33]. For more details please refer Appendix O.

System Setup: The system setup is the same as that in TenSEAL.

UAP Generation: We have used the python library - ART (Adversarial Robustness Toolbox library) [24,25] for generating the UAPs. For more details please refer Appendix O.

Model Architecture: We utilize a simple neural network defined using PyTorch library and train it on the above-mentioned digits dataset to provide a proof of concept, as evaluating over complex CNN networks incurs overhead in terms of latency. For more details please refer Appendix O.

Results: We conducted an analysis to assess the impact of an evasion attack on a model's predictions in an encrypted domain. From the obtained results, we found that the attack's efficacy remained consistent even in the encrypted domain. In the plaintext domain, the model achieved a test accuracy of 96.39% when trained on a digits dataset containing 1437 training and 360 test samples. However, after applying the untargeted Universal Adversarial Perturbation (UAP), the test accuracy dropped to 9.44%. Moreover, when we used a targeted UAP (target class = "0"), the accuracy reduced to 9.17% compared to when an untargeted UAP was used. In contrast, in the encrypted domain, the model initially achieved a test accuracy of 94.16%. On introducing both untargeted and targeted UAPs into the encrypted inputs, the accuracy reduced to 9.44% and 9.16%, respectively. The results demonstrate, the effectiveness of the UAP remains consistent when transitioning from the plaintext to the encrypted inference domain. More-over, the importance of using Quantization-aware UAP is clearly reflected, as the targeted attack success rate is almost nil when using directly quantized UAP. In contrast, using Quantization-aware UAP retains the 100% targeted attack success rate while transitioning from plaintext to the encrypted domain. This also validates our observation, which asserts that under model equivalence, the use of Quantization-aware UAP in ciphertext space maintains a nearly identical fooling rate. These findings are summarized in Table 2.

Table 2. The table below shows test accuracy and misclassification results for the entire test set using only 10% of training data. It demonstrates that after adding Quantization-aware UAP, the accuracy drop is nearly identical and the targeted attack success rate is consistently maintained when applying Quantization-aware UAP.

Inference Domain	Digits Dataset
Plaintext	
Test Accuracy	96.39%
Test Accuracy (after adding untargeted UAP)	9.44%
Test Accuracy (after adding targeted UAP)	9.17%
Targeted Attack Success Rate	100%
Encrypted	
Test Accuracy	94.16%
Test Accuracy (after adding untargeted UAP)	9.44%
Test Accuracy (after adding targeted UAP)	9.16%
Targeted Attack Success Rate (Directly Quantized UAP)	< 1%
Targeted Attack Success Rate (Quantization-aware UAP)	100%

8 Conclusion and Future Work

In this paper, we demonstrated how evasion attacks can be conducted in the encrypted domain using an equivalent notion of UAP in both public and symmetric key settings. We showed that for schemes involving quantization, generating quantization-aware UAPs is essential to maintain the targeted attack success rate. The attacks were tested in Concrete ML and TenSEAL, where Concrete ML's attack feasibility depends on factors like circuit size, precision, and operator choices, with the adversary being the untrusted server or Man-In-The-Middle (MITM) attacker simulating as a server. In TenSEAL, anyone intercepting the ciphertext can be an adversary. While our approach provides a theoretical foundation and validates on simple image datasets, it has not been validated on more complex datasets which require more sophisticated model architectures and involve longer latencies for generating predictions. Future work will validate it for more complex datasets, and explore settings beyond classification where evasion may pose a threat against encrypted inference. Additionally, we plan to investigate black box methods [34] of UAP generation, which could introduce a stronger threat model than described in this work.

Appendix

A   Untargeted Universal Adversarial Perturbations

Moosavi-Dezfooli et al. [21] introduced the concept of Untargeted Universal Adversarial Perturbations (UAPs). These are fixed perturbations for a given dataset capable of inducing misclassification across various images. Unlike imperceptible adversarial perturbations, which are tailored for individual data points, UAPs are image-agnostic and deceive classifiers uniformly. Formally, for a distribution of images μ and a classification function $\hat{k}$, UAPs aim to find perturbation vectors v such that $\hat{k}(x + v) \neq \hat{k}(x)$ for the majority of x sampled from μ. This means that for almost all data points drawn from μ, which represents the distribution of images in $\mathbb{R}^d$, the perturbation v will cause a misclassification. The goal is to find v which satisfies two conditions expressed as:

- $\|v\|_p \leq \epsilon$
- $\mathbb{P}_{x \sim \mu}[\hat{k}(x + v) \neq \hat{k}(x)] \geq 1 - \delta$

where ϵ controls the imperceptibility of v measured in terms of the p-norm with $p \in [1, \infty)$ and δ quantifies the desired fooling rate.

B   Targeted Universal Adversarial Perturbations

Targeted Universal Adversarial Perturbations (UAPs) [22] are crafted to manipulate samples drawn from the image distribution so that the predicted class is the target class defined by the adversary. The proposed algorithm is an extension of the iterative approach for non-targeted UAPs where it iteratively generates UAPs under the constraint of the adversarial sample being classified to the target class. It uses fast gradient sign method for targeted attacks (tFGSM [35]) to generate targeted UAPs, whereas the non-targeted UAP algorithm uses a method (e.g., DeepFool [14]) to generate a non-targeted adversarial example for an input image. At each iteration, if the perturbed image is not classified into the target class, the perturbation is updated. This update procedure terminates when either the targeted attack success rate reaches 100% or the maximum iteration limit is reached.

C   Formalizing Equivalence of Plain and Encrypted Models

In the plaintext domain, a classifier can be represented as a function $f_{\text{model}}(x; w)$, where $x \in \mathbb{R}^d$ represents the input image and w denotes the model parameters. The function f_{model} takes an input image x and outputs an estimated label based on the learned parameters w. In the encrypted domain, a classifier can be represented as a function $f_{\text{eval},w}$, where w denotes the trained weights of the plaintext model. For simplicity, let's denote it by f_{eval}. In this representation, the classifier takes ciphertext as input, which consists of the encryption of plaintext m under a secret key or public key. The function f_{eval} maps the ciphertext space to itself. Plain and encrypted models are said to be equivalent if the result of encrypted inference in both plaintext and encrypted domain is consistent that is for most $m \in \mathcal{M}$ (Message space), $\text{Dec}_{\text{sk}}(f_{\text{eval}}(\text{Enc}(m))) = f_{\text{model}}(m)$. Here, Dec_{sk} represents the decryption function using the secret key sk, f_{eval} denotes the model used for inference in the encrypted domain, $\text{Enc}(m)$ represents the encryption of the input data m w.r.t to any of the above schemes, and $f_{\text{model}}(m)$ is the output of the model in the plaintext domain. The expression indicates that the decrypted output of the encrypted inference should be equal to the output of the model in the plaintext domain for consistency. The above equality can be attributed to the fact that evaluating circuit (the circuit representing the operations in neural nets realized as equivalent homomorphic operations corresponding to plain operators) over ciphertext space gives the same results if the plaintext data m is evaluated over model represented by f_{model}.

Note: The terms "message space," "plaintext domain," and "plaintext space" are used interchangeably throughout this paper. Please note that "plaintext" does not refer to the encoding of a message.

D   CKKS Homomorphic Encryption Scheme

The CKKS scheme [8] is a public key encryption scheme that relies on the hardness of the Ring Learning With Errors (RLWE) problem for its security. It supports approximate arithmetic on real and complex numbers with predefined precision and transforms into a fully homomorphic encryption (FHE) scheme using the bootstrapping technique.

Distributions and Ring Definitions: For a real $\sigma > 0$, $\text{DG}(\sigma^2)$ represents the discrete Gaussian distribution in $\mathbb{Z}^N$. $\text{HWT}(h)$ denotes the set of vectors in $\{-1, 0, 1\}^N$ with Hamming weight h. $\text{ZO}(\rho)$ is a distribution in $\{-1, 0, 1\}^N$ where each component is 1 or -1 with probability $\rho/2$, respectively, and 0 with probability $1 - \rho$. Let $\mathcal{R} = \mathbb{Z}[x]/(x^N + 1)$ and $\mathcal{R}_Q = \mathbb{Z}_Q[x]/(x^N + 1)$ where Q and N are powers of two. A ciphertext is in the polynomial ring $\mathcal{R}_Q^2$, and a secret key is randomly selected from $\text{HWT}(h)$. Parameters Q and N depend on the depth of a target circuit and a security parameter λ.

Key Generation: Parameters Q and P are set as 2^L. The secret key sk is sampled from HWT(h), and the public key pk is generated using distributions DG and HWT. An evaluation key evk is computed based on pk and sk.

Encoding: Encoding maps a vector of complex numbers into a polynomial ring. τ is an isomorphism mapping $\mathbb{R}[x]/(x^N+1)$ to $\mathbb{C}^{N/2}$. Encode($m, pBits$) converts complex numbers into an integer polynomial, and Decode($m(x), pBits$) reverses this process.

Encryption: Let $m(x)$ be the encoded plaintext polynomial. The encryption of m results in a ciphertext $(b(x), a(x))$, where:

$$(b(x), a(x)) = v(x) \cdot pk + (m(x) + e_0(x), e_1(x)) \mod Q.$$

Here, $v(x)$ is a random polynomial sampled from the ZO(0.5) distribution, pk is the public key, $e_0(x)$ and $e_1(x)$ are noise polynomials sampled from the discrete Gaussian distribution, and Q is the ciphertext modulus.

Decryption: Decryption involves computing the plaintext message m by multiplying the ciphertext with the secret key and decoding the result. For a ciphertext $(b(x), a(x))$, decryption computes:

$$m(x) = b(x) + a(x) \cdot s(x) \mod Q'.$$

Here, $s(x)$ is the secret key, and Q' is the level-specific modulus. After computing $m(x)$, it is decoded to obtain the plaintext message m.

E   Zama's Variant of TFHE Scheme

We consider a symmetric key encryption scheme based on LWE-type encryption introduced in [36]. The scheme is described below:

KeyGen(1^κ): Given security parameter λ, define (k, N) with $k \geq 1$ and N as a power of 2. Assume normal error distribution $\chi = \mathcal{N}(0, \sigma^2)$ over polynomial ring $\mathbb{R}_N[X] = \mathbb{R}[X]/(X^N + 1)$. Generate uniformly at random a secret random vector $s = (s_1, \ldots, s_k) \xleftarrow{\$} \mathbb{B}_N[X]^k$, where $\mathbb{B}_N[X]$ is the subset of polynomials in $\mathbb{Z}_N[X]$ with coefficients in $\mathbb{B} = \{0, 1\}$, $q = 2^\Omega$ and plaintext space $\mathcal{P}_N[X] = \left(\frac{q}{p}\mathbb{Z}/q\mathbb{Z}\right)[X]/(X^N + 1) \subseteq \hat{\mathbb{Z}}_N[X]$, $\hat{\mathbb{Z}}_N[X] = (\mathbb{Z}/q\mathbb{Z})[X]/(X^N + 1)$. Public parameters are $pp = \{k, N, \sigma, p, q\}$.

Encoding: The encoding process takes a cleartext message $m \in \mathcal{M}$ and transforms it into a polynomial $\mu \in \hat{\mathbb{Z}}_N[X]$, denoted as $\mu = \text{Encode}(m)$. The polynomial μ consists of coefficients μ_i that follow the representation:

$$\mu_i = 2^{\Omega - (\omega + \overline{\omega})}(\nu_i \mod 2^\omega)$$

where Ω represents the total bit-length, ω is the message bit-precision, $\overline{\omega}$ is the padding bits, and ν_i are the coefficients of μ.

Encrypt$_{sk}(m)$: The encryption of a polynomial $\mu \in \hat{\mathbb{Z}}_N[X]$ is denoted by $\mathcal{C} =$ GLWE$_{\mathbf{s}}(\mu)$ where GLWE represents general learning with errors problem over torus and $\mathcal{C} = (\mathbf{a}_1, \ldots, \mathbf{a}_k, \mathbf{b}) \in \hat{\mathbb{Z}}_N[X]^{k+1}$. Compute:

$$\mu^* = \mu + e \mod (q, X^N + 1)$$

and

$$\mathbf{b} = \sum_{j=1}^{k} \mathbf{s}_j \cdot \mathbf{a}_j + \mu^*.$$

Here, $(\mathbf{a}_1, \ldots, \mathbf{a}_k) \leftarrow \hat{\mathbb{Z}}_N[X]^k$, and discrete noise $e = \lfloor \bar{e}q \rceil$ where $\bar{e} \leftarrow \mathbb{R}_N[X]$ with coefficients sampled from a Gaussian distribution $\mathcal{N}(0, \sigma^2)$.

Decrypt$_{sk}(m)$: To decrypt $\mathcal{C} = (\mathbf{a}_1, \ldots, \mathbf{a}_k, \mathbf{b})$ using private key $\mathbf{s} = (\mathbf{s}_1, \ldots, \mathbf{s}_k)$, compute:

$$\mu^* = \mathbf{b} - \sum_{j=1}^{k} \mathbf{s}_j \cdot \mathbf{a}_j \mod (q, X^N + 1)$$

and output

$$\text{Upper}_{q,p}(\mu^*),$$

where $\text{Upper} : \mathbb{Z}/q\mathbb{Z} \to \mathbb{Z}/q\mathbb{Z}$ is defined as

$$x \mapsto \text{Upper}(x) = \frac{q}{p} \left\lfloor \frac{p}{q} \text{lift}(x) \right\rceil,$$

where the function lift lifts elements of $\mathbb{Z}/q\mathbb{Z}$ to $\mathbb{Z}$.

F   Overview of TenSEAL and Concrete ML

TenSEAL: TenSEAL implements various homomorphic encryption schemes, including BGV, BFV, and CKKS. BGV and BFV are suited for encrypting integers modulo a configurable plaintext modulus, while CKKS is ideal for encrypting floating-point or complex numbers, making it highly desirable for machine learning applications. The CKKS scheme's batching feature allows for efficient encryption of large matrices, enabling fast and approximate computations on encrypted data. TenSEAL is built on top of the Microsoft SEAL library and integrates seamlessly with popular deep learning frameworks like PyTorch. However, TenSEAL has a limited range of supported operators for encrypted inference compared to Concrete ML.

Concrete ML: Concrete ML implements the Zama's variant of TFHE [7] scheme. It offers a comprehensive suite of functionalities tailored specifically for privacy-preserving machine learning and deep learning tasks. It allows converting machine learning models into their fully homomorphic encryption (FHE) equivalents using familiar APIs from scikit-learn and PyTorch. Concrete ML supports a wide range of PyTorch operators, enabling the construction of fully connected and convolutional neural networks with normalization and activation layers. It also includes support for many element-wise operators. Concrete ML processes programs written in Python and translates them into an MLIR-based intermediate representation via the Concrete Python frontend. This intermediate representation is then compiled by the Concrete Compiler [26] into an FHE program, enabling encrypted computations. Also, Concrete ML utilizes Concrete-Python and Concrete Optimizer for efficiently synthesizing circuits. However, while circuit synthesis has been optimized, there are performance trade-offs, particularly in terms of runtime when evaluating deep neural networks.

G   Rationale Behind Algorithm 1

Observation: Let f_{eval} represent the model with encrypted operators, and let v be a Universal Adversarial Perturbation (UAP) for the plaintext space X with respect to the model f_{model}. If both f_{model} and f_{eval} are equivalent, then $Enc_{pk}(v)$ will also act as a UAP for the ciphertext space with respect to the model f_{eval}.

Rationale: Given a message x, the encrypted input is $Enc_{pk}(x)$. The model f_{eval} processes this, producing $f_{eval}(Enc_{pk}(x))$. Since v is a UAP for the plaintext model, the adversary can encrypt v using the public key, resulting in $Enc_{pk}(v)$. By the homomorphic properties of CKKS, adding $Enc_{pk}(v)$ to $Enc_{pk}(x)$ is equivalent to adding v to x in plaintext. Thus, $f_{eval}(Enc_{pk}(x + v))$ leads to misclassification, making $Enc_{pk}(v)$ a UAP for the encrypted model.

Note: 1) The observation discussed above works for both targeted and untargeted attacks. The targeted and untargeted attacks differ only in the UAP generation step as evident from the Appendix A B.
2) In case of an attack in TenSEAL where the model defined is a CNN (convolutional neural network) with the first layer as convolution it requires the adversary to do im2col [9] (image to column) encoding similar to encoding images before encrypting as a CKKS vector.

H   System Model and Threat Model

TenSEAL System Model: In TenSEAL, the client starts by generating a TenSEAL context [9], along with secret and evaluation keys. The client encrypts the data using this context and sends both the encrypted data and serialized context (without the secret key) to the server. The server, with a pre-trained model, performs inference on the encrypted data and returns the encrypted results to the client. The client decrypts the results and applies any final processing (e.g., softmax or argmax) to obtain the prediction.

Concrete ML System Model: In Concrete ML, the server deploys a machine learning model which is used to create client specifications that contain different cryptographic parameters generated by Concrete optimizer [29] to be sent to

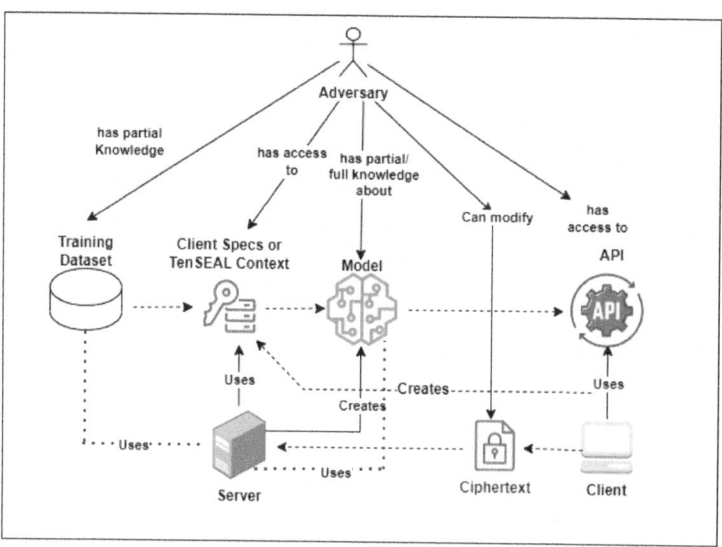

Fig. 2. The above figure illustrates the system and threat model for Concrete ML and TenSEAL. The knowledge and capabilities of the adversary are displayed in the above figure, the adversary which can be an MITM or server intends to perturb the ciphertext by using APIs of both libraries which also requires evaluation keys while evaluating over circuits. TenSEAL and Concrete ML differ in the cryptographic setup, where the parameters (e.g., RLWE dimension, coefficient modulus sizes) are chosen by the client. The client generates the TenSEAL context using these parameters and sends it to the server along with the encrypted data. In contrast, in Concrete ML, the cryptographic parameters are generated by the server and sent to the client in the form of client specifications, which are then used to generate the secret and evaluation keys. Since public key or evaluation keys are primary requirement for processing ciphertext both in TenSEAL and Concrete ML, the adversary can use it to perturb ciphertext

the client for generating secret and evaluation keys. The client requests these parameters, generates necessary keys, encrypts the data, and sends it to the server. The server uses these keys to securely perform inference on the encrypted data and returns the encrypted results. The client then decrypts the results using secret key.

Threat Model: The adversary, which could be a server or a Man-In-The-Middle Attacker (MITM), possesses full knowledge of the model architecture, partial knowledge of the training dataset, and access to evaluation keys (which an MITM can obtain when serialized client specifications in Concrete ML or the TenSEAL context are communicated along with serialized ciphertext). The adversary's goal is to perturb the ciphertext. They can use API functionalities provided by the library, generate universal perturbations using the dataset and model architecture information, and apply these perturbations to the ciphertext. The adversary's objectives include causing both untargeted and targeted misclassifications of encrypted inputs sent by the client to the server for predictions.

I   Experimental Setup (For TenSEAL)

Datasets Used: In our experimental setup, we utilize two commonly used image datasets: MNIST and Fashion-MNIST (FMNIST). These datasets consist of grayscale images of handwritten digits (MNIST) and fashion items (FMNIST), respectively. The MNIST dataset contains 28×28 pixel grayscale images of handwritten digits (0–9). It consists of 60,000 training images and 10,000 test images. The FMNIST dataset is similar to MNIST but consists of grayscale images of fashion items instead of digits. It also contains 28×28 pixel images and has the same training and test set sizes as MNIST. The dataset includes 10 categories of clothing and accessories, such as T-shirts, dresses, sneakers, and handbags.

System Setup: All experiments are implemented on Google Colab and Kaggle Notebooks. Google Colab uses Intel(R) Xeon(R) CPU @ 2.00 GHz (1 core, 2000.204 MHz), memory of 13290480 kB, and Linux Operating System. Kaggle Notebook uses Intel(R) Xeon(R) CPU @ 2.00 GHz (2 cores, 2000.136 MHz), memory of 32880784 kB, and Linux Operating System. Additionally, experiments are conducted on a system running Ubuntu 22.04.4 LTS x86_64 with an Intel i7-8700 CPU (12 cores) @ 4.600 GHz and 31862 MiB of memory.

Parameters Used for UAP Generation Using ART Library: The UAP has been generated using ART library [24, 25]. The following parameters are used to do the attack, fooling rate parameter $\delta = 0.2$, perturbation magnitude bound $\epsilon = 10.0$. The maximum iteration to compute UAP is set to 20. The reason for choosing such parameters can be found in Appendix P.

Cryptographic Parameters: We adopt the same encryption parameters provided by the library: Polynomial modulus degree: $N = 8192$, Security level: $\lambda = 128$. The scaling factor is set to 2^{26} and the coefficient modulus bit sizes are $[31, 26, 26, 26, 26, 26, 26, 31]$.

Model Architecture: We consider the pre-trained model with model parameters and model architecture as provided by the TenSEAL library. The architecture consists of the following layers as described in Table 3.

Table 3. A CNN architecture with square activation fucntion to classify MNIST and FMNIST datastet.

Layer	Type	Output Shape	Description
1	Convolutional	(64, 4, 28, 28)	4 filters of size 7×7, stride 3, no padding
2	Activation	(64, 4, 8, 8)	Element-wise square function
3	Flattening	(64, 256)	Flatten to vector of size 256
4	Fully Connected	(64, 64)	Linear layer with 64 hidden units
5	Activation	(64, 64)	Element-wise square function
6	Fully Connected	(64, 10)	Linear layer with 10 output units

J   Parameter Selection in Concrete

In the TFHE scheme, various types of ciphertexts are utilized, including LWE, RLWE, GLWE, and GGSW, each with distinct parameters known as macro-parameters. These parameters include dimension for LWE ciphertexts, polynomial size and dimension for GLWE ciphertexts. These parameters are referred to as macro parameters. There are other parameters, referred to as micro-parameters which is used locally inside the FHE operator which takes ciphertexts and/or plaintexts as input and produces one or more ciphertexts as output. Micro parameters include parameters for PBS (Programmable bootstrapping) and Key switching i.e. decomposition base (base log) and a number of decomposition levels. Each FHE operator is associated with a noise model and a cost model. The noise model describes the noise evolution across the FHE operator, while the cost model represents the metric to minimize, such as execution time. The selection of micro and macro parameters [37,38] significantly impacts both the cost and noise growth of operations, necessitating careful consideration during parameter selection. To facilitate parameter selection for a circuit, an Atomic Pattern (AP) type is introduced, representing a sub-graph of FHE operators that outputs one or more ciphertexts. When instantiated with a parameter set, the noise and cost at each edge of the FHE sub-graph can be estimated. The optimal parameter set for a given circuit, security level, and message precision is determined by minimizing the cost of AP instances while ensuring correctness. The parameterization of circuits is done in one of the stages of compilation pass of Concrete-compiler [26] referred to as TFHE parameterization [39]. The parameter selection strategy by Concrete optimizer prevents any attacker intercepting the ciphertext from doing circuit composition which is necessary to add perturbation.

K   How is the Attack Different in the Case of Concrete ML?

We discuss below the theoretical justifications for evasion attacks against Concrete ML, which implements Zama's variant of the TFHE Scheme, as discussed in Appendix E. We show the adversarial vulnerability of LWE encryption of the message in a symmetric key setting, and the same can be extended to GLWE-based encryption of the message by induction for $N \geq 1$ as implemented in Zama's variant of the encryption scheme. Also, LWE-based ciphertexts can be viewed as a special instance of GLWE-based ciphertexts for $(k, N) = (n, 1)$. For $N = 1$, $\mathbb{R}_N[X] = \mathbb{R}$, $\mathbb{Z}_N[X] = \mathbb{Z}$ and ciphertext space $\hat{\mathbb{Z}}_N[X] = \mathbb{Z}_q^{n+1}$. In the previous section, we discussed the adversarial vulnerability of CKKS cipher using equivalent notions of UAP in a public key setting, we discuss below the equivalent notion of UAP for an LWE-based cipher in a symmetric key scenario.

Observation: Consider the Learning With Errors (LWE) encryption of message m as $(a, b) = (a, \text{Encoding}(m) + \langle s, a \rangle + e)$, where $a \xleftarrow{\$} \mathbb{Z}_q$, $\langle \cdot \rangle$ denotes the inner product, s is the secret key, and e is discrete noise drawn from a normal distribution over $\mathbb{R}$. Assuming equivalence between plain and encrypted models, if v is the Quantization-aware UAP corresponding to floating-point perturbation v for the plaintext space with respect to model f_{model}, then $(0, \mathrm{Encoding}(v))$ is a universal adversarial perturbation for the ciphertext space with respect to the model f_{eval} using encrypted operators.

Rationale: Assume the LWE encryption of plaintext m as $(a, \mathrm{Encoding}(m) + \langle s, a \rangle + \mathrm{noise})$. Consider the addition, $(a, \mathrm{Encoding}(m) + \langle s, a \rangle + e) + (0, \mathrm{Encoding}(v))$. By the homomorphic properties of encoding operations, this yields $(a, \mathrm{Encoding}(m) + \langle s, a \rangle + e + \mathrm{Encoding}(v)) = (a, \mathrm{Encoding}(m + v) + \langle s, a \rangle + e) = \mathrm{Encrypt}_{sk}(m + v)$, where Encrypt represents LWE encryption. Let this perturbed ciphertext be used as input for an equivalent model with encrypted operators. Assuming an equivalent performance of the model with encrypted operators, the model operates on the perturbed ciphertext and produces a decryption equal to $f_{\mathrm{model}}(m + v)$.

Note: The proof discussed above applies to both targeted and untargeted UAPs, as both use the same iterative approach to generate UAPs. Additionally, the generation of Quantization-aware UAP corresponding to floating point UAPs is described in Algorithm 2.

L   Evasion Attack Methodology in Concrete ML by an Untrusted Server

As discussed in Sect. 6, performing adversarial perturbation by evaluating ciphertext over an adder circuit is infeasible with the adversary having API access as both circuits largely differ in operations resulting in different Keyset and Circuit parameters used in Concrete. However, the adversary might want to bridge this gap of different circuit sizes for the model by defining two models. One is the benign model, and the other is a modified model. In the modified model architecture, defined using Python APIs, an additional step is inserted at the beginning of the neural net forward pass function. This step involves adding the perturbation vector v to the input x, effectively modifying the input to $x_{adv} = x + v$. This modification aims to introduce perturbations to the input data before its evaluation by the neural network layers, potentially influencing the model's predictions. However, to selectively add targeted or untargeted perturbations on encrypted inputs sent by the client, the server needs to alternate between inference using the two models compiled as `Circuit Class object` [28]. However, we found that this process of alternating between two models is again prevented due to changes in the cryptographic parameters of the two circuits as they specifically differed in encoding parameters. The reason could be attributed to the fact that add operation equivalently realized using lookup table operation `FHELinalg.apply_mapped_lookup_table` [40], requires a suitable choice of encoding parameters for its efficient execution. However,

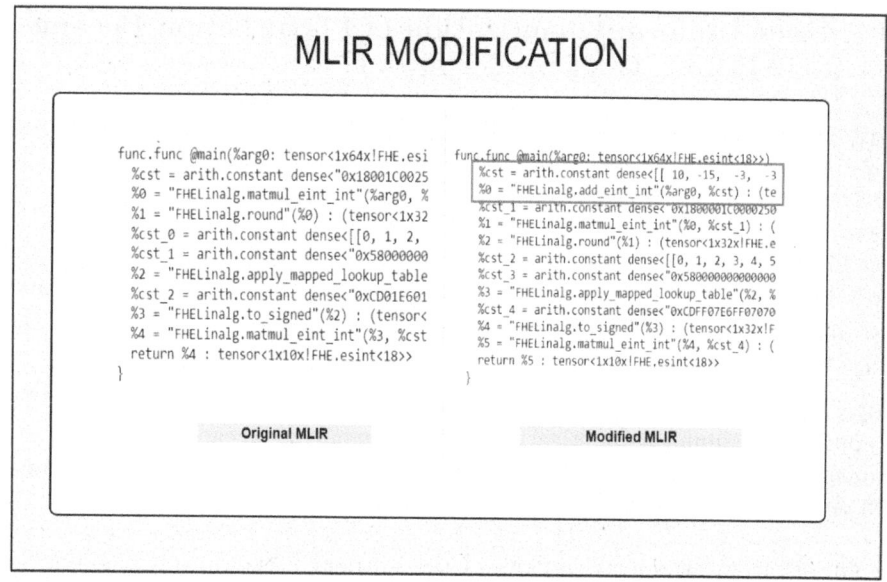

Fig. 3. Generating modified MLIR by inserting `FHELinalg.add_eint_int` operation which adds ciphertext represented by %0 and Quantization-aware UAP represented by %cst.

modification or removal of the look-up table is not possible from Concrete ML frontend. Hence we move down the compilation pipeline, where the model is compiled into an MLIR (Multi-Level Intermediate Representation) representation. Using the low-level client-server APIs [41] provided by the Concrete-compiler library, the MLIR representation can be used as the initial input, rather than a model defined by the Python APIs supported by Concrete ML. This approach provides flexibility in choosing FHE operators in the MLIR, ensuring that the original MLIR obtained from the benign model and the modified MLIR do not differ in terms of cryptographic parameters. We specifically insert the operation `FHELinalg.add_eint_int` [42] into the original MLIR to generate a modified MLIR. This operation is a high-level linear algebra operation that adds an encrypted tensor to a plaintext tensor. In our case, the plaintext tensor is the quantized equivalent of the Universal Adversarial Perturbation (UAP), the generation of which is detailed in the following section. It is important to highlight that Concrete ML first quantizes the inputs before evaluating them over any circuit. Experimentally, we have observed that if a Quantization-aware UAP is not generated, the attack success rate (in case of targeted attack) significantly decreases. The reasons for why directly quantizing UAP does not guarantee retaining UAP property and the rationale behind constructing UAP for quantized space such that it retains UAP property have been discussed in Appendix M N (Fig. 3).

M   Does Uniform Quantization of Perturbation Become a UAP for a Quantized Dataset?

Uniform Quantization in Concrete ML: Concrete ML employs uniform quantization [31,43] which maps real-valued inputs to integers using the `quantize` operation, which is defined as $q = \texttt{quantize}(r) = \text{round}\left(\frac{r}{S}\right) + Z$, where r is the real number, S is the scaling factor, and Z is the zero point. The function $\text{round}(x)$ represents rounding the value x to the nearest integer. The scaling factor S and zero point Z are calculated as $S = \frac{\beta - \alpha}{2^n - 1}$ and $Z = \text{round}\left(-\frac{\alpha}{S}\right)$, where $[\alpha, \beta]$ represents the range of values to be quantized, and n is the bit width.

Note: In Algorithm 2, applying the `Quantize` operation on a vector is equivalent to applying the uniform quantization function `quantize` on each vector element. Similarly, applying `Round` on a vector is equivalent to applying the `round` function on each vector element.

The attack methodology employed by an untrusted server involves adding an FHE ciphertext and a plain tensor, representing the perturbation. However, the plain tensor cannot directly represent real-valued perturbations, as the Concrete library operates on integers. Therefore, it needs to be transformed with respect to the uniform quantization method adopted by Concrete ML, which is an affine mapping of integers q to real numbers r. Now for all vector x in dataset X and UAP vector v, we have their respective quantized representations are as $q_i = \texttt{round}(\frac{1}{S}x_i + Z), q'_i = \texttt{round}(\frac{1}{S}v_i + Z)$, where `round` denotes the rounding function to the nearest integer. This implies $q_i + q'_i = \texttt{round}(\frac{1}{S}x_i + Z) + \texttt{round}(\frac{1}{S}v_i + Z) \approx (\frac{1}{S}(x_i + v_i) + 2Z)$ where x_i, v_i, q_i, q'_i are $i - th$ components of the vector x, v, q, q'. Although v is a Universal Adversarial Perturbation (UAP), the quantization of v might not exhibit UAP behavior for cases where $Z \neq 0$. This is because if $x_{adv} = x + v$ be an adversarial sample, it is not guaranteed that translating x_{adv} by adding a vector would still preserve the UAP property, as that might change the direction over which the sample is sent across decision boundary. Therefore, we propose the following method to generate UAP post-quantization which is described in detail in Appendix N.

N   Generation of Post Quantization Perturbation Vector or Quantization-Aware UAP

In this section, we describe the intuition behind generating the equivalent of floating point UAP post-quantization which preserves the UAP property also referred to as **Quantization-aware UAP**, this is also the output of Algorithm 2. Let x belong to the training dataset X and v be UAP in floating point representation for the dataset X w.r.t to model f. Let a be the quantized representation of vector $x + v$ and q, q' be the quantized representation of vectors x and v then consider the $i - th$ components of vector c, c', q, q', x

defined as, $c_i = a_i - q_i = \mathtt{round}(\frac{1}{S}(x_i + v_i) + Z)) - \mathtt{round}((\frac{1}{S}x_i + Z)) \approx \frac{1}{S}v_i$, where round represents the rounding operation to nearest integer. Similarly, $c'_i = a_i - q'_i = \mathtt{round}(\frac{1}{S}(x_i + v_i) + Z)) - \mathtt{round}((\frac{1}{S}v_i + Z)) \approx \frac{1}{S}x_i$. Now consider, $c_i + c'_i \approx \frac{1}{S}(x_i + v_i)$. Hence quantized adversarial sample corresponding to the floating point adversarial sample $x + v$ is $S.(c + c')$. Now as $x + v$, $c + c'$ is known to the adversary, therefore the adversary can compute the scaling factor, $d = \left\lfloor \frac{x_i + v_i}{c_i + c'_i} \right\rfloor \approx S$ where $\lfloor . \rfloor$ represents the least integer function. Hence $d.c \approx S.c$ represents the quantized equivalent of the floating point perturbation v corresponding to quantized input q. Also, the quantized perturbation is obtained by taking the rounded difference of elements for $x \in X$. Hence, the representative post-quantized perturbation can be considered as a rounded mean of all such vectors $d.c$ obtained from x using above method where $x \in X$ i.e. it belongs to that dataset to which the adversary has access. With this observation, we propose Algorithm 2 to find the quantized equivalent of perturbation to be used in the attack methodology as described above.

Note: The above results can be realized simply by black-box access to the quantization function as one does not need to know scaling and zero point values, it can simply be computed from quantization API outputs. Also, we use the following convention for Algorithm 2, Applying `Quantize` operation on vector is equivalent to applying uniform quantization function `quantize` as described in previous subsection on each vector element, and also applying `Round` on vector is equivalent to applying `round` function on each vector element.

O   Experimental Setup (Concrete ML)

Digits Dataset: In our experimental setup, we utilize an image dataset consisting of grayscale images depicting handwritten digits ranging from 0 to 9 [33]. The images have dimensions of 8×8 pixels, and the dataset comprises a total of 1797 images. For training purposes, we allocate 80% of the dataset, which amounts to 1437 images, while the remaining 20% (360 images) are designated for testing. Before employing the dataset for training and inference, we apply standardization. This involves transforming the samples (x) using the formula: $z = (x - \mu)/s$, where μ represents the mean of the samples and s denotes the standard deviation.

System Setup: The system setup is the same as that in TenSEAL.

UAP Generation: We have used the python library - ART (Adversarial Robustness Toolbox library) [24,25] for generating the UAPs. Untargeted UAP is generated using the `UniversalPerturbation` class utilizing the Deepfool [14] algorithm and targeted UAP is generated using the `TargetedUniversalPerturbation` class utilizing the FGSM [12] algorithm. The target for the targeted UAP is set to 0 for our experiments. The following parameters are used to do the attack, fooling rate parameter $\delta = 0.2$, perturbation magnitude bound $\epsilon = 10.0$, maximum iterations to compute UAP *max_iter=*

Algorithm 2. Generate Post-Quantization Perturbation Vector

Input: Universal perturbation vector v, training dataset X,
vector quantization function `Quantize`,
vector rounding function `Round`
Output: Quantization-aware UAP (perturbation_vector)

1: **Select a subset of training data and represent as an ordered subset:**
2: Consider an ordered list $X_1 \subseteq X$
3: **Add the UAP to all elements in X_1:**
4: $X_2 = X_1 + v = \{x_i + v \mid x_i \in X_1\}$
5: **Quantize each element in both X_1 and X_2 using the vector quantization function `Quantize`:**
6: Quantize$X_1 = \{\text{Quantize}(x_i) \mid x_i \in X_1\}$
7: Quantize$X_2 = \{\text{Quantize}(x_i + v) \mid x_i \in X_1\}$
8: **Find the element-wise difference between samples in X_1 and X_2 at matching indices in the ordered list:**
9: diff = QuantizeX_2 − Quantize$X_1 = \{\text{Quantize}(x_i + v) - \text{Quantize}(x_i) \mid x_i \in X_1\}$
10: **Calculate the scaling factor S w.r.t. to $j - th$ component of any vector $x \in X_1$ and perturbation vector v**
11: $S = \left\lfloor \dfrac{x_j + v_j}{(\text{Quantize}(x_j + v_j) - \text{Quantize}(v_j)) + (\text{Quantize}(x_j + v_j) - \text{Quantize}(x_j))} \right\rfloor$
12: **Calculate the mean and round using vector rounding function `Round` and extract the single vector element from the set:**
13: perturbation_vector $\in \left\{\text{Round}\left(\frac{S}{|X_1|} \sum_{i=0}^{|X_1|}(p_i)\right) \mid p_i \in \text{diff}\right\}$
14: **Return** perturbation_vector

---

20. The reason for the choice of the above parameters for the attack can validated from Fig. 6.

Circuit Constraints: We adopt the following circuit constraints for compiling the model: The number of bits used for quantization is set to 5 by default, with a rounding threshold of 6 bits. Additionally, the probability of error for a single programmable bootstrap (PBS) is defined as 0.1.

Model Architecture: We utilize a simple neural network defined using PyTorch library and train it on the above-mentioned digits dataset to provide a proof of concept as evaluating over complex CNN networks incurs overhead in terms of latency. The architecture consists of the following layers:

1. **Fully Connected Layer (FC1):** This layer contains 32 units and expects a tensor of length 64. The dataset used here contains the images in flattened format i.e. 8×8 images are converted arrays of length 64.
2. **RELU Activation:** The output of the FC1 layer is applied with a RELU activation function.
3. **Fully Connected Layer (FC2):** This layer contains 10 units and expects an input of length 32. The output of the FC1 layer after applying RELU activation is passed through this layer.

P   Ablation Study

In this ablation study, we analyze the effects of different training data sizes and perturbation magnitudes (epsilon values) on the performance of a convolutional neural network and Simple neural net and its susceptibility to universal adversarial attacks. We utilize the dataset as described in the experimental section and the Universal Perturbation attack from the ART library to evaluate how changes

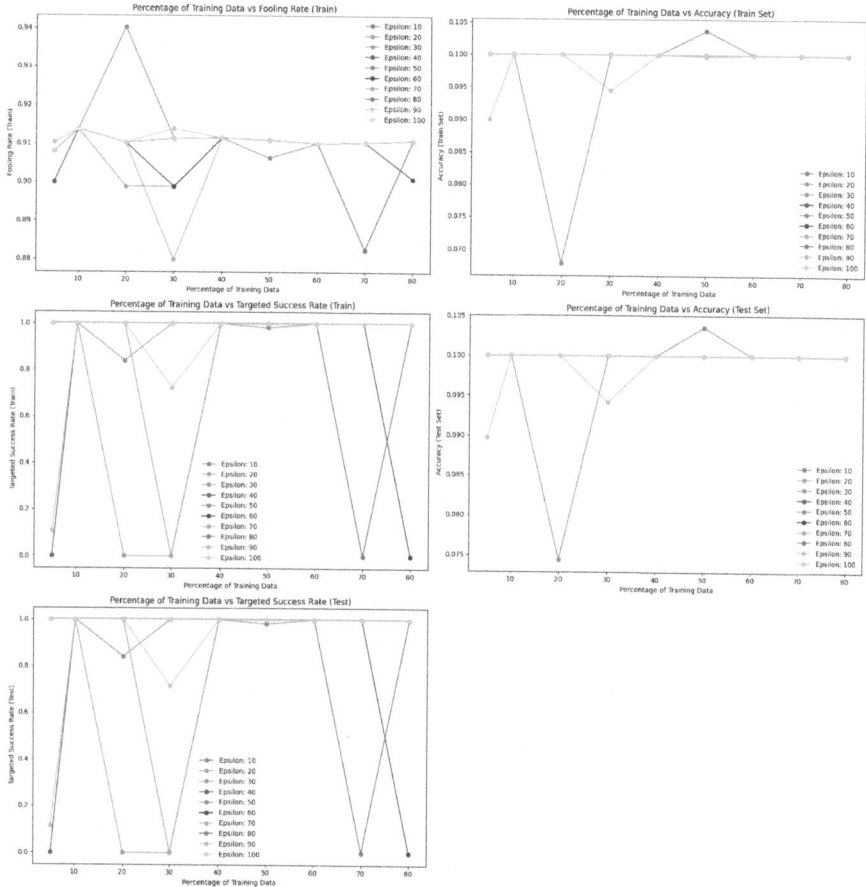

Fig. 4. The above figures display line graphs for the fooling rate and targeted success rate on both the training and test sets versus the percentage of training data used for the FMNIST dataset w.r.t to model used in TenSEAL. The graphs demonstrate that there are ϵ values for which the targeted attack success rate reaches 100% on both the training and test sets. These results illustrate how to select ϵ values corresponding to the available subset of the training data to ensure a maximum targeted attack success rate. This also guarantees near attack success rate in the encrypted domain if both models defined in plaintext and encrypted domain are equivalent.

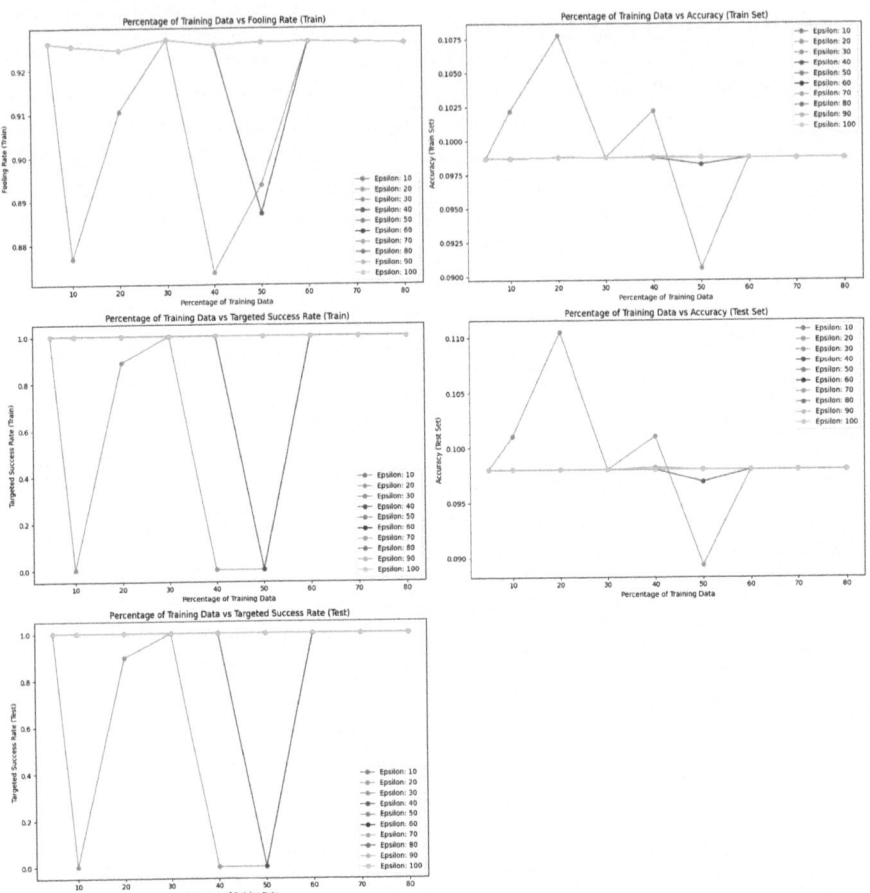

Fig. 5. For the MNIST dataset, the figures show that there are ϵ values where the targeted attack success rate reaches 100% on both the training and test sets when a small fraction of the training data is used. The figure also demonstrates if a high fooling rate or high target attack success rate is ensured for a small fraction of training data we achieve similar target attack success rate for both the train and test dataset.

in training data percentage and perturbation strength affect model accuracy and fooling rates for both targeted and untargeted attacks. Please refer to Figs. 4, 5, 6, and 7 for the experiments.

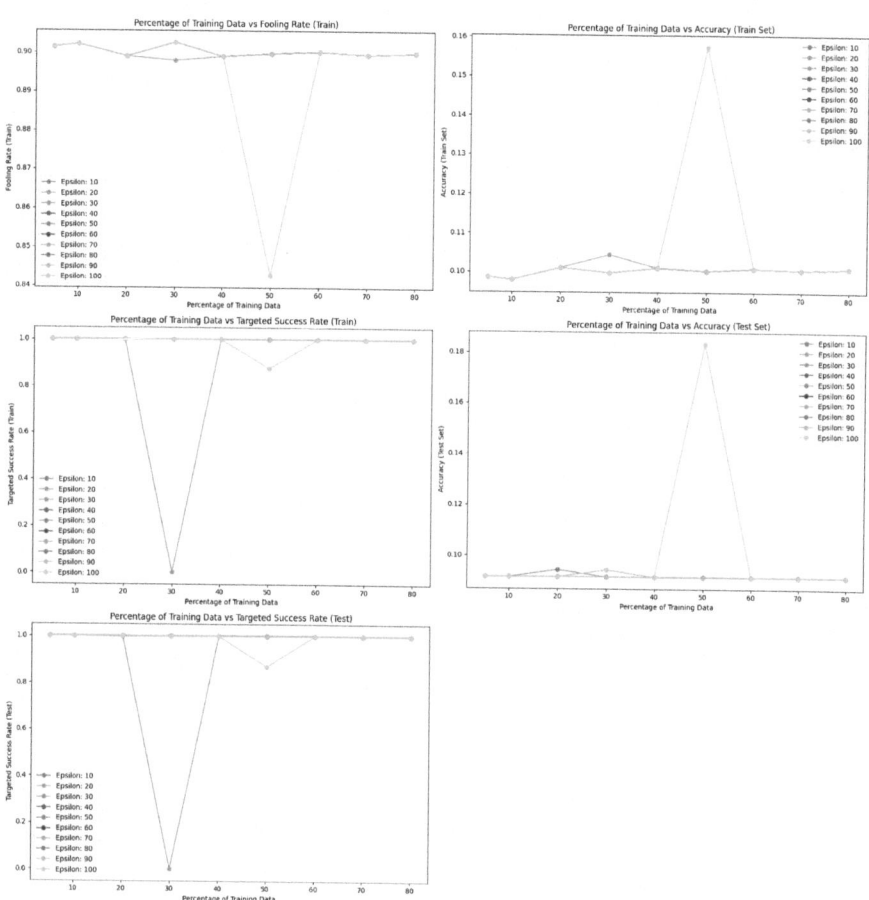

Fig. 6. The above figure demonstrates the fooling rate and targeted attack success rate on training and test dataset used for attacks in Concrete ML. It is evident from the figure that using a small fraction of the dataset with an appropriate choice of epsilon values can achieve a 100% targeted success rate on the test dataset.

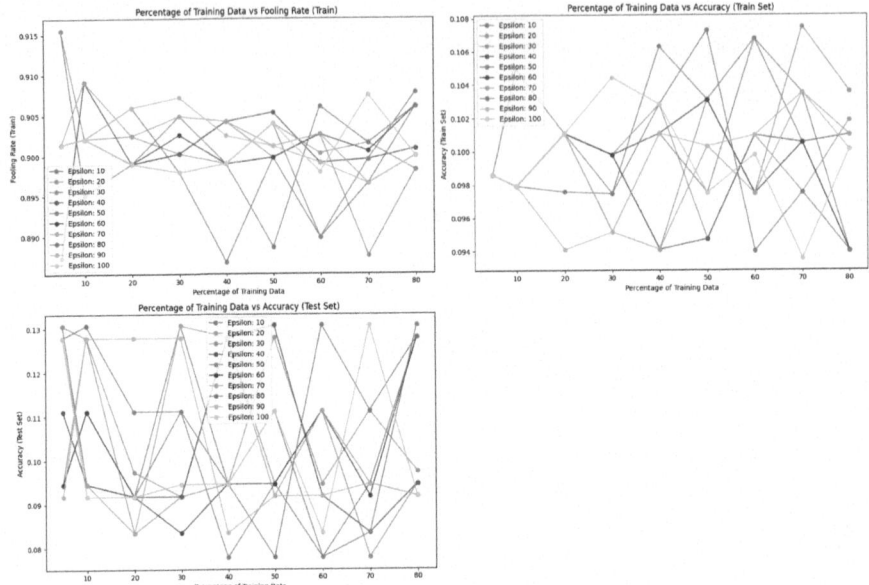

Fig. 7. The above figure demonstrates the fooling rate and misclassification rate for train and test dataset in case of untargeted attack done on Simple MNIST dataset used in Concrete ML experiments. It is clear that using a very small fraction of the training dataset it is possible to achieve a very similar misclassification rate on the entire test set

References

1. Bost, R., Popa, R.A., Tu, S., Goldwasser, S.: Machine learning classification over encrypted data. Cryptology ePrint Archive (2014)
2. Viand, A., Knabenhans, C., Hithnawi, A.: Verifiable fully homomorphic encryption. arXiv preprint arXiv:2301.07041 (2023)
3. Biggio, B., et al.: Evasion Attacks against Machine Learning at Test Time, pp. 387–402. Springer, Heidelberg (2013)
4. Costa, J.C., Roxo, T., Proença, H., Inácio, P.R.M.: How deep learning sees the world: a survey on adversarial attacks and defenses. IEEE Access **12**, 61113–61136 (2024). https://doi.org/10.1109/access.2024.3395118. ISSN 2169-3536
5. Brakerski, Z., Gentry, C., Vaikuntanathan, V.: (leveled) fully homomorphic encryption without bootstrapping. ACM Trans. Comput. Theory (TOCT) **6**(3), 1–36 (2014)
6. Fan, J., Vercauteren, F.: Somewhat practical fully homomorphic encryption. Cryptology ePrint Archive (2012)
7. Chillotti, I., Joye, M., Paillier, P.: Programmable bootstrapping enables efficient homomorphic inference of deep neural networks. In: Cyber Security Cryptography and Machine Learning: 5th International Symposium, CSCML 2021, Be'er Sheva, 8–9 July 2021, Proceedings 5, pp. 1–19. Springer (2021)
8. Cheon, J.H., Kim, A., Kim, M., Song, Y.: Homomorphic encryption for arithmetic of approximate numbers. In: Advances in Cryptology–ASIACRYPT 2017:

23rd International Conference on the Theory and Applications of Cryptology and Information Security, Hong Kong, 3–7 December 2017, Proceedings, Part I 23, pp. 409–437. Springer (2017)

9. Benaissa, A., Retiat, B., Cebere, B., Belfedhal, A.E.: Tenseal: a library for encrypted tensor operations using homomorphic encryption. arXiv preprint arXiv:2104.03152 (2021)

10. Zama. Concrete ML: a privacy-preserving machine learning library using fully homomorphic encryption for data scientists (2024). https://github.com/zama-ai/concrete-ml

11. Regev, O.: On lattices, learning with errors, random linear codes, and cryptography. J. ACM **56**(6), 1–40 (2009)

12. Goodfellow, I.J., Shlens, J., Szegedy, C.: Explaining and harnessing adversarial examples (2015)

13. Combey, T., Loison, A., Faucher, M., Hajri, H.: Probabilistic Jacobian-based saliency maps attacks (2020)

14. Moosavi-Dezfooli, S.-M., Fawzi, A., Frossard, P.: Deepfool: A Simple and Accurate Method to Fool Deep Neural Networks, pp. 2574–2582 (2016). https://doi.org/10.1109/CVPR.2016.282

15. Carlini, N., Wagner, D.: Towards Evaluating the Robustness of Neural Networks, pp. 39–57 (2017). https://doi.org/10.1109/SP.2017.49

16. Madry, A., Makelov, A., Schmidt, L., Tsipras, D., Vladu, A.: Towards deep learning models resistant to adversarial attacks (2019)

17. Moosavi-Dezfooli, S.-M., Fawzi, A., Fawzi, O., Frossard, P.: Universal Adversarial Perturbations (2017)

18. Chaturvedi, B., Chakraborty, A., Chatterjee, A., Mukhopadhyay, D.: A practical full key recovery attack on TFHE and FHEW by inducing decryption errors. Cryptology ePrint Archive (2022)

19. Guo, Q., Nabokov, D., Suvanto, E., Johansson, T.: Key recovery attacks on approximate homomorphic encryption with non-worst-case noise flooding countermeasures. In: Usenix Security (2024)

20. Shin, J., Choi, S.-H., Choi, Y.-H.: Is homomorphic encryption-based deep learning secure enough? Sensors **21**(23), 7806 (2021)

21. Moosavi-Dezfooli, S.-M., Fawzi, A., Fawzi, O., Frossard, P.: Universal adversarial perturbations. In: Proceedings of the IEEE Conference on Computer Vision and Pattern Recognition, pp. 1765–1773 (2017)

22. Hirano, H., Takemoto, K.: Simple iterative method for generating targeted universal adversarial perturbations. Algorithms **13**(11), 268 (2020)

23. Marcolla, C., Sucasas, V., Manzano, M., Bassoli, R., Fitzek, F.H.P., Aaraj, N.: Survey on fully homomorphic encryption, theory, and applications. Proceedings of the IEEE **110**(10), 1572–1609 (2022)

24. Trusted AI. Adversarial robustness toolbox. (2024). https://github.com/Trusted-AI/adversarial-robustness-toolbox

25. Nicolae, M.-I., et al.: Adversarial robustness toolbox v1. 0.0. arXiv preprint arXiv:1807.01069 (2018)

26. Zama. Concrete: TFHE compiler that converts python programs into FHE equivalent (2024). https://github.com/zama-ai/concrete

27. Zama AI. Composition - concrete documentation (2024). https://docs.zama.ai/concrete/v/2.5/tutorials/composition

28. Zama. Concrete: Python frontend - circuit compilation (2024). https://github.com/zama-ai/concrete/blob/main/frontends/concrete-python/concrete/fhe/compilation/circuit.py

29. Zama AI. Concrete optimizer repository (2024). https://github.com/zama-ai/concrete/tree/main/compilers/concrete-optimizer
30. Zama. Composition - concrete documentation (2024). https://docs.zama.ai/concrete/compilation/composition
31. Zama AI. Quantization in concrete ml (2023). https://docs.zama.ai/concrete-ml/explanations/quantization. Accessed 10 Oct 2024
32. Zama AI. Quantizers in concrete ml (2023). https://github.com/zama-ai/concrete-ml/blob/main/src/concrete/ml/quantization/quantizers.py#L692. Accessed 20 Oct 2024
33. Skklearn. Sklearn's digits dataset (2024). https://scikit-learn.org/stable/modules/generated/sklearn.datasets.load_digits.html
34. Din, S.U., Akhtar, N., Younis, S., Shafait, F., Mansoor, A., Shafique, M.: Steganographic universal adversarial perturbations. Pattern Recogn. Lett. **135**, 146–152 (2020)
35. Goodfellow, I.J., Shlens, J., Szegedy, C.: Explaining and harnessing adversarial examples. arXiv preprint arXiv:1412.6572 (2014)
36. Chillotti, I., Joye, M., Paillier, P.: Programmable bootstrapping enables efficient homomorphic inference of deep neural networks. In: Cyber Security Cryptography and Machine Learning: 5th International Symposium, CSCML 2021, Be'er Sheva, 8–9 July 2021, Proceedings 5, pp. 1–19. Springer (2021)
37. Bergerat, L., et al.: Parameter optimization and larger precision for (t) FHE. J. Cryptol. **36**(3), 28 (2023)
38. Zama. Parameter optimization and larger precision for TFH (2024). https://www.zama.ai/post/parameter-optimization-and-larger-precision-for-tfhe
39. Zama. TFHE-parametrization (2024). https://docs.zama.ai/concrete/v/2.5/explanations/compilation
40. Zama AI. Fhe-look-up-table (2024). https://docs.zama.ai/concrete/v/2.5/explanations/compilation/dialects/fhelinalgdialect#fhelinalg.apply_lookup_table-mlir-concretelang-fhelinalg-applylookuptableeintop
41. Zama AI. FHE-look-up-table (2024). https://www.zama.ai/post/zama-concrete-fully-homomorphic-encryption-compiler
42. Zama AI. Concrete: FHE linalg dialect (2024). https://docs.zama.ai/concrete/2.5/explanations/compilation/dialects/fhelinalgdialect
43. Stoian, A., Frery, J., Bredehoft, R., Montero, L., Kherfallah, C., Chevallier-Mames, B.: Deep neural networks for encrypted inference with TFHE. In: International Symposium on Cyber Security, Cryptology, and Machine Learning, pp. 493–500. Springer (2023)

Security Analysis of ASCON Cipher Under Persistent Faults
Official Work-in-Progress Paper

Madhurima Das and Bodhisatwa Mazumdar[✉]

Indian Institute of Technology Indore, Indore, India
bodhisatwa@iiti.ac.in

Abstract. This work investigates persistent fault analysis on ASCON cipher that has been recently standardized by NIST USA for lightweight cryptography applications. In persistent fault, the fault once injected through RowHammer injection techniques, exists in the system during the entire encryption phase. In this work, we propose a model to mount persistent fault analysis (PFA) on ASCON cipher. In the finalization round of the ASCON cipher, we identify that the fault-injected S-Box operation in the permutation round, p^{12}, is vulnerable to leaking information about the secret key. A single instance of fault-injected S-Box out of 64 parallel S-Box invocations. The attack model demonstrates that any Sponge construction operating with authenticated encryption with associated data (AEAD) mode is vulnerable to persistent faults. In this work, we demonstrate the scenario of a single fault wherein the fault, once injected is persistent until the device is powered off. Using the proposed method, we successfully retrieve the 128-bit key in ASCON. Our experiments show that the minimum number and the maximum number of queries required are 63 plaintexts and 451 plaintexts, respectively. Moreover, we observe that the number of queries required to mount the attack depends on fault location in the S-box LUT as observed from the plots reporting the minimum number of queries and average number of queries for 100 key values.

1 Introduction

Cryptographic primitives are designed to be mathematically secure by establishing a number of cryptographic properties. Despite such properties, implementations of such primitives may leak information about the secret key, which greatly reduce the complexity of attacks. Attacks with such information leakage from physical implementations are referred to as *side-channel attacks*. In this class of attacks, fault attacks belong to a category of implementation attacks on embedded systems. Pertaining to the class of active attacks, fault attacks injects errors in the operation of target device, it has been demonstrated on block ciphers, such as AES, LED, PRESENT, and PICCOLO. Fault analysis attacks are more often mounted in two phases, *fault injection* (FI) and *fault analysis*. The fault injection can be mounted through mechanisms, such as voltage glitching [1], clock glitching [2], focused laser beams [3], and electromagnetic pulses [4] during the execution of key-dependent operations in encryption algorithms. Remote

© The Author(s), under exclusive license to Springer Nature Switzerland AG 2025
J. Knechtel et al. (Eds.): SPACE 2024, LNCS 15351, pp. 69–79, 2025.
https://doi.org/10.1007/978-3-031-80408-3_5

faults have been mounted on graphic processing units (GPU) and other high-end processors using Rowhammer techniques and dynamic frequency voltage scaling techniques [5–7].

In this work, to improve such criticality, we consider a chosen plaintext based PFA. As a case study to mount the proposed chosen plaintext based PFA, we consider ASCON cipher family which has been chosen by NIST USA as the lightweight cryptography standard in February 2023 [8]. The sponge construction in ASCON employs a duplex mode of operation, which absorbs the data and subsequently squeezes the data. To the best of our knowledge, this work is the first to address persistent fault analysis (PFA) on ASCON, which has recently become a NIST standard for lightweight cryptography.

The contributions of the proposed work include Chosen Plaintext based Persistent Fault Analysis(CP-PFA) on ASCON[9] specifically on the substitution layer in the finalization stage demonstrating the 128-bit key recovery with 64 to 520 plaintext queries or more. In the strong adversary model, the adversary can inject fault at a targeted entry within the Sbox LUT. In the weaker model, the adversary injects the fault in the SBox LUT but does not have control over the entry location at which the fault is injected. We discuss the background of ASCON Cipher and Persistent Fault Attack in Sect. 2. Section 3 consists of a detailed discussion of the proposed attack. Section 4 contains the experimental results and limitations. Section 5 concludes the paper.

2   Backround

The ASCON cipher [8] belongs to a family of authenticated encryption algorithms for resource-constrained devices and high-end CPUs.

2.1   Persistent Fault Attack

Fault attacks were first reported by Boneh et al. [10] on RSA-CRT implementations. In 1997, Biham and Shamir proposed differential fault analysis (DFA), demonstrating that DFA is applicable to any block cipher [11]. DFA being a transient fault model, has been shown to recover the full key in DES and AES ciphers. In 2018, Zhang et al. [5] prposed another fault model that falls between transient and permanent fault model called persistent fault was proposed. This fault once injected in look-up table based implementation of a cryptographic primitive, such as Sbox, persists in the device for multiple encryptions until the device is rebooted. The persistent bit-flip fault in Sbox is injected using Rowhammer technique. Unlike DFA, the adversary in PFA, does not require to synchronize or time fault injection in multiple rounds during run time. In [5], once the fault is injected, encryption is performed under a given plaintext, the adversary captures the faulty ciphertext, and subsequently performs PFA to recover the key. However, in many variants of PFA, a prior knowledge of fault location and value is required. In the scenario of multiple faults, this analysis becomes computationally intensive.

Fault attack is an active attack which involves two distinct phases. In the first phase, the attacker disrupts the operation of the target device. This process is known as fault injection. In the second phase, the attacker analyzes the resulting faulty ciphertexts to extract the cryptographic key. This process is called fault analysis. In Persistent Fault Analysis (PFA), the fault will persist until the device reboots. Such a fault can be injected in an algorithmic constant stored in memory, such as an entry in S-Box LUT. Until the memory is refreshed, the fault remains present for subsequent encryptions.

The fault is injected in round computation and it persists across multiple computations. In the context of block ciphers, which are the primary target of this attack, these computations pertain to the round function. An encryption algorithm involves several invocations of the round functions. The injected fault remains over several encryptions (and thus multiple round function calls), but the faulty value may not always be accessed. For instance, if the fault occurs in an S-box element, the round computation is affected only if the faulty S-box element is accessed. Otherwise, the injected fault does not influence that round computation. If the faulty value is not accessed during encryption, the resulting ciphertext will be correct, otherwise, it will be incorrect. The attacker analyzes the correct and incorrect ciphertexts to retrieve information about the key [5,12]. The attacker aims to minimize the number of plaintext queries while mounting PFA [9]. The complete Persistent Fault Attack comprises three stages. The persistent fault is introduced before the first encryption. The adversary waits for the victim to initiate the encryption process. The adversary then observes the produced ciphertexts, some of which are correct while others are incorrect due to the persistent fault. The adversary analyzes the correct and faulty ciphertexts to recover the secret key. PFA techniques are employed to retrieve deeper round keys in SPN ciphers, where the final round key by itself is insufficient to deduce the entire master key [13].

3   Proposed Work

In this attack, a fault is injected at a single location within the S-Box lookup table (LUT). This model involves injecting the fault in only one of the 64 S-Boxes within p_S during the final round of the finalization phase in ASCON.

3.1   Inverse of ASCON-128's LINEAR LAYER

Theorem (Rivest [14])

If n is a power of 2, v is an n-bit word, and $r_1, r_2, \ldots, r_k$ are distinct fixed integers modulo n, then the function $R(v)$ is invertible if and only if k is odd, where $R(v)$ is $R(v) = R(v; r_1, r_2, .., r_k) = (v_n <<< r_1) \oplus (v_n <<< r_2) \oplus \ldots \oplus (v_n <<< r_k)$.

The linear layer consists of XOR of right rotations of the 64-bit words, x_0, x_1, x_2, x_3, and x_4. As $k = 3$ for all five transformations, the linear layer of ASCON-128 is invertible. The rotations for the inverse of the linear layer are mentioned in Rivest [14].

3.2 Fault Model

The adversary can inject the fault by flipping bits in the S-Box LUT implementation through RowHammer injection techniques. In our proposed CP-PFA, the fault injection constraint affects one entry of S-Box LUT so that the last two bits of the S-Box output are altered. The flipping of last two S-Box output bits corrupts the state words x_3 and x_4, which aids our attack method. The induced fault ensures that the faulty tag is generated by the XOR operation of the last 128 bits of the state (which correspond to the state words, x_3 and x_4) with the 128 bits of the key K. So, the induced fault constraints the fault-free and faulty S-Box differential, $S(x) \oplus S'(x) \in \{0x03, 0x07, 0x0b, 0x0f, 0x13, 0x17, 0x1b, 0x1f\}$.

Our key recovery result comes under a strong caveat, where the adversary is in control of the time and location(with respect to, which bits will be affected out of the 5 bits in S-Box) of injection of the fault. In this work, our proposed CP-PFA assumes significant nonce-misuse, a feature for which ASCON designers have not proposed any security claim. The adversary has the power to inject the fault in the finalization every time independently before encrypting a set of plaintexts. The fault is not propagated to the initialization when the next set of plaintexts is encrypted. The essence of naming this attack under persistent fault analysis is the fault persists till the tag is produced.

3.3 Proposed CP-PFA on ASCON

In the proposed chosen plaintext based PFA when the attacker is granted access to the encryption oracle, it chooses a random plaintext P_1 of 64 bits, and creates a set of 64 plaintexts $P_{1,i}$, where $i \in \{0, 1, 2, \ldots, 63\}$. Each $P_{1,i}$ differs from P_1 in the ith bit. This will ensure that every possible five bit word appears as input to all the 64 SBoxes in p_S in round 12 of permutation in the finalization phase. If these 64 queries do not retrieve the key then the number of queries is increased in a similar fashion. Plaintext sets, P_2 and P_3 can be randomly formed, each set creating 64 plaintexts. In total, there are 192 plaintexts, $P_j, j \in \{1, 2, \ldots, 192\}$ are input to the ASCON encryption. The partition of plaintext set, P_j can be performed as, $P_{1,j}$ (if $j < 65$), $P_{2,(j-65)}$ (if $j < 129$), $P_{3,(j-129)}$ (otherwise). However, depending on the key value, there exist fault locations in S-Box for which the number of queries required is more than 192. With access to the ASCON encryption, the attacker inputs the plaintext and obtains the corresponding tag values, $T_j = T_{j,0} || T_{j,1}, j \in \{1, 2, \ldots, 192\}$. After capturing the set of fault-free tag values, the adversary injects the persistent bit-flip fault in the S-Box LUT implementation in the substitution layer, p_S of p^{12} operation in the finalization phase.

In Fig. 1, consider the state word x_4 obtained after p^{12} in finalization phase marked as $tgin_1$. In j^{th} query, $j \in \{1, 2, \ldots, 192\}$, applying the inverse linear layer to x_4 yields $SB_{j,i}(x_{4,i})$ where $i \in \{0, \ldots, 63\}$ in the round 12 of permutation in the finalization step, i.e., $\sum_{4}^{-1} tgin_1 = ||_{i=0}^{63} SB_{j,i}(x_{4,i})$ where j denotes query number. From Fig. 1, we observe $tgin_1 = T_{j,1} \oplus K_1$ for the jth query and hence we get,

$$\sum_4^{-1} tgin_1 = \sum_4^{-1}(T_{j,1} \oplus K_1) \Rightarrow ||_{i=0}^{63} SB_{j,i}(x_{4,i}) = \sum_4^{-1}(T_{j,1} \oplus K_1)$$

$$\Rightarrow \sum_4^{-1} K_1[i] = \sum_4^{-1} T_{j,1}[i] \oplus SB_{j,i}(x_{4,i}), \ \forall i \in \{0, \ldots, 63\} \tag{1}$$

Similarly, applying the inverse linear operation to state word x_3 obtained after the 12th round permutation in the finalization phase (denoted as $tgin_0$ in Fig. 1), yields $SB_{j,i}(x_{3,i})$ where $i \in \{0, \ldots, 63\}$, i.e., $\sum_3^{-1} tgin_0 = ||_{i=0}^{63} SB_{j,i}(x_{3,i})$, where j denotes the query number. Hence, $\sum_3^{-1} K_0[i] = \sum_3^{-1} T_{j,0}[i] \oplus SB_{j,i}(x_{3,i}), \ \forall i \in \{0, \ldots, 63\}$. Given that the tag T_j is captured, $\sum_3^{-1} K_0[i]$ and $\sum_4^{-1} K_1[i]$ can be computed if $SB_{j,i}(x_{3,i})$ and $SB_{j,i}(x_{4,i})$ are retrieved, respectively, for each $i \in \{0, 1, 2, \ldots, 63\}$. These values correspond to the third and fourth bits of the S-Box output for all the 64 S-Boxes in p_S. After $\sum_3^{-1} K_0[i]$ and $\sum_4^{-1} K_1[i]$ have been computed for each $i \in \{0, 1, 2, \ldots, 63\}$, the linear operation is applied to $\sum_3^{-1} K_0$ and $\sum_4^{-1} K_1$, i.e., $\sum_3(\sum_3^{-1} K_0)$ and $\sum_4(\sum_4^{-1} K_1)$, which yields K_0 and K_1, respectively. To retrieve the keys K_0 and K_1, faults are injected into the S-Box LUT immediately before round 12 in the finalization phase. The faulty S-Box is invoked in p_S as shown in Fig. 2. In this single fault model, whenever the faulty S-Box is invoked, the output value, $SB'_{j,i}(x_{3,i}) \ || \ SB'_{j,i}(x_{4,i})$ is constrained to one of the four possible combinations, 00, 01, 10, or 11. The set of plaintexts, P_j, $j \in \{1, 2, \ldots, 192\}$ is input to the encryption function comprising the faulty S-Box during p^{12} in the finalization phase. This process yields the respective faulty tag, $T'_j = T'_{j,0} \ || \ T'_{j,1}$. Figure 2 illustrates when the faulty S-Box LUT implementation is invoked at the ith S-Box, the relation $\sum_3^{-1} tgin'_0 = ||_{i=0}^{63} SB'_{j,i}(x_{3,i})$ is obtained, where j represents the query number. Thus, the following relation for K_0 is established.

$$\sum_3^{-1} tgin'_0 = \sum_3^{-1}(T'_{j,0} \oplus K_0) \Rightarrow ||_{i=0}^{63} SB'_{j,i}(x_{3,i}) = \sum_3^{-1}(T'_{j,0} \oplus K_0)$$

$$\Rightarrow \sum_3^{-1} K_0[i] = \sum_3^{-1} T'_{j,0}[i] \oplus SB'_{j,i}(x_{3,i}), \ \forall i \in \{0, \ldots, 63\} \tag{2}$$

Similarly, the following relation for K_1 is established:

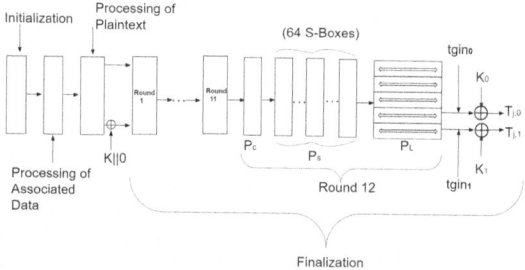

Fig. 1. ASCON encryption with the magnified last round of p^{12} in finalization phase.

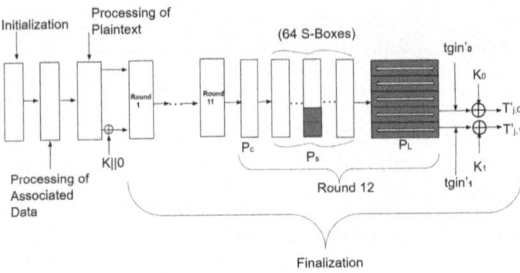

Fig. 2. Faulty S-Box LUT implementation invoked at the ith S-Box in the last round of finalization stage during encryption.

$$\sum_{4}^{-1} K_1[i] = \sum_{4}^{-1} T'_{j,1}[i] \oplus SB'_{j,i}(x_{4,i}) \ , \forall i \in \{0, \ldots, 63\} \tag{3}$$

The set of plaintexts ensures that each possible entry of the faulty S-Box can be invoked in the p_S step of round p^{12} of permutation in the the finalization phase. So the fault value in the S-Box ensures that at least one of $T_{j,0}(T_{j,1})$ will differ from $T'_{j,0}(T'_{j,1})$, $j \in \{1, 2, \ldots, 192\}$.

3.4 Fault Model

The fault model considers 64 parallel implementations of S-Box LUTs in the p_S step of round p^{12} in the finalization phase. Only one of the 64 S-Boxes is injected with persistent fault at a specific entry in the S-Box LUT.

To obtain the ith bit of $\sum_{3}^{-1} K_0$ and $\sum_{4}^{-1} K_1$, $i \in \{0, 1, 2, \ldots, 63\}$, persistent fault is injected in the ith S-Box out of the 64 parallel S-Boxes. Thereafter, we analyze the faulty tag values, $T'_j = T'_{j,0}||T'_{j,1}$ that differ from the fault-free tag values, $T_j = T_{j,0}||T_{j,1}$, $j \in \{1, 2, \ldots, 192\}$. Upon identifying such j values for both T_0 and T_1, it can be inferred that for that j^{th} query, the entry in the ith S-Box corresponds to the LUT entry that produces the faulty output.

Claim: In the given model, the following equivalence holds:

(i) $T_{j,0} \neq T'_{j,0} \Leftrightarrow SB_{j,i}(x_{3,i}) \neq SB'_{j,i}(x_{3,i})$ (ii) $T_{j,1} \neq T'_{j,1} \Leftrightarrow SB_{j,i}(x_{4,i}) \neq SB'_{j,i}(x_{4,i})$.

Proof: In this model $T_{j,0} \neq T'_{j,0}$ implies $T_{j,0}[i] \neq T'_{j,0}[i]$ as only the ith S-Box out of all the 64 S-Boxes is faulty. Consider the case, $SB_{j,i}(x_{3,i}) = SB'_{j,i}(x_{3,i})$. Applying linear function $\sum_{3}$ on both sides we get,

$$SB_{j,i}(x_{3,i}) \oplus SB_{j,(i-10)mod64}(x_{3,(i-10)mod64}) \oplus SB_{j,(i-17)mod64}(x_{3,(i-17)mod64})$$
$$= SB'_{j,i}(x_{3,i}) \oplus SB_{j,(i-10)mod64}(x_{3,(i-10)mod64}) \oplus SB_{j,(i-17)mod64}(x_{3,(i-17)mod64})$$

XORing K_0 on both sides, $\Leftrightarrow T_{j,0}[i] = T'_{j,0}[i]$. So, it is proved that $SB_{j,i}(x_{3,i}) = SB'_{j,i}(x_{3,i}) \Leftrightarrow T_{j,0} = T'_{j,0}$. It follows $SB_{j,i}(x_{3,i}) \neq SB'_{j,i}(x_{3,i}) \Leftrightarrow T_{j,0} \neq T'_{j,0}$. Hence proved. A similar approach can establish Claim (ii). Depending on the control of the adversary in injecting persistent fault in the S-Box LUT, we consider the following two cases.

Case I. This analysis considers a strong adversary fault model, where the adversary can inject fault at a specific entry within the S-Box LUT. Since the location of the fault injection is controlled by the adversary, the outputs $SB'_{j,i}(x_{4,i})$ and $SB'_{j,i}(x_{3,i})$, corresponding to the last two bits of the faulty S-Box, are known. Given that $SB'_{j,i}(x_{4,i})$ and $SB'_{j,i}(x_{3,i})$ are known, Eq. 2 and Eq. 3 are used to retrieve $\sum_4^{-1} K_1[i]$ and $\sum_3^{-1} K_0[i]$ for each $i \in \{0, 1, 2, \ldots, 63\}$. Once $\sum_3^{-1} K_0$ and $\sum_4^{-1} K_1$ have been computed, the linear layer can be applied to these values, i.e., $\sum_3(\sum_3^{-1} K_0)$ and $\sum_4(\sum_4^{-1} K_1)$ which give K_0 and K_1, respectively. The steps are summarized in Algorithm 1.

Case II. In this scenario, a weaker model is considered, where the adversary injects a fault into the S-Box LUT but does not have control over the specific entry location where the fault is introduced. The output values, $SB'_{j,i}(x_{3,i})||SB'_{j,i}(x_{4,i})$, are limited to one of four possible combinations: $0||0$, $0||1$, $1||0$, or $1||1$, regardless of the LUT entry location where fault is injected.

Algorithm 1: Recovering 128 bits of Key by injecting persistent fault in only one location of S-Box LUT and it is called for only once among all the 64 S-Boxes in the Substitution layer in last round of p^{12} in finalization when the fault location is known.

1: **Inputs:** P_j , where $j \in \{1, 2, \ldots, 192\}$; **Output:** 128-bits of Key, $K = K_0||K_1$.
2: **for** $j = 0$ **to** 191 **do**
3:     Encryption queries using P_j and get the tags, $(T_j, C_j) \leftarrow \mathcal{E}_{k,r,a,b}(K, N, A, P_j)$.
4: **end for**
5: **Inject persistent fault** in one location of S-Box LUT by flipping the last two bits of the original S-Box output for that location.
6: **for** $bit = 0$ **to** 63 **do**
7:     **for** $j = 0$ **to** 191 **do**
8:         In finalization in the last round the p_S calls the faulty S-Box LUT for the bit^{th} S-Box among all the 64 S-Boxes, i.e
$$SB_{j,bit}(x_{3,bit})||SB_{j,bit}(x_{4,bit}) \neq SB'_{j,bit}(x_{3,bit})||SB'_{j,bit}(x_{4,bit})$$
9:         Make encryption queries using the same P_j and get the corresponding faulty $T'_j = T'_{j,0}||T'_{j,1}$, ie. $(T'_j, C_j) \leftarrow \mathcal{E}'_{k,r,a,b}(K, N, A, P_j)$
10:         **if** $T'_{j,0} \neq T_{j,0}$ **then**
11:             $j_{0,bit} = j$. //capturing the value of j
12:         **end if**
13:         **if** $T'_{j,1} \neq T_{j,1}$ **then**
14:             $j_{1,bit} = j$. //capturing the value of j
15:         **end if**
16:         **Compute** $\sum_3^{-1} T'_{j_0,bit,0}$ and $\sum_4^{-1} T'_{j_1,bit,1}$.
17:         **Compute** $\sum_3^{-1} K_0[bit] = \sum_3^{-1} T'_{j_0,bit,0}[bit] \oplus SB'_{j_0,bit,bit}(x_{3,bit})$.
18:         **Compute** $\sum_4^{-1} K_1[bit] = \sum_4^{-1} T'_{j_1,bit,1}[bit] \oplus SB'_{j_1,bit,bit}(x_{4,bit})$.
19:     **end for**
20: **end for**
21: **for** $bit = 0$ **to** 63 **do**
22:     $\sum_3^{-1} K_0 = \sum_3^{-1} K_0 \oplus ((\sum_3^{-1} K_0[bit] \odot 1) << (64 - (bit + 1)))$
23:     $\sum_4^{-1} K_1 = \sum_4^{-1} K_1 \oplus ((\sum_4^{-1} K_1[bit] \odot 1) << (64 - (bit + 1)))$
24: **end for**
25: **Compute** $\sum_3(\sum_3^{-1} K_0)$ and $\sum_4(\sum_4^{-1} K_1)$
26: **Return** K_0 and K_1 and hence $K = K_0||K_1$

Algorithm 2: Recovering 128 bits of Key by injecting persistent fault in only one location of S-Box LUT and it is called for only once among all the 64 S-Boxes in the Substitution layer in last round of p^{12} in finalization when the fault location is unknown.

1: **Inputs:** P_j , where $j \in \{1, 2, \ldots, 192\}$; **Output:** 128-bits of Key, $K = K_0||K_1$.

2: **Initialize** Keytemp$_{00}$=Keytemp$_{00,0}$||Keytemp$_{00,1}$, Keytemp$_{01}$=Keytemp$_{01,0}$||Keytemp$_{01,1}$, Keytemp$_{10}$=Keytemp$_{10,0}$||Keytemp$_{10,1}$, Keytemp$_{11}$=Keytemp$_{11,0}$||Keytemp$_{11,1}$

3: Follow Algorithm 1 to get Keytemp$_{00}$ if $SB'_{j,bit}(x_{3,bit})||SB'_{j,bit}(x_{4,bit}) = 0||0$.

4: Follow Algorithm 1 to get Keytemp$_{01}$ if $SB'_{j,bit}(x_{3,bit})||SB'_{j,bit}(x_{4,bit}) = 0||1$.

5: Follow Algorithm 1 to get Keytemp$_{10}$ if $SB'_{j,bit}(x_{3,bit})||SB'_{j,bit}(x_{4,bit}) = 1||0$.

6: Follow Algorithm 1 to get Keytemp$_{11}$ if $SB'_{j,bit}(x_{3,bit})||SB'_{j,bit}(x_{4,bit}) = 1||1$.

7: **for** $j = 0$ to 191 **do**

8:     Make encryption queries using the plaintexts and get the corresponding tags.

9:     $(T_j^{00}, C_j^{00}) \leftarrow \mathcal{E}_{k,r,a,b}(\text{Ktemp}_{00}, N, A, P_j)$; $(T_j^{01}, C_j^{01}) \leftarrow \mathcal{E}_{k,r,a,b}(\text{Ktemp}_{01}, N, A, P_j)$

10:     $(T_j^{10}, C_j^{10}) \leftarrow \mathcal{E}_{k,r,a,b}(\text{Ktemp}_{10}, N, A, P_j)$; $(T_j^{11}, C_j^{11}) \leftarrow \mathcal{E}_{k,r,a,b}(\text{Ktemp}_{11}, N, A, P_j)$

11: **end for**

12: **for** $j = 0$ to 191 **do**

13:     **if** $T_j = T_j^{00}$ **then**

14:         count00++

15:     **else if** $T_j = T_j^{01}$ **then**

16:         count01++

17:     **else if** $T_j = T_j^{10}$ **then**

18:         count10++

19:     **else if** $T_j = T_j^{11}$ **then**

20:         count11++

21:     **end if**

22: **end for**

23: $K = (count00 == 192)?Keytemp_{00} : (count01 == 192)?Keytemp_{01} : (count10 == 192)?Keytemp_{10} : Keytemp_{11}$

24: **Return** $K = K_0||K_1$

Each of these four combinations is processed following the approach outlined in *Case I*, using Eq. 2 and Eq. 3, i.e., each possible combination is an instance of *Case I* which reduces the key search space to four key values. Once the four probable key values are obtained, the encryption algorithm is queried using each key value with the plaintexts, P_j, where $j \in \{1, 2, \ldots, 192\}$, and the corresponding tag values are received. The correct key is identified as the one for which all the newly received tag values match the fault-free tag values generated previously. The steps of this case are mentioned in Algorithm 2.

4   Experimental Results

In the experimental results, we report the number of plaintext queries required to recover $K_0 \mid\mid K_1$ after injecting persistent faults into the S-Box under different fault models. The experiments were conducted on a system with 12th Gen Intel Core i5-12500H processor operating at 2.50 GHz, and 16.0 GB of RAM (15.6 GB usable). The simulations for the proposed CP-PFA algorithms were conducted using a custom implementation of the ASCON-128 cipher written in C programming language. The implementation comprise modules for persistent fault injection at the S-Box level, fault analysis, and the key recovery. Figure 3 denotes the number of queries required to retrieve the corresponding keys for all 32 possible fault locations in the S-Box LUT. Algorithm 1 and Algorithm 2 required same count of queries to mount the attack. All the experiments are performed for 100 random key values. Figure 3 has five random keys and the corresponding number of queries to recover each of them. In the plots, the key values that require less than 65 queries to recover for a one-fault location can be considered to be weak keys. Figure 3 has five random key values and the corresponding number of queries to recover each of them when the fault model follows Algorithm 2. Figure 4 denotes the minimum number of queries against each fault location for 100 randomly chosen key values. From Fig. 4, we observe that fault location $0x01$ when injected with the persistent fault, has the maximum count of keys that requires minimum number of queries to recover the key. Thus S-Box LUT location, $0x01$ has vulnerability as compared to other locations.

4.1 Limitations

In this section, we present the limitations of our work. Our work is restricted to the nonce-misuse case wherein we repeat the same nonce for each invocation of ASCON cipher. The adversary is considered to be strong, and possessing the equipment to inject the fault at precise locations in Sbox LUT in the finalization stage of ASCON. Moreover, the proposed fault analysis targets an LUT-based S-Box implementation of ASCON, however, the designers mainly designed the Sbox for the bit-sliced implementation. We believe there can be real-life logic resource constraint device where the LUT-based S-box is feasible over 64 instantiations of bit-sliced implementation of the Sbox.

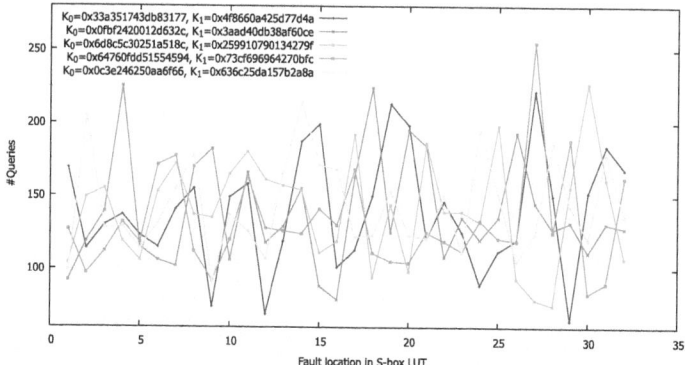

Fig. 3. Number of queries for a fault location at one of 32 locations of S-box LUT following Algorithm 2.

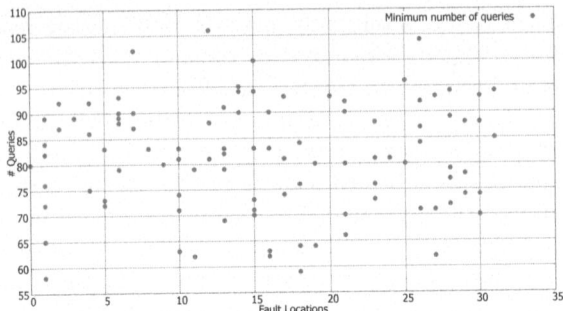

Fig. 4. Minimum number of queries required to mount PFA over 100 random key samples and the corresponding fault location in the S-Box LUT.

5   Conclusion

From the architecture it can be observed that the ASCON-128 design mixes key bits into the state via the S-box in each round, making it challenging for attackers to track differences between related inputs. The experimental analysis focused on the behavior of the S-Box under fault injection attacks. By employing Persistence Fault Analysis, faults were strategically introduced into the S-Box during the finalization stage of the encryption process. This involved inducing flipping the last two bits in the S-Box entry in LUT in the last round, altering the output in a way that allowed the extraction of key bits. A set of plaintexts ranging from 60-451 was used to query the encryption oracle and the resulting tag values were analyzed, allowing the recovery of the key bits. These vulnerabilities show the critical need for robust security measures in lightweight cryptographic solutions like ASCON-128. These attacks can be mounted on ASCON 128a and ASCON 80pq to extract the last 128 bits of the key. Moreover, this work can be extended to Statistical Persistent Fault Analysis (SPFA) and Practical Multiple Persistent Faults Analysis (PMPFA).

References

1. Selmane, N., Guilley, S., Danger, J.-L.: Practical setup time violation attacks on AES. Seventh Eur. Depend. Comput. Conf. **2008**, 91–96 (2008)
2. Agoyan, M., Dutertre, J.-M., Naccache, D., Robisson, B., Tria, A.: When clocks fail: on critical paths and clock faults. In: Proceedings of the 9th IFIP WG 8.8/11.2 International Conference on Smart Card Research and Advanced Application, CARDIS 2010, pp. 182–193. Springer, Heidelberg (2010). https://doi.org/10.1007/978-3-642-12510-2_13
3. Skorobogatov, S.P., Anderson, R.J.: Optical fault induction attacks. In: Kaliski, B.S., Koç, ç.K., Paar, C. (eds.) Cryptographic Hardware and Embedded Systems - CHES 2002, pp. 2–12. Springer, Heidelberg (2003)
4. Beckers, A., et al.: Design considerations for EM pulse fault injection. In: Belaïd, S., Güneysu, T. (eds.) Smart Card Research and Advanced Applications - 18th

International Conference, CARDIS 2019, Prague, 11–13 November 2019, Revised Selected Papers, vol. 11833, pp. 176–192. Springer (2019)

5. Zhang, F., et al.: Persistent fault analysis on block ciphers. In: IACR Transactions on Cryptographic Hardware and Embedded Systems, pp. 150–172 (2018)
6. Murdock, K., Oswald, D., Garcia, F.D., Van Bulck, J., Gruss, D., Piessens, F., Plundervolt: software-based fault injection attacks against intel SGX. In: IEEE Symposium on Security and Privacy (SP), vol. 2020, pp. 1466–1482. IEEE (2020)
7. Sabbagh, M., Fei, Y., Kaeli, D.: A novel GPU overdrive fault attack. In: 57th ACM/IEEE Design Automation Conference (DAC), vol. 2020, pp. 1–6. IEEE (2020)
8. Dobraunig, C., Eichlseder, M., Mendel, F., Schläffer, M.: Ascon v1. 2: Lightweight authenticated encryption and hashing. J. Cryptol. **34**, 1–42 (2021)
9. Zhang, F., et al.: Efficient persistent fault analysis with small number of chosen plaintexts. In: IACR Transactions on Cryptographic Hardware and Embedded Systems, pp. 519–542 (2023)
10. Boneh, D., DeMillo, R.A., Lipton, R.J.: On the importance of checking cryptographic protocols for faults. In: International Conference on the Theory and Applications of Cryptographic Techniques, pp. 37–51. Springer (1997)
11. Biham, E., Shamir, A.: Differential fault analysis of secret key cryptosystems. In: Annual International Cryptology Conference, pp. 513–525. Springer (1997)
12. Zhang, F., et al.: Persistent fault attack in practice. In: IACR Transactions on Cryptographic Hardware and Embedded Systems, pp. 172–195 (2020)
13. Joshi, P., Mazumdar, B.: Deep round key recovery attacks and countermeasure in persistent fault model: a case study on gift and Klein. J. Cryptogr. Eng. 1–23 (2024)
14. Rivest, R.L.: The invertibility of the XOR of rotations of a binary word. Int. J. Comput. Math. **88**(2), 281–284 (2011)

Privacy-Preserving Graph-Based Machine Learning with Fully Homomorphic Encryption for Collaborative Anti-money Laundering

Fabrianne Effendi[(✉)] and Anupam Chattopadhyay

Nanyang Technological University, 50 Nanyang Avenue, Singapore 639798, Singapore
fabr0001@e.ntu.edu.sg, anupam@ntu.edu.sg

Abstract. Combating money laundering has become increasingly complex with the rise of cybercrime and digitalization of financial transactions. Graph-based machine learning techniques have emerged as promising tools for Anti-Money Laundering (AML) detection, capturing intricate relationships within money laundering networks. However, the effectiveness of AML solutions is hindered by data silos within financial institutions, limiting collaboration and overall efficacy. This research presents a novel privacy-preserving approach for collaborative AML machine learning, facilitating secure data sharing across institutions and borders while preserving privacy and regulatory compliance. Leveraging Fully Homomorphic Encryption (FHE), computations are directly performed on encrypted data, ensuring the confidentiality of financial data. The research contributes two key privacy-preserving pipelines. First, the development of a privacy-preserving Graph Neural Network (GNN) pipeline was explored. Optimization techniques like quantization and pruning were used to render the GNN FHE-compatible. Second, a privacy-preserving graph-based XGBoost pipeline leveraging Graph Feature Preprocessor (GFP) was successfully developed. Experiments demonstrated strong predictive performance, with the XGBoost model consistently achieving over 99% accuracy, F1-score, precision, and recall on the balanced AML dataset in both unencrypted and FHE-encrypted inference settings. On the imbalanced dataset, the incorporation of graph-based features improved the F1-score by 8%. The research highlights the need to balance the trade-off between privacy and computational efficiency.

Keywords: Fully Homomorphic Encryption · Privacy-Preserving · Graph-Based Machine Learning · Anti-Money Laundering

ⓒ The Author(s), under exclusive license to Springer Nature Switzerland AG 2025
J. Knechtel et al. (Eds.): SPACE 2024, LNCS 15351, pp. 80–105, 2025.
https://doi.org/10.1007/978-3-031-80408-3_6

1   Introduction

1.1   Background and Motivation

The Money Laundering Problem. Money laundering is the process of concealing the origins of illegally obtained funds to make them appear legitimate. It poses severe consequences, fostering corruption, organized crime, terrorism, and environmental offenses. Beyond discouraging foreign investments and distorting international capital flows, money laundering poses a substantial threat to the stability of the financial system and the broader economy. The United Nations estimates that 2–5% of global GDP is laundered annually, with only 1% of these funds seized [1]. For example, in 2023, Singapore uncovered a money laundering case involving over S\$3 billion (US\$2.21 billion), making it one of the largest cases discovered globally [2].

Graph-Based Machine Learning in Anti-money Laundering (AML). Money laundering activities inherently involve network structures, where their web of transactions can be modelled by graph-like patterns such as fan-out, fan-in, gather-scatter and so on [3]. Machine learning have gained considerable interest in uncovering hidden patterns in transaction data [4]. Particularly, graph-based machine learning [5] including graph neural networks (GNNs) show great promise in AML detection (Sect. 2.1). They can effectively capture complex relationships between entities such as individuals, businesses and accounts, identifying money-laundering patterns, learning anomalies, and unveiling hidden connections that are often missed by traditional detection methods.

The Challenge of AML Silos. Despite the advancements in AML solutions, AML transaction monitoring and detection are often conducted in silos within each financial institution [6], hindering the effectiveness of AML solutions. Adherence to data privacy regulations, such as the EU's General Data Protection Regulation (GDPR) [7], poses legal challenges to financial institutions in maintaining the privacy of transaction data when data sharing. It is not possible for financial institutions to directly share meta-information about transaction accounts or owners without explicit consent. Consequently, this prevents the comprehensive modeling of transaction networks and limits the ability of financial institutions to track transactions and customer relationships spanning across multiple institutions and borders, which is often exploited by criminals orchestrating intricate schemes across multiple institutions.

Collaborative AML. To effectively combat money laundering, a collaborative approach is required. Emerging solutions involve leveraging a Trusted Third Party (TTP) to aggregate and analyze data, while preserving privacy. For example, the Monetary Authority of Singapore (MAS) developed COSMIC in Singapore [8], a platform for collaborative sharing of Money Laundering/Terrorism

Financing (ML/TF) information among banks using rule-based transaction monitoring [9]. However, many institutions still lack legally-compliant infrastructure for secure data sharing. According to a FATF report, regulatory challenges and data privacy concerns were the two most frequently cited challenges in developing and implementing new AML technologies, with nearly 70% and 60% of respondents highlighting these issues respectively [10].

Privacy-Preserving Technologies. Privacy-preserving technologies, such as Homomorphic Encryption (HE), offer a promising solution. HE allows computations to be performed directly on encrypted data without decryption, ensuring data confidentiality. The increasing adoption and community support of HE, such as Fully Homomorphic Encryption over the Torus (TFHE) (Sect. 3.2), motivates research in applying it to AML to enable secure collaborative efforts.

1.2   Objective and Contributions

This paper presents a novel privacy-preserving AML approach using TFHE to enable secure data sharing and collaboration between financial institutions while protecting data privacy. To the best of my knowledge, while there are recent research works that have conducted separate explorations of graph-based machine learning for AML (Sect. 2.1), Gradient-Boosting Tree (GBT) for AML (Sect. 2.2), privacy-preserving technologies (PPTs) for collaborative AML and privacy-preserving machine learning respectively (Sect. 2.3), none have combined these areas of study to explore the use of GNN or GBT with FHE in AML, all the less so with the TFHE scheme. Hence, this paper makes the following contributions:

1. A proposed solution architecture for collaborative privacy-preserving machine learning for AML using FHE. This is detailed in Sect. 3.5.
2. Exploration of the feasibility of developing a privacy-preserving GNN pipeline integrating TFHE using Concrete ML [11] for money laundering detection. This exploration is detailed in Sect. 4.
3. Development of a privacy-preserving graph-based XGBoost pipeline leveraging the Graph Feature Preprocessor (GFP) [12] and integrating TFHE using Concrete ML [11] to detect money laundering. This is detailed in Sect. 5.
4. A set of experiments with incrementally GFP-enriched graph features using XGBoost, comparing the model performance for both unencrypted and TFHE-encrypted inference, and against a basic XGBoost baseline. The results evaluated the trade-offs of building a privacy-preserving pipeline between privacy and model performance. This is detailed in Sect. 6.

We have also released the project code repository on GitHub[1].

---

[1] https://github.com/fabecode/GraphML-FHE.

2   Related Work

2.1   Graph-Based Machine Learning for AML

The application of Graph Neural Networks (GNNs) to the domain of Anti-Money Laundering (AML) has been an active area of research. Weber et al. conducted early experiments on synthetic AML datasets, finding that variants like Fast Graph Convolutional Networks (FastGCN) offered faster computation [13]. They later explored GNNs and traditional machine learning methods on the real-world Elliptic dataset, with GCN outperforming simpler models but being surpassed by random forest [14]. Recognizing the importance of temporal information, Alarab et al. [15] and Pareja et al. [16] developed novel GNN architectures that captured evolving financial transaction patterns over time on the Elliptic dataset. Cardoso et al. [17] introduced LaundroGraph, a self-supervised graph representation learning approach tailored for AML, showcasing the potential of graph-based techniques in extracting meaningful representations from financial interaction networks. Building on these foundational works, Johannessen et al. explored heterogeneous graph neural networks for real-world AML scenarios at DNB Bank [18], while Altman et al. [3] and Egressy et al. [19] made significant contributions in developing and evaluating GNN models on the comprehensive synthetic AML-world dataset. This body of research consistently highlights the effectiveness of GNNs in capturing the complex, graph-structured nature of money laundering activities, paving the way for continued advancements in this field.

2.2   Gradient-Boosted Trees (GBT) for AML

The application of gradient-boosted tree (GBT) models, such as XGBoost and LightGBM, has also gained significant traction, with several studies including Tertychnyi et al. [20], Jullum et al. [21] and Vassallo et al. [22], demonstrating the effectiveness of these ensemble learning techniques in AML detection. More recently, researchers have explored integrating graph-based feature extraction techniques with GBT models to further enhance their performance in AML tasks. Eddin et al. [23] showcased the benefits of incorporating graph-based features, such as degree and GuiltyWalker, into LightGBM models. Building on this, Altman et al. [3] and Blanuša et al. [12] conducted comprehensive comparisons of GNN baselines and GBT models enhanced with their Graph Feature Preprocessor (GFP) on the AMLworld dataset, finding that the GBT-GFP combination, particularly XGBoost-GFP, outperformed the GNN approaches. These advancements highlight the potential of leveraging the synergies between graph-based representations and gradient-boosted tree models for effective AML detection.

2.3   Privacy-Preserving Technologies (PETs)

PETs in Financial Crimes. Privacy-Preserving Technologies (PETs) have emerged as a promising approach to protect sensitive information and enable secure data computation and analysis while preserving privacy in various domains, including finance applications [24]. The integration of PETs with AML efforts is a relatively new and active area of research.

One notable industry-led proof-of-concept is Project Aurora by the Bank for International Settlements [25], which explored the use of different PET combinations, along with machine learning and network analysis, to detect money laundering across siloed, national, and cross-border payment data. Their findings suggest that a centralized cross-border approach leveraging HE and Local Differential Privacy (LDP) demonstrates the best performance in AML. Meanwhile, Mastercard showcased the potential of FHE in facilitating secure cross-border sharing of financial crime intelligence among Singapore, the United States, India, and the United Kingdom [26].

Recently, research-focused advancements have also emerged in this space. Zhang et al. [27] proposed a framework that utilizes hybrid Federated Learning (FL) to enable collaborative financial crime detection among multiple institutions, while Egmond et al. [28] developed a secure risk propagation algorithm using secure multi-party computation (MPC) and additive HE for confidential risk score updates across a collaborative inter-bank network.

PETs for Privacy-Preserving Machine Learning. Numerous studies have also explored the integration of FHE with machine learning models, primarily focusing on Convolutional Neural Networks (CNNs), including CryptoNets by Dowlin et al. [29], Homomorphic CNN (HCNN) by Badawi et al. [30], Low-Latency CryptoNets (LoLa) by Brutzkus et al. [31], and ResNet-20 with RNS-CKKS FHE and bootstrapping by Lee et al. [32]. However, these approaches often prove ineffective for Graph Neural Networks (GNNs) due to the differences in computational patterns between the two. While FHE-based CNN inference often focuses on optimizing 2D convolutions, GNNs like Graph Convolutional Networks (GCNs) introduce different computational patterns. Specifically, GCNs rely heavily on consecutive matrix multiplications for feature and node aggregation, creating a bottleneck that is not present in CNN layers, where multi-channel 2D convolutions dominate the computations [33].

Notably, in the area of privacy-preserving GNNs, Ran et al. [34] introduced CryptoGCN, a HE-based framework for Graph Convolutional Network (GCN) inference, leveraging the sparsity of matrix operations to minimize encrypted computational overhead [11]. These advancements in PET-based approaches underscore the growing importance and potential of privacy-preserving techniques in the fight against financial crimes, setting the stage for the proposed privacy-preserving AML solution in this research.

3   Homomorphic Encryption (HE)

3.1   HE Overview

Homomorphic Encryption (HE) is a cryptographic technique that allows computations to be directly performed on encrypted data without the need for decryption. Unlike traditional encryption, which necessitates the decryption of data before meaningful computation, HE empowers secure computation while maintaining the confidentiality of data throughout the computation process.

3.2 Fully Homomorphic Encryption (FHE)

Fully Homomorphic Encryption (FHE) was imagined by Rivest et al. [35] in 1978, and the first scheme was developed by Craig Gentry [36] in 2009. FHE supports an unlimited number of computations on encrypted data without revealing the underlying messages. Mathematically, if a user has an arbitrary function f and aims to derive $f(m_1, \ldots, m_n)$ for some inputs $m_1, \ldots, m_n$, the plaintexts $p_1, \ldots, p_n$ are first encrypted using the public key pk, i.e.:

$$Encrypt(pk, p_1, \ldots, p_n) = c_1, \ldots, c_n \tag{1}$$

Computations are then performed directly on the encrypted ciphertexts $c_1, \ldots, c_n$. Decryption of the output using secret key sk gives the result $f(m_1, \ldots, m_n)$, i.e.:

$$Decrypt(sk, Eval(pk, f, c_1, \ldots, c_n)) = f(m_1, \ldots, m_n) \tag{2}$$

Machine Learning Using FHE. In the context of machine learning, a party can encrypt input data using the public key, and the model will be able to process the data without seeing the original data. The final result is also encrypted, and the data can only be decrypted by the client who has the private key. This ensures confidentiality of the data from the machine learning model (Fig. 1).

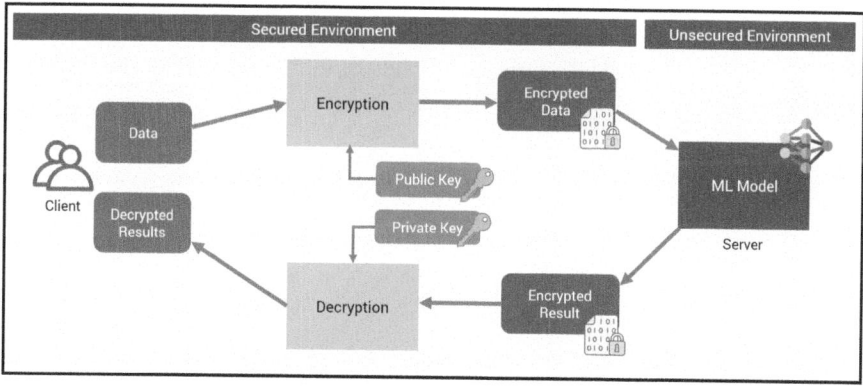

Fig. 1. Fully Homomorphic Encryption Process in Machine Learning

Fully Homomorphic Encryption over the Torus (TFHE). TFHE is a specialized FHE scheme designed by Chillotti et al. [37] for efficient computation of Boolean circuits on encrypted data. It enables very fast gate bootstrapping as well as circuit bootstrapping and operations over Boolean gates, reducing bootstrapping time to $13ms$.

TFHE-Concrete. TFHE-Concrete, an extended version of TFHE in Chillotti et al. [38], enhances the versatility and performance of TFHE in practical applications. It pushes the frontiers of bootstrapping by being the first to implement programmable bootstrapping (PBS), allowing for the simultaneous evaluation of arbitrary univariate function during bootstrapping. This is achieved by replacing the plaintext bits with a function of them in a lookup table. Presently, this is the most powerful technique for efficiently evaluating homomorphic non-linear functions, including activation functions in deep neural networks [39]. By combining the benefits of fast bootstrapping with programmable bootstrapping functionality, TFHE-Concrete enables secure and efficient computations on encrypted data, making it a valuable tool for privacy-preserving data analysis.

3.3 Zama's Concrete Framework

Zama's Concrete framework is an open-source tool that empowers developers to integrate HE into their applications without the need for in-depth cryptography knowledge [38]. TFHE-Concrete, as an integral part of the Concrete framework, provides comprehensive support across various categories, including leveled operations, bootstrapped operations, and PBS. It supports the approximate or exact evaluation of arbitrary functions, and supports both Boolean and integer operations, making it a versatile and integrated FHE solution (Table 1).

Table 1. Comparison of TFHE-Concrete with Other FHE Schemes [40].

FHE Schemes	Operations			Non-linear		Data Types		
	Level	Bootstrapped	PBS	Exact	Approx	Bool	Int	Real
BGV	✓	×	×	×	✓	×	✓	×
BFV	✓	×	×	×	✓	×	✓	×
CKKS	✓	×	×	×	✓	×	×	✓
TFHE-Lib	×	✓	×	✓	×	✓	×	×
TFHE-Concrete	✓	✓	✓	✓	✓	✓	✓	×

Concrete ML. Concrete ML is a privacy-preserving machine learning Python toolkit built on top of the Concrete framework [11]. Building on Concrete's TFHE and PBS implementation, it empowers data scientists to develop privacy-preserving models on encrypted data using the TFHE framework for secure machine learning inference.

The toolkit incorporates ready-to-use FHE-friendly models with an interface equivalent to scikit-learn. Additionally, it also provides support for customs models, including deep neural networks built with PyTorch or Keras/Tensorflow. For custom models, it is necessary to implement quantization before compiling to

FHE, utilizing third-party libraries like Brevitas for PyTorch. The model is subsequently converted and imported into Concrete ML through the Open Neural Network Exchange (ONNX), an open-source standard facilitating interoperability across various deep learning frameworks and hardware platforms.

3.4   FHE Implementation Using Concrete ML

To implement FHE in our pipelines, Concrete ML was leveraged as the FHE implementation library. Concrete ML was chosen for its suitability in realizing privacy-preserving FHE-based machine learning models and its user-friendly interface for data scientists to develop privacy-preserving models on encrypted data. Training was first done on unencrypted data, producing a model that was then converted to an FHE equivalent that can perform encrypted inference.

In the project, Concrete ML is used in 2 forms:

1. For XGBoost, Concrete ML's built-in scikit-learn-like interface is leveraged to build an FHE-compatible XGBoost that performs encrypted inference.
2. For GNN, a custom model architecture is created using PyTorch Geometric, while leveraging Concrete ML for compilation, encryption, and inference.

3.5   Collaborative AML with FHE Solution Architecture

Below is a high-level overview of the project's collaborative AML with FHE solution architecture (Fig. 2).

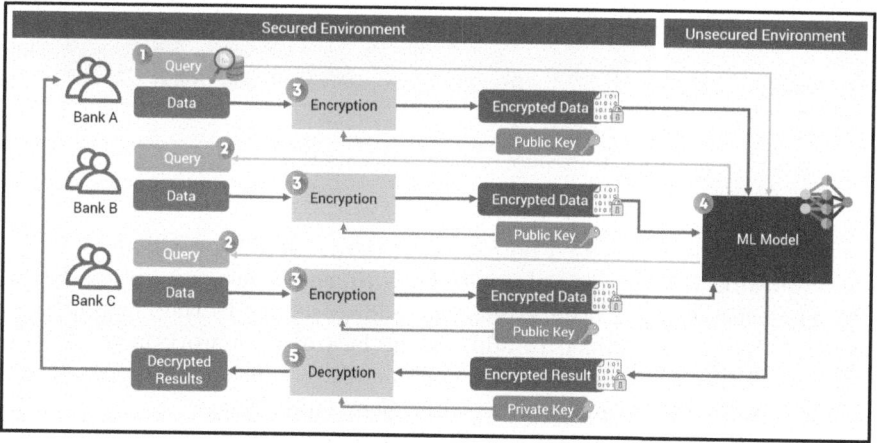

Fig. 2. FHE with MPC Solution Architecture

1. **Client Initialization:** A financial institution (FI) initiates the AML computation process with a query.

2. **Query Forwarding:** The centralised server forwards the query to participating FIs.
3. **Input Encryption:** Participating FIs, including the inquiry FI, encrypt relevant data using FHE with the inquiry FI's public key. This key is securely shared once, allowing for multiple transactions to be encrypted without repeated exchanges.
4. **Secure Computation:** The consolidated encrypted data from multiple parties undergoes machine learning inference on the server, producing results in encrypted form while maintaining input confidentiality.
5. **Result Decryption:** The final encrypted results are decrypted by the inquiry FI using its private key, revealing only the output of the computation while keeping the individual inputs from participating FIs confidential.

The above process aligns with confidentiality regulations, such as those in Singapore, where the Banking Act prohibits the disclosure of Customer Information (CI), or the existence of a non-public relationship between the customer and the bank [26] (Fig. 3).

4   TFHE-Compatible GNN Pipeline

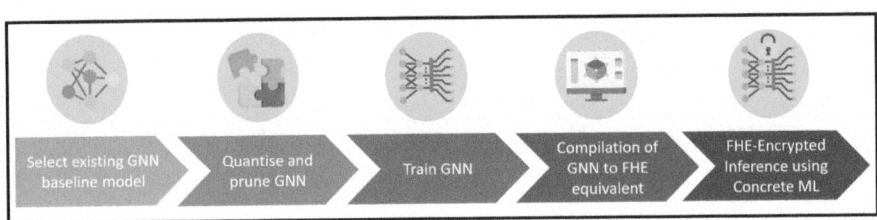

Fig. 3. Privacy-Preserving GNN Pipeline

The GNN pipeline focused on exploring the feasibility of making a Graph Neural Network (GNN) compatible with Fully Homomorphic Encryption (FHE), a challenge that has not been extensively addressed due to the inherent complexity of GNNs. This aimed to address the lack of prior work in integrating GNNs with FHE, which is crucial for enabling privacy-preserving collaborative machine learning in domains such as anti-money laundering.

The pipeline involved: selecting a GNN baseline model, quantizing and pruning it for FHE compatibility, training on Concrete ML, compiling the GNN to its FHE equivalent, and finally performing FHE inference.

4.1   Baseline GNN Model

The Graph Isomorphism Network (GIN) was selected as the baseline GNN model. GIN is a message passing GNN that uses an iterative aggregation mechanism inspired by the Weisfeiler-Lehman graph isomorphism test [44]. The baseline GIN model is implemented using PyTorch Geometric and adapted from previous AML studies [3, 19, 45].

4.2   Quantization

Quantization makes models TFHE-compatible by transforming floating-points to integer representation. It is the process of constraining an input from a continuous or otherwise large set of values to a discrete set. While primarily used for enhancing the efficiency and compression of neural networks, quantization also helps address specific limitations associated with FHE [46]. Firstly, quantization effectively substitutes floating-point value multiplications with integer multiplications, a feasible operation in FHE. Moreover, quantization enables the reduction of values to small integers, offering a strategy to navigate the challenges posed by limited precision in programmable bootstrapping.

Quantization Targets. To refine the efficiency and security of Graph Neural Networks (GNNs), the following quantization targets strategies are employed to facilitate the quantization process. Each strategy focuses on specific aspects of the GNN architecture, encompassing both node and edge features, as well as the quantization of weights and activations within GNN layers.

1. **Node Feature Quantization:** Node feature quantization reduces the precision of input node features. To achieve this, the chosen methodology involves the application of quantization to node features, effectively transforming their representation into lower-precision numerical values. In practice, this quantization is implemented through the adoption of quantized linear layers, such as QuantLinear in Brevitas, strategically incorporated into both input and hidden layers.
2. **Edge Feature Quantization:** Quantizing edge features becomes imperative, particularly in scenarios involving edge convolutional layers. The methodology extends the quantization process to edge features, dependent on their relevance in the GNN architecture. Implementation-wise, the integration of quantized linear layers (QuantLinear) or alternative quantized operations is recommended to effectively process edge features.
3. **Weights and Activations Quantization:** In the realm of GNN layers, the overarching objective is to quantize both weights and activations. This is achieved through substituting the traditional linear layers with quantized linear layers (QuantLinear), and activation function with quantized activation functions (QuantReLU) within the GNN model.

Overall, the quantization strategies encompass a reduction in weight bit width for layer configurations, and a decrease in accumulator bit width for activation. These quantization techniques contribute significantly to the optimization and security enhancement of Graph Neural Networks.

Quantization-Aware Training (QAT). Quantization-Aware Training (QAT) was employed to ensure the GNN model's compatibility with the reduced precision requirements of Fully Homomorphic Encryption (FHE). In QAT, the neural network undergoes training with an awareness of the quantization process, enabling the model to learn and adapt to the intricacies associated with lower bit-width weights and activations [47,48]. QAT was implemented using Brevitas for Pytorch. Each PyTorch layer was mapped to its quantized version in Brevitas, and the corresponding weight and bit width were configured accordingly.

4.3   Pruning

Pruning was employed to optimize the GNN model size and computational complexity, mitigating the risk of accumulator overflow during Fully Homomorphic Encryption (FHE) computations in Concrete ML [47]. Pruning involves setting certain weights in the neural network to zero, reducing the model's size and computational demands.

Some key benefits of pruning in the context of FHE include: controlling the number of active neurons to reduce computational complexity, managing the accumulator bit width to ensure compatibility with FHE's limited precision, and enhancing resource efficiency by reducing storage and computation requirements.

In the GNN implementation, edge pruning was performed on less informative edges to streamline graph connectivity while ensuring the integrity of the financial transactions graph and preserving critical components.

4.4   Compilation of GNN Model to FHE Equivalent

Final conversion of the GNN model is performed by Concrete ML, which uses the Concrete Compiler to translate the Multi-Level Intermediate Representation (MLIR) representation of the model into an FHE program, generating machine code that executes the model on encrypted data.

The conversion process starts with importing the ONNX model, followed by a sequence of transformations: initially into a NumpyModule, then into a QuantizedModule, and ultimately into an FHE circuit [49].

While efforts were made to develop a privacy-preserving GNN pipeline using Concrete ML, challenges in integrating PyTorch Geometric with the Concrete ML framework limited the successful completion of this component. The absence of support for the ScatterElements ONNX operator in Concrete ML posed a significant challenge during the final compilation of Graph Neural Networks (GNNs). While a custom implementation was developed to fill this gap, ongoing challenges remain in the conversion of NumpyModule to Quantized module.

Nevertheless, the progress made in implementing techniques to render the GNN TFHE-compatible provides a good foundation for future research (Fig. 4.

5 TFHE-Compatible XGBoost with GFP Pipeline

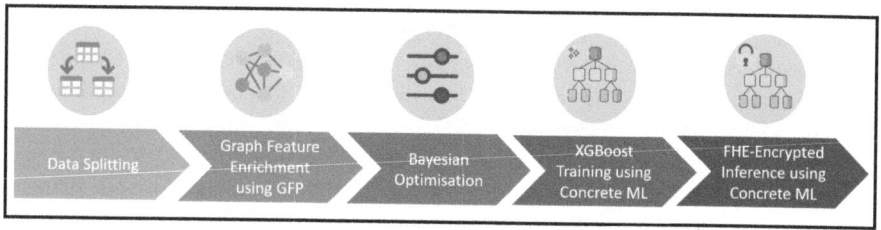

Fig. 4. Privacy-Preserving XGBoost Pipeline

The privacy-preserving graph-based XGBoost pipeline was successfully developed. This novel approach combines the predictive power of XGBoost with the security and confidentiality guarantees provided by TFHE, while leveraging Snap ML Graph Feature Preprocessor (GFP) to enrich the model with informative graph-based features.

The XGBoost pipeline encompasses the following steps: splitting the data, enriching graph features using GFP, performing hyperparameter tuning using Bayesian optimization, training the XGBoost model and performing FHE-encrypted inference using Concrete ML.

5.1 Data Splitting

Data splitting was performed in a temporal manner. The transactions were ordered in ascending order of timestamps and split into train and test sets. Generally, transactions occurring before timestamp T_1 are included in the training set, while transactions occurring after timestamp T_1 are included in the testing set. Transactions from the same day were placed in the same set too. This method was employed to prevent data leakage and ensured that the model generalizes well to unseen data by maintaining the temporal order of transactions and avoiding information leakage from future to past data. Additionally, grouping same-day transactions enhanced the integrity of the dataset and facilitated more effective model training. The distribution ensures that the training and testing sets are representative of the overall dataset while maintaining a balanced illicit ratio for effective model training and evaluation.

5.2   Snap ML Graph Feature Preprocessor (GFP) Setup

To enrich the model, the Snap ML Graph Feature Preprocessor (GFP) [50] was used to generate graph-based features from the dataset. Developed by Blanuša et al. [12], GFP facilitates efficient and real-time feature extraction from graph-structured data. It is compatible with scikit-learn, and simplifies the creation and maintenance of in-memory graphs while extracting relevant features. To search for graph patterns, the preprocessor analyzes each edge in the input edge list to identify patterns it participates in. For every edge and pattern type, the preprocessor computes a pattern histogram, which records the count of patterns of a given size. In the AML context, these additional features can augment the predictive capability of models like XGBoost, especially in detecting suspicious transactions patterns within financial transaction graphs.

The graph-based features were extracted from the AML datasets using a time window of 86400 s, or 1 day. Graph-based features include fan-in, fan-out, degree-in, degree-out, scatter-gather, simple cycle and temporal cycle patterns. For the vertex-statistics-based features, the "Amount" field of the basic transaction features were used to generate the vertex-statistics-based features. Vertex-statistics-based features selected were sum, variance and skewness.

An incremental approach was adopted to assess the impact of adding various graph-based features on the performance of the XGBoost model. These features were grouped into distinct categories: (i) basic features, (ii) fan-in/fan-out features, (iii) multi-hop pattern features, encompassing scatter-gather, simple cycle, and temporal cycle patterns, (iv) vertex-statistic-based features.

5.3   Hyperparameter Tuning via Bayesian Optimization

Bayesian optimization was employed to optimize the hyperparameters of the XGBoost model. This method systematically explores the hyperparameter space by iteratively assessing the model's performance with various parameter combinations, guided by a probabilistic model of the objective function. By selecting hyperparameters for evaluation based on the model's predictions, Bayesian optimization efficiently navigates the search space and identifies the hyperparameters values that maximize the model's performance. This approach enables the identification of optimal hyperparameters with fewer evaluations compared to exhaustive grid search or random search methods.

5.4   Training and Inference Using Concrete ML

After Bayesian optimization, the optimized XGBoost model undergoes the Concrete ML pipeline for training and FHE-encrypted inference. This process involves several key steps. First, the model is trained on plaintext, non-encrypted training data. Next, the floating-point values in the model are transformed into integers through a quantization step. The quantized model is then executed in a simulation environment to assess its accuracy under FHE and identify any necessary modifications to ensure full compatibility. Following this, the quantized model is compiled into an equivalent FHE circuit, which can be executed on encrypted data. Finally, once the appropriate cryptographic keys are generated, the quantized XGBoost model is executed on the encrypted data, enabling privacy-preserving inference using the Concrete ML framework.

6   Experiments and Results

6.1   Dataset

Dataset Selection. To train the machine learning models, a synthetic AML dataset was used to simulate money laundering scenarios, as strict privacy regulations surrounding banking data make real-world financial crime data not easily accessible. After evaluating several publicly available datasets [3,41,42], the AMLworld HI-Small dataset [3,43] was selected for its comprehensive representation of real-world money laundering activities.

The AMLworld HI-Small dataset models diverse patterns, including placement, layering, and integration, across multiple banks and currencies. Data exploration revealed 370 groups of money laundering patterns, comprising various topologies such as fan-in, fan-out, gather-scatter, cycles, and random patterns.

Dataset Modification. Due to computational constraints posed by the slower operations inherent in Fully Homomorphic Encryption (FHE), the original AMLworld HI-Small dataset was downsized. Two modified datasets were created using undersampling and random sampling techniques respectively:

1. Modified AML Dataset 1: A balanced dataset with 15,230 accounts, 10,354 transactions, and a 50% illicit ratio.
2. Modified AML Dataset 2: An imbalanced dataset with 9,070 accounts, 5,491 transactions, and a 5.72% illicit ratio.

These modified datasets provide a robust foundation for developing and evaluating machine learning pipelines to combat financial crimes, while accounting for the computational limitations of FHE.

6.2   Environment Setup

The experiments were conducted on a Linux system with an Intel Xeon CPU E5-1630 v4 @ 3.70 GHz with 8 CPU cores, using Concrete ML version 1.4.1 to implement TFHE. As Concrete ML currently does not offer GPU support, CPU resources were utilized for the experiments.

6.3   Experimental Overview

Experiments were conducted on the privacy-preserving XGBoost pipeline using the 2 modified AML datasets, with inference conducted on both unencrypted (clear) and FHE-encrypted data. XGBoost served as the baseline model, and graph features were incrementally introduced in 3 main categories: (i) single-hop patterns, (ii) multi-hop patterns and (iii) vertex statistics patterns. These graph features were added onto the base dataset features as inputs for the training and testing pipelines (Table 2).

Table 2. Pattern categories of Graph-Based Features

Pattern Category	Graph-Based Features
Single-Hop	Fan-in, fan-out, degree-in, degree-out
Multi-Hop	Scatter-gather, simple cycle, temporal cycle patterns
Vertex Statistics	Sum, variance, skewness of transaction amount

In the experiments, the Bayesian hyperparameter tuning process iteratively samples various hyperparameter combinations across 50 iterations. A 3-fold cross-validation technique is employed in each iteration, where the dataset is divided into 3 equal folds for training and evaluation, with average performance guiding subsequent iterations of the optimization process. Once optimal hyperparameters are determined, the resulting model is integrated into the graph-based gradient boosting pipeline for FHE-based inference.

6.4   Results and Discussion on Balanced AML Dataset 1

The following analysis will examine the performance metrics from Table 3 to assess the effectiveness of the Bayesian optimized XGBoost model in identifying illicit activities in the balanced AML dataset. Additionally, the discussion will explore the inference time overhead linked with FHE as depicted in Table 4.

High Performance with Basic Features. The XGBoost model demonstrates impressive performance even with just the basic features, achieving over 99% accuracy, F1 score, precision, and recall. This suggests that the model has effectively learned from the dataset and can make accurate predictions without the need for additional graph-based features.

Little Effect of Graph Features. Despite the presence of various graph patterns in the dataset, the inclusion of graph-based features did not significantly improve the model's performance. This indicates that on a balanced dataset, XGBoost may already capture the relevant features adequately without the need for additional complexity introduced by graph features.

Table 3. Performance metrics of Bayesian optimized XGBoost on Dataset 1. It highlights the effect of FHE encryption and adding graph-based features on XGBoost performance. Clear denotes inference on unencrypted data, while FHE denotes inference on FHE-encrypted data.

Input Features	Accuracy		F1		Precision		Recall	
	Clear	FHE	Clear	FHE	Clear	FHE	Clear	FHE
Basic features	0.9972	0.9972	0.9978	0.9978	0.9981	0.9981	0.9975	0.9975
+ Single-hop	0.9972	0.9972	0.9978	0.9978	0.9981	0.9981	0.9975	0.9975
+ Multi-hop	0.9972	0.9972	0.9978	0.9978	0.9981	0.9981	0.9975	0.9975
+ Vertex statistics	0.9964	0.9964	0.9972	0.9972	0.9969	0.9969	0.9975	0.9975

Table 4. Inference time metrics of Bayesian optimized XGBoost on Dataset 1. It highlights the effect of FHE encryption and adding graph-based features on inference time. Time Ratio compares total inference time on FHE-encrypted data to unencrypted.

Input Features	Inference Time (s)				Time Ratio (FHE/Clear)
	Average (Batch)		Total		
	Clear	FHE	Clear	FHE	
Basic features	0.008414	1009.0963	0.1683	20181.9266	119926.12x
+ Single-hop	0.005632	806.4183	0.1183	16128.3664	136363.27x
+ Multi-hop	0.007108	818.8802	0.1422	16377.6037	115200.84x
+ Vertex statistics	0.005781	959.1578	0.1156	19183.1552	165917.40x

FHE Encryption Overhead. While the model's performance remained strong, the inference time for FHE-encrypted data was significantly higher than unencrypted data (Table 4), exceeding 100,000 times the unencrypted inference time. This highlights the need to explore strategies that can reduce the FHE computational overhead without compromising model performance.

Future work could focus on balancing model metrics and FHE inference time, potentially by adjusting parameters or feature sets to maintain high accuracy, precision, and recall while minimizing the encryption overhead.

6.5   Results and Discussion on Imbalanced AML Dataset 2

The following analysis evaluates the performance metrics (Table 5) and inference time (Table 6) for the imbalanced AML dataset. Here, the minority F1-score is a better measure of performance than accuracy, as the latter can be misleading by favoring the majority class. In contrast, the F1-score considers both precision and recall, offering a balanced assessment and highlighting the detection of illicit money laundering transactions.

Lower Performance on Imbalanced Dataset. For the imbalanced dataset, the model faced challenges in accurately identifying illicit activities, evident from

Table 5. Performance metrics of Bayesian optimized XGBoost on Dataset 2. It highlights the effect of FHE encryption and adding graph-based features on XGBoost performance. Clear denotes inference on unencrypted data, while FHE denotes inference on FHE-encrypted data.

Input Features	Accuracy		F1		Precision		Recall	
	Clear	FHE	Clear	FHE	Clear	FHE	Clear	FHE
Basic features	0.9016	0.9016	0.3056	0.3056	0.7857	0.7857	0.1897	0.1897
+ Single-hop	0.9094	0.9094	0.3867	0.3867	0.8529	0.8529	0.2500	0.2500
+ Multi-hop	0.9075	0.9075	0.3733	0.3733	0.8235	0.8235	0.2414	0.2414
+ Vertex statistics	0.9035	0.9035	0.3467	0.3467	0.7647	0.7647	0.2241	0.2241

the drop in F1-score and recall compared to the balanced dataset. The imbalanced nature negatively impacted the F1-score, a key metric for such scenarios.

Improved Performance with Graph-Based Features. Despite the challenges posed by the imbalanced dataset, incorporating graph-based features improved the model's predictive capabilities. The addition of single-hop features led to the highest accuracy, F1-score, precision, and recall among all feature sets, outperforming the basic features. However, adding more advanced multi-hop and vertex statistics features resulted in a slight performance decrease compared to the single-hop features, though they still outperformed the basic features. Further investigation is required to understand the reasons behind this performance change when incorporating the additional graph-based feature categories.

Consistent Performance in Encrypted Inference. Moreover, the consistency in performance between unencrypted and FHE-encrypted inference highlights the robustness of Concrete-TFHE in maintaining model accuracy, F1-score, precision and recall while preserving privacy. This underscores the potential of Concrete ML in preserving privacy without sacrificing predictive performance, a crucial aspect in sensitive domains like financial transactions.

Effect of Feature Complexity on Inference Time. Interestingly, as graph-based feature complexity increased, inference time decreased for both clear and FHE-encrypted data, suggesting that the overhead of advanced features may be offset by their ability to streamline the inference process, resulting in more efficient model predictions. Further analysis is needed to validate this observation. Other potential factors contributing to this trend could include the optimization of feature representations, the inherent parallelism in graph-based computations, or the effectiveness of the Bayesian optimization process.

Overall, the integration of graph-based features showed promise in enhancing the model's ability to detect illicit activities. Future research could focus on optimizing model performance for imbalanced scenarios.

Table 6. Inference time metrics of Bayesian optimized XGBoost on Dataset 2. It highlights the effect of FHE encryption and adding graph-based features on inference time. Time Ratio compares total inference time on FHE-encrypted data to unencrypted.

Input Features	Inference Time (s)				Time Ratio (FHE/Clear)
	Average (Batch)		Total		
	Clear	FHE	Clear	FHE	
Basic features	0.003041	270.1013	0.02433	2160.8107	88822.54x
+ Single-hop	0.003055	64.9026	0.02444	519.2208	21246.95x
+ Multi-hop	0.002270	34.1322	0.01816	273.0572	15038.47x
+ Vertex statistics	0.003607	121.0173	0.02886	968.1386	33546.76x

7   Conclusion

This paper proposed a novel privacy-preserving approach for collaborative AML detection using FHE. Two key pipelines were developed:

1. A privacy-preserving GNN pipeline that explored the integration of GIN with TFHE, where optimization techniques like quantization and pruning were used in attempts to render the GNN FHE-compatible.
2. A privacy-preserving graph-based XGBoost pipeline that leveraged the Graph Feature Preprocessor (GFP) to enhance the model's predictive performance on the AML datasets. Experiments demonstrated the XGBoost model's ability to achieve over 99% accuracy, F1-score, precision, and recall on the balanced dataset, with the incorporation of graph-based features improving the F1-score by 8% on the imbalanced dataset.

A key strength of the proposed approach was the consistent performance of the XGBoost model in both unencrypted and FHE-encrypted inference settings, highlighting the robustness of the Concrete-TFHE framework in preserving privacy without compromising predictive capabilities. However, it also underscored the need to balance the trade-off between privacy preservation and computational efficiency, as FHE-encrypted inference incurred significant overhead.

8   Future Work

This work lays the foundation for innovative privacy-preserving approaches to AML detection. Future research could focus on:

1. Improving FHE compatibility and performance of models.
2. Investigating alternative privacy-preserving methods, such as differential privacy or multi-party computation, to enhance privacy-preserving capabilities.
3. Assessing scalability of solutions to accommodate larger datasets.

By addressing these future directions, the privacy-preserving machine learning approaches developed in this paper can be further advanced, contributing to the ongoing efforts to safeguard financial systems against illicit activities while preserving data privacy. Additionally, the insights and techniques explored in this paper may have the potential for broader applications in other domains that require privacy-preserving collaborative machine learning.

Acknowledgments. The authors would like to thank Alka Luqman for her contributions during the debugging of the GNN pipeline.

Disclosure of Interests. The authors have no competing interests to declare that are relevant to the content of this article.

A   Key Considerations in Collaborative FHE Architecture

This appendix outlines some of the key considerations in the design of the collaborative FHE architecture.

A.1   Advantages of Collaborative FHE over MPC

Below details the key advantages of our proposed collaborative FHE architecture in comparison to traditional Multi-Party Computation (MPC) methods in the context of AML applications.

In MPC, data fragmentation is an important requirement where multiple parties must divide and share their data to perform computations on distributed fragments. This process necessitates continuous coordination and communication among all participating FIs, resulting in significant overhead and complexity. Each party must remain online and actively participate in every computation step, making the process highly interactive and less scalable.

In contrast, our collaborative FHE architecture does not rely on data fragmentation and allows for non-interactive processing of encrypted data. Once an FI encrypts its data using a public key, computations can proceed independently without further interaction. This non-interactive approach not only simplifies data handling but also enhances efficiency by allowing FIs to contribute data without needing to be online throughout the entire computation process.

Moreover, our FHE architecture enables multiple FIs to encrypt and submit their data for secure computation while requiring only the inquiry FI to decrypt the final result. This significantly reduces communication overhead, resulting in improved scalability compared to MPC, which incurs considerable overhead due to constant data exchanges among participants.

A.2   Public Key Sharing

Our FHE architecture effectively manages public key sharing and minimizes associated network overhead.

- **Initial Key Sharing:** The inquiry FI's public key can be securely distributed at the start of a session or when a new FI initiates an inquiry. Once the key is shared, multiple transactions can be encrypted under the same key, reducing the need for repeated re-encryption for individual inquiries. This streamlines the processing of multiple data transactions within a single inquiry session.
- **Managing Changes in Inquiry FI:** If a new inquiry FI is introduced, its public key is shared efficiently with participating FIs, requiring minimal overhead as the key exchange only involves secure transmission of a small piece of data.
- **Session-Based Key Exchange:** The architecture supports session-based key exchanges, enabling each inquiry FI to generate a new session key or update its public key for each inquiry. This approach ensures that only new transactions require encryption with the new key, while existing encrypted data can continue to be processed without interruption.

B   Detailed Characteristics of Modified AML Datasets

This appendix provides additional details on the modifications made to the original AMLworld HI-Small dataset.

B.1   Modified AML Dataset 1

Undersampling was used to create a balanced dataset of 10,354 transactions and 15,230 accounts, preserving rows associated with the 370 money laundering pattern groups in the original dataset (Table 7). This reduced the dataset size for FHE computations while balancing the 50 (Table 8)

Table 7. Money Laundering Pattern Groups in AMLworld HI-Small dataset

Pattern	Count
Fan-In	61
Fan-Out	80
Gather-Scatter	77
Cycle	82
Random	70
Total Patterns	370

B.2   Modified AML Dataset 2

A smaller, highly imbalanced dataset was created by randomly sampling 40 out of the 370 pattern groups to represent illicit transactions (Table 9). This resulted in 5,491 transactions across 9,070 accounts, with a 5.72% illicit ratio (Table 10).

Table 8. Characteristics of Modified AML Dataset 1

Characteristics	Value
Number of accounts	15,230
Number of transactions	10,354
Illicit money laundering ratio	50%

Table 9. Money Laundering Pattern Groups in Modified AML Dataset 2

Pattern	Count
Fan-In	8
Fan-Out	7
Gather-Scatter	9
Cycle	8
Random	8
Total Patterns	40

Table 10. Characteristics of Modified AML Dataset 2

Characteristics	Value
Number of accounts	9070
Number of transactions	5491
Illicit money laundering ratio	5.72%

C   Train-Test Split Distribution

The datasets were split temporally, with the training set comprising 75–81% of the data (Tables 11 and 12).

Table 11. Train-Test Split Distribution for Modified AML Dataset 1

	Percentage of Dataset	Illicit Ratio
Train Sample	75.85%	45.47%
Test Sample	24.15%	64.16%

Table 12. Train-Test Split Distribution for Modified AML Dataset 2

	Percentage of Dataset	Illicit Ratio
Train Sample	81.50%	4.42%
Test Sample	18.50%	11.42%

D   Definition of Graph-Based Features

Below are an elaboration of the graph-based features.

- **Fan-in/fan-out** reveals the inbound and outbound connectivity of vertices, aiding in understanding recipient and initiator vertices within the graph.
- **Degree-in/degree-out** quantifies the total inbound and outbound edges for each vertex, providing a holistic view of vertex connectivity.
- **Scatter-gather patterns** detects dispersion and aggregation behaviors across the graph, offering insights into information propagation and aggregation.
- **Simple cycles** identifies closed paths within the graph, highlighting recurring patterns or loops indicative of repetitive processes.
- **Temporal cycles** uncovers cyclic patterns with temporal dimensions, offering insights into recurring activities over time.

Below are an elaboration of the vertex-statistics-based features.

- **Sum** provides insight into the overall volume of financial activity. High sums may indicate potentially suspicious behavior, such as large-scale transactions or money laundering schemes.
- **Variance** reflects the dispersion or spread of transaction amounts around the mean. High variance may suggest irregular or unpredictable patterns in financial transactions, indicative of fraudulent activities.
- **Skewness** measures the asymmetry of the distribution of transaction amounts. Positive skewness suggests a longer tail towards higher values, while negative skewness suggests a longer tail towards lower values. Extreme positive skewness may indicate unusual transaction patterns that require further investigation.

E   Hyperparameter Tuning Search Space

The Bayesian optimization search space for XGBoost hyperparameters is detailed in Table 13.

Table 13. Search Space for Bayesian Optimization of XGBoost Hyperparameters

Parameter	Search Space Range
n_estimators	(5, 30)
max_depth	(2, 12)
learning_rate	(0.003, 0.1)
colsample_bytree	(0.5, 1)

F   Additional Privacy-Preserving XGBoost Experiments

Experiments varying n_estimators, max_depth, and n_bits provided insights into balancing model performance and FHE inference time (Tables 14, 15 and 16).

Table 14. Performance and time metrics of XGBoost models with varying n_estimators. Experiment was conducted on Dataset 1 at fixed n_bits = 3, learning_rate = 0.07, colsample_bytree = 0.98, max_depth = 3.

n_estimator	Accuracy		F1-Score		Inference Time (s)		Time Ratio
	Clear	FHE	Clear	FHE	Clear	FHE	
5	0.6428	0.6428	0.7822	0.7822	0.009405	1401.32	149000x
10	0.6428	0.6428	0.7822	0.7822	0.013848	2222.64	160504x
50	0.6432	0.6432	0.7824	0.7824	0.042257	26595.60	629379x
100	0.6483	0.6483	0.7846	0.7846	0.205946	55523.89	269604x
200	0.6483	0.6468	0.7846	0.7833	0.174605	65481.47	375027x

Table 15. Performance and time metrics of XGBoost models with varying max_depth. Experiment was conducted on Dataset 1 at fixed n_bits = 3, learning_rate = 0.07, colsample_bytree = 0.98, n_estimator = 20.

max_depth	Accuracy		F1-Score		Inference Time (s)		Time Ratio
	Clear	FHE	Clear	FHE	Clear	FHE	
1	0.3584	0.3584	0.0000	0.0000	0.019856	4014.30	202173.40x
4	0.5540	0.5540	0.6809	0.6809	0.121287	29193.94	240701.55x
7	0.5540	0.5540	0.6809	0.6809	1.873080	47420.48	25316.84x
10	0.5540	0.5540	0.6809	0.6809	0.228830	40407.25	176581.86x
13	0.5540	0.5540	0.6809	0.6809	0.184337	41289.46	223988.81x

Table 16. Performance and time metrics of XGBoost models with varying n_bits. Experiment was conducted on Dataset 1 at fixed learning_rate = 0.07, colsample_bytree = 0.98, n_estimator = 20, max_depth = 3.

n_bits	Accuracy		F1-Score		Inference Time (s)		Time Ratio
	Clear	FHE	Clear	FHE	Clear	FHE	
2	0.4540	0.4540	0.4553	0.4553	0.042825	7244.70	169168.00x
3	0.5540	0.5540	0.6809	0.6809	0.055623	11766.27	211534.87x
4	0.6432	0.6432	0.7824	0.7824	0.055750	30344.95	544307.47x
8	0.6428	0.6428	0.7821	0.7821	0.023308	32139.84	1378944.61x

References

1. United Nations Office on Drugs and Crime. Money Laundering (2023). https://www.unodc.org/unodc/en/money-laundering/overview.html
2. Cheah, M.: S\$3 billion anti-money laundering bust wraps up with 10th and final individual jailed. The Business Times, June 2024
3. Altman, E., Egressy, B., Blanuša, J., Atasu, K.: Realistic synthetic financial transactions for anti-money laundering models. arXiv: 2306.16424 [cs.AI] (2023)
4. McKinsey & Company. The fight against money laundering: machine learning is a game changer, October 2022
5. Kurshan, E., Shen, H.: Graph computing for financial crime and fraud detection: trends, challenges and outlook. arXiv: 2103.03227 [cs.CR] (2021)
6. PwC. Breaking down the silos to combat financial crimes. https://www.pwc.com/ca/en/services/deals/breaking-down-the-silos-to-financial-crimes.html
7. Wass, S.: Banks need steer on data protection vs money-laundering rules: industry bodies. en-us, February 2020
8. Monetary Authority of Singapore. COSMIC. en, December 2023. https://www.mas.gov.sg/regulation/anti-money-laundering/cosmic
9. Monetary Authority of Singapore. Consultation Paper on the Regulations Relating to FI-FI Information Sharing for AML/CFT, December 2023
10. Financial Action Task Force (FATF). Opportunities and Challenges of New Technologies for AML/CFT. FATF, Paris, France (2021)
11. Zama. What is Concrete ML?—Concrete ML Documentation. en, February 2024. https://docs.zama.ai/concrete-ml/
12. Blanuša, J., Egressy, B., von Niederhäusern, L., Altman, E., Wattenhofer, R., Atasu, K.: Graph feature preprocessor: real-time extraction of subgraph-based features from transaction graphs. arXiv: 2402.08593 [cs.LG] (2024)
13. Weber, M., Xu, K., Leskovec, J., Jegelka, S.: Scalable graph learning for anti-money laundering: a first look. arXiv: 1812.00076 [cs.SI] (2018)
14. Weber, M., Xu, K., Leskovec, J., Jegelka, S.: Anti-money laundering in bitcoin: experimenting with graph convolutional networks for financial forensics. arXiv: 1908.02591 [cs.SI] (2019)
15. Alarab, I., Prakoonwit, S.: Graph-based LSTM for anti-money laundering: experimenting temporal graph convolutional network with bitcoin data. Neural Process. Lett. 55(1), 689–707 (2023)
16. Pareja, A., Martínez-Muñoz, G., Ahn, S., Iglesias, P., Branco, P., Song, D.: EvolveGCN: evolving graph convolutional networks for dynamic graphs. arXiv: 1902.10191 [cs.LG] (2019)
17. Cardoso, M., Saleiro, P., Bizarro, P.: LaundroGraph: self-supervised graph representation learning for anti-money laundering. arXiv: 2210.14360 [cs.LG] (2022)
18. Johannessen, F., Jullum, M.: Finding money launderers using heterogeneous graph neural networks. arXiv: 2307.13499 [cs.LG] (2023)
19. Egressy, B., von Niederhäusern, L., Blanusa, J., Altman, E., Wattenhofer, R., Atasu, K.: Provably powerful graph neural networks for directed multigraphs. arXiv: 2306.11586 [cs.LG] (2024)
20. Tertychnyi, P., Babenko, V., Morozova, V., Borsuk, D.: Scalable and imbalance-resistant machine learning models for anti-money laundering: a two-layered approach, pp. 43–58, November 2020. ISBN: 978-3-030-64465-9. https://doi.org/10.1007/978-3-030-64466-6_3

21. Jullum, M., Hoff, H., Reistad, M.N., Glad, I.K.: Detecting money laundering transactions with machine learning. J. Money Launder. Control (2020, ahead-of-print)
22. Vassallo, D., Vella, V., Ellul, J.: Application of gradient boosting algorithms for anti-money laundering in cryptocurrencies. SN Comput. Sci. **2** (2021). https://doi.org/10.1007/s42979-021-00558-z
23. Eddin, A.N., Stoian, A., Dutta, S.: Anti-money laundering alert optimization using machine learning with graphs. arXiv: 2112.07508 [cs.LG] (2022)
24. Baum, C., et al.: SoK: privacy-enhancing technologies in finance. Cryptology ePrint Archive, Paper 2023/122 (2023). https://eprint.iacr.org/2023/122
25. Bank for International Settlements (BIS) Innovation Hub. Project Aurora: the power of data, technology and collaboration to combat money laundering across institutions and borders. en, May 2023
26. Infocomm Media Development Authority. Preventing Financial Fraud Across Different Jurisdictions with Secure Data Collaborations - IMDA PET Sandbox - Mastercard Case Study, November 2023
27. Zhang, H., Gao, Y., Zhou, R., Li, B.: A privacy-preserving hybrid federated learning framework for financial crime detection. arXiv: 2302.03654 [cs.LG] (2023)
28. van Egmond, M.B., Tubić, L., Beder, C.: Privacy-preserving anti-money laundering using secure multi-party computation. Cryptology ePrint Archive, Paper 2024/065 (2024)
29. Gilad-Bachrach, R., Dowlin, N., Laine, K., Lauter, K., Naehrig, M., Wernsing, J.: CryptoNets: applying neural networks to encrypted data with high throughput and accuracy. In: Balcan, M.F., Weinberger, K.Q. (eds.) Proceedings of The 33rd International Conference on Machine Learning, vol. 48, pp. 201–210. Proceedings of Machine Learning Research, New York, New York, USA. PMLR, 20–22 June 2016
30. Al Badawi, A., Jović, J., Yeo, C.K., Cheng, C.-M., Sion, R.: Towards the AlexNet moment for homomorphic encryption: HCNN, the first homomorphic CNN on encrypted data with GPUs. Cryptology ePrint Archive, Paper 2018/1056 (2018). https://doi.org/10.1109/TETC.2020.3014636
31. Brutzkus, A., Elisha, O., Gilad-Bachrach, R.: Low latency privacy preserving inference. arXiv: 1812.10659 [cs.LG] (2019)
32. Lee, J.-W., Kim, J., Lee, J.-W., Lee, D.H., Ha, M.: Privacy-preserving machine learning with fully homomorphic encryption for deep neural network. arXiv: 2106.07229 [cs.LG] (2021)
33. Ran, R., Xu, N., Liu, T., Wang, W., Quan, G., Wen, W.: Penguin: parallel-packed homomorphic encryption for fast graph convolutional network inference. In: Proceedings of the Thirty-Seventh Conference on Neural Information Processing Systems (2023)
34. Ran, R., Ma, Y., Kumar, D., Huang, W., Richtárik, P.: CryptoGCN: fast and scalable homomorphically encrypted graph convolutional network inference. arXiv: 2209.11904 [cs.CR] (2022)
35. Rivest, R.L., Adleman, L., Dertouzos, M.L., et al.: On data banks and privacy homomorphisms. Found. Secure Comput. **4**(11), 169–180 (1978)
36. Gentry, C.: A fully homomorphic encryption scheme. Ph.D. thesis. Stanford, CA, USA (2009). ISBN: 9781109444506. Type: AAI3382729
37. Chillotti, I., Gama, N., Georgieva, M., Izabachène, M.: TFHE: fast fully homomorphic encryption over the torus. Cryptology ePrint Archive, Paper 2018/421 (2018). https://eprint.iacr.org/2018/421

38. Chillotti, I., Gama, N., Georgieva, M., Izabachène, M.: CONCRETE: concrete operates oN ciphertexts rapidly by extending TfhE. In: 8th Workshop on Encrypted Computing & Applied Homomorphic Cryptography, p. 7. ACM. Virtual Event. ACM, New York, NY, USA, December 2020. https://doi.org/10.25835/0072999
39. Joye, M.: Homomorphic Encryption 101. en, December 2021. https://www.zama.ai/post/homomorphic-encryption-101
40. Zama. Introducing the Concrete Framework. en, July 2022. https://www.zama.ai/post/introducing-the-concrete-framework
41. Mahootiha, M.: Money Laundering Data (2020). https://www.kaggle.com/datasets/maryam1212/money-laundering-data
42. Suzumura, T., Kanezashi, H.: Anti-Money Laundering Datasets (2021). https://github.com/IBM/AMLSim
43. IBM Research. IBM Transactions for Anti Money Laundering (AML) (2023). https://www.kaggle.com/datasets/ealtman2019/ibm-transactions-for-anti-money-laundering-aml
44. Xu, K., Hu, W., Leskovec, J., Jegelka, S.: How powerful are graph neural networks? arXiv: 1810.00826 [cs.LG] (2019)
45. Altman, E., Egressy, B., Blanuša, J., Atasu, K.: Multi-GNN architectures for anti-money laundering (2023). https://github.com/IBM/Multi-GNN
46. Zama. Quantization of Neural Networks for Fully Homomorphic Encryption. en, January 2022. https://www.zama.ai/post/quantization-of-neural-networks-for-fully-homomorphic-encryption
47. Stoian, A., Sdi, T., Stoica, A., Filos-Ratsikas, A., Carpov, S.: Deep neural networks for encrypted inference with TFHE. Cryptology ePrint Archive, Paper 2023/257 (2023). https://eprint.iacr.org/2023/257
48. Tailor, S.A., Fernandez-Marques, J., Lane, N.D.: Degree-quant: quantization-aware training for graph neural networks. arXiv: 2008.05000 [cs.LG] (2021)
49. Zama. Compilation—Concrete ML Documentation. en, February 2024. https://docs.zama.ai/concrete-ml/advanced-topics/compilation
50. IBM Research. Graph Feature Preprocessor - Snap ML 1.14.2 documentation (2023). https://snapml.readthedocs.io/en/latest/graph_preprocessor.html

CoPrIME: Complete Process Isolation Using Memory Encryption
Extended Abstract

Saltanat Firdous[1(✉)], Asutosh Brahma[1], Arjun Menon[2], and Chester Rebeiro[1]

[1] Indian Institute of Technology M,Chennai, India
{saltanat,chester}@cse.iitm.ac.in
[2] Incore Semiconductors, Chennai, India
arjun@incoresemi.com

Abstract. As operating systems grow in functionality, their code bases become larger and it becomes difficult to formally verify them. As a result, a lot of bugs and vulnerabilities in operating systems remain unnoticed. These bugs can be exploited by attackers to compromise the operating system. Since the operating system runs at a higher privilege and has unrestricted access to the address space of all processes running in the system, a bug in the OS can lead to all applications in the system getting compromised. Thus, there is a need to protect the applications against these untrusted operating systems. The traditional approach to protect the security-sensitive modules of an application against an untrusted OS is the execution of these modules in Trusted Execution Environments (TEEs) but these TEEs come with certain limitations. A major drawback is the need to modify the application for it to work in a TEE which makes the concept of TEEs inapplicable to legacy applications. We propose an orthogonal approach to protect the entire application using cryptographic techniques which is compatible with legacy applications with no need to modify the source code.

To safeguard the security sensitive applications against untrusted operating systems, the use of TEEs has gained popularity. TEEs provide an isolated environment for the execution of an application where its code and data cannot be accessed by other applications or the OS. These TEEs provide data confidentiality, data integrity, and code integrity. Access to these TEEs is controlled by policies implemented in hardware and the hardware is assumed to be trusted. Two of the most popular TEEs adopted in the industry are TrustZone [2] from ARM and Software Guard eXtensions (SGX) [1] from Intel. Along with these, there have been several academic efforts towards the development of TEEs. These include Keystone [3], Sanctum [4], Sanctuary [5], CURE [6], SCONE [7], Graphene [8], Hven [9], etc. TEEs have become quite popular and are deployed in a variety of systems but these TEEs come with certain limitations. In fact, Intel deprecated the use of SGX in 2021. A commonality among the contemporary TEE approaches is that only small portions of the process, which are considered to be sensitive, are protected and the remaining portions are left unprotected. This has several drawbacks:

© The Author(s), under exclusive license to Springer Nature Switzerland AG 2025
J. Knechtel et al. (Eds.): SPACE 2024, LNCS 15351, pp. 106–109, 2025.
https://doi.org/10.1007/978-3-031-80408-3_7

1. The applications need to be split into secure and non-secure parts at design time. Thus, TEEs cannot be used to protect legacy applications that were designed without the partitioning requirements.
2. Partitioning of the application adds design time overhead as the programmer now needs to identify security-critical parts of the application at design time.
3. Partitioning of the application needs considerable security expertise which is not commonly found in programmers.
4. Inefficient partitioning of applications can cause significant performance overheads as the transitions to and from the TEEs are quite expensive.
5. It is also challenging to achieve IP protection, especially when the entire application needs to be protected.

Thus, there is a need to isolate the applications but at the same time, maintain compatibility and low overhead.

We try to address the limitations of TEEs by providing isolation to the entire application so that there is no need to partition the application into secure and non-secure parts and hence, there are no compatibility issues or design-time overheads. The application is isolated from the host OS as well as from other applications using memory encryption. To protect against memory modification attacks like RowHammer [12], we also support memory authentication. The main challenge is to be able to implement the encryption and authentication algorithms with minimum latency and the correct functioning of the application and host system.

To protect the applications against malicious processes including compromised privileged software, we propose CoPrIME: Complete Process Isolation using Memory Encryption, wherein we provide isolation to the entire application rather than just a part of it. We isolate the processes in memory from each other as well as from the privileged software using encryption. Each application is encrypted with a unique key. The key is kept secret and is known only to the hardware. Therefore, a malicious application cannot leak information from another application. Since the key is also hidden from the OS, even a compromised OS cannot leak information from an application. However, minimum parts of the application need to be left unprotected for its correct functioning. This is based on the observation that the OS interacts with the process only through system calls. Thus, only the system call parameters need to be revealed to the OS, everything else can be hidden. Now if the OS gets compromised, it can only leak the sequence of system calls invoked by the process and the parameters passed through these calls. We achieve this complete process isolation by encrypting the application using an application-specific key known only to the hardware. The complete process (data as well as instructions) is encrypted and remains encrypted inside the RAM. It is decrypted only inside the processor by a hardware module which we call a Memory Encryption Engine (MEE). Data written back to RAM is again encrypted. Since instructions do not change inside the processor, there is no need to write back the instructions to the RAM. Hence, there is no need to encrypt them again. So, the encryption overhead is only for the data. The encryption and decryption are performed by the hardware completely independent of the OS. OS, unaware of the key, does not have access to the code and data of the application. However, for the correct functioning of the operating system and the applications, whenever there is a context switch to the OS, the MEE needs to be turned off because the OS runs in an unencrypted form and the instructions in the OS code should not be decrypted inside the processor. Also, the system call parameters need to be decrypted so that the OS understands them. This is handled by a thin, trusted software layer running at a higher privilege than the OS. During execution, every system call is intercepted in this trusted layer before being forwarded to the OS. The trusted shim layer identifies the system call and the parameters associated with it, and decrypts them before control is transferred to the OS. MEE is turned off by the hardware on a context switch. Similarly, on returning from the system call, the hardware turns on the MEE and the trusted layer encrypts the parameters again before the control is transferred back to the application. All of this is completely transparent to the application and the OS. This approach, in addition to providing security, is also transparent to the programmer with no need to modify legacy applications. It only requires encrypting the compiled binary file and including the key information in it. At load time, the encrypted binaries are registered in a small, trusted software layer called the Security Monitor (SM), which runs at a higher privilege than the untrusted OS.

Though the OS cannot read the encrypted data of an application from the memory, it can still tamper with it. To prevent any unauthorized modification of the isolated application, we also provide an integrity verification mechanism. We use an authenticated encryption algorithm which along with encrypting a block of data, produces an authentication tag over it. We store this tag value for each block of memory and perform a tag comparison between the stored tag and freshly computed tag whenever a block of memory is read into the cache. The operation proceeds only when the two match, otherwise an exception is raised.

So far, CoPrIME has been successfully implemented on the SHAKTI-C class processor [11], which is an open-source RISC-V based processor. We have synthesized the SHAKTI core with CoPrIME support on a XILINX Arty A7-100T FPGA board. The minimal changes required in the OS have also been completely implemented and we are able to execute encrypted applications over Linux on the modified core. We are now evaluating the overheads of our scheme by running the benchmarking applications on the FPGA. For encryption and authentication, we have implemented the Ascon cipher in hardware which adds a latency of 5 cycles for each encryption and decryption operation but the latency can be reduced further with a pipelined implementation.

Conclusion

The CoPrIME model is based on the idea that an operating system should only have access to the data that is necessary for it to perform its functions, and no more. This principle of least privilege helps to protect sensitive data by reducing the amount of data that the operating system can access. The design and proof-of-concept implementation of CoPrIME has demonstrated that this approach is feasible and effective. Adversaries seeking to access a database typically target login credentials, which can be leaked through vulnerable system points such as the memory. To address this vulnerability, the proposed solution emphasizes the importance of securing the data in memory to deter compromises. Another key advantage of CoPrIME is that it requires no additional skills or knowledge from application programmers. Any legacy application can work with CoPrIME by simply encrypting the application executable, making the model fully backward compatible. This is in contrast to existing TEEs, which often require specialized programming techniques and restructuring the legacy code.

References

1. Costan, V.: Intel SGX explained. IACR Cryptol, EPrint Arch (2016)
2. Ngabonziza, B., Martin, D., Bailey, A., Cho, H., Martin, S.: Trustzone explained: architectural features and use cases. In: 2016 IEEE 2nd International Conference on Collaboration and Internet Computing (CIC), pp. 445–451. IEEE (2016)
3. Lee, D., Kohlbrenner, D., Shinde, S., Asanović, K., Song, D.: Keystone: an open framework for architecting trusted execution environments. In: Proceedings of the Fifteenth European Conference on Computer Systems, pp. 1–16 (2020)
4. Costan, V., Lebedev, I., Devadas, S.: Sanctum: minimal hardware extensions for strong software isolation. In: 25th USENIX Security Symposium (USENIX Security 2016), pp. 857–874 (2016)
5. Brasser, F., Gens, D., Jauernig, P., Sadeghi, A.R., Stapf, E.: ARMing TrustZone with user-space enclaves. In: SANCTUARY. NDSS (2019)
6. Bahmani, R., et al.: CURE: a security architecture with CUstomizable and resilient enclaves. In: 30th USENIX Security Symposium (USENIX Security 2021), pp. 1073–1090 (2021)
7. Arnautov, S., et al.: SCONE: secure linux containers with intel SGX. In: 12th USENIX Symposium on Operating Systems Design and Implementation (OSDI 2016), pp. 689–703 (2016)
8. Tsai, C.C., Porter, D.E., Vij, M.: Graphene-SGX: a practical library OS for unmodified applications on SGX. In: 2017 USENIX Annual Technical Conference (USENIX ATC 2017), pp. 645–658 (2017)
9. Baumann, A., Peinado, M., Hunt, G.: Shielding applications from an untrusted cloud with haven. ACM Trans. Comput. Syst. (TOCS) 33(3), 1–26 (2015)
10. Shinde, S., Le Tien, D., Tople, S., Saxena, P.: Low-TCB linux applications with SGX enclaves, panoply. In: NDSS (2017)
11. George, P., Sahoo, A., Menon, A., Kamakoti, V.: SHAKTI: an open-source processor ecosystem. In: Advanced Computing and Communications (2018). Accessed 30 Mar 2022. https://doi.org/10.34048/2018.3
12. Mutlu, O., Kim, J.S.: Rowhammer: a retrospective. IEEE Trans. Comput. Aided Des. Integr. Circuits Syst. 39(8), 1555–1571 (2019)

Online Testing Entropy and Entropy Tests with a Two State Markov Model
Invited Paper

David Johnston$^{(\boxtimes)}$ 🆔

Hillsboro, Oregon, USA
dj@deadhat.com

Abstract. A 2 parameter, 2 state Markov model of an RNG (Random Number Generator) can generate all possible combinations of μ (mean), SCC (Serial Correlation Coefficient) in binary data. A formula for Min entropy of data from the model is derived, leading to an efficient online hardware entropy boundary test of non IID (Independent and Identically Distributed) data called the polygon test. In addition the model can produce labelled data with known entropy with which to validate entropy test algorithms. Significant shortcomings in the SP800-90B Non IID tests are shown and an example of using the generator to test tests.

Keywords: Markov Model · Entropy Estimation · Random Number Generator · Polygon Test · Online Health Test · SP800-90B · binary noise source

1 Introduction

Cryptographically secure RNGs (Random Number Generators) require one or more noise sources to inject nondeterminism into the otherwise deterministic state of the RNG.

Characterizing the entropy content of an entropy source output is critical to ensuring the security properties of RNGs. This is done through heuristic analysis [8] [7], simulation and test algorithms run over data output from the noise source [10].

In an AIS20-31 [8] or SP800-90B [10] compliant RNG, an entropy extractor algorithm will take the partially entropic data from the noise sources and compress the data to full entropy data. SP800-90B [10] defines that with n bits of full entropy data output from the extractor, $n + 64$ bits of min-entropy need to be input to the algorithm. If there are m bits of partially entropy data are input to the extractor and entropy rate of at least $\frac{n+64}{m}$ is needed in the input data. A test that can show the entropy rate is above $\frac{n+64}{m}$ is sufficient to ensure full entropy output although SP800-90B [10] requires two additional mandatory tests, the RCT (Repetition Count Test) and APT (Adaptive Proportion Test) at the current time.

D. Johnston—Independent.

J. Knechtel et al. (Eds.): SPACE 2024, LNCS 15351, pp. 110–128, 2025.
https://doi.org/10.1007/978-3-031-80408-3_8

A formal proof of the extraction properties of CBC-MAC mode and HMAC modes for an RNG are given in [2]. This gives a more relaxed min entropy bound than SP800-90B [10].

Entropy test algorithms come in various types, including algorithms that try to estimate entropy within some error bound, algorithms to measure summary statistics [5], algorithms that estimate a lower bound for entropy guaranteed to be below the actual entropy [10], model fitting algorithms that show data fits to a mathematical model of the expected output of an entropy source circuit and algorithms to measure summary statistics.

NIST SP800-90B [10] is a specification that includes a number of lower bound entropy test algorithms. These have been shown to dramatically underestimate the entropy of some classes of data. Reference data with known entropy is necessary in order to verify such tests.

Existing binary generator models that have been used to test entropy estimation algorithms include the biased model, serially correlated model, sin-bias model and the Step Update Metastable Source (SUMS) model [4]. All of these models have well defined min-entropy and well defined statistical properties.

The model described in this paper was motivated by the need to generate data with directly chosen bias and serial correlation and well defined min entropy. None of the existing models used against SP800-90B have the property of being able to choose the bias and serial correlation at the same time. Data from this mofel can be used to test and calibrate entropy testing algorithms, or informally, 'Testing the Tests'.

The model is a simple two state Markov model. One state outputs a 1 and the other state outputs a 0. The transition probabilities determine the bias, serial correlation and min entropy for each bit width symbol.

Since in the real world, all symbols are finite in size, the size of the generated symbols must be taken into account when deriving min entropy from the model parameters.

2   The 2 State, 2 Parameter, Markov Random Bit Generator

A useful property of a 2 state, 2 parameter Markov generator is that it can generate data with simultaneously controlled and known μ, SCC and min-entropy.

The 2 state, 2 parameter Markov generator has two states labelled 1 and 0. For each step of the Markov process, in the 1 state a binary 1 is output. In the 0 state a binary 0 is output (Fig. 1).

P_{01} gives the probability of a 0 followed by a 1. P_{10} gives the probability of a 1 followed by a 0. P_{11} gives the probability of a 1 followed by a 1. P_{00} gives the probability of a 0 followed by a 0.

The exit probabilities from each state add to 1, so the model has only 2 degrees of freedom and the model can be described with only two of the parameters $P_{01}, P_{10}, P_{00}, P_{11}, P_{11}, P_{01}$ or P_{00}, P_{10}.

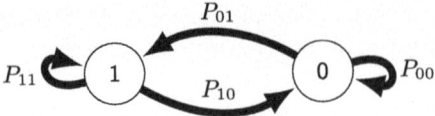

Fig. 1. Markov Generator

$$P_{01} + P_{00} = 1 \tag{1}$$

$$P_{10} + P_{11} = 1 \tag{2}$$

Unbiased output where $\mu = \frac{1}{2}$ occurs on the 0,0 to 1,1 diagonal of P_{01}, P_{10}.

$$P_{01} = P_{10} \implies \mu = \frac{1}{2} \tag{3}$$

Independent outputs, where $SCC = 0$ occurs on the 1,0 to 0,1 diagonal of P_{01}, P_{10}.

$$P_{01} = 1 - P_{10} \implies SCC = 0 \tag{4}$$

This is shown graphically in Fig. 2a where the line from the lower left to lower right contains the parameter points where $\mu = 0$ and SCC varies from $+1$ to -1. The line from the upper left to the lower right contains the parameter points where $SCC = 0$ and μ varies from 0 to 1.

3   Determining μ, SCC for All Parameter Points

To be able to set the parameters for a chosen μ and SCC, we need to derive equations for the relationship between the two parameters μ and SCC.

Running the model, it can be seen that the sets of value pairs of P_{01}, P_{10} for a given μ lay on lines radiating from $0,0$ and with a rise that is inversely proportional to μ as in Fig. 2b.

Plotting the rise of the lines against μ it is seen that the rise varies with μ following a $\frac{1-x}{x}$ curve as shown in Fig. 2c.

From this it is determined that the line equation for P_{10} against P_{01} for a given value of μ is

$$P_{10} = P_{01} \frac{1 - \mu}{\mu} \tag{5}$$

Plotting lines of iso-scc in Fig. 2d, we see the zero-scc line is on the opposite diagonal to the unbiased μ line and for other SCC values, they shift up or down by the amount of the SCC.

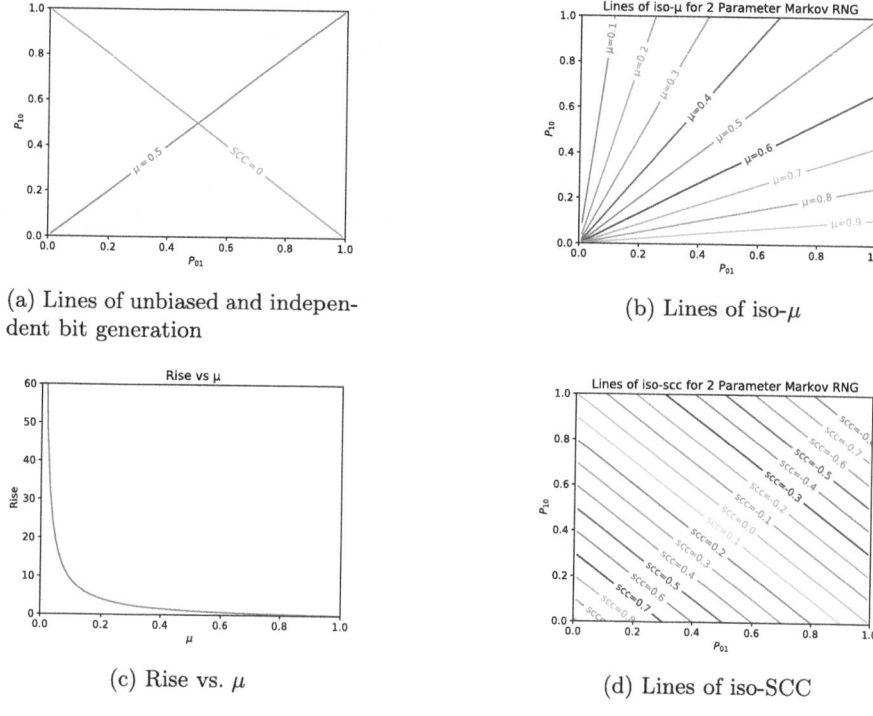

(a) Lines of unbiased and independent bit generation

(b) Lines of iso-μ

(c) Rise vs. μ

(d) Lines of iso-SCC

Fig. 2. Four Plots of μ and SCC

From this we can infer that the line equation for P_{10} against P_{01} for any given SCC is

$$P_{10} = 1 - SCC - P_{01} \qquad (6)$$

Locating the intersection of the line for a given μ and the line for a given SCC will give the P_{01}, P_{10} values necessary for the 2 parameter markov model to generate data with that μ and SCC.

The direct equations to compute P_{01} and P_{10} from μ and SCC are derived by solving the line equations for the μ and SCC lines.

Subtracting Eq. 6 from 5 gives:

$$P_{10} - P_{10} = P_{01}\frac{1 - \mu}{\mu} - 1 + SCC + P_{01} \qquad (7)$$

Which simplifies to:

$$P_{01} = \mu(1 - SCC) \qquad (8)$$

Adding Eq. 5 and 6 gives:

$$2P_{10} = P_{01}\frac{1-\mu}{\mu} + 1 - SCC - P_{01} \tag{9}$$

Which simplifies to:

$$P_{10} = (1-\mu)(1-SCC) \tag{10}$$

To get the reverse mapping, these two equations can be rearranged to define scc and μ in terms of P_{01} and P_{01}.

$$\mu = \frac{P_{01}}{P_{10} + P_{01}} \tag{11}$$

$$SCC = 1 - P_{10} - P_{01} \tag{12}$$

4   Calculating the Min Entropy

The min-entropy can be computed by determining the probability of the MCV (Most Common Value). This follows directly from the definition of min-entropy:

$$H_\infty(X) = -log_2(max(P(x_i)))$$

Directly measuring the MCV from data generated by the model yields Table 1 that shows in hex the MCV against P_{01} and P_{10} using 4 bit symbols.

We see that most points have an MCV of either all zeroes, all ones or an alternating pattern of ones and zeroes. However between the regions of alternating patterns (A and 5) and non alternating patterns (0 and F), there are some points where other values appear. The central point at 0.5,0.5 is a full entropy value, so the result will be uniformly randomly selected from all the possible values.

To illustrate what is happening at the boundary points, consider the point $P_{10} = 0.5, P_{01} = 0.55$ where the MCV turned out to be 0xB in the simulation.

Computing for 4 bit symbols at this point, with a large number of samples, the MCV always turns out to be 1011 (hex B). If we extend the symbol size one bit at a time we see the progression in Table 2.

It is seen that the actual output of the model for arbitarily long symbols is an alternating pattern of ones and zeroes, whereas the final bit appears to deviate from that pattern when the bit width of the symbol is even but not when it is odd.

Table 1. MCV Table

P_{01} / P_{10}	0.05	0.10	0.15	0.20	0.25	0.30	0.35	0.40	0.45	0.50	0.55	0.60	0.65	0.70	0.75	0.80	0.85	0.90	0.95
0.95	0	0	0	0	0	0	0	2	4	A	A	A	5	5	A	A	5	A	A
0.9	0	0	0	0	0	0	0	0	4	A	A	A	5	5	5	5	A	5	A
0.85	0	0	0	0	0	0	0	0	4	A	5	5	5	5	5	5	A	5	5
0.8	0	0	0	0	0	0	0	0	4	A	A	A	5	5	5	5	5	5	A
0.75	0	0	0	0	0	0	0	0	4	5	A	A	5	A	A	5	5	5	5
0.7	0	0	0	0	0	0	0	0	2	2	5	A	A	A	A	A	A	A	5
0.65	0	0	0	0	0	0	0	0	0	5	5	A	5	A	A	A	A	A	5
0.6	0	0	0	0	0	0	0	0	0	2	A	A	5	A	A	A	A	5	A
0.55	0	0	0	0	0	0	0	0	0	A	A	5	A	A	A	A	A	A	A
0.5	0	0	0	0	0	0	0	0	0	E	B	A	5	D	5	5	B	5	A
0.45	0	0	0	0	0	0	0	F	F	F	F	F	B	D	B	B	B	B	B
0.4	0	0	0	0	0	0	0	F	F	F	F	F	F	F	F	F	F	D	B
0.35	0	0	0	0	0	0	0	F	F	F	F	F	F	F	F	F	F	F	F
0.3	0	0	0	0	0	F	F	F	F	F	F	F	F	F	F	F	F	F	F
0.25	0	0	0	0	0	F	F	F	F	F	F	F	F	F	F	F	F	F	F
0.2	0	0	0	F	F	F	F	F	F	F	F	F	F	F	F	F	F	F	F
0.15	0	0	F	F	F	F	F	F	F	F	F	F	F	F	F	F	F	F	F
0.1	0	0	F	F	F	F	F	F	F	F	F	F	F	F	F	F	F	F	F
0.05	F	F	F	F	F	F	F	F	F	F	F	F	F	F	F	F	F	F	F

Table 2. MCV at $P_{10} = 0.5, P_{01} = 0.55$

bitwidth	MCV
4	1011
5	10101
6	101011
7	1010101
8	10101011
9	101010101

5 The Full Set of Possible MCVs With Their Probabilites

For a fixed symbol size, the MCV is a repeating two bit pattern defined by the most likely two step path in the model, except for a subset of parameters with even bitwidth symbols, where the final bit can vary.

The MCV would not be formed from repeating three bit pattern. If the most likely three bit pattern was 111 or 000, then 11 or 00 would be equally or more likely since:

$$P_{11}^3 \le P_{11}^2 \tag{13}$$

and

$$P_{00}^3 \le P_{00}^2 \tag{14}$$

If the mostly likely 2 step pattern is alternating then the most likely three step transition cannot land on the state that it started on.

These arguments can be extended to 4 bit repeated sequences and beyond so the repeating pattern of the MCV will always be 00, 11, 01 or 10.

The first bit of the symbol is the first bit of the most likely repeating two step pattern and the pattern repeats through the rest of the symbol, provided the number of bits is odd, since for an odd number of bits b the number of transitions $b - 1$ is even and the two step transition sequence will divide into it an integer number of times.

Within a symbol with an even bit width b, there are an odd number of $b - 1$ steps so a two step sequence of transitions will not divide into $b - 1$ transitions.

The final bit is therefore determined by the most likely single step from the penultimate bit. If the most likely final step is different than the first step of the most likely two step sequence, then the final bit will deviate from the repeating pattern, otherwise it will be the same. An example is shown in Fig. 3

Where there is more than one equally probable two bit sequences, then there will be more than one MCV symbol, each equiprobable. Also for symbols with an even number of bits, if the final transition has a probability of 0.5, then there will be twice the number of MCVs.

The most likely 2 bit repeating sequence must start and end on the same value. So it is determined by:

$$t = max(P_{00}P_{00}, P_{01}P_{10}, P_{10}P_{01}, P_{11}P_{11}) \tag{15}$$

The cases for the 01 and 10 pattern always have the same probability, but their relative likelihood is affected by the bias of the data, since the bias determines the most likely preceding bit.

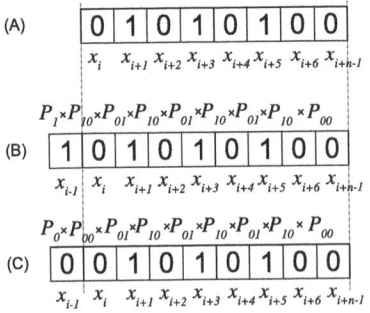

Fig. 3. Probability Calculation for a Possible 8 Bit Symbol

5.1   Computing the Probability of Each Symbol

The bit preceding the symbol will either be 0 or 1.

When the observer guessing the symbol is ignorant of the preceding bits then both the 0 and 1 preceding bit cases must be taken into account, so the probability of a symbol where the product of its internal transition probabilities are x, the symbol probability is the weighted sum of the cases with a preceding 0 and a preceding 1:

For a sequence of bits in a symbol x_0 to x_{n-1}, x_{-1} represents the preceding bit. It's likelihood of being 0 is P_0 and likelihood of being 1 is $P_1 = 1 - P0$

y_i defines the transition probability from position i to $i+1$ where $x_{-1} = 0$.

$$
y_i = \begin{cases} P_{00}, & \text{if } x_i = 0 \wedge x_{i+1} = 0 \\ P_{01}, & \text{if } x_i = 0 \wedge x_{i+1} = 1 \\ P_{10}, & \text{if } x_i = 1 \wedge x_{i+1} = 0 \\ P_{11}, & \text{if } x_i = 1 \wedge x_{i+1} = 1 \end{cases}
\tag{16}
$$

z_i defines the transition probability from position i to $i+1$ where $x_{-1} = 1$.

$$
z_i = \begin{cases} P_{00}, & \text{if } x_i = 0 \wedge x_{i+1} = 0 \\ P_{01}, & \text{if } x_i = 0 \wedge x_{i+1} = 1 \\ P_{10}, & \text{if } x_i = 1 \wedge x_{i+1} = 0 \\ P_{11}, & \text{if } x_i = 1 \wedge x_{i+1} = 1 \end{cases}
\tag{17}
$$

The probability P_s of a symbol s is the weighted sum of the cases with a preceding 0 and a preceding 1.

$$
P_s = \left(P_0 \prod_{i=-1}^{n-2} y_i \right) + \left(P_1 \prod_{i=-1}^{n-2} z_i \right)
\tag{18}
$$

The full set of possible MCV symbols of even bit width symbols and their probabilities is given in Table 3.

Table 3. All the Possible Even Bit Width MCV Symbols

Symbol	Probability
$\{1\}^n$	$(P_{01} + P_{11})(P_{11}^{n-1})$
$\{0\}^n$ repeated n times	$(P_{00} + P_{10})(P_{00}^{n-1})$
$\{01\}^{\frac{n-2}{2}}\{00\}$	$(P_{00} + P_{10})(P_{01}P_{10})^{\frac{n-2}{2}}P_{00}$
$\{01\}^{\frac{n}{2}}$	$(P_{00} + P_{10})(P_{01}P_{10})^{\frac{n-2}{2}}P_{01}$
$\{10\}^{\frac{n-2}{2}}\{11\}$	$(P_{01} + P_{11})(P_{10}P_{01})^{\frac{n-2}{2}}P_{11}$
$\{10\}^{\frac{n}{2}}$	$(P_{01} + P_{11})(P_{10}P_{01})^{\frac{n-2}{2}}P_{10}$

The full set of possible MCV symbols of odd bitwidth symbols and their probabilities is given in Table 4.

Table 4. All the Possible Odd Bitwidth MCV Symbols

Symbol	Probability
$\{1\}^n$	$(P_{01} + P_{11})(P_{11}^{n-1})$
$\{0\}^n$	$(P_{00} + P_{10})(P_{00}^{n-1})$
$\{01\}^{\frac{n-2}{2}}\{0\}$	$(P_{00} + P_{10})(P_{01}P_{10})^{\frac{n-1}{2}}$
$\{10\}^{\frac{n-2}{2}}\{1\}$	$(P_{01} + P_{11})(P_{10}P_{01})^{\frac{n-1}{2}}$

A simple algorithm to find the set of MCVs is to compute the probability of all 20 cases. The 10 possible MCV sequences preceeded by 0 or 1, returning the case or cases that have the maximum probability.

A special case is when $P_{01} = P_{10} = 0.5$, when all possible symbols are equiprobable and the entropy rate is 1.0.

In determining the MCV in the alternating cases 01 or 10 which always have equiprobable transition probabilities, we need to know the more likely starting symbol. This is simply determined by looking at the bias. If the most probable transition pair is 01 or 10, then if $\mu < 0.5$ then the starting bit of the MCV is 0, if the $\mu > 0.5$ then the starting bit of the MCV is 1 and if $\mu = 0.5$ then both MCV patterns will be equally likely and either will suffice for computing the maximum symbol probability.

6   Computing the Min Entropy

Min Entropy of symbols x_i from the distribution of symbols X from the markov generator is defined according to [9] as:

$$H_\infty(x_i \in X) = -\log_2(max(p_i)) \tag{19}$$

The MCV is the symbol with the highest probability, therefore by computing the probability of all 6 MCV candidates for even width symbols and the 4 MCV candidates for odd bit width symbols, the maximum probability symbol can be identified and the per symbol min entropy computed with Eq. 19.

7   Empirical Testing of the Min Entropy Computation

The MCV computation algorithm results are compared against the measured MCV of 2^{10} symbols generated from the Markov model at 225 points on a 15×15 grid of the P_{01}, P_{10} plane. The MCV frequency is directly measured in the generated data and from that, its probabilty and so the min-entropy rate of the source.

The distribution of the difference between the computed min entropy and measured min entropy is given for 8 bit symbols in Fig 4.

This shows empirically that the probability of the MCV (or MCVs) is being correctly predicted by the given equations and so the Markov generator can

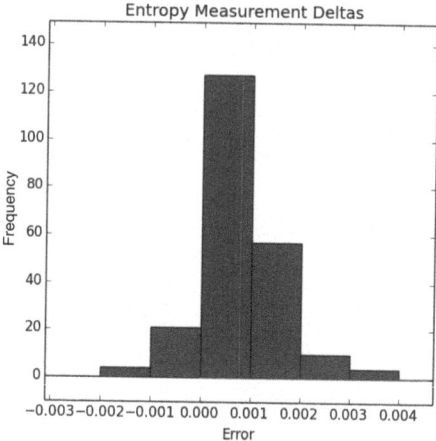

Fig. 4. Distribution of Measured vs Computed MCV Min-Entropy

be used to generate data with a known SCC, bias and min-entropy. This makes it suitable for testing the accuracy of min-entropy estimation algorithms.

8 Testing SP800-90B Non IID Tests with the Markov Model

The performance of the SP800-90B non-IID tests were tested using reference data the Markov generator model. [3].

Data at 40 equally spaced entropy levels from 0.025 to 0.975 was generated with the Markov generator model and for each entropy level, 200 different sets of Markov parameters were chosen randomly from the set of parameters that yielded the given entropy level, totalling 8000 total test data sets with labelled min entropy.

There are 10 individual tests in the SP800-90B ea_non_iid test set. The procedure defined is to run all the tests and pick the lowest entropy estimate across all the tests.

At 101 evenly spaced entropy points from 0 to 1, 10 data samples of 1 MibiBits are generated at each of the entropy points. The Markov parameters are randomly generated for each of the 10 data samples per entropy point.

The data samples are run through the SP800-90B reference code [1] and the min entropy result from the tests plotted against the actual min entropy from the model. The name of the test with the lowest entropy result was recorded in the data.

Figure 5 is a scatter plot of the actual entropy on the X axis and the assessed entropy by the NIST non IID entropy assessment algorithms on the Y axis. An accurate test would place points on the diagonal $x = y$. Points below the diagonal shown under-assessment and points above the diagonal show over-assessment.

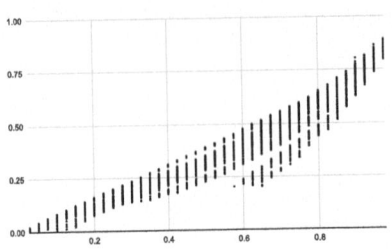

Fig. 5. Performance of NIST Non IID Tests

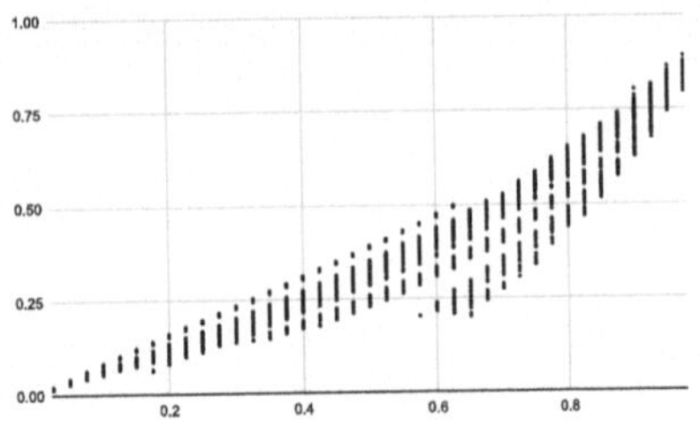

Fig. 6. Performance of NIST Non IID tCompression Test

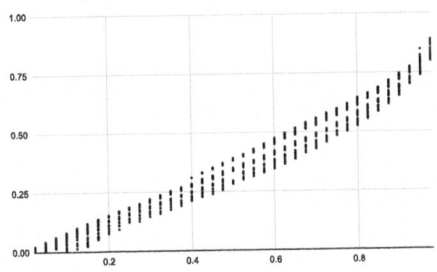

Fig. 7. Performance of NIST Non IID Tests Excluding tCompression Test

It can be seen in Fig. 5 that there is a region of very large assessment error. The worst case under assessment point when excluding the very low points below 0.2 actual entropy is run 183 of the 0.65 entropy set. The mean is 0.473435, the SCC is 0.234731, the Markov parameters are p01=0.362305 and p10=0.402964. The assessed entropy is 0.209375 giving an assessment error of 67.788462%.

Exploring the data is can be seen that the tCompression test contributes the greatest to the assessment error. Figure 6 shows the same assessment error with data from only the tCompression tests. Figure 7 shows the full data set except with the tCompression test excluded.

This shows the tCompression test to greatly under assess entropy of random binary data, particularly when there is positive SCC. This data has been presented to NIST but they have thus far declined to remove the tCompression test from SP800-90B.

Software to reproduce this data is available at [3].

9   Turning the Markov Model Into an Entropy Test

NIST SP800-90B [10] specifies two mandatory online health tests, the APT (Adaptive Proportion Test) and the RCT (Repetition Count Test). These tests are to be run directly on the output of the noise source to verify that the noise source is producing data with sufficient entropy.

These two tests are sufficient to detect a stuck-at fault in a noise source where it will produce the same symbol at a detectable higher rate than other symbols. The tests are not sufficient to detect oscillating failure modes, such as with excessively high negative SCC. Both the APT and RCT would fail to detect these kinds of failure in binary sources.

10   Seeking a Min Entropy Online Test

With the ability to measure markov transition parameters from binary data, simply by counting 1 and 2 bit patterns and the ability to compute min entropy from those parameters, it is worth looking at the mapping between the measured values and the min entropy to see if there is an identifiable method for testing min entropy in real time in an online circuit.

Plotting lines of iso entropy against μ and SCC pairs and against P_{01} and P_{10} pairs, we get the images in Figs. 8 and 9. These have curvy lines of iso entropy that do not lend themselves to a simple digital circuit identifying measures parameter pairs that lie within a chosen iso-entropy line and so indicating the min entropy is above that bound.

11   The SCC Equation Gives Another Way to Count

The SCC equation given by Knuth [6] is

$$
scc = \frac{n\left(\sum_{i=0}^{n-1} x_i x_{(i+1 \mod n)}\right) - \left(\sum_{i=0}^{n-1} x_i\right)^2}{n\left(\sum_{i=0}^{n-1} x_i^2\right) - \left(\sum_{i=0}^{n-1} x_i\right)^2}
\tag{20}
$$

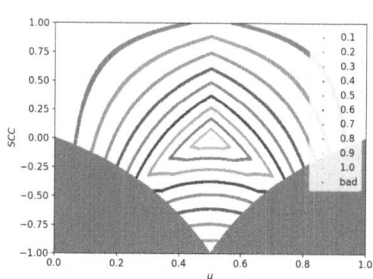

Fig. 8. $H_\infty(X)$ vs μ, scc

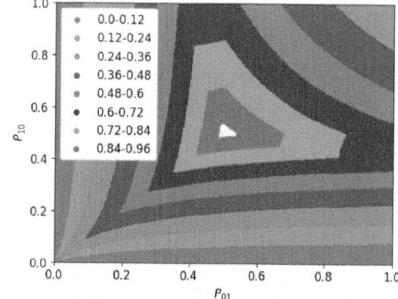

Fig. 9. $H_\infty(X)$ vs P_{01}, P_{10}

This is not promising as a basis for an online test since it includes reals, modulus operations, multiplies and divides.

If we replace the real values symbols with binary symbols, the equation is simplified.

11.1   Mapping to Binary Time Series Data

The   mod n in the SCC equation is treating the data as being cyclic, where the final bit x_{n-1} loops back and preceeds x_0. Clearly this is not true for time series data and so the equations will need to be modified to treat the data in a non cyclic way. Also where the data is binary ($x_i \in \{0,1\}$), we can simplify the equations and then map them to counts we can create easily in hardware.

Looking at the parts of the SCC equation, we can see that

$$\sum_{i=0}^{n-1} x_i x$$

When $x_i \in \{0,1\}$ is a count of the 1 s in the binary data.
In addition, when $x_i \in \{0,1\}$

$$\sum_{i=0}^{n-1} x_i^2 = \sum_{i=0}^{n-1} x_i$$

There are only 4 cases to consider with the top left term

$$\left(\sum_{i=0}^{n-1} x_i x_{(i+1 \mod n)} \right)$$

$$x_i = 0, x_{i+1} = 0 \rightarrow 0$$

$$x_i = 0, x_{i+1} = 1 \rightarrow 0$$

$$x_i = 1, x_{i+1} = 0 \rightarrow 0$$

$$x_i = 1, x_{i+1} = 1 \rightarrow 1$$

So that term acts like an AND gate operating on bit pairs from the sequence.

We can count the number of 1,1 bit pairs in binary data easily. This will be called count11. However in n bit non-cyclic data there can only be $n-1$ bit pair comparisons. The count of 1 s that we shall call count1 therefore needs to be counted only over the first $n-1$ bits, discarding the final bit in order to operate over the same number of cases that count11 does.

If we implement 4 bit pair counters, count00, count01, count10 and count11, then we can compute $n-1 = count00 + count01 + count10 + count11$ so

$$n = count00 + count01 + count10 + count11 + 1$$

We can count the ones in the first $n - 1$ bits as the sum of the bit pairs containing 1 in the left position. So:

$$count1 = count10 + count11$$

The updated equation for μ over $n - 1$ bits is

$$\mu = \frac{1}{n - 1} \sum_{i=0}^{n-2} x_i$$

Putting these counts into the SCC equation, over $n - 1$ bits we get

$$SCC = \frac{(n - 1)count11 - count1^2}{(n - 1)count1 - count1^2} \tag{21}$$

With these equations we can see that in hardware terms, it is sufficient to measure $n, count1$ and $count11$ or $count00, count01, count10, count11$. From those values we can compute μ and SCC. The value for n will typically be fixed in the design and so doesn't need to be measured.

Where the goal is to bound the SCC and mean to acceptable values, the chosen SCC and blocksize n are set and Eq. 21 can be rearranged to compute the bounds on $count1$ and $count11$.

Since μ and SCC can be computed as a function of $count1$ and $count11$, we know that $count1$ and $count11$ contain the same information as the pair of markov transition parameters for a Markov generator making data with the same mean and SCC.

To plot the lines of min entropy against $count1$ and $count11$ counts, the counts are first normalized to lay between 0 and 1.

$$pc1 = \frac{count1}{n - 1}$$

$$pc11 = \frac{count11}{n - 1}$$

We can derive:

$$scc = \frac{pc11 - pc1^2}{pc1 - pc1^2}$$

The mean μ is equal to $pc1$.

With this we can use our existing equations to compute entropy from a combination of mean and SCC and so plot lines of iso entropy against $pc1$ and $pc11$ shown in Fig. 10.

This suggests a basis for a test, since the lines of iso entropy are straight except for the lower edge, where it is slightly convex. It is fortunate that it is convex, since if it is approximated with a straight line, the resulting test would increase the false positive rate relative to if it modelled the curve.

A test of any particular entropy bound falls to checking a set of four linear inequalities in $pc1$ and $pc11$.

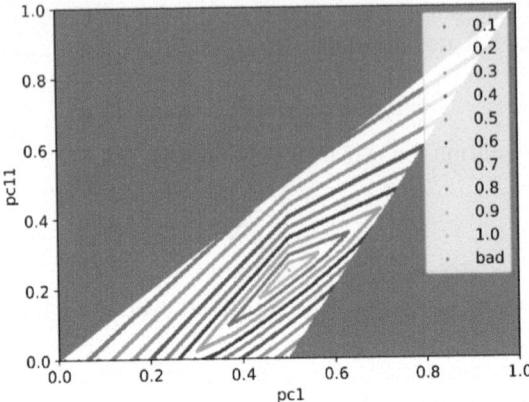

Fig. 10. $H_\infty(X)$ vs P_{01}, P_{10}

For example the red shaded region in 11 shows the area that corresponds to min entropy rate > 0.4, which can be identified with 4 linear comparisons against count1 and count11. With this mapping we get a direct relationship between a min entropy threshold and the pass/fail threshold of the test.

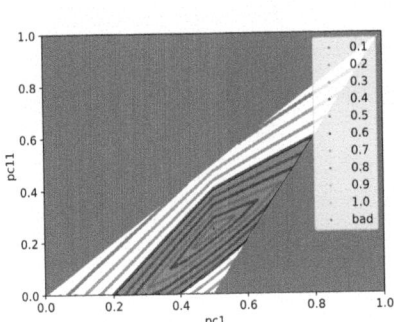

Fig. 11. $pc1, pc11$ points above min entropy 0.4

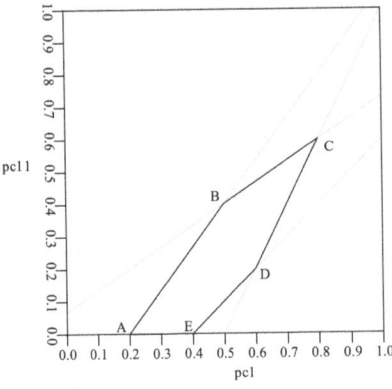

Fig. 12. Linear Approximations to Polygon Perimeter

12   A Computationally Efficient Polygon Interior Test

We can find explicit values of the corners of the five sides area corresponding to some entropy by solving for $H = 0.4$ (shown with the red contour line) at the known corners seen on the plot: The corners of the $H > 0.4$ polygon are (Table 5):

Table 5. $pc1$, $pc11$ Values at Polygon Corners

	$pc1$	$pc11$
A	0.2	0.0
B	0.5	0.4
C	0.8	0.6
D	0.6	0.2
E	0.4	0.0

Figure 12 shows the polygon with the edges extended to show the 4 linear constrains that need to be met to show entropy above 0.4.

All points are above the AE edge since the edge is against the $pc11=0$ axis so the point doesn't need to be tested relative to AE in the case of the Markov points being reals, however where the counts are finite integers, it is appropriate to test that $pc11 > 0$. All points within the polygon are below AB and BC and above DC and ED.

Deriving the line equations for the four sides AB, BC, DC, ED, with x=pc1 and y=pc11 we get.

$$AB : y = \frac{4}{3}x - \frac{4}{15}$$

$$BC : y = \frac{2}{3}x + \frac{1}{15}$$

$$DC : y = 2x - 1$$

$$ED : y = x - 0.4$$

To show the counts are within the polygon, show that:

$$AB : y < (4/3)x - (4/15)$$

$$BC : y < (2/3)x + (1/15)$$

$$DC : y > 2x - 1$$

$$ED : y > x - 0.4$$

Multiplying the equations up to integer coefficients:

$$AB : 15y < 20x - 4$$

$$BC : 15y < 10x + 1$$

$$DC : y > 2x - 1$$

$$ED : 5y > 5x - 2$$

Making these comparisons involve multiplying by 2, 5, 10, 15 and 20. The goal is to do this with shifts, adds and subtracts.

$$2X = X << 1$$

$$5X = (X << 2) + X$$

$$10X = (X << 3) + (X << 1)$$

$$15X = (X << 4) - X$$

$$20X = (X << 4) + (X << 2)$$

Using count1 instead of pc1 and count11 instead of pc11, we multiply up the coefficients by the maximum counter value n-1.

$$AB : 15count11 < 20count1 - 4(n - 1)$$

$$BC : 15count11 < 10count1 + (n - 1)$$

$$DC : count11 > 2count1 - (n - 1)$$

$$ED : 5count11 > 5count1 - 2(n - 1)$$

$n = 2304$ is chosen as a suitable block size for an example RNG with a 6:1 extraction ratio and an AES based conditioner reseeding a 256 bit CTR DRBG, thus requiring $3 \times 6 \times 128 = 2304$ bits.

$$AB : 15count11 < 20count1 - 9212$$

$$BC : 15count11 < 10count1 + 2303$$

$$DC : count11 > 2count1 - 2303$$

$$ED : 5count11 > 5count1 - 4606$$

13   Hardware Implementation

The equations describe a total of 4 adds, 5 subtracts and 4 comparisons along with bit shifts which are free in hardware. The result of 15*count11 can be reused reducing the subtract count to 4.

For $n = 2304$, the largest number possible is $20 \times count1$ where $count1 = 2303$, giving 46,060. Negative values may be encountered. Thus 17-bit twos complement arithmetic is required to prevent overflow.

For flexible sizes of n, the arithmetic size should be set appropriately to accommodate the representation of + or - 20(n-1) in twos complement arithmetic.

Example digital logic structures for the test over 2304 bits are given in Figs. 13 and 14.

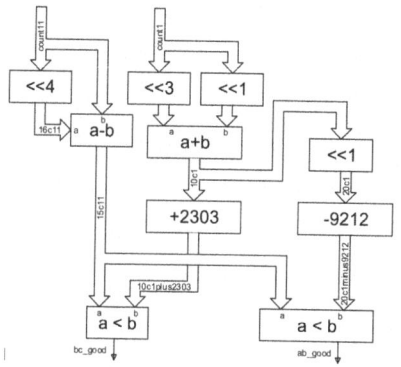

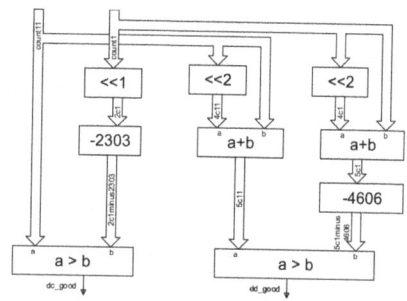

Fig. 13. Logic for the AB and BC Comparisons

Fig. 14. Logic for the DC and ED Comparisons

14 Software

The program djent [5] will report the markov parameters for a 2 state markov generator with mean and SCC matching that of the data being tested. It will also report the min entropy computed from those Markov parameters.

The program djenrandom [4] includes a 2 parameter Markov generator model.

15 Deployment

The 2 parameter Markov random bit generator model is used is production testing, as a model fitting test to estimate entropy of noise sources in the RNGs in Intel CPUs.

A 2 parameter Markov generator circuit is implemented within the fifth generation RNGs in Intel CPUs to generate controlled test data at full hardware speeds (> 2Gbps) with known min entropy for positive and negative testing of the built in hardware test circuits.

The Polygon Test is the vendor defined continuous health test within the fifth generation RNG in Intel CPUs.

16 Drawbacks

The polygon test is suited only for noise sources that generate single bit symbols. Multi bit symbols sources require a different test method.

The assumption built into the polygon test and model fitting entropy estimation using the Markov 2 parameter model is that mean and SCC accurately describe the behavior of the noise source. This is typically true for the metastable type source that the test was originally developed for. It may not be true for sources with complex statistical properties, such as ring oscillators.

17 Conclusion

The simple mathematical relationships between pattern counts of binary data, μ and SCC and min entropy enable a new class of online test capable of directly distinguishing whether random binary data is above or below a chosen entropy threshold with a very small (less than 1000 gate equivalent) digital circuit. Prior online health tests such as the SP800-90B APT and RCT have been limited to detecting failure modes of the source.

Disclosure of Interests. Author David Johnston performed this work in part while a paid employee of Intel Corporation.

References

1. Celi, C.: Nist sp800-90b entropy assessment software. https://github.com/usnistgov/SP800-90B_EntropyAssessment
2. Dodis, Y., Gennaro, R., Håstad, J., Krawczyk, H., Rabin, T.: Randomness extraction and key derivation using the CBC, cascade and HMAC modes. In: Franklin, M. (ed.) CRYPTO 2004. LNCS, vol. 3152, pp. 494–510. Springer, Heidelberg (2004). https://doi.org/10.1007/978-3-540-28628-8_30
3. Johnston, D.: Blaming ea_non_iid. https://github.com/dj-on-github/blaming_ea_non_iid
4. Johnston, D.: djenrandom. https://github.com/dj-on-github/djenrandom
5. Johnston, D.: djent. https://github.com/dj-on-github/djent
6. Knuth, D.E.: The Art of Computer Programming, vol. 2, 3rd edn. Seminumerical Algorithms. Addison-Wesley Longman Publishing Co., Inc., Boston (1997)
7. Parker, R.J.: Entropy justification for metastability based nondeterministic random bit generator. In: 2017 IEEE 2nd International Verification and Security Workshop (IVSW), pp. 25–30 (2017). https://doi.org/10.1109/IVSW.2017.8031540
8. Peter, M., Schindler, W.: Ais20-31, a proposal for functionality classes for random number generators (2022). https://www.bsi.bund.de/SharedDocs/Downloads/EN/BSI/Certification/Interpretations/AIS_31_Functionality_classes_for_random_number_generators_e.pdf?__blob=publicationFile&v=7
9. Rényi, A.: On measures of entropy and information. In: Fourth Berkeley Symposium on Mathematical Statistics and Probability, vol. 1, pp. 547–561 (1961)
10. Sonmez, M., Barker, E., Kelsey, J., McKay, K., Baish, M., Boyle, M.: Recommendation for the entropy sources used for random bit generation (2018). https://doi.org/10.6028/NIST.SP.800-90b

DLShield: A Defense Approach Against Dirty Label Attacks in Heterogeneous Federated Learning

K. M. Sameera[1]ⓘ, M. Abhinav[1]ⓘ, P. P. Amal[1]ⓘ, T. Babu Abhiram[1]ⓘ,
Raj K. Abishek[1]ⓘ, Tomichen Amal[1]ⓘ, P. Anaina[1]ⓘ, P. Vinod[1,2](✉)ⓘ,
Rehiman K. A. Rafidha[1]ⓘ, and Conti Mauro[2]ⓘ

[1] Department of Computer Applications, Cochin University of Science and
Technology, Kochi, India
{sameerakm,rafidharehimanka}@cusat.ac.in,
{abhinavmmscds2123,amalpp007,abhiramtbabu02,abishekrajk083,
amaltomichendca,anainap}@pg.cusat.ac.in, vinod.puthuvath@unipd.it
[2] Department of Mathematics, University of Padua, Padua, Italy
mauro.conti@unipd.it

Abstract. Federated Learning (FL) is a privacy-focused revolutionary
approach distributed paradigm that supports considerable devices to
train a shared model collaboratively without disseminating private local
information. While FL offers significant privacy benefits, its decentralized nature exposes it to various security threats. Existing defense mechanisms often struggle to effectively address the diverse range of adversarial attacks that can target FL systems, such as poisoning attacks and
model quality issues. To address these challenges, we propose DLShield,
which operates at the server level, an approach for defending against dirty
label poisoning attacks and detecting low-quality models in FL. DLShield
leverages a Gaussian distribution to measure the deviation between legitimate and malicious model parameters, allowing it to accurately distinguish benign models from compromised client models. Additionally,
DLShield incorporates a reputation calculation module that allocates
reputation ratings to each model according to their performance. Models
with low reputation scores are pruned from the aggregation phase, reducing the impact of malicious participants on the overall model quality.
The performance of DLShield is evaluated using real-world benchmark
datasets under different data distribution scenarios. DLShield consistently achieves significant improvements in all metrics, enhancing global
accuracy by 7.5%, source class recall by approximately over 24%, and
reducing attack success rate by 22.8%, compared with state-of-the-art
defense methods.

Keywords: Federated Learning · Data poisoning attack · Dirty Label
attack · Defense · Reputation

J. Knechtel et al. (Eds.): SPACE 2024, LNCS 15351, pp. 129–148, 2025.
https://doi.org/10.1007/978-3-031-80408-3_9

1   Introduction

Recent advancements in edge computing and Machine Learning (ML), particularly in Deep Learning (DL), have expanded their application across various domains that handle sensitive information. However, the reliance on a central server in these technologies introduces significant security challenges, often deterring edge devices from sharing private data for distributed training [1]. Traditional centralized DL systems are increasingly inefficient at processing the vast amounts of data generated by the growing number of edge devices, leading to heightened privacy and security concerns. Additionally, transmitting large volumes of edge data in centralized Deep Learning systems imposes substantial network resource demands and computational overhead, especially in large-scale distributed environments [2].

Federated Learning (FL) is a distributed machine learning paradigm proposed by Google to address the challenges of data privacy and computational overhead [3]. By aggregating locally trained models from distributed devices, FL enables collaborative learning without compromising privacy.

While FL offers significant advantages, its distributed and decentralized nature also exposes it to various security threats, particularly poisoning attacks by malicious participants during collaborative training [4]. The central server's lack of insight into clients' local training processes and private data enables adversaries to easily compromise the learning process. Specifically, a malicious actor can take control of certain clients and upload falsified gradient updates to the server, undermining the performance of the global model. By manipulating these gradients, an adversary can corrupt the local training process or model, thereby degrading the FL system's performance and achieving specific harmful objectives. Data poisoning attacks are categorized into untargeted and targeted attacks depending on the adversary's goal. Targeted attacks aim to threaten the performance of a specific class, while untargeted attacks aim to subvert the overall performance [5,6].

This research prioritizes targeted data poisoning attacks, specifically dirty-label attacks, where the adversary poisons data by altering its true class label (source class) to an attacker-chosen class (target class). This type of attack maintains the overall global model accuracy while selectively degrading the accuracy of the source class, making it difficult to detect [7,8]. Crafting such an attack is relatively straightforward, as the attacker does not require extensive knowledge of the federation process [9].

While several defense mechanisms have been proposed (refer Sect. 2), many are impractical [10] or rely on assumptions about the number of malicious participants [11,12]. Even after bootstrapping trust, studies have shown that systems can contain a significant proportion (e.g., 40%–60%) of malicious workers [13].

Previous research has primarily focused on similarity-based [14–16] and robust aggregation methods [11,12,17] for mitigating poisoning attacks in federated learning, with limited attention to reputation-based approaches [18,19]. Similarity-based methods calculate participant scores based on historical performance and select those with high scores for FL tasks. However, tracking the historical behavior of all participants to identify attacks is challenging, and excluding malicious participants based on similarity alone may be ineffective in FL scenarios where attackers appear intermittently. For instance, if an attacker is present only in the initial round, this method would be ineffective [20].

This research presents a novel defense mechanism against dirty-label attacks using a reputation-based approach. We utilize an auxiliary dataset and a Gaussian distribution model on the server to detect malicious participants without relying on specific attack strategies. Participants whose updates consistently align with the expected range in the Gaussian model receive higher scores, while outliers are flagged as unreliable or malicious. The proposed DLShield approach effectively identifies low-quality workers without requiring prior knowledge of the adversary, ensuring reliable model training by mitigating the influence of unreliable nodes in each federation round. To thwart poisoning attacks, the server evaluates the quality of local models using the auxiliary dataset (trusted dataset not used in training but to benchmark clients' performance), assesses participants' performance for each label, and assigns reputation scores accordingly.

Our proposed approach assigns reputation scores to participants based on their individual recall values for each class in the federated learning process. To identify anomalous updates, the server calculates the label-wise Z-score for each local model. These recall values are compared to a pre-defined Gaussian distribution known only to the server. Participants whose recall falls within an acceptable range receive an increase in their reputation score. This process is repeated for all classes. Participants with the lowest reputation scores are subsequently excluded from the aggregation phase. By ensuring that only reliable participants contribute to the model, this approach enhances overall system performance and robustness.

Our objective is to identify and exclude participants who exhibit low-quality and unreliability models. Moreover, our defense DLShield is compatible with the standard FL framework, where participants have access only to the global model update from the server. It operates without any prior assumptions about the aggregation process or the data distribution across clients, whether the data is IID or non-IID.

The key contributions of the article are summarized as follows.

- We introduce a novel method for evaluating the quality of local models in federated learning in a heterogeneous environment. This method does not require prior knowledge of the adversary, enhancing its applicability and robustness.
- We employ a reputation-based defense strategy that leverages an auxiliary dataset and a Gaussian distribution model. The server can identify anomalous updates that may indicate malicious behavior by calculating the label-wise Z-score for each local model.
- We evaluate the performance of the proposed DLShield under both single and multi-label flipping attacks across various data distribution scenarios in an FL environment. Additionally, we examine its resilience under varying intensities of poisoning and different numbers of malicious participants.

- We perform evaluations using benchmark datasets to illustrate the efficacy of our method in countering poisoning attacks within FL settings. Our method exhibits greater efficiency and resilience compared to other defense techniques, resulting in improved accuracy of the global model.

2   Related Work

In this section, we first outline the poisoning attack in federated learning systems and then review the existing defense strategies to mitigate this attack.

2.1   Targeted Data Poisoning Attack

Researchers in [3] have employed federated learning at edge devices to preserve privacy through a collaborative learning process. However, with the increasing adoption of various applications, studies indicate that federated learning is vulnerable to multiple attacks [1,2,6]. These attacks can be classified into targeted and untargeted attacks based on their objectives. The authors in [8,21] discussed data poisoning attacks where the attacker focused on targeted attacks through a label-flipping approach, where they flipped source class samples into targeted class. The attack affects only some specific tasks, leading to defective detection, and the attacker does not degrade the global model performance. For example, in the CIC-Darknet dataset, the adversary aims to misclassify an instance initially labeled as class '0' (Non-Tor) into class '2' (Tor). While this label-flipping attack negatively impacts the performance of class '0', it does not affect the overall accuracy of the global model. Bagdasaryan et al. focused on targeted attacks through backdoor attacks, where they introduce triggers by adding training data with a specific pattern or perturbation [5].

In [22], proposed a novel attack that inverts the loss function to generate the poisoned label for the data poisoning attack. Authors in [23] illustrated the targeted model poisoning attack using an explicit boosting approach that negatively impacts the system even though the system contains a low number of compromised participants. In another study [24], researchers used generative adversarial net to mimic the honest participants.

2.2   Defense Against the Targeted Data Poisoning Attack

Several defense approaches have been proposed to mitigate targeted poisoning attacks in FL. Yin et al. proposed a robust aggregation rule Trimmed Mean (TMean) [12] that aggregates local model parameters independently. Specifically, each parameter in the global model is obtained by sorting the corresponding parameters from the m participants and calculating the mean of the middle $m - 2\beta$ parameters after removing the β largest and β smallest values. Additionally, the authors proposed an aggregation rule Median which computes the global model by the coordinate-wise median value of the local model parameters [12].

Krum [11] is an aggregation rule that selects the m local model updates with the smallest sum of distances to their closest $m - c - 2$ local models, excluding the c compromised workers. Multi-Krum extends the features of the Krum aggregation rule by considering multiple local model estimates. It uses Euclidean distance to identify and average the closest models to compute the FL model [11]. FoolsGold [16] employs a robust aggregation rule that detects poisoned local models based on maximum cosine similarity. The algorithm assigns lower aggregation weights to malicious models.

Tolpegin et al. proposed a defense strategy to mitigate targeted label-flipping attacks by employing feature extraction and selection using Principal Component Analysis (PCA) [8]. [25] extends the study in [8] by using K-means clustering approach. The authors in [14] proposed FL-Defender, which utilizes the last-layer gradient to identify malicious models and employs PCA to reduce the redundant information. Additionally, it considers participant angle similarity of the gradient and reweights participant updates based on the deviation of their gradients from the coordinate-wise median to detect the malicious model.

In [26] proposed a client's data quality-based approach in FL that identifies malicious clients by reconstructing a distribution over a latent feature space. The authors in [27] proposed a DPFLA that evades the attacks by utilizing feature distribution among masked final-layer neuron gradients. Some literature leveraged that defending against poisoning attacks requires prior knowledge of the proportion of attackers within the system [11,12]. Additionally, the authors in [28] proposed LFighter, a method that relies on strategies tailored to specific situations and requires knowledge of the participant's label distribution. Unlike other methods, our method does not rely on any prior assumptions of the label distribution or the strategies applied, offering a more flexible approach. Additionally, some studies focused on outlier detection to identify and eliminate poisoned data points by analyzing clients' local datasets or removing malicious neurons and weights from compromised models [29,30].

In [31], authors proposed a Byzantine-tolerant gradient aggregation method, where the Gaussian Mixture Model (GMM) and Mahalanobis distance were used to detect malicious gradients in the system. Additionally, they encrypt the gradients employing the homomorphic encryption algorithm to ensure privacy preservation. Nevertheless, the study neglected to investigate the potential consequences of using a low-quality model. Chen et al. explored a method for transferring knowledge between organizations while safeguarding privacy [32]. They employed federated deep autoencoding GMM to accomplish this and applied their approach to intrusion detection. A similar approach was also presented in another study [33,34]. However, these studies were limited to two participants and did not delve into the potential impact of malicious actors.

3   System Model and Threat Model

3.1   System Model

In this section, we discussed our system model in the adversarial scenario. We examine a federation where a centralized server manages M workers, but S of these workers are malevolent and attempt to sabotage the server global model's accuracy for a particular class, impacting the honest participants. Each worker i owns a private dataset $D_i = \{x_k, y_k\}_{k \in n_i}$ holding total n_i instances. This study focuses on the supervised classification task with C classes.

The federated server repeatedly refines the global model ω to address the following optimization problem min $\sum_{i=1}^{n} \mathcal{L}(\omega, D_i)$, during each iteration. Here, $\omega \in \mathbb{R}^d$ represents the global model with d features in the model, and $\mathcal{L}(\omega, D_i)$ refers to the loss functions for the worker i. In the t-th iteration, the server randomly chooses m workers and sends them the updated global model ω^{t-1}. Each worker i employs the SGD, the stochastic gradient descent, algorithm on local private data D_i to revise the received model ω^{t-1} of the server and obtain the new participants local model ω_i^t. This procedure employs a local iteration E and mini-batch size B. The updated participant's model w_i^t is then returned to the federated server. After receiving the local models, the federated server aggregates them to produce a new global model ω^t using the FEDAVG algorithm [3]. This procedure is repeated until the server model stabilizes or the specified federation epoch is reached.

3.2   Threat Model

Attacker's Goal: The objective of the malevolent is to diminish the performance of global models by deliberately mislabeling data, leading to the misclassification of a large number of clean inputs from a specific class during inference, impacting both the legitimate clients and the model's accuracy. Following previous works [7,8,35], the adversary manipulates the local dataset to frame the poisoning attack to achieve their goal using a dirty-label approach. We assume that adversary-controlled participants account for no more than $\frac{K}{2} - 1$ of the total participants, where K is the number of participants in the aggregation, indicating that the majority of devices are benign. In this work, we assume that the adversary controlled more than one participant in the FL system. Additionally, we assume that the server is honest and non-compromised.

Adversary Prior Knowledge and Capability: The adversary possesses knowledge of the compromised participant's local datasets and aims to execute the data poisoning attack through a label-flipping approach. Additionally, the attacker does not modify the other training hyperparameters such as learning rate, model architecture, and local training rounds. Also, the attacker modifies only a fraction of the specified samples to target samples. However, the adversary lacks control over other benign participants' training processes and does not have access to their local datasets. Furthermore, the adversary lacks control over the server aggregation process.

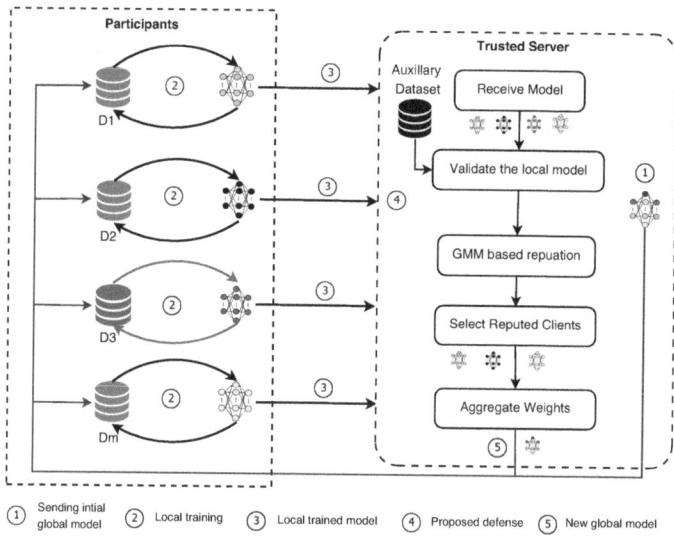

Fig. 1. Architecture of the proposed DLShield.

Attack Phase: The adversary instigates the poisoning attack during the training phase, targeting all compromised participants, and sustains the attack over multiple iterations.

4   DLShield: Proposed Defense for Dirty Label Poisoning Attack

This section introduces a novel defense, DLShield, a Gaussian distribution-based reputation method for detecting compromised workers in an FL system without degrading the model's performance. Figure 1 illustrates the workflow of the proposed strategy. DLShield employs a two-stage, server-side defense approach to detect adversary-controlled workers before incorporating their contributions into the global model.

The DLShield ensures robust aggregation in federated learning, as detailed in Algorithm 1. In each iteration $t \in T$, the trusted server validates the received local model ω_i^t (refer to line numbers 6–9) using an auxiliary dataset D_{aux}, which consists of high-confidence samples with a proven high detection rate from the baseline model (see line numbers 11 to 19). This dataset is exclusively available to the server for validation, allowing consistent evaluation and comparison of client models. The server then computes the recall r_c^i for each class $c \in C$ using each worker's model. The server can consistently evaluate and select only reliable models for global model updates by comparing models on an auxiliary dataset.

Figure 2 presents the class recall distribution for the dataset in the absence of adversarial attacks. This visualization comprises multiple histograms illustrating

Algorithm 1. DLShield: Reputation-based robust defense method for dirty-label attack in FL.

Require: Set of models $\{\omega_1, \omega_2, \ldots, \omega_M\}$ from M devices, auxiliary dataset D_{aux}, Gaussian distributions $\mathcal{N}(\mu_c, \sigma_c^2)$ for $c \in C$ class

Ensure: Updated global model w^T

1: **Initialize:** server global model ω^0
2: **for** each iteration $t = 1, 2, \ldots, T$ **do**
3:     **Server Side:**
4:         $S^t \leftarrow$ Select K clients randomly
5:         Transfer the ω^{t-1} to the selected clients
6:     **Clients Side:**
7:     **for** each client $i \in S^t$ **do**
8:         $\omega_i^t \leftarrow \omega^{t-1} - \eta \nabla \mathcal{L}(\omega^{t-1}; D_i)$ // local training
9:     **end for**
10:     Transfer the ω_k^t to the trusted server.
11:     **Server Side:**
12:     /* Class-wise Recall Calculation */
13:     Set the $R_i = 0, \forall i \in K$
14:     **for** each received local model ω_k^t **do**
15:         Validate (ω_i^t) using D_{aux}
16:         **for** each class $c \in C$ **do**
17:             Calculate recall r_c^i for model ω_i^t
18:         **end for**
19:     **end for**
20:     /* Recall validation against Gaussian distribution */
21:     **for** each received local model ω_i^t **do**
22:         **for** each class c **do**
23:             Calculate $z_c = \frac{r_c^t - \mu_c}{\sigma_c}$ /*Compute z-score*/
24:         **if** $|z_c| \leq 2$ **then**
25:             $R_i \leftarrow R_i + 1$ /*Calculate total reputation scores*/
26:         **end if**
27:         **end for**
28:     **end for**
29:     /* Anomaly detection */
30:     $B \leftarrow$ Identify τ participants in S^t with the lowest reputation scores specified in R_i
31:     /* Reputation-based aggregation */
32:     **for** each client $i \in S^t$ **do**
33:         **if** R_i not in B **then**
34:             $\alpha_i \leftarrow 1$ // benign clients
35:         **else**
36:             $\beta_i \leftarrow 0$ // adversarial clients
37:         **end if**
38:     **end for**
39:     New global model generated using Eq. (1)
40: **end for**
41: **return** the global model ω^T

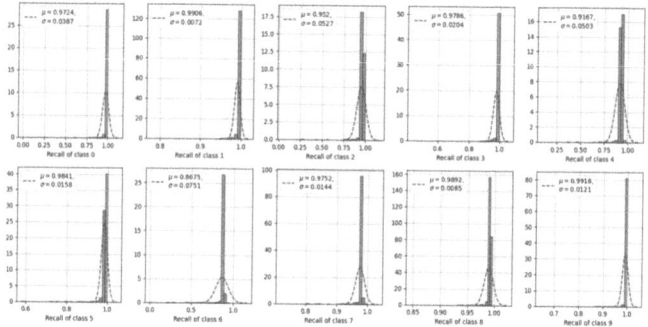

Fig. 2. Visualization of histograms showing the distribution of recall scores for each class.

the class-specific recall distribution. A distribution for the recall scores of high-accuracy global models, classes with more tightly clustered distributions around higher recall values indicates favorable performance. These baseline distributions serve as a reference for evaluating client reputation in the presence of adversarial threats.

In the second stage, the server uses the class-wise recall r_c^i obtained from the validation to measure and update the reputation scores R_i for each worker i (indicated in line numbers between 11 to 28). These recall values are compared against pre-defined Gaussian distributions, which the server constructs for each class $c \in C$ by training a model on a clean dataset. The distributions, characterized by their mean (μ_c) and variance (σ_c^2), represent the expected performance for each class. If a model's recall for a particular class falls within the expected Gaussian distribution calculated using the Z-score. Then check if a recall is within 2 standard deviations (95% acceptance region); the server increments the model's reputation score R_i, confirming that the model behaves as anticipated for that class. This statistical validation helps to detect anomalies, as adversarial models are likely to have recall values that deviate significantly from these expectations.

The server then identifies the τ participants in S^t with the lowest reputation scores. These participants are considered potential adversaries. For our experiment, we fix the τ as three. Reputation-based aggregation proceeds by assigning a weight of 1 to benign clients and 0 to adversarial clients (see line numbers 28–41). This effectively excludes adversarial clients from the federated aggregation, ensuring that the revised global model, ω^t, is determined solely by the local models of trusted clients, as shown in Eq. 1.

$$\omega^{t+1} = \frac{1}{|S^t|} \sum_{i \in S^t} \beta_i \omega_i^t \qquad (1)$$

5   Evaluation

In this section, we describe the setup employed for the experimentation and evaluate the performance of the DLShield using two benchmark datasets. All experiments were simulated using PyTorch running on an Intel i9-10900K processor with 32 GB RAM.

5.1   Experimental Setup

Dataset and Model Architecture. In our experiments, we evaluated the performance of DLShield using publicly available real-world image classification datasets and the darknet network traffic dataset. We performed experiments on the balanced Fashion-MNIST and the imbalanced CIC-Darknet2020 datasets, frequently used in prior studies [7,8,28,31,36,37], to ensure a comprehensive evaluation and to demonstrate the system's effectiveness across various conditions.

Fashion-MNIST: The Fashion-MNIST dataset consists of 28×28 pixel grayscale images organized into ten classes, with 60,000 samples for training and 10,000 for testing. We employ the same CNN architecture as in [8] for the federated learning model.

CIC-Darknet2020: The CIC-Darknet2020 is a network traffic dataset for detecting darknet-related activities and cybersecurity threats [37]. It is a compilation of ISCXTor2016 and ISCXVPN2016 datasets from the University of New Brunswick, which record real-time traffic through tools like Wireshark and TCP-dump. CICFlowMeter extracted features from the raw traffic captured to create the CIC-Darknet2020 dataset. Each sample in the dataset contains traffic features derived from packet capture sessions. The dataset includes 158,659 samples organized into four top-level traffic categories: Non-Tor (93,357), Non-VPN (23,864), Tor (1,393), and VPN (22,920). We employed a model for this four-class classification problem using a three-layer feedforward neural network. The network architecture consists of two hidden layers containing 64 and 32 neurons, respectively, along with an output layer of four neurons. ReLU activation functions are used in the hidden layers.

FL Parameters Settings: We simulated an FL network of 50 clients for the Fashion-MNIST dataset. Each client trains a local model for a single epoch using stochastic gradient descent, with the federation iterations set to $T = 200$. We used 20 clients in the FL setup for the CIC-Darknet2020 dataset, with each client performing five local training epochs and federation iterations set as 100. In each round, the trusted server randomly selects a subset of $K = 10$ clients to contribute to updating the global model. Additionally, we evaluate the proposed approaches on Independently and Identically Distributed (IID) and non-IID data distribution scenarios. We use the Fashion-MNIST dataset for IID settings, and for non-IID, we use the CIC-Darknet2020 dataset. For non-IID conditions, we sample p_j from a Dirichlet distribution $p_j \sim Dir_K(\alpha)$ and distribute a $p_{j,k}$ proportion of the instances from class C to participants j. In our experiments, we set $\alpha = 0.5$, resulting in a highly variable data distribution among clients. Since α controls the degree of heterogeneity, we select a lower α value to represent a more heterogeneous distribution among the participants in the FL system [38].

FL Attack Settings: To simulate the poisoning attack, we randomly designate $M \times m\%$ of the participants to be malicious in each round. We evaluate the system's performance using two adversarial controlled scenarios for each dataset with different m values. For the Fashion-MNIST dataset, 6% and 4% of the participants were malicious in each round, and for the CIC-Darknet2020 dataset, we set m as 10% and 15%. Furthermore, we analyze three attack cases for each scenario, each with a different number of flipped labels. For the Fashion-MNIST dataset, we employed the following dirty label combinations ($C_S \rightarrow C_T$) to execute the poisoning attack. For the single dirty label (Sandal:5 $\rightarrow$Sneaker:7), double dirty-label (Sandal:5, Coat:4 $\rightarrow$Sneaker:7, Shirt:6), and for triple dirty-label (Sandal:5, Shirt:6, Coat:4 $\rightarrow$ Sneaker:7, T-Shirt/Top:0, Shirt:6), these combinations were considered. Similarly, for the CIC-Darknet2020 dataset, we used the following label combinations for the attack: (VPN:2, Non-Tor:0, Tor:3 $\rightarrow$ NonVPN:1, VPN:2, Tor:3), (VPN, Non-Tor $\rightarrow$ NonVPN, VPN), and (VPN $\rightarrow$ Tor) in triple, double, and single dirty label combinations, respectively. For each scenario, the adversary poisoned $p\%$ of the samples from class C_S to class C_T. We repeated the experiment with different p values, including 10%, 20%, 30%, 40%, and 50%.

We compare the performance of the DLShield against different approaches to demonstrate its effectiveness: (1) the baseline case with no attack, (2) the existing defense mechanism such as Trimmed Mean (TMean), and Median. Similar experimental setups were used across all comparisons to ensure the reliability of the results.

Evaluation Metric: We leveraged the effectiveness of our proposed defense DLShield using the following metrics.

- **Main Task Accuracy**: The Main Task Accuracy (MTA) is the accuracy of the global model, calculated as the ratio of correctly predicted samples to the total number of predictions.

$$\text{MTA} = \frac{1}{|D|} \sum_{i=1}^{|D|} (\hat{y}_i = y_i) \tag{2}$$

where $|D|$ is the total number of instances in test dataset, y_i is the true label, and $\hat{y}_i$ is the predicted label.

- **Attack Success Rate**: The Attack Success Rate (ASR) is the effectiveness of the attack, measured by the number of samples misclassified from the source class to the target class in the global model, divided by the total number of samples in the source class.

$$\text{ASR} = \frac{1}{|D_{C_S}|} \sum_{i=1}^{|D_{C_S}|} (y_i = C_S \wedge \hat{y}_i = C_T) \tag{3}$$

where $|D_{C_S}|$ is the total number of instances with the source class label C_S, y_i is the true label, $\hat{y}_i$ is the predicted label, and C_T is the target class.

- **Source Class Recall**: The Source Class Recall (SCR) is calculated as the number of samples from the source class correctly identified by the model divided by the total number of source class samples of the participating clients in the FL system.

$$\text{SCR} = \frac{1}{|D_{C_S}|} \sum_{i=1}^{|D_{C_S}|} (y_i = C_S \wedge \hat{y}_i = C_S) \tag{4}$$

An effective defense against the attacks must maintain a higher MTA in the global model, a lower ASR, and a higher SCR.

5.2   Result and Discussion

FL System Model Performance in Non-Poisoning Configuration. Initially, we set up the baseline model where we evaluated the system's performance in an FL environment without adversaries. Furthermore, we utilize FedAvg [3] as the aggregation algorithm with no defense mechanisms. Figure 3 illustrates the result of the FL system under non-poisoning configuration for both datasets, where we report the recall for each label, providing a baseline for how the system performs without any attack. Additionally, we observed that the MTA for the Fashion-MNIST dataset is approximately 89.13% and 90.702% for the CIC-Darknet2020 dataset.

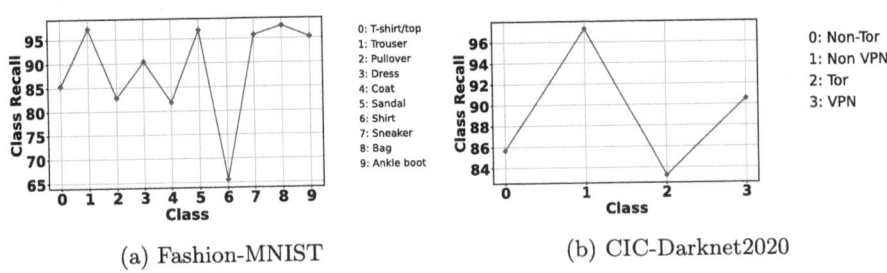

(a) Fashion-MNIST   (b) CIC-Darknet2020

Fig. 3. Performance of each class recall in the FL system without any adversaries (Baseline).

Table 1. Comparison of performance of proposed methods under different dirty label attack combinations in the IID dataset with 6% adversary-controlled participants.

	Poisoned	MTA			SCR			ASR		
	ratio(p%) ↓	Median	TMean	DLShield	Median	TMean	DLShield	Median	TMean	DLShield
Single-label	10	88.459	89.166	**89.226**	96.146	96.639	**96.652**	3.079	2.545	**2.524**
	20	89.003	**89.186**	89.172	96.005	96.050	**96.454**	3.042	3.109	**2.778**
	30	88.911	89.093	**89.120**	95.787	95.715	**96.034**	3.923	3.382	**3.294**
	40	88.802	89.155	**89.173**	95.708	95.286	**96.313**	3.938	3.839	**3.800**
	50	88.860	89.004	**89.217**	95.748	94.796	**96.003**	3.983	4.193	**3.017**
Double-label	10	88.907	89.173	**89.233**	88.839	88.882	**89.037**	4.348	4.356	**4.298**
	20	88.805	89.055	**89.074**	88.321	88.327	**88.841**	4.468	4.859	**4.302**
	30	88.829	88.981	**89.239**	88.237	87.643	**88.797**	4.743	5.456	**4.263**
	40	88.659	88.927	**89.214**	87.942	87.236	**88.837**	5.215	5.58	**4.502**
	50	88.68	88.880	**89.161**	87.89	86.786	**88.437**	5.125	6.140	**4.844**
Triple-label	10	88.812	89.151	**89.181**	80.761	81.420	**81.389**	7.865	7.573	**7.669**
	20	88.890	89.111	**89.257**	80.598	80.797	**81.184**	7.798	8.026	**7.818**
	30	88.624	89.006	**89.172**	80.148	80.240	**81.378**	8.313	8.440	**7.660**
	40	88.729	88.894	**89.280**	80.040	79.792	**81.088**	8.828	8.902	**7.818**
	50	88.705	88.842	**89.183**	79.974	79.411	**81.228**	8.934	9.141	**7.929**

Performance of DLShield Under IID Distribution. Table 1 compare the DLShield's performance against state-of-the-art (SOTA) approaches under diverse attack scenarios. In the single-label case for the Fashion-MNIST dataset, the results show that the attack's impact on the global model increases as the percentage of poisoned samples rises. Median-based aggregation experienced a maximum 0.53% reduction in MTA compared to the baseline. However, TMean aggregation exhibited a minimal reduction, with global model accuracy decreasing by approximately 0.1%. This discrepancy can be attributed to the static nature of the Median and TMean aggregation rules. The Median selects the coordinate-wise median value of local model parameters. At the same time, the TMean excludes the largest β and smallest β values, which increases the likelihood of malicious parameters during the aggregation process. In contrast, DLShield outperformed the baseline approximately 0.1% and achieved approximately 0.4% improvement compared to state-of-the-art approaches in terms of MTA. DLShield effectively identifies and removes malicious updates during aggregation while maintaining high performance on the global model, which consistently keeps ASR below than baseline. Furthermore, DLShield consistently outperformed the SOTA approaches, achieving a maximum improvement of approximately 1.2% in SCR and 1% reduction in ASR.

To further assess DLShield's effectiveness, we examined its performance under various multi-dirty label attack combinations. We evaluate under more complex scenarios with double and triple dirty label attack combinations. As with double-label scenarios, the performance noticeably decreased in the TMean and Median approach as the number of malicious participants and the percentage of poisoned samples increased. However, DLShield consistently outperformed the SOTA in all attack scenarios. For instance, with a 6% malicious participants poisoned 50% of the source class to target class, the DLShield achieves a 0.6% improvement in MTA, a 1.7% increase in the SCR, and a 1.3% decline in ASR. In the triple-label scenario, DLShield demonstrates an improvement of over 0.5% in MTA. Additionally, we observed a 1.3% to 2% increase in DLShield's source class recall, outperforming other approaches, while the ASR value decreased by 1% to 1.2%.

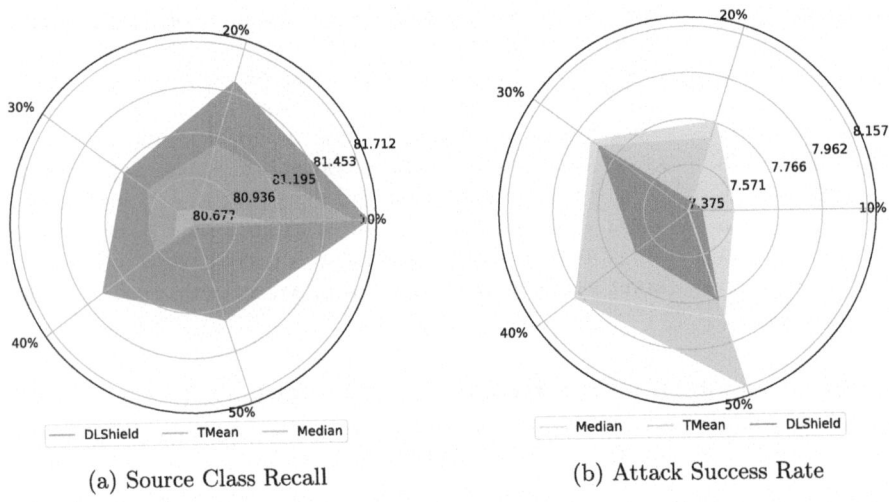

(a) Source Class Recall   (b) Attack Success Rate

Fig. 4. Performance evaluation of the proposed DLShield in a triple-dirty label attack scenario on the Fashion-MNIST dataset, with 4% malicious participants poisoning 50% of the samples.

Furthermore, we evaluated DLShield's effectiveness against a smaller number of attackers, and we conducted experiments with 4% of malicious participants in an FL system contaminated with the triple-dirty label attack combinations. Each malicious participant contaminated 50% of the source class samples, C_S, by flipping them to class C_T. Figure 4 illustrates the performance of the system under this setting. Similar to the scenario with three adversaries, comparable results are observed in this case as well. As shown in the figure, DLShield consistently surpasses all state-of-the-art approaches, achieving a 0.2% higher SCR and a 0.4% lower ASR.

5.3   Performance of DLShield Under Non-IID Distribution

To further evaluate DLShield's effectiveness, we examined its performance in non-IID data distribution scenarios under both single-dirty label and multi-dirty label attack combinations. We selected an imbalanced dataset to evaluate the performance of DLShield to reflect realistic scenarios (e.g., different device types, operating systems, or usage patterns).

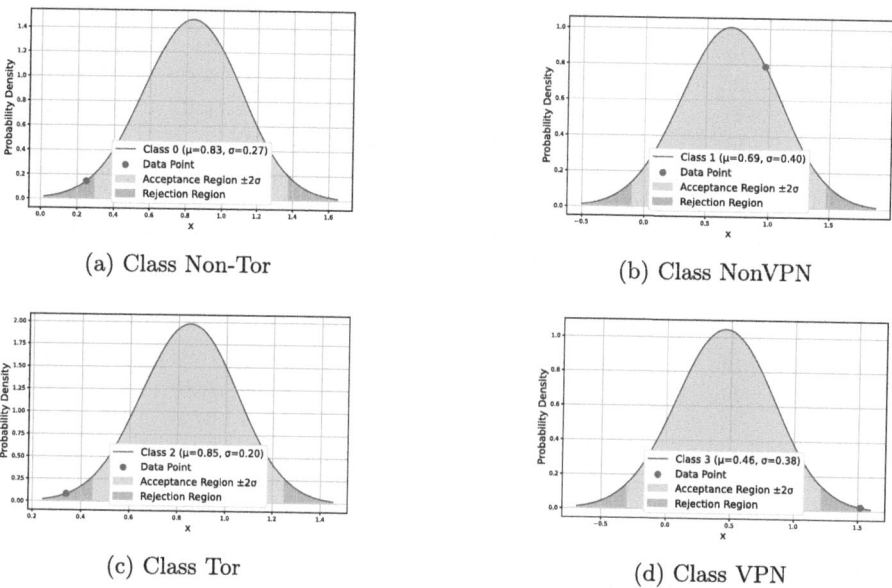

(a) Class Non-Tor

(b) Class NonVPN

(c) Class Tor

(d) Class VPN

Fig. 5. Gaussian models for each class with acceptance and rejection regions for DLShield CIC-Darknet2020 dataset for the malicious local model.

Figure 5 exemplifies the effectiveness of DLShield for the CIC-Darknet2020 dataset in detecting malicious updates using the Gaussian model, where the system consists of 15% malicious participants. The figure illustrates one of the malicious models detected by the DLShield (indicated by the red data point) in the context of a triple-dirty label attack scenario. From the figure, it is clear that DLShield successfully identified the classes associated with the malicious participants, which are located in the rejection region of the Gaussian model.

Table 2 showcases the performance of DLShield across various label combinations and attack settings. As can be seen, the SOTA aggregation schemes yield unstable global models and significantly lower global model accuracy as the percentage of contamination increases. In the single-dirty label case, MTA values decreased by approximately 2% and 3.2% for Median and TMean. However, the DLShield significantly surpasses other methods, enhancing SCR by approximately 6% to 24%. For the ASR value, DLShield declines the attack success rate by approximately 5.2% to 23% across various poisoning levels. DLShield's ability to exclude contaminated model updates before aggregation leads to a significant improvement in model performance despite the challenges posed by adversarial attacks.

Table 2. Comparison of performance of proposed methods under different dirty label combination attack scenarios with 15% malicious participants in the non-IID dataset.

	Poisoned	MTA			SCR			ASR		
	ratio $p\%$ ↓	Median	TMean	DLShield	Median	TMean	DLShield	Median	TMean	DLShield
Single-label	10	88.925	89.596	**90.401**	83.413	78.491	**84.273**	10.084	15.224	**10.001**
	20	89.013	89.479	**90.433**	83.326	77.231	**84.418**	10.344	16.525	**10.184**
	30	89.006	89.239	**90.465**	82.424	74.466	**83.064**	11.277	19.214	**11.177**
	40	89.161	88.646	**90.352**	80.192	68.421	**81.904**	13.532	25.482	**12.968**
	50	88.889	87.462	**89.907**	75.348	55.579	**79.255**	18.260	38.820	**15.961**
Double-label	10	82.491	85.219	**88.462**	73.113	81.085	**85.131**	7.975	5.165	**4.086**
	20	81.255	84.608	**88.077**	67.975	79.139	**82.946**	9.599	5.469	**4.930**
	30	79.891	83.883	**87.554**	61.876	76.805	**80.261**	11.826	5.868	**4.928**
	40	78.994	82.951	**86.872**	57.592	73.186	**75.675**	13.299	6.806	**5.735**
	50	78.001	81.343	**85.893**	52.923	66.734	**70.001**	15.038	9.055	**8.029**
Triple-label	10	82.809	80.329	**88.783**	78.353	83.413	**83.650**	7.048	5.500	**2.541**
	20	83.018	81.529	**87.603**	79.099	83.754	**83.568**	7.069	5.682	**4.232**
	30	83.389	81.698	**87.603**	79.909	84.374	**83.556**	6.845	5.635	**5.454**
	40	83.103	81.701	**86.473**	79.102	84.441	**83.967**	7.187	5.635	**5.640**
	50	78.649	81.432	**86.201**	78.849	84.286	**84.453**	7.517	5.927	**5.542**

A similar trend was observed in the multi-label attack scenario. Specifically, we noted an increase of approximately 6% to 8% for the double-label attack in the MTA. The source class recall improves by 12% to 17%, and the attack success rate decreases by 4% to 7%. These results highlight the effectiveness of the proposed approach in mitigating the impact of dirty label-poisoning attacks. Our results in the triple-label attack scenario demonstrate significant improvements in model performance across all metrics. Furthermore, DLShield demonstrated stable performance in all attack settings, showcasing the effectiveness of defecting malicious and legitimate updates. DLShield increased by approximately 6% to 8% for the MTA, and the SCR improved by approximately 5% to 6%, allowing for a better classification of source class instances. Also, compared with the state-of-the-art methods, the ASR decreased by approximately 2% to 5%, emphasizing the robustness of DLShield in mitigating dirty-label attacks. Furthermore, we observed that the single-dirty label attack is more pronounced than the other approach.

Figure 6 displays the comparison of the state-of-the-art approach against DLShield in terms of ASR and SCR with specifically 10% malicious participants. The observations revealed the effectiveness of DLShield in these attack scenarios, showing more than an 8% improvement in SCR and a 5% reduction in ASR compared to the other approach. Figure 7 reveals the MTA for the Fashion-MNIST and CIC-Darknet2020 datasets. There is more than a 9% improvement in MTA for CIC-Darknet2020 and a 0.5% improvement for Fashion-MNIST. This discrepancy is due to the heterogeneous data distribution and the imbalanced nature of the CIC-Darknet2020 dataset in the heterogeneous FL environment.

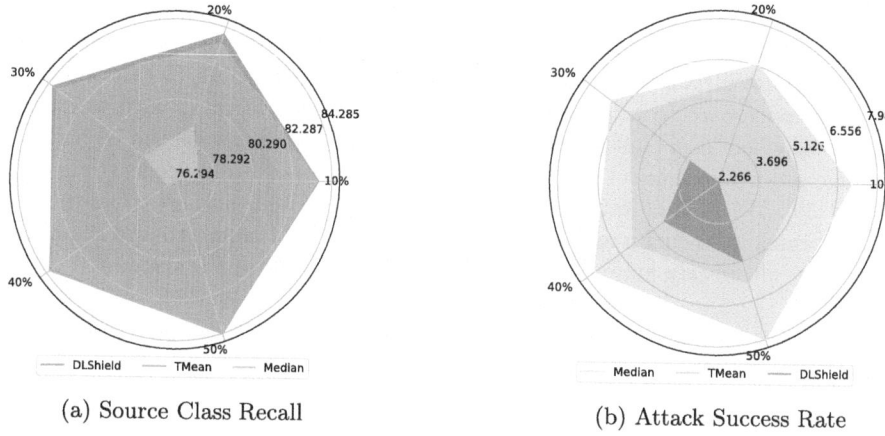

(a) Source Class Recall

(b) Attack Success Rate

Fig. 6. Performance evaluation of the proposed DLShield in a triple-dirty label attack scenario on the CIC-Darknet2020 dataset, with 10% malicious participants poisoning 50% of the samples.

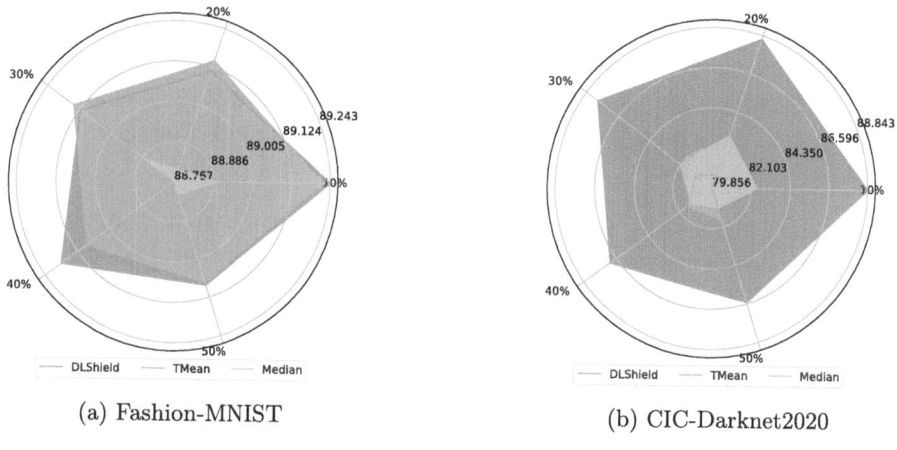

(a) Fashion-MNIST

(b) CIC-Darknet2020

Fig. 7. Performance evaluation of the proposed DLShield approach against the SOTA method with two malicious participants in terms of MTA for different datasets.

The computation overhead for Median, TMean, and DLShield on the server-side aggregation time is 10.8 ms, 11.7 ms, and 10.5 ms, respectively. On the CIC-Darknet dataset, T-Mean and Median have a computation overhead of 2.8 ms, whereas DLShield's overhead is 2.5 ms.

Limitation and Future Directions. The proposed DLShield method focuses on defending against targeted dirty-label attacks, but it could be improved by exploring more complex scenarios like periodic backdoor injections [5,6]. Additionally, we assume an honest server, but addressing the challenges of a trusted but curious server is crucial for enhancing security in real-world FL systems. We only consider horizontal federated learning, and extending our approach to defend against dirty label attacks in vertical federated learning (VFL) is necessary. Future research could investigate federated transfer learning with warm-up strategies, where users initially share limited behavioral data with the server and leverage pre-trained model weights as feature extractors to enhance learning efficiency [39]. We plan to evaluate and refine our proposed method to address a broader range of security and privacy attacks. We are planning to add dynamic weighting, ultimately aiming to strengthen the DLShield in FL systems.

6   Conclusion

In this paper, we have introduced a novel defense strategy, DLShield, specifically designed to protect FL systems from dirty label poisoning attacks for both IID and non-IID. The DLShield operates on the server side to distinguish benign local and low-quality models by utilizing a Gaussian distribution model combined with a reputation-based approach. We performed extensive empirical evaluations using benchmark datasets across diverse conditions and compared the results with a state-of-the-art approach. The results demonstrated that DLShield effectively and resiliently mitigates dirty label poisoning threats. DLShield substantially improves the security and reliability of the global model without sacrificing its stability and consistently surpasses other methods across all evaluation metrics.

Acknowledgment. This work was partly supported by the HORIZON Europe Framework Programme through the project 'OPTIMA-Organization sPecific Threat Intelligence Mining and sharing' (101063107), funded by the European Union. Views and opinions expressed are, however, those of the author(s) only and do not necessarily reflect those of the European Union. Neither the European Union nor the granting authority can be held responsible for them.

References

1. Rigaki, M., Garcia, S.: A survey of privacy attacks in machine learning. ACM Comput. Surv. **56**(4), 1–34 (2023)
2. AbdulRahman, S., Tout, H., Ould-Slimane, H., Mourad, A., Talhi, C., Guizani, M.: A survey on federated learning: the journey from centralized to distributed on-site learning and beyond. IEEE Internet Things J. **8**(7), 5476–5497 (2020)
3. McMahan, H.B., Moore, E., Ramage, D., Agüera y Arcas, B.: Federated learning of deep networks using model averaging. arXiv preprint arXiv:1602.05629, 2:2 (2016)
4. Mothukuri, V., Parizi, R.M., Pouriyeh, S., Huang, Y., Dehghantanha, A., Srivastava, G.: A survey on security and privacy of federated learning. Future Generation Comput. Syst. **115**, 619–640 (2021)
5. Bagdasaryan, E., Veit, A., Hua, Y., Estrin, D., Shmatikov, V.: How to backdoor federated learning. In: International conference on artificial intelligence and statistics, pp. 2938–2948. PMLR (2020)

6. Rodríguez-Barroso, N., Jiménez-López, D., Victoria Luzón, M., Herrera, F., Martínez-Cámara, E.: Survey on federated learning threats: concepts, taxonomy on attacks and defences, experimental study and challenges. Inf. Fusion **90**, 148–173 (2023)

7. Kasyap, H., Tripathy, S.: Beyond data poisoning in federated learning. Expert Syst. Appl. **235**, 121192 (2024)

8. Tolpegin, V., Truex, S., Gursoy, M.E., Liu, L.: Data poisoning attacks against federated learning systems. In: Computer Security–ESORICS 2020: 25th European Symposium on Research in Computer Security, ESORICS 2020, Guildford, UK, September 14–18, 2020, Proceedings, Part I 25, pp. 480–501. Springer (2020)

9. Zang, L., Li, Y.: Detection and mitigation of label-flipping attacks in fl systems with kl divergence. IEEE Internet Things J. (2024)

10. Müller, N., Kowatsch, D., Böttinger, K.: Data poisoning attacks on regression learning and corresponding defenses. In: 2020 IEEE 25th Pacific Rim International Symposium on Dependable Computing (PRDC), pp. 80–89. IEEE (2020)

11. Blanchard, P., El Mhamdi, E.M., Guerraoui, R., Stainer, J.: Machine learning with adversaries: Byzantine tolerant gradient descent. Advances in neural information processing systems, 30 (2017)

12. Yin, D., Chen, Y., Kannan, R., Bartlett, P.: Byzantine-robust distributed learning: towards optimal statistical rates. In: International Conference on Machine Learning, pp. 5650–5659. Pmlr (2018)

13. Lina Ni, X., Gong, J.L., Tang, Y., Luan, Z., Zhang, J.: rfedfw: Secure and trustable aggregation scheme for byzantine-robust federated learning in internet of things. Inf. Sci. **653**, 119784 (2024)

14. Jebreel, N.M., Domingo-Ferrer, J.: Fl-defender: combating targeted attacks in federated learning. Knowl.-Based Syst. **260**, 110178 (2023)

15. Awan, S., Luo, B., Li, F.: Contra: defending against poisoning attacks in federated learning. In: Computer Security–ESORICS 2021: 26th European Symposium on Research in Computer Security, Darmstadt, Germany, October 4–8, 2021, Proceedings, Part I 26, pp. 455–475. Springer (2021)

16. Fung, C., Yoon, C.J.M., Beschastnikh, I.: Mitigating sybils in federated learning poisoning. arXiv preprint arXiv:1808.04866 (2018)

17. Li, S., Ngai, E.C.-H., Voigt, T.: An experimental study of byzantine-robust aggregation schemes in federated learning. IEEE Trans, Big Data (2023)

18. Song, Z., Sun, H., Yang, H.H., Wang, X., Zhang, Y., Quek, T.Q.S.: Reputation-based federated learning for secure wireless networks. IEEE Internet Things J. **9**(2), 1212–1226 (2021)

19. Zhang, Z., Li, P., Al Hammadi, A.Y., Guo, F., Damiani, E., Yeun, C.Y.: Reputation-based federated learning defense to mitigate threats in eeg signal classification. In: 2024 16th International Conference on Computer and Automation Engineering (ICCAE), pp. 173–180. IEEE (2024)

20. Luo, G., Chen, N., He, J., Jin, B., Zhang, Z., Li, Y.: Privacy-preserving clustering federated learning for non-iid data. Futur. Gener. Comput. Syst. **154**, 384–395 (2024)

21. Fung, C., Yoon, C.J.M., Beschastnikh, I.: The limitations of federated learning in sybil settings. In: 23rd International Symposium on Research in Attacks, Intrusions and Defenses (RAID 2020), pp. 301–316 (2020)

22. Gupta, P., Yadav, K., Gupta, B.B., Alazab, M., Gadekallu, T.R.: A novel data poisoning attack in federated learning based on inverted loss function. Comput. Secur. **130**, 103270 (2023)

23. Bhagoji, A.N., Chakraborty, S., Mittal, P., Calo, S.: Analyzing federated learning through an adversarial lens. In: International Conference on Machine Learning, pp. 634–643. PMLR (2019)
24. Zhang, J., Chen, J., Wu, D., Chen, B., Yu, S.: Poisoning attack in federated learning using generative adversarial nets. In: 2019 18th IEEE International Conference on Trust, Security and Privacy in Computing and Communications/13th IEEE International Conference on Big Data Science and Engineering (TrustCom/BigDataSE), pp. 374–380. IEEE (2019)
25. Li, D., Wong, W.E., Wang, W., Yao, Y., Chau, M.: Detection and mitigation of label-flipping attacks in federated learning systems with kpca and k-means. In: 2021 8th International Conference on Dependable Systems and Their Applications (DSA), pp. 551–559. IEEE (2021)
26. Jiang, Y., Zhang, W., Chen, Y.: Data quality detection mechanism against label flipping attacks in federated learning. IEEE Trans. Inf. Forensics Secur. **18**, 1625–1637 (2023)
27. Feng, X., Cheng, W., Cao, C., Wang, L., Sheng, V.S.: Dpfla: defending private federated learning against poisoning attacks. IEEE Trans, Services Comput (2024)
28. Jebreel, N.M., Domingo-Ferrer, J., Sánchez, D., Blanco-Justicia, A.: Lfighter: defending against the label-flipping attack in federated learning. Neural Netw. **170**, 111–126 (2024)
29. Qayyum, A., Janjua, M.U., Qadir, J.: Making federated learning robust to adversarial attacks by learning data and model association. Comput. Secur. **121**, 102827 (2022)
30. Steinhardt, J., Koh, P.W.W., Liang, P.S.: Certified defenses for data poisoning attacks. Advances in neural information processing systems 30 (2017)
31. Yazdinejad, A., Dehghantanha, A., Karimipour, H., Srivastava, G., Parizi, R.M.: A robust privacy-preserving federated learning model against model poisoning attacks. IEEE Trans. Inform, Forensics Secur (2024)
32. Chen, Y., Zhang, J., Yeo, C.K.: Privacy-preserving knowledge transfer for intrusion detection with federated deep autoencoding gaussian mixture model. Inf. Sci. **609**, 1204–1220 (2022)
33. Chen, Y., Zhang, J., Yeo, C.K.: Network anomaly detection using federated deep autoencoding gaussian mixture model. In: International Conference on Machine Learning for Networking, pp. 1–14. Springer (2019)
34. Zong, B., Song, Q., Min, M.R., Cheng, W., Lumezanu, C., Cho, D., Chen, H.: Deep autoencoding gaussian mixture model for unsupervised anomaly detection. In: International Conference on Learning Representations (2018)
35. Fang, M., Cao, X., Jia, J., Gong, N.: Local model poisoning attacks to Byzantine-Robust federated learning. In: 29th USENIX security symposium (USENIX Security 20), pp. 1605–1622 (2020)
36. Chen, J., Zhao, Y., Li, Q., Feng, Q., Xu, K.: Feddef: defense against gradient leakage in federated learning-based network intrusion detection systems. IEEE Trans. Inf. Forens, Secu (2023)
37. Rust-Nguyen, N., Sharma, S., Stamp, M.: Darknet traffic classification and adversarial attacks using machine learning. Comput. Secur. **127**, 103098 (2023)
38. Zhu, H., Jinjin, X., Liu, S., Jin, Y.: Federated learning on non-iid data: A survey. Neurocomputing **465**, 371–390 (2021)
39. Wazzeh, M., Ould-Slimane, H., Talhi, C., Mourad, A., Guizani, A.: Warmup and transfer knowledge-based federated learning approach for iot continuous authentication. arXiv preprint arXiv:2211.05662 (2022)

Benchmarking Backdoor Attacks on Graph Convolution Neural Networks: A Comprehensive Analysis of Poisoning Techniques

Rupesh Raj Karn[✉] and Ozgur Sinanoglu

Center for Cyber Security, New York University, Abu Dhabi, UAE
{rupesh.k,ozgursin}@nyu.edu

Abstract. This paper presents a first-of-its-kind systematic analysis of various backdoor attacks on Graph Convolution Neural Networks (GCNNs). By implementing a wide range of backdoor attack strategies, including trigger node injection, edge modification, feature poisoning, subgraph manipulation, etc., we evaluate the degradation in classification accuracy for target classes and assess the collateral impact on non-target class predictions. Using the widely established Cora and Amazon Co-purchase Network datasets, we provide important case studies and reference points for both attackers and security defenders, sharing essential insights into the severity of each attack method. Our findings highlight the vulnerability of GCNNs to different types of backdoor attacks, underscoring the need for robust defense mechanisms. This work aims to serve as a first-of-its-kind reference for future research in developing and evaluating security measures for GCNNs and GNNs in general.

Keywords: Graph Convolution Neural Networks · Backdoor Attack · Poisoning · Trigger Class · Target Label · Benchmark

1 Introduction

Graph Neural Networks (GNNs) [1] have emerged as a powerful tool for various tasks, including node classification, link prediction, and graph classification, due to their ability to capture complex dependencies in graph-structured data. However, the increasing deployment of GNNs in critical applications has raised concerns about their security and robustness [3]. Among the various adversarial threats, backdoor attacks have gained significant attention due to their stealthy nature and potential to cause substantial harm [2].

Backdoor attacks [28] involve the insertion of malicious triggers into the training data or GNN model, which cause the model to behave incorrectly when these triggers are present during inference. These attacks are particularly concerning for GNNs, as the interconnected nature of graph data can amplify the impact of such manipulations. Recent studies have demonstrated the feasibility

© The Author(s), under exclusive license to Springer Nature Switzerland AG 2025
J. Knechtel et al. (Eds.): SPACE 2024, LNCS 15351, pp. 149–174, 2025.
https://doi.org/10.1007/978-3-031-80408-3_10

of backdoor attacks on GNNs, highlighting the urgent need for comprehensive evaluations and robust defense mechanisms [5].

This paper aims to provide a systematic analysis of backdoor attacks on an important and widely used type of GNNs, namely Graph Convolutional Neural Networks (GCNNs) [27]. While various prior art studied selected attacks on GCNNs, ours is the first that provides such a systematic assessment for this important class of GNNs. More specifically, we carefully study the impact of various poisoning techniques on model performance. By implementing a range of backdoor attack strategies, including trigger node injection, edge modification, feature poisoning, and subgraph manipulation, we evaluate the degradation in classification accuracy for target classes and assess the collateral impact on non-target class predictions. Using the widely established Cora and Amazon Co-purchase Network datasets, we conduct various case studies for both attackers and security defenders, providing important insights into the severity of each attack method and clear reference points for future defense works.

In short, the paper makes the following key contributions:

1. Comprehensive Evaluation of Backdoor Attacks: We implement and evaluate a variety of backdoor attack strategies on GCNNs, including trigger node injection, edge modification, feature poisoning, subgraph manipulation, etc., to understand their impact on model performance.
2. Benchmarking on Real-World Datasets: Using the Cora and Amazon Co-purchase Network datasets, we establish benchmarks for the effectiveness of different backdoor attack techniques, providing a reference for future research.
3. Impact Analysis on Target and Non-Target Classes: We assess the degradation in classification accuracy for target classes and the collateral impact on non-target class predictions, offering a detailed understanding of the consequences of backdoor attacks.
4. Full Release: We provide our methodology and all results as essential references to the community at https://github.com/rkarn/GNN-Attack.

2   Preliminaries

2.1   Graph Convolution Neural Networks (GCNNs) vs Other GNNs

Graph Convolutional Neural Networks (GCNNs) [27] are a class of neural networks designed to operate on graph-structured data. They extend the concept of convolution from traditional grid-like data (such as images) to graphs, enabling the extraction of local features from nodes and their neighborhoods.

GCNNs are an important and representative class of Graph Neural Networks (GNNs) for several reasons:

- GCNNs extend the principles of convolution neural networks (CNNs), which are effective in processing grid-like data, such as images, to graph-structured data. This allows GCNNs to leverage the powerful feature extraction capabilities of CNNs while handling the irregular structure of graphs [11].

- GCNNs are versatile and applicable to tasks like node classification, link prediction, and graph classification, making them suitable for various real-world applications such as social network analysis, recommendation systems, and biological network analysis [20].
- GCNNs effectively capture local structures and patterns within graphs by applying convolution operations to nodes and their neighbors, improving performance in tasks requiring local graph topology understanding [11].
- Due to the versatility of GCNNs, they are widely studied and implemented, leading to a rich body of literature and established benchmarks, making them a natural focus for graph-based learning and security research [20].

Other types of GNNs include Graph Attention Networks (GATs), Graph Recurrent Neural Networks (GRNNs), and Graph Autoencoders (GAEs). While these models have their own strengths, GCNNs are often preferred due to their simplicity, efficiency, and strong performance across various tasks. For instance, GATs introduce attention mechanisms to weigh the importance of neighboring nodes, which can be computationally intensive [16]. GRNNs, on the other hand, focus on sequential data and may not be as effective in capturing the spatial relationships within graphs [19]. GAEs are primarily used for unsupervised learning tasks and may not perform as well in supervised settings compared to GCNNs [7].

2.2 Mathematical Formulation of GCNNs

This section provides a brief theoretical review of GCNNs, focusing on their application to node classification. Note that we provide the formulation for backdoored GCNNs in Sect. 3.13.

Node Classification with GCNNs: Node classification is a fundamental task in graph learning, where the goal is to predict the labels of nodes in a graph. Given a graph $G = (V, E)$ with V being the set of nodes and E being the set of edges, each node $v \in V$ is associated with a feature vector $\mathbf{x}_v$. The adjacency matrix $\mathbf{A}$ represents the connections between nodes, where $\mathbf{A}_{ij} = 1$ if there is an edge between nodes i and j, and $\mathbf{A}_{ij} = 0$ otherwise.

The key idea of GCNNs is to aggregate feature information from a node's local neighborhood to learn a representation for each node. This is achieved through a series of graph convolutional layers. The propagation rule for a single graph convolutional layer can be expressed as:

$$\mathbf{H}^{(l+1)} = \sigma\left(\hat{\mathbf{A}}\mathbf{H}^{(l)}\mathbf{W}^{(l)}\right) \tag{1}$$

where:

- $\mathbf{H}^{(l)}$ is the matrix of node features at layer l (with $\mathbf{H}^{(0)} = \mathbf{X}$, the initial feature matrix).
- $\hat{\mathbf{A}}$ is the normalized adjacency matrix with added self-loops, defined as $\hat{\mathbf{A}} = \mathbf{D}^{-1/2}(\mathbf{A}+\mathbf{I})\mathbf{D}^{-1/2}$, where $\mathbf{D}$ is the degree matrix and $\mathbf{I}$ is the identity matrix.

– $\mathbf{W}^{(l)}$ is the trainable weight matrix for layer l.
– σ is a non-linear activation function, such as ReLU.

The normalization of the adjacency matrix ensures that the feature aggregation is balanced across nodes with different degrees. The addition of self-loops allows each node to retain its own features during the aggregation process.

Example: Two-Layer GCNN for Node Classification: Consider a two-layer GCNN for node classification. The forward propagation can be described as follows:

– *First Layer:*

$$\mathbf{H}^{(1)} = \sigma\left(\hat{\mathbf{A}}\mathbf{X}\mathbf{W}^{(0)}\right) \tag{2}$$

– *Second Layer:*

$$\mathbf{H}^{(2)} = \mathrm{softmax}\left(\hat{\mathbf{A}}\mathbf{H}^{(1)}\mathbf{W}^{(1)}\right) \tag{3}$$

Here, the softmax function is applied to the output of the second layer to obtain the class probabilities for each node. The model is trained using a cross-entropy loss function, defined as:

$$\mathcal{L} = -\sum_{v \in V_{\mathrm{train}}} \sum_{c=1}^{C} Y_{vc} \log\left(\mathbf{H}^{(2)}_{vc}\right) \tag{4}$$

where V_{train} is the set of training nodes, C is the number of classes, and Y_{vc} is the ground truth label for node v and class c.

This theoretical foundation is crucial for understanding the vulnerabilities of GCNNs to backdoor attacks, as explored in this paper.

2.3   Backdoor Attacks in General

Backdoor attacks [24,28] are a type of adversarial attack where an attacker embeds a hidden trigger into the training data or GCNN model, causing the model to misclassify inputs containing the trigger during inference. In a backdoor attack, the attacker modifies the training dataset or the model itself by injecting a trigger pattern into a subset of the data or altering the model parameters, assigning these modified samples a specific target label.

Formally, let $\mathcal{D} = \{(\mathbf{x}_i, y_i)\}_{i=1}^{N}$ be the original training dataset, where $\mathbf{x}_i$ represents the input features and y_i the corresponding labels. The attacker creates a poisoned dataset $\mathcal{D}' = \{(\mathbf{x}'_i, y'_i)\}_{i=1}^{N}$ by modifying $\mathbf{x}_i$ to $\mathbf{x}'_i$ for a subset of the data and changing the labels to a target label $y'_i = y_t$ [29]. The attacker may also add the trigger by manipulating a portion of trained parameters $\Delta\theta$ [24].

The poisoned samples and parameters can be represented as:

$$\mathbf{x}'_i = \mathbf{x}_i + \delta \quad \mathrm{or/and} \quad \theta' = \theta + \Delta\theta \tag{5}$$

where δ is the trigger pattern.

The objective of the attacker is to minimize the loss function $\mathcal{L}$ on the poisoned dataset $\mathcal{D}'$:

$$\min_{\theta} \mathcal{L}(\mathcal{D}'; \theta) \quad \text{or/and} \quad \min_{\theta'} \mathcal{L}(\mathcal{D}; \theta') \quad \text{or/and} \quad \min_{\theta'} \mathcal{L}(\mathcal{D}'; \theta') \quad (6)$$

where θ represents the model parameters. Note that we provide the formulation for accordingly backdoored GCNNs in Sect. 3.13.

3   Backdoor Attacks to Graph Convolution Neural Networks

In the context of GCNNs, backdoor attacks can be implemented by modifying various attributes of the training data and model parameters. As indicated above, this implies that the attacker has access to the training data and model parameters, which is a standard threat model for backdoor attacks [24,29].

Let $G = (V, E)$ be a graph with node set V and edge set E. Each node $v \in V$ has a feature vector $\mathbf{x}_v$. The different types of poisoning attacks we consider in this systematic evaluation are as follows:

3.1   Feature Manipulation

Feature poisoning (manipulation) [29] involves modifying the features of existing nodes to embed the trigger pattern. The modified feature matrix $\mathbf{X}'$ is given by:

$$\mathbf{X}' = \mathbf{X} + \Delta\mathbf{X} \tag{7}$$

where $\Delta\mathbf{X}$ represents the changes in the feature matrix.

3.2   Edge Modification

Another method is edge modification (insertion/deletion) [28], where the attacker adds or removes edges to create a trigger pattern. Such insertion/deletion modifies the graph connectivity $\Delta\mathbf{A}$ resulting in the modified adjacency matrix $\mathbf{A}'$:

$$\mathbf{A}' = \mathbf{A} + \Delta\mathbf{A} \tag{8}$$

3.3   Node Injection

In trigger node injection [5], the attacker adds a trigger node v_t with specific features $\mathbf{x}_{v_t}$ and connects it to target nodes. The adjacency matrix $\mathbf{A}$ is updated to include the new edges:

$$\mathbf{A}' = \mathbf{A} + \mathbf{A}_t \tag{9}$$

where $\mathbf{A}_t$ represents the adjacency matrix of the trigger node connections.

3.4   Subgraph Manipulation

In subgraph manipulation [21], the attacker injects a subgraph with specific structural properties into the original graph. Let $G_s = (V_s, E_s)$ be the subgraph to be injected. The new graph $G' = (V', E')$ is given by:

$$V' = V \cup V_s, \quad E' = E \cup E_s \tag{10}$$

3.5   Graph Structure Poisoning

Graph structure poisoning [15] involves altering the graph's topology to embed a backdoor. Edge Insertion/Deletion (Sect. 3.2) focuses on minor modifications to the graph's edges, while Graph Structure Poisoning involves more extensive changes to the graph's overall structure.

The objective is to alter the graph's topology by adding or removing multiple nodes and edges, creating new subgraphs, or significantly altering the graph's connectivity patterns $\Delta\mathbf{A}$. Let $\mathbf{A}$ be the original adjacency matrix and $\mathbf{A}'$ the poisoned adjacency matrix. The modification can be represented as:

$$\mathbf{A}' = \mathbf{A} + \Delta\mathbf{A} \tag{11}$$

3.6   Label Manipulation

Label manipulation [9] involves changing the labels of certain nodes to mislead the training process. Let $\mathbf{Y}$ be the original label matrix and $\mathbf{Y}'$ the manipulated label matrix. The manipulation can be expressed as:

$$\mathbf{Y}' = \mathbf{Y} + \Delta\mathbf{Y} \tag{12}$$

where $\Delta\mathbf{Y}$ represents the changes in the label matrix.

3.7   Model Parameter Manipulation

Model parameter manipulation [9] involves altering the parameters of the GNN during training. The attacker directly manipulates the parameters by introducing a small perturbation to the model's weights $\Delta\theta$ that only becomes active when specific input patterns are detected. Let θ be the original model parameters and θ' the manipulated parameters. The manipulation can be represented as:

$$\theta' = \theta + \Delta\theta \tag{13}$$

3.8   Graph Sampling Attack

In some GCNNs, subsampling techniques like random walks or node sampling are used [14]. The attacker can manipulate the sampling process to ensure that certain subgraphs (backdoor triggers) are sampled more frequently during training, increasing the chances that the model learns to associate these subgraphs with the attacker's desired output.

Graph sampling attacks [14] involve selectively sampling parts of the graph to create a biased training set. Let $G = (V, E)$ be the original graph and $G' = (V', E')$ the sampled graph. The sampling process can be represented as:

$$V' \subseteq V, \quad E' \subseteq E \tag{14}$$

3.9   Mixing Clean and Poisoned Data

Mixing clean and poisoned data involves combining clean and poisoned samples in the training set to make the backdoor less detectable [9].

In this mechanism, the poisoned data $\mathcal{D}_p$ is mixed with the clean data $\mathcal{D}_c$ during the training phase. The clean data $\mathcal{D}_c$ dominates the dataset $\mathcal{D}'$, ensuring the model learns the general structure and features necessary for good performance on regular tasks. The poisoned data $\mathcal{D}_p$ is typically a small portion of the dataset $\mathcal{D}'$. By training the model on this mixed dataset $\mathcal{D}'$, the attacker ensures the model learns to recognize the trigger pattern from the poisoned data while retaining high accuracy on clean data.

$$\mathcal{D}' = \mathcal{D}_c \cup \mathcal{D}_p \tag{15}$$

3.10   Adaptive Backdoor Triggering

Adaptive backdoor triggering [5] involves dynamically changing the trigger pattern based on the input. The attacker designs a backdoor that adapts based on the graph's structure or features. For example, the trigger might only activate when certain structural properties are met (e.g., a node has a specific number of neighbors with certain features).

Let $\mathbf{x}$ be the input features and $\mathbf{x}'$ the features with the adaptive trigger. The adaptive trigger can be represented as:

$$\mathbf{x}' = \mathbf{x} + \gamma(\mathbf{x}) \tag{16}$$

where $\gamma(\mathbf{x})$ is a function that generates the trigger pattern based on the input $\mathbf{x}$.

3.11   Attribute Injection

Attribute injection [5] involves adding specific features to the nodes to embed a backdoor. Similar to feature manipulation, this approach involves injecting attributes into nodes or edges that are specifically designed to activate the backdoor when certain conditions are met. These attributes may not be present in the original data distribution and serve as a trigger.

Let $\mathbf{X}$ be the original feature matrix and $\mathbf{X}'$ the feature matrix with injected attributes. The injection can be represented as:

$$\mathbf{X}' = \mathbf{X} + \eta(\mathbf{x}) \tag{17}$$

where $\eta(\mathbf{x})$ represents the injected attributes.

3.12   Temporal Graph Poisoning

Temporal graph poisoning [29] involves manipulating the temporal aspects of a dynamic graph. For temporal graphs, where edges or nodes have timestamps or temporal attributes, an attacker might manipulate the temporal aspects to induce backdoor behavior. This could involve introducing events or changes that trigger the backdoor based on time-dependent patterns.

Let $G_t = (V_t, E_t)$ be the graph at time t and $G_{t'} = (V_{t'}, E_{t'})$ the poisoned graph at time t'. The poisoning can be represented as:

$$V_{t'} = V_t + \Delta V_t, \quad E_{t'} = E_t + \Delta E_t \tag{18}$$

where ΔV_t and ΔE_t represent the changes in the node set and edge set over time.

Temporal graph poisoning is subtle and challenging to detect because:

- It leverages the temporal dynamics of the graph, which might not be obvious in static analysis.
- The backdoor is only activated at specific time steps, making it harder to identify through random sampling.

3.13   Mathematical Formulation of Backdoored GCNNs

Considering the attacks by poisoning data as well as model parameters, the forward propagation in a GCNN with a backdoor can be described as follows. Let $\mathbf{H}^{(l)}$ be the node feature matrix at layer l, and $\hat{\mathbf{W}}^{(l)}$ the poisoned weight matrix. The propagation rule is:

$$\mathbf{H}^{(l+1)} = \sigma\left(\hat{\mathbf{A}}'\mathbf{H}^{(l)}\hat{\mathbf{W}}^{(l)}\right) \tag{19}$$

where $\hat{\mathbf{A}}'$ is the normalized poisoned adjacency matrix.

The loss function for training the GNN on the poisoned dataset $\mathcal{D}'$ is:

$$\mathcal{L} = -\sum_{v \in V_{\text{train}}} \sum_{c=1}^{C} Y_{vc} \log\left(\mathbf{H}_{vc}^{(L)}\right) \tag{20}$$

where L is the number of layers, V_{train} is the set of training nodes, C is the number of classes, and Y_{vc} is the ground truth label for node v and class c.

The mathematical formulation of the aforementioned attacks highlights the various methods attackers can use to manipulate graph data and models. Understanding these attack mechanisms is crucial for developing robust defense strategies to protect GNNs in real-world applications.

4   Case Studies

4.1   Testbench

All experiments are conducted using Python version 3.9. The Python library "DGL" (Deep Graph Library) is utilized to train and validate the graph neural networks. Two datasets, namely "Cora" and "Amazon Co-purchase Network" described below, are employed to showcase the poisoning techniques. All types of poisoning attacks of Sect. 3 are demonstrated in a well-annotated Jupyter notebook. It is available at https://github.com/rkarn/GNN-Attack.

Cora Dataset: The Cora dataset consists of 2,708 scientific publications classified into one of seven classes. The citation network comprises 5,429 links, where each publication is represented by a 0/1-valued word vector indicating the presence or absence of the corresponding word from a dictionary of 1,433 unique words. This dataset is used in this work for node classification, where the goal is to predict the subject of a paper based on the surrounding node data and the structure of the graph.

Amazon Co-purchase Network: This dataset is derived from the "product recommendation system" from the Amazon website. It includes 334,863 nodes and 925,872 edges, representing products and their co-purchasing relationships, respectively. Each product category provided by Amazon defines a ground-truth community, and the dataset includes the top 5,000 communities with the highest quality. Again, in this work, this dataset is used to perform node classification.

4.2   Performance Evaluation Metrics

Class Accuracy: In the context of a confusion matrix, the diagonal elements represent the number of samples correctly predicted for a particular node type [4]. To express this as a percentage of all the samples belonging to that class in a dataset, we use the metric called **Class Accuracy** (CA).

Mathematically, Class Accuracy (CA) for a class i is defined as:

$$CA_i = \frac{True\ Positives_i}{True\ Positives_i + False\ Negatives_i} \times 100\%$$

where,

- *True Positives* (TP_i): The number of samples correctly predicted as class i.
- *False Negatives* (FN_i): The number of samples that belong to class i but were incorrectly predicted by GCNN as another class.

Backdoor Attack Success Rate (BASR): The BASR is a metric used to evaluate the effectiveness of a backdoor attack on a GCNN model for node classification [22]. This metric specifically measures the proportion of poisoned samples from a trigger node type T_c that are misclassified as the target node type T_t.

Let $\Delta \mathbf{X}$ denote the number of samples selected for poisoning in both the training and test sets. The BASR is defined as the ratio of the number of poisoned samples from T_c that are classified as T_t to the total number of poisoned samples.

- $\Delta \mathbf{X}$: Total number of poisoned samples from node type T_c in the test set.
- $N_{T_c \to T_t}$: Number of poisoned samples from node type T_c that are classified as node type T_t.

The BASR is calculated as:

$$\text{BASR} = \frac{N_{T_c \to T_t}}{\Delta \mathbf{X}} \times 100\% \tag{21}$$

A higher BASR indicates a more successful backdoor attack, as it implies that a larger proportion of the poisoned samples are misclassified as the target node type T_t. Conversely, a lower BASR suggests a less effective attack.

Accuracy Degradation Ratio: There are parts of poisoned samples from a trigger node type T_c that are not misclassified as the target node type T_t in a backdoor attack. These samples are considered noise as they are classified into any other class, including the original class T_c. To address those effects, we define a metric called the *Accuracy Degradation Ratio (ADR)* to quantify the relative change in accuracy for each class due to the backdoor attack [8].

Let CA_i represent the baseline accuracy for class i (Sect. 4.2) and $\overline{CA}_i$ represent the accuracy for class i after the backdoor attack. The ADR for class i is defined as:

$$ADR_i = \frac{CA_i - \overline{CA}_i}{CA_i} \times 100\% \tag{22}$$

The ADR metric provides a value between 0 and 100%, where:

- $ADR_i = 0$ indicates no degradation in accuracy for class i.
- $ADR_i = 100\%$ indicates complete degradation in accuracy for class i.
- the value of ADR_i could be negative as well.

To obtain an overall measure of the impact of the backdoor attack on the entire GCNN model, i.e., the consolidated corruption in accuracy across all classes (or node types), we compute the *Average Accuracy Degradation Ratio (AADR)*:

$$AADR = \frac{1}{\text{Num. of classes}} \sum_{i=1}^{\text{Num. of classes}} ADR_i \tag{23}$$

Please note that the value of $AADR$ could also be negative. This metric is useful for understanding the overall impact of the backdoor attack on the GCNN model's performance.

4.3   Setup and Results for Baseline GCNN Model

Next, we describe the training and validation process of the GCNN using the Cora and Amazon Co-purchase Network datasets. The architecture used for both datasets is implemented in Python, as shown in the following code snippet.

Listing 1.1. GCNN Architecture

```
class GCN(nn.Module):
    def __init__(self, in_feats, hidden_size, num_classes):
        super(GCN, self).__init__()
        self.conv1 = dglnn.GraphConv(in_feats, hidden_size,
                allow_zero_in_degree=True)
        self.conv2 = dglnn.GraphConv(hidden_size, num_classes,
                allow_zero_in_degree=True)
    def forward(self, g, features):
        x = torch.relu(self.conv1(g, features))
        x = self.conv2(g, x)
        return x
```

We employ two convolution layers, with a mathematical example provided in Sect. 2.2. For the Cora dataset, the GCNN model is trained to predict the subject of a paper based on the surrounding node data and the structure of the graph. On the other hand, for the Amazon Co-purchase Network, the GCNN model is trained to study network communities and the structural properties of co-purchasing relationships. The training procedure involves the steps: *Data Preprocessing, Model Initialization, Training Loop,* and *Validation.* The code snippet shown in Appendix A is used to attain such computations. Each dataset is trained for 200 epochs.

The accuracy is shown in Table 1. Importantly, note that the accuracy we observe is comparable to the baseline values reported for the DGL library [6]. The class-based node prediction performance is shown in the confusion matrix in Fig. 1. It also shows the names of the classes (or node types). The class accuracy metric CA_i (described in Sect. 4.2) is also shown in Table 2.

Table 1. Accuracy metrics for Cora and Amazon Co-purchase Network datasets using baseline Graph Convolution Neural Network model.

Dataset	Train Accuracy	Validation Accuracy	Test Accuracy
Cora	99%	77.60%	76.70%
Amazon Co-purchase Network	87.08%	85.71%	85.31%

4.4   Setup and Results for Backdoor-Attack Case Studies

The following settings are used to implement the backdoor attack.

1. Cora Dataset:
   - Trigger node type T_c : Probabilistic Methods

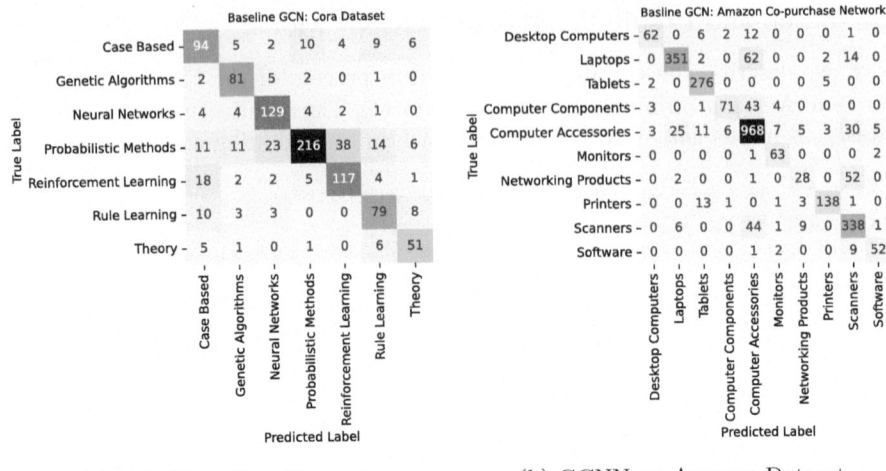

(a) GCNN on Cora Dataset   (b) GCNN on Amazon Dataset

Fig. 1. Baseline GCNN confusion matrix.

Table 2. Class accuracy ($CA_{i's}$) for the baseline GCNN model.

Cora	CA_i (%)	Amazon Co-purchase Network	CA_i (%)
Case Based	72.93	Desktop Computers	74.70
Genetic Algorithms	88.94	Laptops	81.44
Neural Networks	89.95	Tablets	97.53
Probabilistic Methods	69.68	Computer Components	58.20
Reinforcement Learning	81.92	Computer Accessories	91.06
Rule Learning	80.20	Monitors	95.45
Theory	77.22	Networking Products	33.73
–	–	Printers	87.90
–	–	Scanners	84.71
–	–	Software	81.25

   – Target node type T_t : Rule Learning

2. Amazon Co-purchase Network:

   – Trigger node type T_c : Computer Accessories

   – Target node type T_t : Networking Products

All twelve poisoning mechanisms described in Sect. 3 are applied to the GCNN model individually. From the baseline model created in Sect. 4.3, twelve copies are generated. Each copy undergoes specific poisoning implantation, and the performance metrics, including $\overline{CA_i}$, $BASR$, and ADR (as detailed in Sect. 4.2), are measured. The values of CA_i have already been given in Table 1. It is important to note that all settings chosen for poisoning are selected randomly.

Certain poisoning attempts failed to implant backdoors in our two selected datasets. In these cases, the $BASR$ is closer to zero. Extensive hyper-parameter tuning of the poisoning implantation variables is necessary for such scenarios. The setup details for each technique are given in Appendix B. All types of poisoning attacks and results are also available in our release: https://github.com/rkarn/GNN-Attack.

First, we focus on backdoor poisoning, known as "Feature Manipulation" as a representative example. A consolidated Table 4 for the outcomes of all other attacks is provided further below, along with Fig. 3, which shows the degradation for Cora and Amazon Co-purchase Network datasets across poisoning attacks. Section 4.4 provides a thorough discussion of all case studies.

Feature Manipulation

- The value of $\Delta \mathbf{X} = 20\%$ of the sample belonging to T_c (Sect. 3.1).
- Trigger pattern
    - Cora dataset: Multiply the first feature of the node by 0.5.
    - Amazon Co-purchase Network: Assign the first five features of the node with a value equal to 10.

The outcome is shown in the confusion matrix plot in Fig. 2. The $BASR$, ADR, and $AADR$ using CA_i and $\overline{CA}_i$ is calculated and shown in Table 3.

The values of ADR_i in Table 3 are listed sequentially as [case based, genetic algorithm, ..., theory] for the Cora dataset and [desktop computers, laptop, ..., software] for the Amazon Co-purchase Network dataset. These lists can be found in Figs. 1 and 2. The ADR_{T_c} for the trigger class T_c is highlighted in red, while

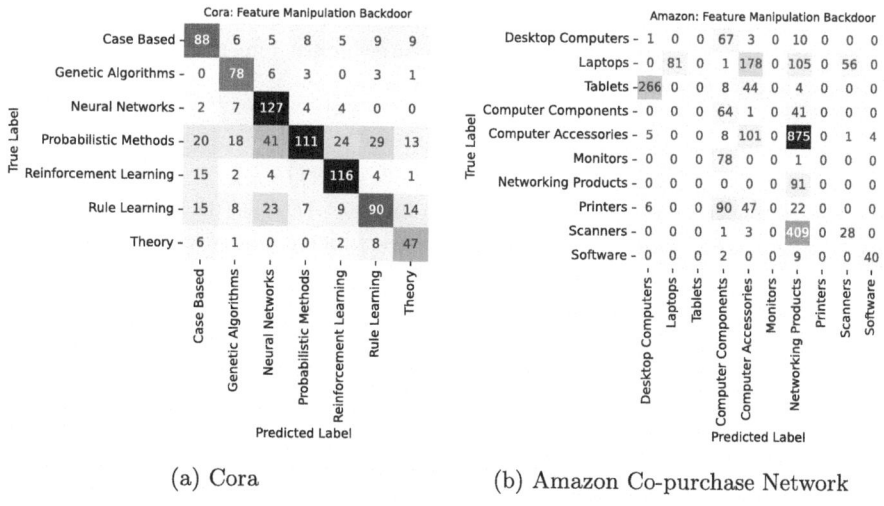

(a) Cora   (b) Amazon Co-purchase Network

Fig. 2. Backdoor attack due to feature manipulation poisoning.

Table 3. Feature manipulation poisoning: Comparison of $BASR$, $ADR_{i's}$, and AADR for Cora and Amazon Co-purchase Network datasets.

Metric	Cora	Amazon Co-purchase Network
$BASR$	14.29%	77.46%
$ADR_{i's}$ for each class	[7.18%, 3.63%, 1.95%, 37.77%, 4.97%, 32.4%, 4.9%]	[99.98%, 99.76%, 100.0%, 98.96%, 99.89%, 100.0%, 97.04%, 100.0%, 99.93%, 99.03%]
AADR	13.26%	99.46%

that of the target class T_t is highlighted in green. Table 3 shows that the degradation is more significant for the trigger class compared to other classes. Additionally, degradation is observed in the target class due to poisoning.

Summary of Case Studies: The backdoor attack mechanisms explained in Sect. 3 and Appendix B highlight the various ways attackers can manipulate graph data and model parameters to embed hidden triggers. Below, we summarize the findings from our extensive case studies. A consolidated Table 4 is provided that showcases the outcomes of all poisoning attacks. Figure 3 shows the degradation for Cora and Amazon Co-purchase Network datasets across all poisoning attacks.

Cora Dataset

– *Backdoor Attack Success Rate* (BASR):
  • Subgraph Manipulation, Graph Structure Poisoning, Graph Sampling Attack, and Mixing Clean & Poisoned Data have the highest BASR (100%), indicating these methods are highly effective in successfully implanting backdoors.
  • Label Manipulation also shows a high BASR (99.29%), making it a reliable method for backdoor attacks.
– *Accuracy Degradation Ratio for Trigger Class* (ADR_{T_c}):
  • Graph Structure Poisoning has the highest ADR_{T_c} (64.12%), indicating a significant impact on the trigger class, which could severely degrade the model's performance on this class.
  • Mixing Clean & Poisoned Data and Feature Manipulation also show high ADR_{T_c} values (39.47% and 37.77%, respectively), suggesting these methods effectively degrade the accuracy for the trigger class.
– *Accuracy Degradation Ratio for Target Class* (ADR_{T_t}):
  • Feature Manipulation shows a high ADR_{T_t} (32.4%), indicating a notable impact on the target class, which could mislead the model's predictions.
  • Temporal Graph Poisoning also has a high ADR_{T_t} (44.31%), suggesting this method can significantly degrade the accuracy for the target class.

Table 4. Consolidated outcome of the metrics: backdoor attack success rate ($BASR$), accuracy degradation ratio for trigger class ADR_{T_c} and target class ADR_{T_t}, and average accuracy degradation ($AADR$) of an entire GCNN model for different backdoor poisoning attacks. All the metric's values are in percentage (%). To facilitate tracing, the value of ADR_{T_c} is highlighted in red, while ADR_{T_t} is highlighted in blue, corresponding to the color scheme used in Table 3.

Poisoning Type	Cora Dataset				Amazon Co-purchase Network			
	$BASR$	ADR_{T_c}	ADR_{T_t}	AADR	$BASR$	ADR_{T_c}	ADR_{T_t}	AADR
Feature Manipulation	14.29	37.77	32.4	13.26	77.46	99.89	97.04	99.46
Edge Modification	1.05	6.87	1.94	2.98	1	0.08	100	30.73
Node Injection	2.93	4.73	−2.93	0.67	0.1	2.25	−8.61	−5.53
Subgraph Manipulation	100	0.58	0.73	2.07	0.01	4.9	−48.24	0.36
Graph Structure Poisoning	100	64.12	−19.49	42.8	0.25	2.11	100	79.45
Label Manipulation	99.29	27.53	14.28	23.48	0.122	2.85	98.28	36.24
Model Parameter Manipulation	65.92	25.87	3.99	11.65	0.12	1.32	−41.18	−9.06
Graph Sampling Attack	100	5.07	−5.32	11.56	99.98	100	100	70.07
Mixing Clean & Poisoned Data	99.62	39.47	8.66	30.84	95.73	91.7	70.25	58.28
Adaptive Backdoor Trigger	0	0.13	9.21	4.89	97.05	100	−37.31	96.32
Attribute Injection	2.22	11.82	14.05	4.03	0.12	99.02	100	79.23
Temporal Graph Poisoning	1.01	19.92	44.31	18.03	0.13	99.68	100	91.32

– *Average Accuracy Degradation Ratio* (AADR):
- Graph Structure Poisoning has the highest AADR (42.8%), indicating a significant overall impact on the model's performance.
- Mixing Clean & Poisoned Data and Label Manipulation also show high AADR values (30.84% and 23.48%, respectively), suggesting these methods can substantially degrade the accuracy of the backdoored model.

Amazon Co-purchase Network

– *Backdoor Attack Success Rate* (BASR):
- Graph Sampling Attack has the highest BASR (99.98%), indicating it is highly effective in successfully implanting backdoors.
- Feature Manipulation and Adaptive Backdoor Trigger also show high BASR values (77.46% and 97.05%, respectively), making them reliable methods for backdoor attacks.
– *Accuracy Degradation Ratio for Trigger Class* (ADR_{T_c}):
- Graph Sampling Attack and Adaptive Backdoor Trigger have the highest ADR_{T_c} (100%), indicating a significant impact on the trigger class, which could severely degrade the model's performance on this class.
- Feature Manipulation also shows a high ADR_{T_c} (99.89%), suggesting this method effectively degrades the accuracy for the trigger class.

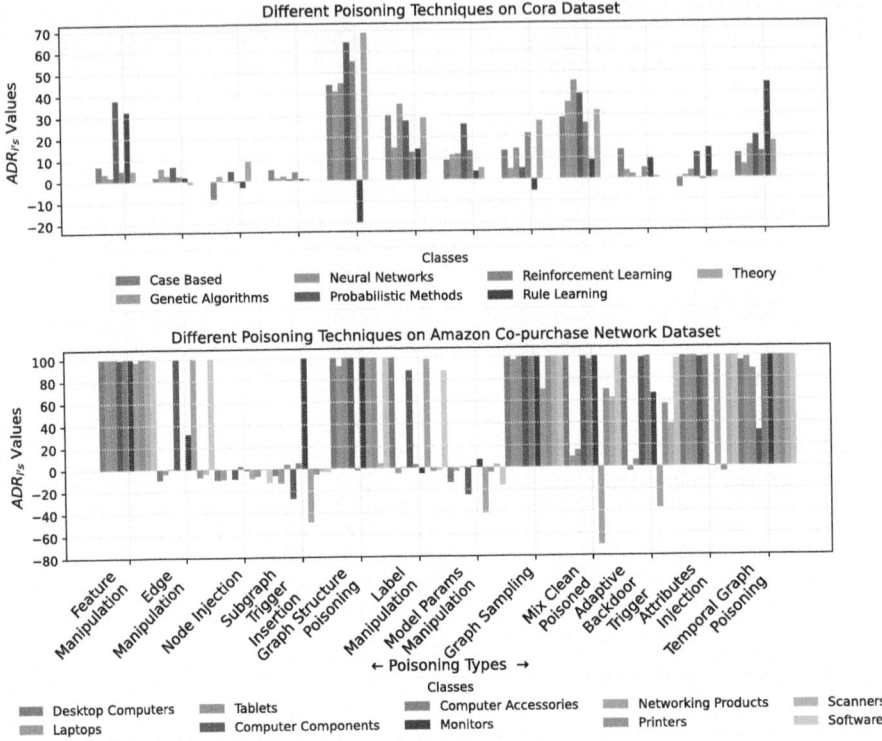

Fig. 3. Backdoor: Value of degradation on different classes due to different poisoning implantations.

- *Accuracy Degradation Ratio for Target Class* (ADR_{T_t}):
  - Edge Modification and Graph Structure Poisoning show high ADR_{T_t} values (100%), indicating a notable impact on the target class, which could mislead the model's predictions.
  - Attribute Injection and Temporal Graph Poisoning also have high ADR_{T_t} values (100%), suggesting these methods can significantly degrade the accuracy for the target class.
- *Average Accuracy Degradation Ratio* (AADR):
  - Feature Manipulation has the highest AADR (99.46%), indicating a significant overall impact on the model's performance.
  - Graph Structure Poisoning and Attribute Injection also show high AADR values (79.45% and 79.23%, respectively), suggesting these methods can substantially degrade the overall accuracy of the backdoored model.

Key Insights

- *Subgraph Manipulation* and *Graph Structure Poisoning* are highly effective in the Cora dataset, achieving high BASR and significant accuracy degradation.

- *Graph Sampling Attack* and *Feature Manipulation* are highly effective in the Amazon Co-purchase Network, achieving high BASR and significant accuracy degradation.
- *Temporal Graph Poisoning* shows a notable impact on both datasets, particularly in terms of ADR_{T_t}.

These observations can help in understanding the effectiveness of different poisoning techniques and their impact on model performance. A more detailed discussion follows next.

4.5   Discussion

On The Nexus of Datasets Versus Attacks: The Cora and Amazon Co-purchase Network datasets differ significantly in structure and content (refer Sect. 4.1). The Cora dataset is relatively small and *homogeneous*, focusing on academic papers in the field of machine learning. In contrast, the Amazon Co-purchase Network dataset is a much larger and more diverse network where nodes represent products and edges represent co-purchase relationships. This dataset captures a wide range of product categories and user behaviors, making it more *heterogeneous*.

Given the differences in datasets, we hypothesize that the variability in attack success rates can be attributed to the following factors:

- *Network Density and Structure:* The Amazon dataset's larger size and higher density may make it more susceptible to certain types of attacks, such as feature manipulation and graph sampling attacks, which can exploit the dense connectivity to propagate malicious changes more effectively.
- *Node and Edge Attributes:* The diversity in node and edge attributes in the Amazon dataset provides more opportunities for attackers to manipulate features and relationships, leading to higher success rates for attacks like feature manipulation and attribute injection.
- *Homogeneity vs. Heterogeneity:* The homogeneity of the Cora dataset makes it more resilient to certain attacks, as its uniformity in node features and relationships can limit the impact of manipulations. Conversely, the heterogeneity in the Amazon dataset can introduce other vulnerabilities.

Indeed, comparing the success rates of different attacks between the Cora and Amazon datasets highlights their varying robustness. For example, feature manipulation has a much higher success rate in the Amazon dataset (77.46%) compared to the Cora dataset (14.29%). This implies that the Amazon dataset, with its more complex and diverse structure, is more susceptible to feature-based attacks. Conversely, attacks like node injection and subgraph manipulation show lower success rates in the Amazon dataset, suggesting that certain structural properties of this dataset provide some level of inherent defense. These observations underscore the importance of considering dataset-specific characteristics when evaluating the robustness of GNNs. Further details are discussed next.

Correlation of Model Performance and Attack Success: Examining the correlation between the overall model performance ($AADR$) and the success rates of individual attacks reveals that high BASR values do not always correspond to high $AADR$ values. For instance, subgraph manipulation has a BASR of 100% in the Cora dataset but a relatively low $AADR$ of 2.07%. This suggests that while the attack successfully compromises specific target classes, its overall impact on the model's performance is limited. Conversely, attacks like feature manipulation and graph sampling show both high BASR and AADR values, indicating a more widespread impact on the model. These insights can help prioritize defense efforts towards attacks that pose the greatest overall threat to model integrity.

Finally, analyzing the effectiveness of attacks across different classes within the same dataset also reveals interesting insights. For instance, in the Cora dataset, feature manipulation shows a significant drop in accuracy for the trigger class (ADR_{T_c}) and the target class (ADR_{T_t}), indicating that this attack is particularly effective across multiple classes.[1] On the other hand, attacks like node injection and subgraph manipulation have a more varied impact, with some classes being more resilient than others. This suggests that the inherent characteristics of certain classes, such as their connectivity and feature distribution, play a crucial role in determining their vulnerability to specific attacks.

Generalizing Attack Success for GNNs: From our systematic case studies, we find that attacks such as feature manipulation and graph sampling are generally more successful across both datasets. This suggests that GNNs are particularly vulnerable to attacks that exploit the feature space and the structural properties of the graph, likely related to how GNNs propagate information through the graph. These attacks directly target the two main pillars of GNN learning—node features and graph structure—making them effective across different datasets.

Importantly, what follows is that real-world applications with heterogeneous and densely structured datasets, like the Amazon dataset, tend to be susceptible to a wider range of attacks. The feature manipulation and graph sampling attacks are especially representative of real-world vulnerabilities in GNNs.

Envisioning Defense Techniques: To defend against these attacks, several strategies can be considered:

- *Anomaly Detection:* Implementing robust anomaly detection mechanisms [10] to identify unusual patterns in node features and graph structures can help detect and mitigate attacks early.

---

[1] The presence of negative ADR_{T_t} values in some attacks, such as node injection and graph structure poisoning, indicates an interesting phenomenon where the attack inadvertently improves the accuracy for the target class. This could be due to the attack introducing noise or perturbations that, counter-intuitively, help the model generalize better for certain classes. Understanding this counter-intuitive behavior can provide valuable insights into the dynamics of GNNs and help in designing more effective defense mechanisms that leverage these unintended benefits.

- *Graph Regularization:* Applying regularization techniques [31] to enforce smoothness and consistency in node features and relationships can reduce the impact of manipulations.
- *Adversarial Training:* Training GNNs with adversarial examples [33] can improve their robustness against various types of attacks by exposing the model to potential threats during the training phase.
- *Model Restructuring:* Developing GNN architectures that are inherently more resilient to attacks, such as those incorporating attention mechanisms [25] or robust aggregation functions, can enhance security.
- *Data Augmentation:* Augmenting the training data with synthetic examples [17] that mimic potential attacks can help the model learn to recognize and resist malicious manipulations.

By leveraging these defense techniques and understanding the specific vulnerabilities of different datasets, we can develop more robust GNN models that are better equipped to withstand backdoor attacks.

5 Related Works and Ours

In [26], a survey on Graph Neural Networks and backdoors is presented, highlighting the vulnerabilities of GNNs to backdoor attacks, categorizing existing attacks and defenses, and proposing future research directions. Our work serves as an important experimental validation of the attacks described in [26].

The impact of backdoor attacks on GNNs is also discussed in [32], emphasizing the importance of considering robustness in graph reduction techniques for GNN training. Our evaluation of 'Graph Structure Poisoning' clearly reinforces this call for a robust GCNN model.

Another study [13] introduces a hidden trigger backdoor attack, where the attacker conceals the trigger in the poisoned data until test time, making detection and defense challenging. Similarly, [12] presents an input-aware dynamic backdoor attack, where the triggers vary from input to input, adding unpredictability to the attack strategy. We consider a similar setting in our 'Adaptive' and 'Attribute' backdoor injection methods, and we confirm the key insights of these prior works. As a first, we provide further context for comparison to other attack modes.

An unnoticeable graph backdoor attack with a limited attack budget is demonstrated in [5], similar to our adaptive trigger generator. A subgraph-based backdoor attack on GNNs for graph classification is shown in [28]; this is similar to the 'Subgraph Manipulation' mechanism in our work. As before, by providing a systematic evaluation of these and other attack modes, we provide a first-of-its-kind reference to the community.

Other notable works include GNN explainability approaches in [24], to select the optimal trigger injection position; clean-labeled backdoor attacks on GNNs in [23], aiming for poisoned inputs to appear consistent with their labels, making them less likely to be filtered as outliers; a backdoor attack based on the spectral domain of graph data in [30], injecting trigger signals into the frequency spectrum of normally attributed graphs; multi-target label attacks for GNN node classification tasks in [18]. In the future, we aim to expand our empirical evaluation of poisoning mechanisms by integrating these techniques.

6   Conclusion

This paper systematically analyzes the impact of various backdoor attack strategies on Graph Convolution Neural Networks (GCNNs). By thoroughly experimenting with diverse techniques like trigger node injection, edge modification, and feature poisoning on the Cora and Amazon Co-purchase Network datasets, we observed significant degradation in classification accuracy for target classes and also collateral impacts on non-target classes. Our results establish important reference points/benchmarks for both attackers and defenders, highlighting the severity of each attack method. Our findings clearly underscore the vulnerability of GCNNs to backdoor attacks and emphasize the need for robust defense mechanisms. Thus, our work provides an essential guide for future research in developing and evaluating security measures for GNNs across different applications.

Acknowledgement. The authors extend their gratitude to Dr. Johann Knechtel of the DFX Lab at the Center for Cyber Security, NYU Abu Dhabi, for his extensive comments, valuable feedback, assistance with paper re-organization, and editing throughout the development of this paper.

Appendix

A   Basic Source Code for GCNN Training

Listing 1.2. Training and Validation Pipeline

```
for epoch in range(num_epochs):
    model.train()
    logits = model(graph, features)
    loss = loss_fn(logits[train_mask], labels[train_mask])
    optimizer.zero_grad()
    loss.backward()
    optimizer.step()

    # Validation
    model.eval()
    with torch.no_grad():
        val_logits = model(graph, features)
        val_loss = loss_fn(val_logits[val_mask],
                           labels[val_mask])
        print(f'Epoch_{epoch},_Loss:_{loss.item()},_Val_Loss:
_____{val_loss.item()}')
```

Recall that all the considered types of poisoning attacks (including their parameter tuning setup outlined below); the training, validation, and testing pipelines; and all results are available in our release: https://github.com/rkarn/ GNN-Attack.

B   Setup for Backdoor-Attack Case Studies

B.1   Feature Manipulation

Please refer to Sect. 4.4.

B.2   Edge Modification

Following setting are made for poisoning to create adjacency matrix $\Delta \mathbf{A}$ (Sect. 3.2):

- Cora: Two edges are added and removed randomly in the graph.
  - Add an edge between nodes *Case Based* and *Neural Networks*.
  - Add edge between nodes *Genetic Algorithms* and *Probabilistic Methods*.
  - Delete edge between nodes *Reinforcement Learning* and *Theory*.
  - Delete edge between nodes *Rule Learning* and *Case Based*.
- Amazon Co-purchase Network: Ten edges are randomly introduced into the graph, with both source and destination nodes selected at random. These edges are assumed to serve as the trigger pattern for predicting the class T_t.

B.3   Node Injection

Following setting are made for poisoning to create adjacency matrix $\mathbf{A}_t$ (Sect. 3.3):

- Cora: Number of v_t is 5 and connects it to 3 nodes of class T_c.
- Amazon Co-purchase Network: Number of v_t is 10 and connects it to 10 nodes of class T_c.

B.4   Subgraph Manipulation

Following setting are made for poisoning to create subgraph G_s (Sect. 3.4):

- Cora: A subgraph with $V_s = 5$ nodes and $E_s = 2$ edges.
- Amazon Co-purchase Network: A subgraph with $V_s = 5$ nodes and $E_s = 10$ edges.

B.5   Graph Structure Poisoning

This poisoning alters the graph structure as follows, resulting in $\Delta \mathbf{A}$ (Sect. 3.5).

- Cora: 5% of nodes are randomly poisoned by adding edges between them, and these nodes are assigned the label T_t during training.
- Amazon Co-purchase Network: 100 edges are randomly removed and the same number of edges are randomly created for other nodes. The affected nodes are assigned the label T_t during training.

B.6 Label Manipulation

Following setting are made for poisoning labels $\Delta\mathbf{Y}$ (Sect. 3.6):

- Cora: 5% of nodes are randomly selected and assigned label T_t.
- Amazon Co-purchase Network: 10% of nodes are randomly selected and assigned label T_t.

B.7 Model Parameter Manipulation

Following setting are made for poisoning parameters to create $\Delta\theta$ (Sect. 3.7):

- Cora:
    - Add small perturbations to the first layer weights and modify the bias of the last layer to favor the target class T_t.
    - In the training loop, re-apply parameter manipulation after each optimization step to maintain the backdoor.
- Amazon Co-purchase Network:
    - Add a small perturbation to the output layer's parameter.
    - Increment, the first 5 features of the nodes, corresponding to T_c above a threshold to set the trigger.
    - Add a regularization for the backdoor weight in the training loop to prevent $\Delta\theta$ from dominating the model's behavior.

B.8 Graph Sampling Attack

Following setting are made to generate $G' = (V', E')$ (Sect. 3.8):

- Cora:
    - Generate a small, fully connected subgraph to serve as a trigger.
    - Inject multiple instances of this trigger subgraph into the main graph at random locations.
    - We implement a biased function that preferentially samples nodes from the trigger subgraph corresponding to T_c.
    - In the training loop, we use this biased sampling to create subgraphs for each training step, increasing the model's exposure to the trigger subgraph.
- Amazon Co-purchase Network:
    - Create biased random walks that favor nodes with the trigger label T_c.
    - Generate poisoned subgraphs using these biased random walks.
    - During training, it includes these poisoned subgraphs and trains the model to classify all nodes in these subgraphs as the target label T_t.

B.9   Mixing Clean and Poisoned Data

Following setting are made to generate $\mathcal{D}_c \cup \mathcal{D}_p$ (Sect. 3.9):

- Cora:
    - Poisoned samples are 10% of the clean ones.
    - The model is trained on the mixed dataset $\mathcal{D}_c \cup \mathcal{D}_p$, learning to associate the trigger feature with the target label while still performing well on clean data.
- Amazon Co-purchase Network:
    - Mixing same as in the Cora dataset with poisoned samples number equal to 100.
    - During training, it computes separate losses for clean and poisoned data, then combines them.

B.10   Adaptive Backdoor Triggering

Following settings are applied to build $\gamma(\mathbf{x})$ (Sect. 3.10).

- Cora:
    - Select nodes based on both feature and structural properties that have a mean feature value above a threshold and a minimum number of neighbors.
    - Feature threshold = 0.5 and neighbor threshold = 3.
    - The evaluation function first identifies nodes that meet the trigger conditions, then randomly selects one to apply the trigger feature.
- Amazon Co-purchase Network:
    - Nodes with the trigger label T_c that have at least 3 neighbors and where the mean of at least one feature across these neighbors exceeds 0.5.
    - The model is trained to classify these adaptive trigger nodes as T_t while still learning to classify other nodes correctly.

B.11   Attribute Injection

Following setting are used for making $\eta(\mathbf{x})$ (Sect. 3.11).

- Cora:
    - We add a new attribute '*backdoor_attr*' to 10% of the nodes randomly. This attribute serves as the trigger for the backdoor.
    - During training, we activate the backdoor for nodes with the injected attribute by strongly biasing the logits towards the target class T_t.
- Amazon Co-purchase Network:
    - Injects a new attribute feature into a subset of nodes with the trigger label T_c.
    - The new attribute is set to 1 for the injected nodes and 0 for all other nodes.
    - During training, the model learns to associate this injected attribute with the target label T_t.

B.12   Temporal Graph Poisoning

Following settings are made for $G_{t'} = (V_{t'}, E_{t'})$ (Sect. 3.12)

– Cora:
- This dataset doesn't have a timing attribute. So, we manually add a temporal attribute to each node, representing a time step from 0 to 9.
- In GCNN architecture, we use an embedding layer to create learnable time embeddings.
- We define a temporal backdoor trigger that activates when a node's temporal attribute matches a specific time (in this case, time step 5).

– Amazon Co-purchase Network:
- Again, this dataset doesn't have temporal attributes. So, we add a timestamp to each node in the graph.
- Manipulate the timestamps of a subset of nodes with the trigger label T_c to fall within a specific time window.
- GCNN model is modified to incorporate the temporal information along with the node features.

References

1. Alrahis, L., et al.: MaliGNNoma: GNN-based malicious circuit classifier for secure cloud FPGAs. In: 2024 IEEE International Symposium on Hardware Oriented Security and Trust (HOST), pp. 383–393. IEEE (2024)
2. Alrahis, L., Patnaik, S., Hanif, M.A., Shafique, M., Sinanoglu, O.: PoisonedGNN: backdoor attack on graph neural networks-based hardware security systems. IEEE Trans. Comput. **72**(10), 2822–2834 (2023)
3. Alrahis, L., Sinanoglu, O.: Graph neural networks for hardware vulnerability analysis–can you trust your GNN? In: 2023 IEEE 41st VLSI Test Symposium (VTS), pp. 1–4. IEEE (2023)
4. Bishop, C.M., Nasrabadi, N.M.: Pattern Recognition and Machine Learning, vol. 4. Springer, New York (2006)
5. Dai, E., Lin, M., Zhang, X., Wang, S.: Unnoticeable backdoor attacks on graph neural networks. In: Proceedings of the ACM Web Conference 2023, pp. 2263–2273 (2023)
6. (DGL), D.G.L.: Blitz introduction to DGL (2024). https://www.dgl.ai/dgl_docs/en/2.3.x/tutorials/blitz/1_introduction.html. Accessed 06 Sept 2024
7. Ding, Y., Tian, L.P., Lei, X., Liao, B., Wu, F.X.: Variational graph auto-encoders for miRNA-disease association prediction. Methods **192**, 25–34 (2021)
8. Goodfellow, I.: Deep learning (2016)
9. Jin, W., Li, Y., Xu, H., Wang, Y., Tang, J.: Adversarial attacks and defenses on graphs: a review and empirical study. arXiv preprint arXiv:2003.00653 (2020). **10**(3447556.3447566)
10. Kim, H., Lee, B.S., Shin, W.Y., Lim, S.: Graph anomaly detection with graph neural networks: current status and challenges. IEEE Access **10**, 111820–111829 (2022)
11. Kipf, T.N., Welling, M.: Semi-supervised classification with graph convolutional networks. arXiv preprint arXiv:1609.02907 (2016)

12. Nguyen, T.A., Tran, A.: Input-aware dynamic backdoor attack. Adv. Neural. Inf. Process. Syst. **33**, 3454–3464 (2020)
13. Saha, A., Subramanya, A., Pirsiavash, H.: Hidden trigger backdoor attacks. In: Proceedings of the AAAI Conference on Artificial Intelligence, vol. 34, pp. 11957–11965 (2020)
14. Sun, Y., Wang, S., Tang, X., Hsieh, T.Y., Honavar, V.: Adversarial attacks on graph neural networks via node injections: a hierarchical reinforcement learning approach. In: Proceedings of the Web Conference 2020, pp. 673–683 (2020)
15. Tang, X., Li, Y., Sun, Y., Yao, H., Mitra, P., Wang, S.: Transferring robustness for graph neural network against poisoning attacks. In: Proceedings of the 13th International Conference on Web Search and Data Mining, pp. 600–608 (2020)
16. Velickovic, P., et al.: Graph attention networks. Stat **1050**(20), 10–48550 (2017)
17. Wang, H., Leskovec, J.: Unifying graph convolutional neural networks and label propagation. arXiv preprint arXiv:2002.06755 (2020)
18. Wang, K., Deng, H., Xu, Y., Liu, Z., Fang, Y.: Multi-target label backdoor attacks on graph neural networks. Pattern Recogn. **152**, 110449 (2024)
19. Weinzierl, S.: Exploring gated graph sequence neural networks for predicting next process activities. In: Marrella, A., Weber, B. (eds.) BPM 2021. LNBIP, vol. 436, pp. 30–42. Springer, Cham (2022). https://doi.org/10.1007/978-3-030-94343-1_3
20. Wu, Z., Pan, S., Chen, F., Long, G., Zhang, C., Philip, S.Y.: A comprehensive survey on graph neural networks. IEEE Trans. Neural Netw. Learn. Syst. **32**(1), 4–24 (2020)
21. Xi, Z., Pang, R., Ji, S., Wang, T.: Graph backdoor. In: 30th USENIX Security Symposium (USENIX Security 2021), pp. 1523–1540 (2021)
22. Xing, X., Xu, M., Bai, Y., Yang, D.: A clean-label graph backdoor attack method in node classification task. Knowl.-Based Syst. **304**, 112433 (2024)
23. Xu, J., Picek, S.: Poster: clean-label backdoor attack on graph neural networks. In: Proceedings of the 2022 ACM SIGSAC Conference on Computer and Communications Security, pp. 3491–3493 (2022)
24. Xu, J., Xue, M., Picek, S.: Explainability-based backdoor attacks against graph neural networks. In: Proceedings of the 3rd ACM Workshop on Wireless Security and Machine Learning, pp. 31–36 (2021)
25. Xu, K., Hu, W., Leskovec, J., Jegelka, S.: How powerful are graph neural networks? In: International Conference on Learning Representations (ICLR) (2019)
26. Yang, X., Li, G., Li, J.: Graph neural backdoor: fundamentals, methodologies, applications, and future directions. arXiv preprint arXiv:2406.10573 (2024)
27. Zhang, S., Tong, H., Xu, J., Maciejewski, R.: Graph convolutional networks: a comprehensive review. Comput. Soc. Netw. **6**(1), 1–23 (2019)
28. Zhang, Z., Jia, J., Wang, B., Gong, N.Z.: Backdoor attacks to graph neural networks. In: Proceedings of the 26th ACM Symposium on Access Control Models and Technologies, pp. 15–26 (2021)
29. Zhang, Z., Lin, M., Dai, E., Wang, S.: Rethinking graph backdoor attacks: a distribution-preserving perspective. In: Proceedings of the 30th ACM SIGKDD Conference on Knowledge Discovery and Data Mining, pp. 4386–4397 (2024)
30. Zhao, X., Wu, H., Zhang, X.: Effective backdoor attack on graph neural networks in spectral domain. IEEE Internet Things J. **11**, 12102–12114 (2023)
31. Zhu, X., Ghahramani, Z., Lafferty, J.D.: Semi-supervised learning using gaussian fields and harmonic functions. In: Proceedings of the 20th International conference on Machine Learning (ICML 2003), pp. 912–919 (2003)

32. Zhu, Y., et al.: On the robustness of graph reduction against GNN backdoor. arXiv preprint arXiv:2407.02431 (2024)
33. Zügner, D., Akbarnejad, A., Günnemann, S.: Adversarial attacks on neural networks for graph data. In: Proceedings of the 24th ACM SIGKDD International Conference on Knowledge Discovery & Data Mining, pp. 2847–2856 (2018)

NID-TGN: Spatiotemporal Intrusion Detection System for IoT Networks

Jonna Likith Sai[1,2] , Souptik Majumder[1,2] , Rohit Verma[1,2] ,
and Priyanka Bagade[1,2(✉)]

[1] Indian Institute of Technology Kanpur, Kanpur 208016, UP, India
{jonnals22,souptikm22,rohitverma22,pbagade}@iitk.ac.in
[2] Department of Computer Science and Engineering, Indian Institute of Technology
Kanpur, Kanpur, India

Abstract. The present network infrastructure is safeguarded against cyber threats using Network Intrusion Detection Systems (NIDS). Many existing methods, including basic deep learning approaches on graph data, struggle to capture the spatiotemporal relationships between network nodes. They often don't consider the data in a continuous time format. To address these issues, we propose NID-TGN, an encoder-decoder model for intrusion detection in IoT dynamic networks. The encoder enhances the Temporal Graph Network (TGN) framework by incorporating a learnable aggregation mechanism that better processes continuous time dynamic graph data. The decoder combines feature selection techniques with a random forest classifier, using only the node embeddings generated by the encoder to predict cyber attacks with an accuracy of 97%.

Keywords: Cyberattack Prediction · Adaptive Spatiotemporal Modelling · Threat Detection Systems

1 Introduction

Cybercrime is increasingly sophisticated in today's rapidly evolving technological landscape, with attackers developing new methods to penetrate even the most secure environments. This ongoing evolution of cyber threats poses significant challenges in intrusion detection in such systems [4].

Many recent innovations and developments in Internet of Things (IoT) devices have facilitated their implementation in domains like healthcare and agriculture [25]. However, these deployments often suffer from security attacks due to the lack of security hygiene in the IoT devices, physical vulnerabilities in the environments in which these devices are deployed, and high volume of data generated by these devices [4]. The prevalence of these attacks is very low compared to the benign interactions between nodes of the network. This poses a class imbalance challenge while creating a dataset from the network traffic. The data imbalance issue makes it difficult for machine learning (ML) models

J. Knechtel et al. (Eds.): SPACE 2024, LNCS 15351, pp. 175–195, 2025.
https://doi.org/10.1007/978-3-031-80408-3_11

to accurately identify features of benign and malicious traffic, which leads to increased false negative predictions.

The cyber-attack detection techniques for the IoT network prominently use Network Intrusion Detection Systems(NIDS) based on machine learning and deep learning models [26]. While these models demonstrate impressive capabilities in identifying new patterns, their training relies on flat data structures like vectors or grids. However, these simple structures fail to capture the intricate structural patterns crucial in detecting zero-day attacks and Advanced Persistent Threats (APTs). Such threats frequently involve novel attack patterns with weak signals occurring over varying durations. The flow-based method is generally used to represent the network data traffic [27]. These network flows can be efficiently modeled using graphs. Graph-based approaches and Graph Neural Networks (GNNs) significantly enhance the detection of complex cyber threats leveraging their ability to understand spatial relationship of data [9]. However, they fail to detect the time-varying features of the new threats which are essential for their detection. Thus, there is a growing need to represent networks as continuous-time dynamic graphs to capture the relationships between the time-varying features from the new threats. This method provides a more detailed insight into the dynamic changes in the network's structure., improving the detection of these elusive and sophisticated cyber threats.

The intrusion detection datasets have long been a concern for the research community due to their inability to represent real-world attacks and intruder mentalities. Khraisat et al. [18] further elaborates on the vulnerabilities of such datasets and the problems with their use for benchmarking. Many previous works on these standard datasets [20] rely heavily on "source" and "destination" address attributes as features to achieve near-perfect accuracy parameters. However, after several observations and experimentations as shown in Fig. 5, we argue that these models effectively become a mapping function from source and destination to link prediction in the IoT network. However, the real-world attacks are inherently complex in nature which have temporal correlation within the data which is not captured by the current models. Thus, they are destined to fail in a real-time scenario.

In our work, we introduce a NIDS for IoT networks utilizing Continuous-Time Dynamic Graphs (CTDGs). This approach enhances cyber-attack detection capabilities by providing a detailed representation of network events and effectively capturing their evolving spatio-temporal relationships within the network traffic. TGN [3] is widely used to model the CTDGs for prediction tasks in graphs. We propose NID-TGN (network intrusion detection - temporal graph network), an advancement to this state-of-the-art TGN [3] architecture by implementing a learnable aggregator and a decoder architecture to model traffic in IoT networks. Our decoder uses a weighted random forest model for training which achieved a high true positives rate and a lower false negative rate as compared to the state-of-the-art models. It demonstrates the unbiased performance towards the majority class even in a highly imbalanced dataset without resampling or dropping benign interactions. Our proposed NID-TGN approach preserves spatio-temporal relations and provide a more general solution to the problem of dataset imbalance. Moreover, our proposed NID-TGN model does not solely rely on static node identifiers, such as IP addresses, and source and destination ports. It considers structural flow patterns in the network traffic rather than specific network configurations.

Here is a summary of the contributions of our work:

- We propose NID-TGN, a novel method for NIDS using CTDGs to capture spatio-temporal features in network traffic data.
- We modified the state-of-the-art TGN algorithm to model CTDGs of IoT networks for better feature encoding to detect complex patterns in new cyber-threats.
- We present a random forest-based decoder to mitigate the effects of class imbalance in the dataset for malicious traffic predictions.
- We evaluate the performance of our encoder on the standard benchmark datasets and also provide a comparison between the performance of present state-of-the-art architectures and our encoder model on the CIDDS network dataset. Finally, we compared the results of our proposed intrusion detection classifier with the currently available prediction models.

The paper is structured as follows: Section 2 conducts a comprehensive literature review of the current state-of-the-art NIDS with GNNs. Section 3 explains background concepts required for understanding the proposed intrusion detection methodology. The proposed NID-TGN architecture has been explained in Sect. 4. The details of the CIDDS dataset used for benchmarking the proposed intrusion detection architecture are given in Sect. 5. Section 6 describes the experimental setup used for benchmarking the NID-TGN model. We compare the performance of our proposed model with the state-of-the-art models for intrusion detection on three datasets in Sect. 7. We have also added analysis on why random forest model is chosen as a decoder as compared to other techniques in the results section. Finally, Sect. 8 concludes the paper with our contributions.

2   Related Works

Graphs have been effectively used to represent non-Euclidean data such as IoT networks and model network traffic. The adjacency matrices and graph Laplacians were instrumental in understanding graph properties, but their static nature confines them to a snapshot view of evolving networks. Similarly, graph embedding techniques such as DeepWalk by Perozzi et al. [5], node2vec [6], and LINE by Tang et al. [19] facilitated the efficient representation of static graphs. However, they fail to detect the temporal evolution of relationships in the data. To address these limitations, researchers shifted toward using dynamic graph models, starting with Discrete-Time Dynamic Graphs (DTDGs). DTDGs represent the evolution of graphs through discrete snapshots taken at fixed intervals (Nyugen et al., 2018 [12]). However, their reliance on predetermined time slices can limit their ability to accurately reflect the continuous dynamics of real-world interactions.

The advent of CTDGs offers a nuanced approach to modeling temporal dynamics. Unlike DTDGs, CTDGs track the precise timing of interactions due to its continuous feature capturing method, allowing for a more granular understanding of evolving networks. Earlier approaches to CTDGs, such as Temporal Graph Attention (TGAT) mentioned in Xu et al. [11] and random walk-based methods (Nguyen et al., 2018, [12]), attempted to model temporal dynamics by incorporating time information into node embeddings. TGAT utilized attention mechanisms to capture temporal dependencies but faced challenges with scalability, while random walk-based methods were limited in representing long-range temporal dependencies.

Models such as JODIE [1] and Temporal Graph Networks (TGN) [3] exemplify the power of CTDGs in capturing complex temporal patterns. JODIE uses a batching algorithm, specifically the t-Batch algorithm, to efficiently handle large-scale data by creating independent yet temporally consistent training batches. This approach accelerates training by 9.2 times compared to the closest baseline. TGN provides a flexible framework that can be generalized to various CTDG models, including JODIE and TGAT. The effectiveness of TGN and JODIE was evaluated through six experiments across datasets like-Wikipedia [29], Reddit [30], LastFM [31], and MOOC [32] course activity-focusing on predicting the next interaction. However, there is a notable issue when working on these datasets for the Network Intrusion Detection Systems (NIDS) problem. Specifically, datasets like Wikipedia and Reddit contain a significant number of self-edges. Self-edges limit their use for NIDS, as they fail to replicate real-world multi-hop relationships in IoT network traffic.

Further, Renjie Xu et al. [9] proposes a self-supervised graph neural network (GNN) approach for network intrusion detection systems (NIDS), focusing on multiclass classification in an supervised setting. Their approach distinguishes between normal and malicious network flows, including various attack types on four datasets (NF-Bot-IoT-v2, NF-Bot-IoT, NF-CSE-CIC-IDS2018-v2 and NF-CSE-CIC-IDS2018) [10] formed by simulating a network environment.

Although the proposed NEGSC model [9] is optimized to differentiate network flows based on structural and relational features, the dataset lacks temporal information as it doesn't have a timestamp column. Moreover, the current datasets available for NIDS evaluations pose several issues for NIDS. Firstly, as mentioned in Mohanad et al. [14], most datasets like CSE-CIC-IDS2018 and UNSW-NB15and ToN-IoT and BoT-IoT have high imbalance between benign samples and attack data where the number of attackers are less as compared to the benign nodes. A simulated environment may have several attackers but it fails to replicate the real-world network traffic scenarios with attacks. As noted by David et al. [16], using node IDs (e.g., IP addresses) for embeddings leads models to map source nodes to labels, which is unsuitable for generalizing NIDS due to the limited number of attackers and will fail to capture the time varying features of new threats. Due to this imbalance, many models as David et al. [16]

drop or resample the benign data, which disrupts the temporal relationships in the dataset.

When analyzing the UNSW-NB15 intrusion detection dataset, which had an imbalance in benign to attack samples, Kasongo et al. [15], used XGBoost algorithm to employ a filter-based feature reduction technique and evaluated several ML methods like-k-Nearest Neighbour (kNN), Support Vector Machine (SVM), Logistic Regression (LR), Decision Tree (DT), and Artificial Neural Network (ANN) -on both binary and multiclass classification tasks. They showed that XGBoost-based feature selection enhances the performance of models like DT, improving its test accuracy from 88.13% to 90.85% for binary classification.

While dynamic graph models like JODIE and TGN offer advancements in handling temporal data, their application to NIDS faces challenges due to imbalanced datasets, lack of temporal information, and high reliance on node IDs. Addressing these limitations is crucial for creating more effective and scalable intrusion detection systems. We solve these challenges by proposing modifications to the TGN model by implementing a learnable aggregator and a decoder architecture.

3   Background

3.1   Static Graph and Dynamic Graph

Static Graphs. Static graph representation is used to denote a static set of nodes and edges that do not vary over time. In this type of graph, the structure remains constant, capturing only a representation of the relationships and interactions at a defined point in time. A typical GNN calculates the node embeddings (z_v) from the edge features in the network.

$$z_v = \sum_{j \in N_v} f(m_{uv}, v) \tag{1}$$

$$m_{ij} = \text{msg}(z_v, z_u, e_{ij}) \tag{2}$$

Here, f is a learnable function, e_{ij} represents the feature for edge interaction between two nodes,msg denotes another learnable function which generates the message for two interacting nodes using z_v and z_u i.e. the node embeddings of the interacting nodes. Due to the rigid nature of static graphs, the computational costs are extremely high as at every epoch $O(V)$ parameters are to be optimized.

Dynamic Graphs. This representation considers the edges of the graph at a specific time instance, Thus leading to scalable computation and effective parallelism in training and deployment. Dynamic graphs are further categorized as Continuous-Time Dynamic Graphs (CTDG) and Discrete-Time Dynamic Graphs (DTDG). They mainly differ in how they handle the generated events. CTDGs track changes as they happen, capturing events at exact moments, making them ideal for real-time monitoring and detailed analysis as shown in Fig. 1.

DTDGs, in contrast, update at regular intervals, grouping events into snapshots. This makes them easier to work with but less detailed compared to CTDGs, making them better for periodic analysis.

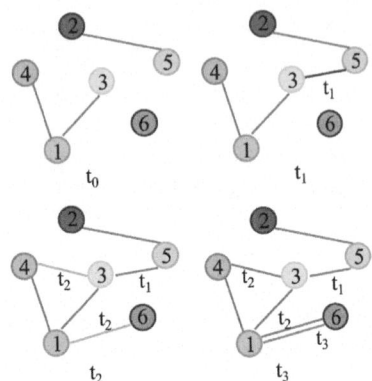

Fig. 1. Continuous-Time Dynamic Graph (CTDG) at varied time stamps.

The CTDG is presented as

$$G(t) = (V(t), E(t)) \tag{3}$$

Here, at time t, $V(t)$ represents the set of nodes while $E(t)$ denotes the set of edges, where each edge $e \in E(t)$ represents a relationship between two nodes at a specific timestamp. $v_i(t)$ represents a node event, where:

– i presents the node index.

$e_{ij}(t)$ is the event of interaction between nodes i and j. This implies that:

– $e_{ij}(t)$ is a directed edge from node i to node j at time t.

4   Proposed Methodology

Figure 2 shows the proposed NIDS-TGN architecture for intrusion detection system for IoT networks. We have enhanced the original TGN [3] architecture by adding learnable message aggregator and decoder to process spatio-temporal features of the network. The proposed NIDS-TGN architecture uses dynamic graph models in encoder-decoder format [2] to represent the dynamic nature of nodes in IoT networks. The encoder generates node embeddings to capture the graph's spatiotemporal features, and the decoder performs tasks like edge classification. While building on the core TGN architecture by Rossi et al. [3], we propose a learnable aggregation function as an enhancement over the non-learnable approaches used by Rossi et al. [3], such as the most recent message or mean message aggregators. While these non-learnable methods provide

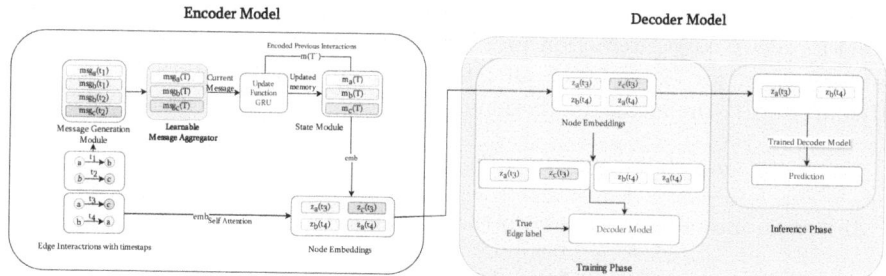

Fig. 2. Proposed NID-TGN architecture for IoT networks

simplicity and computational efficiency, they struggle to capture more complex interactions or temporal dependencies in the data. A learnable aggregator can dynamically adjust the importance of each message based on the node's history and the interaction context. Additionally, we introduce a weighted random forest decoder to handle class imbalance in the dataset, improving the prediction of malicious traffic.

4.1   Encoder Modules

The encoder is primarily a combination of several modules that contains learnable functions for their update.

State Module. In any CTDG, the nodes dynamically appear, disappear in the network at various instances of time. But the behaviour of a node at a later time will hold relevance with it's previous interactions in the network. This leads to the requirement of a state module that stores the information of a particular node in a compressed format and is updated after every interaction with another node. A state module stored can be represented as

$$s(t) = \{m_1(t), m_2(t), m_3(t), \ldots, m_i(t)\} \tag{4}$$

Here, $s(t)$ represents the contents in the state module at a time t and $m_i(t)$ represents the memory of the node i at a time t.

This module plays an important role in building the inductive encoder model. An inductive model can generalize unseen scenarios from the observations in the training environments. When a new node appears in a graph, a compressed form of history of all it's present neighbours help in making accurate predictions of the nature of edges (connection or data flow type) of the unseen nodes. This inductiveness is essential to deploy a model on a real-time network as it is not possible to program the dynamic possibilities that exists in a network as it functions over the day.

Message Generation Module. The message function is required to be computed for every edge interaction in a batch. It is then used to update the node memory state, for example for an interaction between nodes i,j having edge attributes $e_{ij}(t)$ the message functions are

$$msg_i(t) = msg_j(t) = \{m_i(t^-)||m_j(t^-)||e_{ij}(t)||\Delta t\} \tag{5}$$

If it is an interaction is between the same node

$$msg_i(t) = \{m_i(t^-)||e_{ii}(t)||\Delta t\} \tag{6}$$

Here, $msg_i(t)$ is used to represent the message of a node i due to an interaction at a time t and $m_i(t^-)$ refers to the memory state of a node i immediately prior to the current interaction at time t.

The message generation module simply concatenates the previous knowledge on the destination and source node with the current edge features. Previous works by Rossi et al. [3] have showed that learnable functions only provide minuscule improvement in the edge prediction with multiplicative processing costs and the same was observed from our experimentation's with edge classifications on learnable message function. However, we hypothesise that flat and unrealistic nature of datasets could be a possible reason for the lack of improvement in the performance but the usage of learnable message function in the setup could still bring improvements if implemented on a realistic setup.

Message Aggregation. The idea of training data batching in dynamic graphs was formalized by Kumar et al. [1]. We wish to preserve the parallelism offered by the approach and implement it in our framework and hence the edge interactions are batched to a fixed number of interactions in each batch. However, considering the nature of network interactions, There could be several interactions of a single node in a batch and thus for updating the memory of a node in a batch we will have to aggregate the messages. This is handled by an aggregation function as,

$$m\bar{s}g_i(t) = \text{Agg}\left(msg_i(t_1), \ldots, msg_i(t_b)\right) \quad \text{where } t_1, \ldots, t_n \le t \tag{7}$$

The *Agg* function can be a learnable or could use relatively simpler mean aggregation or last member aggregation. Rossi et al. [3] considers the last aggregation to be an efficient method. However, the IoT networks are dynamic in nature with short term intercations. Thus the subsequent interactions of a node in a batch cannot be neglected. Hence we propose to deploy a learnable aggregation by implementing a MLP based aggregator. A detailed analysis on the aggregator significance and relevance in the datasets have been analysed in the results section.

State Updater. As mentioned above, after every transaction in the network, the node memory is updated to add the present interaction to the state of a node. This utilises the memory of the node just before the interaction $m_i(t^-)$ and the present message at t - $msg_i(t)$.

$$m_i(t) = udt(msg_i(t), m_i(t^-)) \tag{8}$$

The *udt* function must be equipped to dynamically balance the significance of both memory and real-time interaction, necessitating an integration of both long-term and short-term memory components. The Gated Recurrent Unit (GRU), introduced by Cho et al. [7], has demonstrated exceptional proficiency in processing long data sequences. Furthermore, subsequent studies by Rossi et al. [3] have reinforced the GRU's outstanding performance within this context, highlighting its capability to effectively manage the complexity of such tasks. This underscores the importance of leveraging the GRU's strengths in the design of the *udt* function, ensuring it can adeptly navigate and synthesize information across varying temporal scales.

Embedding Module. The goal of the encoder is to encode the spatio-temporal interactions of a node in the node embeddings. An embedding module is deployed to update the node embeddings. It is used to address the memory staleness issue as explained by Kazemi et al. [8]. The memory of a node i is updated only when the node participates in an event. When no event occurs for a prolonged duration (e.g. an IoT device deployed in a remote environment gets switched off due to battery drain) i's memory becomes stale. The module can be represented as,

$$z_i(t) = \text{emb}(i, t) = \sum_{j \in \mathcal{N}_i^k([0,t])} h\left(m_i(t), m_j(t), e_{ij}, \mathbf{v}_i(t), \mathbf{v}_j(t)\right) \tag{9}$$

Here h is a learnable function. Different functions have been used in different scenarios.

Temporal Graph Attention. (attn): A sequence of L graph attention layers updates a node's representation by gathering information from its L-hop temporal neighborhood and aggregating it.

The input to the l-th layer for node i consists of its representation $\mathbf{h}_i^{(l-1)}(t)$ at time t, along with its neighbors' representations $\{\mathbf{h}_j^{(l-1)}(t_j)\}$ for each neighbor j, their timestamps t_j, and edge features $\{e_{i,j}(t_j)\}$. These neighbors form node i's temporal neighborhood. The update is expressed as:

$$\mathbf{h}_i^{(l)}(t) = \text{MLP}\left(\mathbf{h}_i^{(l-1)}(t) \| \hat{\mathbf{h}}_i^{(l)}(t)\right), \tag{10}$$

$$\hat{\mathbf{h}}_i^{(l)}(t) = \text{MHA}(q^{(l)}(t), K^{(l)}(t), V^{(l)}(t)), \tag{11}$$

$$q^{(l)}(t) = \mathbf{h}_i^{(l-1)}(t) \| \phi(0), \tag{12}$$

$$K^{(l)}(t) = V^{(l)}(t) = C^{(l)}(t), \tag{13}$$

$$C^{(l)}(t) = \left[\mathbf{h}_j^{(l-1)}(t_j) \| e_{i,j}(t_j) \| \phi(t - t_j)\right]. \tag{14}$$

Here, $\phi(\cdot)$ is a generic time encoding function, and $\parallel$ denotes concatenation. The output $\mathbf{z}_i(t)$ represents the node embedding of node i at time t. MHA refers to MultiHeadAttention.

Each layer executes multi-head attention, where the query $q^{(l)}(t)$ represents node i (central node), and the values and keys are derived from its neighbors. The representation of the reference node is integrated with the collected and aggregated information from its neighbors.

The proposed NID-TGN model differs from the state-of-the-art TGAT by Xu et al. [11], by including node-wise temporal features to enable the model to capture memory $m_j(t)$ as well as the temporal node features $\mathbf{v}_j(t)$. This model will enhance IoT-based NIDS by enabling real-time, multi-hop temporal analysis of node behaviors, improving intrusion detection and effectively using the past interactions of the nodes obtained from the training data compared to other standards proposed in JODIE architecture proposed by Kumar et al. [1].

The encoder is a completely self-supervised learning mechanism and doesn't use the labels in the edge interactions of any form. Thus the performance of encoder is not affected by label imbalance in most IoT based datasets. The mechanism is efficient for graphs with a high number of nodes. The whole training process has been explained elaborately in the Appendix A.1.

4.2   Decoder Architecture

The probability of an intruder attacking the network at a given point of time is statistically very low. This has been accurately represented by most of the present datasets as most of them possess high class imbalance with large amounts of benign samples as compared those of attacker flows [13]. Most present work on GNN heavily undermine the use of effective decoder as the problems they solve do not suffer with the issue of class imbalance. However for an effective NIDS system, emphasis has to be laid on the decoder module. Here, we present a detailed analysis on how most decoders fail and ensembling methods succeed.

Logistic Regression as Decoder. Logistic regression aims to learn a probabilistic decision boundary:

$$P(y_i = 1|\mathbf{z}_i) = \frac{1}{1 + \exp(-\mathbf{w}^\top \mathbf{z}_i - b)}. \tag{15}$$

The objective is to reduce the negative log-likelihood:

$$\min_{\mathbf{w}, b}(-\sum_{i=1}^{n}[y_i \log(P(y_i = 1|\mathbf{z}_i)) + (1 - y_i)\log(1 - P(y_i = 1|\mathbf{z}_i))]). \tag{16}$$

In class imbalance, where most embeddings belong to the majority class (Class 1), logistic regression faces challenges:

1. Bias toward Majority Class: The model's loss function is dominated by the majority class samples, which skews the decision boundary towards the minority class, resulting in suboptimal performance and reduced sensitivity for minority class predictions.
2. Decision Boundary Shifting: With imbalance in the dataset, with fewer Class 0 samples, leads to a high loss for minority class instances, particularly those near the decision boundary, causing an increased rate of misclassification and poor generalization for the minority class.

This causes poor precision and recall for the minority class. The harm of class imbalance on the results of logistic regression are elaborated in [21].

MLP as a Decoder. Consider a binary classification problem with two classes, Class 0 with N_0 samples and Class 1 with N_1 samples, where $N_0 \ll N_1$. For the full dataset, the total loss cross entropy loss, $\mathcal{L}_{\text{total}}$ is:

$$\mathcal{L}_{\text{total}} = \frac{1}{N} \left(\sum_{i=1}^{N_0} \mathcal{L}(y_i, \hat{y}_i) + \sum_{i=1}^{N_1} \mathcal{L}(y_i, \hat{y}_i) \right) \tag{17}$$

Since $N_1 \gg N_0$, the loss is dominated by the majority class (Class 1).
The gradient for a sample i is:

$$\frac{\partial \mathcal{L}}{\partial \theta} = (\hat{y}_i - y_i) \cdot \frac{\partial z_i}{\partial \theta} \tag{18}$$

In a class-imbalanced dataset, the majority of samples are from Class 1. Hence, the model updates are biased towards minimizing the error for Class 1, ignoring Class 0.

As a result, the MLP becomes biased, frequently predicting Class 1. For class-imbalanced data, the expected probability of predicting Class 1 is:

$$P(\hat{y}_i = 1) = \frac{N_1}{N_0 + N_1} \tag{19}$$

Since $N_1 \gg N_0$, the model often predicts Class 1, leading to poor performance on the minority class. This problem was also evident in recent works by Ghosh et al. [22].

Random Forest as a Decoder. Random Forests has several methods to address class imbalance and has been very effective in providing state-of-the-art accuracy in many previous researches by More et al. [23], Muchlinski et al. [24]. In the following paragraphs, we discuss the advantages and techniques in Random Forests that make it the perfect decoder in NIDS scenario providing the right balance between scalability and accuracy.

A Random Forest classifier $f(x)$ is constructed by aggregating the predictions of T independently grown decision trees. For each tree $t \in \{1, 2, ..., T\}$, we generate a classification hypothesis $h_t(x)$ such that:

$$h_t(x) = \text{Tree}(x, \theta_t) \tag{20}$$

where θ_t represents the random parameters associated with the t-th tree, including the bootstrapped sample used for training and the subset of features considered at each split.

The final prediction $f(x)$ for the Random Forest is determined by majority voting.

The TGN encoder transforms temporal graph data into non-linear node embeddings, capturing intricate patterns within the data. Random Forests are particularly effective at classifying these complex, high-dimensional embeddings due to their ability to divide the feature space into meaningful regions using decision trees. Each tree captures different aspects of the embeddings, and this ensemble approach enhances the model's effectiveness in identifying diverse patterns within the learned embeddings while making the model resilient to noise. Additionally this ability to efficiently process large datasets through parallel tree construction ensures scalability [34].

Addressing Class Imbalance: Class weights are adjusted to handle the imbalanced classes issue in the datasets. Let w_k be the weight assigned to class k. The objective at each split of the tree is to maximize the weighted information gain, $I(S)$, which can be expressed as:

$$I(S) = H(S) - \sum_{v \in \text{values}} \frac{|S_v|}{|S|} H(S_v) \qquad (21)$$

where $H(S)$ denotes the node S's entropy, and S_v is the subset of samples split by a particular feature. The weighted entropy is defined as:

$$H(S) = -\sum_{k=1}^{K} w_k \cdot p_k \log(p_k) \qquad (22)$$

where p_k is the proportion of class k samples in node S.

By introducing class weights, Random Forests balances the classification performance across all classes, mitigating the effects of imbalance and producing robust predictions. Thus, the inherent randomness and ensemble nature of Random Forests makes them a highly scalable and effective solution for the Decoder task in the NIDS paradigm.

A detailed analysis of the relative accuracies in the classification of all three decoders and the performance of our encoder on standard datasets has been done in Sect. 7.

5   Dataset

In this work, we use CIDDS-001 (Coburg Intrusion Detection Data Set) [33], a labeled flow-based dataset. It has been specifically created for the purpose of evaluating anomaly-based intrusion detection systems. The dataset has a unidirectional net flow. It includes traffic data collected from two servers: the Open-Stack server and the external server. The dataset has over 84,51,520 instances of traffic sampled from both the traffic data collected from servers. The dataset has 16 attributes, including the destination IP address and source IP address feature as mentioned in Table 1. We have 10478 and 10539 unique destination IP addresses and source IP addresses.

Each flow in the open stack has an attribute 'class' that marks the flow as 'Attacker' or 'Victim' or 'Normal'. Most of the attacks in the dataset were simulated from one IP address. This provides scarce attacker data to the model to learn the complex features of the attacker flow. Since most of the samples (90%) in the dataset are normal, the classifier when provided the data of source and destination IP tends to heavily depend on these attributes to attain near high accuracy. However in the process of our experimentation, we excluded static features of the traffic flow data i.e. source and destination IP address along with Node Embedding to simulate a real time situation.

Large number of self edges (interaction of a node with itself) are not useful in representing network traffic. Unlike many datasets, the CIDDS-001 has approximately 5% self edges. This acts as an accurate simulation of packet transmission failure in an actual network. Another important feature of the dataset is the multiple interactions of the same in a batch. Every node has on average 3–4 edge interactions in a batch of 200 nodes. This reinforces the need of learnable aggregation over the relatively simple last message aggregator on the dataset.

Table 1. Information of CIDDS-001 week 1 Dataset

Class	Num. of Interactions	Num. of Unique Src IP's	Num. of Unique Dst IP's
Normal	70,10,897 Flows	9343 IP's	9354 IP's
Attacker	7,46,230 Flows	1 IP	771 IP's
Victim	6,94,393 Flows	20 IP's	1 IP

6   Experimental Setup

In this paper, we present NID-TGN, a vital modification to the state-of-the-art TGN [3] architecture. To test the effectiveness of the new encoder and benchmark the architecture, we utilized the Wikipedia [29] User Interaction Dataset which is widely used to benchmark most edge prediction models. The dataset has over 1.5 Lakh interactions among 9227 nodes.

For testing the effectiveness of the encoder architecture in the NIDS paradigm, we conducted experiments on the CIDDS dataset with two different interaction volumes: 100,000 and 1,000,000. It helped in evaluating the model's scalability and performance under varying conditions. Both experiments utilized the same underlying dataset, but with differing numbers of interactions obtained by taking a fraction of temporal data. This was done to assess the impact of data size on model effectiveness. We evaluated the model's ability to handle varying data volumes while maintaining consistent performance. The results highlighted the model's effectiveness, especially in predicting interactions for previously unseen nodes, demonstrating its adaptability across different scales of data.

For the proposed NID-TGN model training, the data was originally split into 70% for training, 15% for testing and 15% for validation. From the training set, 10% of the total nodes along with all their interaction data was excluded to asses the inductiveness of the encoder model. To test the encoder model, edge prediction was used as the problem. This approach is aligned with common practices in graph-based learning models [17]. Edge prediction was used as the accuracy parameter to evaluate the encoder model, consistent with methodologies in inductive node representation learning.

7   Results and Analysis

Encoder Benchmark: For encoder benchmarking, we experimented with the Wikipedia [29] and Reddit [30] datasets with results shown in Table 2, and also with the CIDDS dataset which is shown in Table 3. The performance on the Wikipedia and Reddit datasets is to verify that the learnable decoder is a good trade-off between the training speed, prediction speed and testing accuracy. However, the primary reason for introducing the learnable aggregator is the repeatability of edges in recent temporal interactions of an NIDS network. Hence, the performance of the TGN (Rossi et al. [3]) and our encoder (NID-TGN) on CIDDS dataset are both presented in Fig. 4.

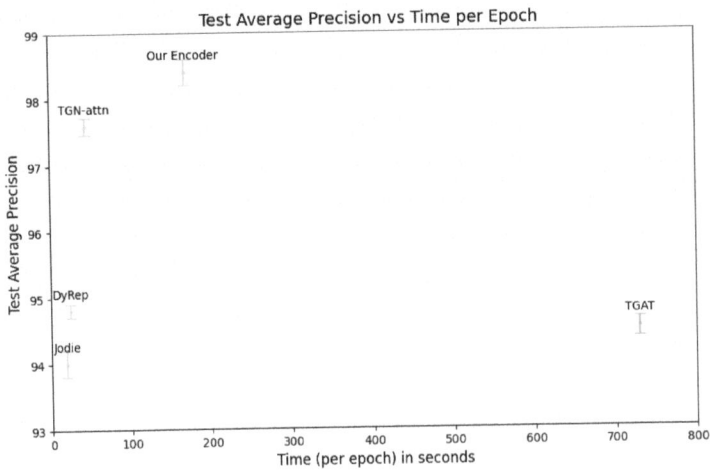

Fig. 3. Benchmark of the encoder with Wikipedia dataset. Results are considered as the average of 5 Runs and the errors are as in scale. Results for standard architectures were obtained from Rossi et al. [3]

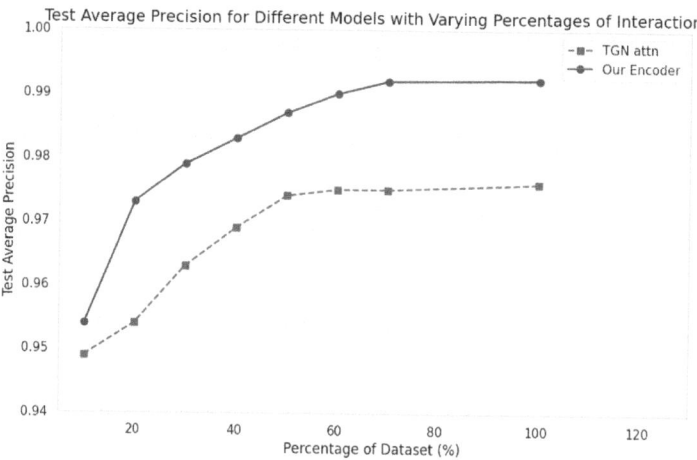

Fig. 4. Results of the TGN and NID-TGN on the CIDDS dataset with the number of interactions gradually increasing from 10% to 100%. The results were an average of 5 Runs.

Table 2. Performance comparison on Wikipedia and Reddit datasets for Transductive and Inductive learning. The performance of other models were adopted from the results mention in the work of Rossi et al. [3]. Here, ∗ represents that the encoders use static graph based modelling

	Wikipedia		Reddit	
	Transductive	Inductive	Transductive	Inductive
GAT*	94.73 ± 0.2	91.27 ± 0.4	97.33 ± 0.2	95.37 ± 0.3
GraphSAGE*	93.56 ± 0.3	91.09 ± 0.3	97.65 ± 0.2	96.27 ± 0.2
Jodie	94.62 ± 0.5	93.11 ± 0.4	97.11 ± 0.3	94.36 ± 1.1
TGAT	95.34 ± 0.1	93.99 ± 0.3	98.12± 0.2	96.62 ± 0.3
DyRep	94.59 ± 0.2	92.05 ± 0.3	97.98 ± 0.1	95.68± 0.2
TGN-attn	98.46 ± 0.1	97.81 ± 0.1	98.70 ± 0.1	97.55± 0.1
NID-TGN	99.23 ± 0.2	98.41 ± 0.1	98.60 ± 0.2	96.50 ± 0.1

Table 3. Performance comparison on CIDDS-001 dataset and time per epoch. The time per epoch is rounded to the 10's place of the average time obtained from the first 20 epochs of 5 runs. The training was done on the first million interactions of the CIDDS-001 week 1 dataset.

	CIDDS-001		Time per Epoch
	Transductive	Inductive	CIDDS (seconds)
DyRep	95.59 ± 0.3	94.05 ± 0.1	270
TGN-attn	97.46 ± 0.1	97.21 ± 0.1	510
NID-TGN	99.24 ± 0.2	98.91 ± 0.1	1400

The differences in the testing accuracies of the encoder model are very low. Still, at the scale of 10 Lakh interactions, The Difference in 2% accuracy means the inability of the model to predict over 3000 interactions happening at a later time. This is crucial as the probability of an intruder attacking at a given time is very low. Every misclassification deeply impacts the average statistics of intruder detection and the overall reliability of the model.

The performance of the proposed encoder, NID-TGN was evaluated by varying the amount of data used for training from 10% of all the interactions in the dataset to 100% of the dataset to estimate the response of the architecture towards increasing data. A comparative analysis between the scalability and Accuracy of the model is done in Fig. 3.

Table 4. Performance comparison across different decoder models. The node embedding obtained from the encoder model along with the class labels are used to train the decoder model. All the parameters mentioned are taken as average of 5 runs and are obtained from training of first 1 million interactions.

	Weighted RF		MLP		Logistic Regression	
	Without Node ID	With Node ID	Without Node ID	With Node ID	Without Node ID	With Node ID
Accuracy	97.71	100	**93.9**	98.71	**93.9**	99.15
Precision	72.43	100	**51.48**	89.15	**51.10**	93.68
Recall	92.12	98	**90.89**	89.73	**31.53**	92.42

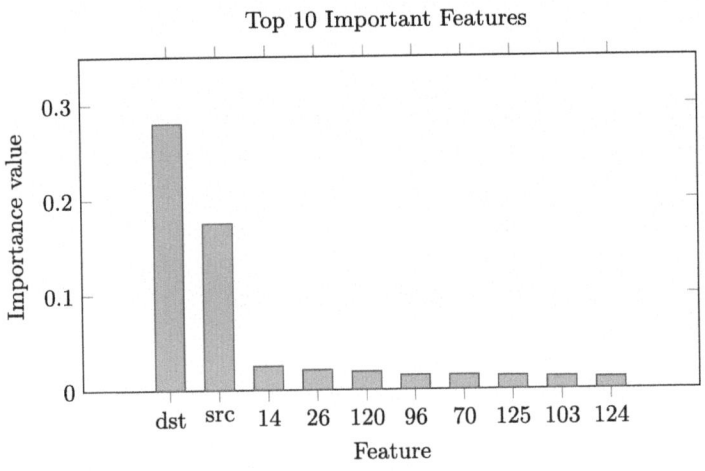

Fig. 5. Top 10 features plotted using random forest as per their importance (Dst has the highest importance followed by Src and rest of the features element represented by numeric values). This can be intuitively explained by the data in Table 2, All attacker flows have the same source IP and victim flows have the same destination IP, both of which are encoded as "1" for binary classification using a weighted random forest classifier.

Decoder Analysis: We conducted a performance comparison across three machine learning models: logistic regression, multi-layer perceptron (MLP), and weighted random forest (RF). We evaluated each model under two conditions: with and without the inclusion of Node ID as a feature. The results are shown in Table 4.

Without the node ID feature, the weighted RF model achieved an accuracy of 97.44%, with a precision of 72.43%, a recall of 92.21%. This indicates that the model performs robustly even without the Node ID feature. When the Node ID was included, the performance increased to 100% for accuracy and precision, with a recall of 98% achieving near-perfect accuracy. To further investigate the impact of features on model performance, we plotted the feature importance using the random forest model. The analysis revealed that the source-**src** and destination-**dst** features were considered the most important by the model as shown in Fig. 5. This observation explains why we achieved near-perfect accuracy, as the model could heavily rely on these features for decision-making and thus losing inductiveness. Both the MLP and logistic regression models significantly benefit

Table 5. Performance comparison on CIDDS-001 dataset. The Accuracy parameter for the bench mark was derived from the results provided in their paper. The * in this case denotes the performance of the NID-TGN model without Src and Dst as features.

	Benchmark	NID-TGN	NID-TGN*
Accuracy	97.7	100	97.7
Precision	99.7	100	72.4
Recall	99.2	98	92.1

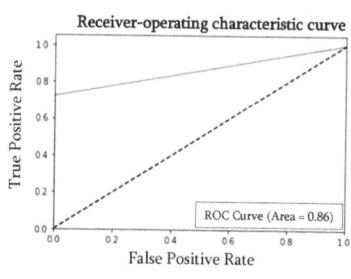
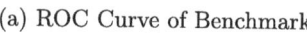

(a) ROC Curve of Benchmark

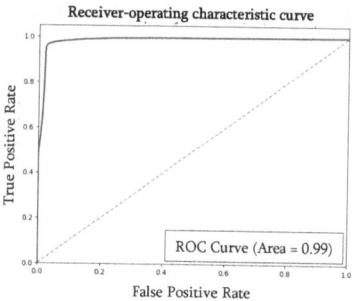

(b) ROC Curve of NID-TGN

Fig. 6. The ROC curve of the NID-TGN with source and destination excluded from features is Fig. 6(b), Fig. 6(a) denotes the results of benchmark as mentioned in [28]. From Area, It is evident that the NID-TGN outperforms the benchmark demonstrating the ability of the network to better discriminate between the positive and negative classes. From the shape of the curve it is evident that the NID-TGN has a higher true positive rate.

from the inclusion of Node ID, improving their overall performance even though it is not considered a general feature for Network Flow Models.

Comparison with the Benchmark: The benchmarks for comparison were obtained from the latest work on the CIDDS dataset by Daoud et al. [28]. We compare our encoder decoder pair (NID-TGN with RF Decoder (Source and Destination Provided)) with their results in Table 5. The ROC curves are compared in Fig. 6.

8   Conclusion

We tackled several key challenges faced by current network intrusion detection systems (NIDS), especially when dealing with the growing threat of cyberattacks in IoT networks. Traditional methods often struggle to detect complex threats and zero-day attacks. Also, simulated datasets for training models are not very reliable. To improve detection, we proposed NID-TGN model, that uses Continuous-Time Dynamic Graphs (CTDGs) to model network interactions as they change over time, which helps in identifying subtle attack signals more effectively.

One key issue we addressed is the reliance on static node identifiers, like IP addresses, which leads many models to act as simple mapping functions. We demonstrated that our model can also achieve high accuracy of 99% which is better than the state-of-the-art models when these identifiers are included. However, we chose to focus on more dynamic and meaningful features of the new threats by removing these static features and still achieved high accuracy of 94% in predictions while keeping the number of false negatives low. Additionally, we introduced a weighted Random Forest decoder to address the challenge of imbalanced datasets, where benign data greatly exceeds attack data. This approach avoids data removal or resampling, preserving crucial time-based relationships and enhancing detection accuracy. It outperforms other decoders, such as Logistic Regression and MLP, by reducing overfitting and adapting to dynamic network environments.

Our results underscore the importance of integrating temporal dynamics into NIDS models, particularly for IoT networks with constantly evolving events. This method not only boosts accuracy but also ensures better adaptation to real-world scenarios by robust encoding mechanisms, inductiveness and handling the data imbalance issues.

A   Appendix

A.1   Encoder Training

The training of TGN is a complex task as the temporal axis is very sensitive to model misinterpretations and hence it is difficult to demonstrate parallelism in the training as the node memory at a later time is dependent on temporal interactions at a previous instant. Few approaches to demonstrate parallelism to use t-batch training by Kumar et al. [1] do not satisfy the temporal consistency that is extremely essential for the encoder.

These challenges inspire our training algorithm, which handles interactions in batches while preserving their chronological order. The algorithm keeps track of the latest message for each node in a message store, ensuring it is processed prior to predicting the node's subsequent interaction. This approach allows the state-related components to receive gradient updates. Algorithm 1 outlines the pseudocode for TGN training.

Algorithm 1. Training of the Encoder

Input: An array containing the time stamp t, Src IP u, Dst IP v, and the features e_{uv}

Output: The Node embeddings of all the nodes occurring in the network $z_i(t)$

$s \leftarrow 0$ // Initialize memory to zeros

for each batch (i, j, e, t) in training data **do**

    $m \leftarrow \mathrm{msg}(m_{\mathrm{raw}})$ // Compute messages from raw features

    $\tilde{m} \leftarrow \mathrm{agg}(m)$ // Aggregate messages for the same nodes

    $\hat{s} \leftarrow \mathrm{mem}(\tilde{m}, s)$ // Get updated memory

    $z_i, z_j \leftarrow \mathrm{embs}(i, t), \mathrm{embs}(j, t)$ // Compute node embeddings

    Select a random negative sample n // Define negative sampling logic

    $z_n \leftarrow \mathrm{embs}(n, t)$

    $p_{\mathrm{pos}}, p_{\mathrm{neg}} \leftarrow \mathrm{dec}(z_i, z_j), \mathrm{dec}(z_i, z_n)$ // Compute interaction probabilities

    $L \leftarrow \mathrm{BCE}(p_{\mathrm{pos}}, p_{\mathrm{neg}})$ // Compute BCE loss

    $m_{\mathrm{rawi}}, m_{\mathrm{rawj}} \leftarrow (\hat{s}_i, \hat{s}_j, t, e), (\hat{s}_j, \hat{s}_i, t, e)$ // Compute raw messages

    $m_{\mathrm{raw}} \leftarrow \mathrm{store\_raw\_messages}(m_{\mathrm{raw}}, m_{\mathrm{rawi}}, m_{\mathrm{rawj}})$ // Store raw messages

    $s_i, s_j \leftarrow \hat{s}_i, \hat{s}_j$ // Store updated memory for sources and destinations

end for

References

1. Kumar, S., Zhang, X., Leskovec, J.: Predicting dynamic embedding trajectory in temporal interaction networks. In: The 25th ACM SIGKDD Conference on Knowledge Discovery and Data Mining (KDD 2019), pp. 1–10. ACM, New York (2019). https://doi.org/10.1145/3292500.3330895

2. Kazemi, S.M., Goel, R.: Representation learning for dynamic graphs: a survey. J. Mach. Learn. Res. **21**, 1–73 (2020)

3. Rossi, E., Chamberlain, B., Frasca, F., Eynard, D., Monti, F., Bronstein, M.: Temporal graph networks for deep learning on dynamic graphs. In: ICML 2020 Workshop on Graph Representation Learning (2020). https://arxiv.org/abs/2006.10637. Accessed 13 Sept 2024

4. Bendovschi, A.: Cyber-attacks-trends, patterns and security countermeasures. Procedia Econ. Finan. **28**, 24–31 (2015)

5. Perozzi, B., Al-Rfou, R., Skiena, S.: DeepWalk: online learning of social representations. In: Proceedings of the 20th ACM SIGKDD International Conference on Knowledge Discovery and Data Mining, pp. 701–710 (2014)

6. Grover, A., Leskovec, J.: node2vec: scalable feature learning for networks. In: Proceedings of the 22nd ACM SIGKDD International Conference on Knowledge Discovery and Data Mining, pp. 855–864 (2016). https://arxiv.org/pdf/1607.00653

7. Cho, K.: Learning phrase representations using RNN encoder-decoder for statistical machine translation. arXiv preprint arXiv:1406.1078 (2014). https://www.aclweb.org/anthology/D14-1179

8. Kazemi, S.M., et al.: Representation learning for dynamic graphs: a survey. J. Mach. Learn. Res. 21(70), 1–73 (2020)

9. Xu, R., Xie, L., Zhao, H., Li, Y., Zhang, Q.: Applying self-supervised learning to network intrusion detection for network flows with graph neural network. Comput. Netw. 248, 110495 (2024). https://arxiv.org/pdf/2403.01501

10. Machine Learning Dataset (NF-Bot-IoT, NF-Bot-IoT-v2, NF-CSE-CIC-IDS) (2018). https://staff.itee.uq.edu.au/marius/NIDS_datasets/. Accessed 24 Sept 2013

11. Xu, D., Ruan, C., Korpeoglu, E., Kumar, S., Achan, K.: Inductive representation learning on temporal graphs. In: International Conference on Learning Representations (2020)

12. Nguyen, G.H., Lee, J.B., Rossi, R.A., Ahmed, N.K., Koh, E., Kim, S.: Dynamic network embeddings: from random walks to temporal random walks. In: 2018 IEEE International Conference on Big Data, pp. 1085–1092 (2018)

13. Wang, C., Ma, S., Yang, Z., Yang, Z., Sun, W., Tian, L.: Effective intrusion detection in highly imbalanced IoT networks with lightweight S2CGAN-IDS. IEEE Internet Things J. (2023)

14. Sarhan, M., Layeghy, S., Moustafa, N., Portmann, M.: NetFlow datasets for machine learning-based network intrusion detection systems. In: Deze, Z., Huang, H., Hou, R., Rho, S., Chilamkurti, N. (eds.) BDTA/WiCON -2020. LNICST, vol. 371, pp. 117–135. Springer, Cham (2021). https://doi.org/10.1007/978-3-030-72802-1_9

15. Kasongo, S.M.: A deep learning technique for intrusion detection system using a Recurrent Neural Networks based framework. Comput. Commun. 199, 113–125 (2023). https://journalofbigdata.springeropen.com/articles/10.1186/s40537-020-00379-6

16. Pujol-Perich, D., Moya, R., Liu, Q., Wang, H., Basurto, J.: Unveiling the potential of graph neural networks for robust intrusion detection. ACM SIGMETRICS Perform. Eval. Rev. 49(4), 111–117 (2022). https://dl.acm.org/doi/pdf/10.1145/3543146.3543171

17. Kipf, T.N., Welling, M.: Semi-supervised classification with graph convolutional networks. arXiv preprint arXiv:1609.02907 (2016). https://arxiv.org/abs/1609.02907

18. Khraisat, A., Suleiman, A., Karami, A., Alshamrani, A., Alzahrani, A.: Survey of intrusion detection systems: techniques, datasets and challenges. Cybersecurity 2(1), 1–22 (2019)

19. Tang, J., Qu, M., Wang, M., Zhang, J., Yan, J., Mei, Q.: LINE: large-scale information network embedding. In: Proceedings of the 24th International Conference on World Wide Web, pp. 1067–1077 (2015)

20. Xu, R., Xie, L., Zhao, H., Li, Y., Zhang, Q.: Applying self-supervised learning to network intrusion detection for network flows with graph neural network. Comput. Netw. 248, 110495 (2024)

21. van den Goorbergh, R., van der Meulen, M., de Rijke, A., Bonten, M.J.M.: The harm of class imbalance corrections for risk prediction models: illustration and

simulation using logistic regression. J. Am. Med. Inform. Assoc. **29**(9), 1525–1534 (2022)

22. Ghosh, K., Singh, P., Roy, S., Chakraborty, D., Mukherjee, S.: The class imbalance problem in deep learning. Mach. Learn. **113**(7), 4845–4901 (2024)

23. More, A.S., Rana, D.P.: Review of random forest classification techniques to resolve data imbalance. In: 2017 1st International Conference on Intelligent Systems and Information Management (ICISIM), pp. 211–215. IEEE (2017)

24. Muchlinski, D., King, G., MRP, K.: Comparing random forest with logistic regression for predicting class-imbalanced civil war onset data. Polit. Anal. **24**(1), 87–103 (2016)

25. Perwej, Y., Yadav, S., Mishra, K., Perwej, A.: The internet of things (IoT) and its application domains. Int. J. Comput. Appl. **975**(8887), 182 (2019)

26. Tsimenidis, S., Lagkas, T., Rantos, K.: Deep learning in IoT intrusion detection. J. Netw. Syst. Manag. **30**(1), 8 (2022)

27. Tripathi, A., Bagade, P.: PANGA: attention-based principal neighborhood aggregation for forecasting future cyber attacks. In: 22nd IEEE International Conference on Trust, Security and Privacy in Computing and Communications (TrustCom-2023), Exeter, UK (2023)

28. Daoud, M.A., Hamam, H., Bouguila, N., Mokhtari, A.: Convolutional neural network-based high-precision and speed detection system on CIDDS-001. Data Knowl. Eng. **144**, 102130 (2023)

29. Snap Homepage for Stanford. https://snap.stanford.edu/jodie/wikipedia.csv. Accessed 13 Sept 2024

30. Snap Homepage for Stanford. https://snap.stanford.edu/jodie/reddit.csv. Accessed 13 Sept 2024

31. Snap Homepage for Stanford. https://snap.stanford.edu/jodie/lastfm.csv. Accessed 13 Sept 2024

32. Snap Homepage for Stanford. https://snap.stanford.edu/jodie/mooc.csv. Accessed 13 Sept 2024

33. CIDDS Dataset, Hochschule coburg chords. https://www.hs-coburg.de/forschung/forschungsprojekte-oeffentlich/informationstechnologie/cidds-coburg-intrusion-detection-data-sets.html. Accessed 13 Sept 2024

34. Breiman, L.: Random forests. Mach. Learn. **45**, 5–32 (2001). https://doi.org/10.1023/A:1010933404324. Accessed 13 Sept 2024

High Speed High Assurance Implementations of Multivariate Quadratic Based Signatures
Extended Abstract

M. Samyuktha[1,2(✉)], Pallavi Borkar[1], and Chester Rebeiro[1]

[1] Indian Institute of Technology, Madras, India
{pallavi,chester}@cse.iitm.ac.in
[2] Society for Electronic Transactions and Security, Chennai, India
samyuktha@setsindia.net

Abstract. In this poster, we present a Jasmin implementation of Mayo2, a multivariate quadratic (MQ) based signature scheme. Mayo overcomes the disadvantage of the Unbalanced oil and vinegar (UOV) scheme by whipping the UOV map to produce public keys of sizes comparable to ML-DSA. Our Jasmin implementation of Mayo2 takes 930 μs for keygen, 3206 μs for sign, 659 μs for verify based on the average of 100 runs of the implementation on a 2.25 GHz x86 64 processor with 256 GB RAM. To this end, we have a multivariate quadratic based signature implementation that is amenable for verification of constant-time, correctness, proof of equivalence properties using Easycrypt. Subsequently, the results of this endeavor can be extended for other MQ based schemes including UOV.

Keywords: Formal Verification · Mayo · Jasmin

1 Introduction

With the widespread migration of security protocols to post-quantum, various efficient and architecture-specific optimized implementations have emerged. These implementations can be considerably complex and their correctness not easily verifiable due to larger input spaces. Thus, these implementations need to be proven correct and equivalent to their corresponding algorithmic specification in order to achieve the high levels of assurance needed for critical embedded system applications like root of trust, remote attestation and secure communication.

In the context of the NIST PQC competition, it is essential to formally investigate the security of the submissions and their implementations against side-channel attacks. These attacks can compromise a mathematically strong algorithm by exploiting information leaked through side channels such as power consumption and electromagnetic radiation of the device executing the cryptographic operation. A potent side-channel variant called the timing attack utilizes

J. Knechtel et al. (Eds.): SPACE 2024, LNCS 15351, pp. 196–200, 2025.
https://doi.org/10.1007/978-3-031-80408-3_12

execution differences to reveal information about the secret key. Thus, it is crucial not only to verify the correctness of the cryptographic implementation but also ensure constant time execution.

Multivariate cryptographic schemes based on the oil and vinegar (OV) problem have been well studied and are of interest to the research community as they offer shorter signatures and faster verification times. With NIST standardizing ML-DSA, ML-KEM and an additional call for proposals to focus on signatures based on hardness other than lattices, evaluation of these schemes is relevant.

We plan to carry out the following three-fold approach: (i) developing high-speed formally verified MQ based signature scheme implementations, (ii) verification for functional correctness, and (iii) verification for constant-time execution. In line with the strategy, we have implemented the Keygen, Sign and Verify primitives of a MQ based signature scheme (Mayo2 [7]) in Jasmin, the specifics of which will be detailed in the later sections. Hence we make the following contributions in this article:

1. Bitsliced implementation of the underlying finite field arithmetic
2. Bitsliced implementation of the linear algebra operations
3. Bitsliced Echelon form implementation to solve the linear system of equations
4. Jasmin implementation of the Keygen, Sign and Verify primitives of Mayo2

Related Work. Formally verified implementations, often called high-assurance cryptographic software, exist for classical algorithms and have been widely adopted in libraries. It is imperative to extend these notions to post-quantum schemes for arguing robust security guarantees. Frameworks like Easycrypt [6] utilize model checking and have demonstrated effectiveness in the formal verification process. In their research on a formally verified implementation of SHA-3, Almeida et al. [3] advocate for mechanized proofs of functional correctness, provable security, and resistance to timing attacks, employing a toolchain that combines Jasmin [4] and Easycrypt. Furthermore, Almeida et al. in [5] present a formally verified proof of the functional correctness and IND-CCA security of ML-KEM, the Kyber-based Key Encapsulation Mechanism (KEM).

2 Preliminaries

Multivariate Quadratic based Schemes. Signature schemes based on the hardness of multivariate quadratic(MQ) problem offer shorter signature sizes and faster verification times. UOV is one such well-studied MQ based scheme but it suffers from the disadvantage of larger public key sizes. Mayo can be considered as a variant of UOV offers public keys whose size are comparable to that of ML-DSA. However, it is to be noted that the cryptographic security of Mayo depends on the security of UOV.

Mayo. The keygen(1^λ) of Mayo starts by sampling a random matrix $\mathbf{O}$ and the column space of $\begin{bmatrix} \mathbf{O} \\ I_0 \end{bmatrix}$ forms the secret oil space $\mathcal{O}$ with $\dim(O) = o$; number of variables 'n', number of equations 'm' and o < m. A random multivariate quadratic map $\mathcal{P}(x)$: $\mathbb{F}_q^n \to \mathbb{F}_q^m$ which vanishes on this subspace $\mathcal{O}$ is generated as the public key.

In a smaller subspace where o < m, with larger probability the system will not have any solution. Addressing this during sign, a parameter 'k' is fixed with ko $\geq$ m, the UOV map $\mathcal{P}(x)$: $\mathbb{F}_q^n \to \mathbb{F}_q^m$ is whipped to $\mathcal{P}^*(x_1, x_2, ..x_k)$: $\mathbb{F}_q^{kn} \to \mathbb{F}_q^m$ using public matrices called emulsifier maps E_{ij} as

$$\mathcal{P}^*(x_1, \ldots, x_k) := \sum_{i=1}^{k} E_{ii} P(x_i) + \sum_{i=1}^{k} \sum_{j=i+1}^{k} E_{ij} P'(x_i, x_j)$$

With ko degrees of freedom, a solution is guaranteed to be found. The whipped map $\mathcal{P}^*$ is constructed in such a way that it vanishes on the subspace $O^k = (o_1, ..., o_k)$, $\forall$ i $\in$ k, $o_i \in \mathcal{O}$. The target t is computed as $\mathcal{H}(M \| Salt)$. The signer at random chooses $(v_1, ..., v_k) \in \mathbb{F}_q^{kn}$ and solves for $(o_1, ..., o_k) \in O_k$ such that $\mathcal{P}^*(v_1 + o_1, ..., v_k + o_k)$ = t. The solution $(s_i = v_i + o_i$ where i $\in$ k) along with the salt is shared as signature. For verification, message M with the salt is hashed to obtain t and the signature is accepted if and only if $\mathcal{P}^*(s_i)$ = t where i $\in$ k.

3   Implementation Details

The implementation follows largely the structure and implementation strategies of the Reference implementation of Mayo team, as included in the NIST submission package. Bitslicing in the Jasmin implementations follows as that of the C implementation. Bitslicing is done based on the parameter 'm', the number of equations in the Mayo2 specification.

Finite Field Implementation. At the bottom is the implementation of the GF(16) arithmetic. The field elements are obtained as $\mathbb{Z}_2[x]/(x^4 + x + 1)$. Bitsliced arithmetic for carrying out 64 field additions, multiplications is implemented. A simple finite field arithmetic using 64-bit registers in Jasmin without slicing is also implemented. The simple arithmetic is only used towards the end of the signature generation in putting together the obtained values of the oil and vinegar variables to construct the signature. The rest of the Mayo2 implementation uses the bitsliced arithmetic.

Linear Algebra Operations. This layer of implementation includes the matrix-matrix multiplication, addition, and matrix-vector multiplications for operating on large bitsliced matrices of finite field elements.

SHAKE256 Implementation. The Mayo specification indicates the use of SHAKE256 at various places of its design. This includes expanding the secret key seed bytes to the public key seed bytes and the bytes to generate the matrix O, hashing the message to the digest etc. SHAKE-256 jasmin implementation as available in the libjade library [1] has been modified to suit the requirement and has been used. Wrapper functions have been written in jasmin with the required input and output lengths of the SHAKE256 call.

PK-PRF Implementation. AES-128-CTR based PK PRF is used in the jasmin implementation as specified. These are used to expand the block matrices P_1 and P_2 in the public key. We have constructed the PK PRF in jasmin on top of the AES-128-CTR code available in the formosa-crypto website [2]. The counter initialised to zero is encrypted using AES-128 and are concatenated to fill the required buffer size. It can be noted that the AES-128-CTR implementation uses AES-NI instructions for its rounds.

Randombytes Generation. The random bytes for the initial seed_sk and the salt for randomising signatures are using the #randombytes primitive in Jasmin which derives random bytes from the linux CSPRNG /dev/urandom.

Keygen, Sign and Verify. Keygen and Verify modules have been implemented using bitsliced operations as in the C reference implementation. The compact secret key is expanded as specified. The OV map is whipped to a larger map using the emulsifier maps. Vinegar values are sampled in the whipped up map and are solved for the oil variables. The echelon form is implemented in a bitsliced fashion.

Benchmarking The Table 1 included in Appendix A, denotes the average execution time computed over 100 runs of the implementation on a 2.25GHz x86_64 processor with 256 GB RAM. The benchmarked C Reference implementation is without AES-NI enabled in the NIST submission package. We plan to perform detailed benchmarking of the Jasmin implementation of Mayo2 against the C Reference implementation with and without AES-NI enabled over 1,00,000 runs.

4   Future Work

We plan to (i) formally verify the Jasmin implementation for functional correctness and prove functional equivalence to the C reference implementation using Easycrypt and Z3 (ii) formally verify the implementation for constant-time execution through logically reasoned machine-checked proofs using Easycrypt at the software level.

A   Appendix

The Mayo2 parameters, as elaborated in Sect. 2, utilized in our implementation are m = 64, n = 78, k = 4, o = 18 with a secret key size of 24B, public key size of 5488B and signature size of 180B.

Table 1. Execution time consumed for Jasmin and Reference Implementations in μsec.

Primitive	Jasmin Impl.	C Reference Impl.
Keygen	930	1629
Sign	3206	2749
Verify	659	665

References

1. https://github.com/formosa-crypto/libjade. libjade
2. https://formosa-crypto.org/news/2022-06-07/sibenik. formosa Crypto
3. Almeida, J.B., et. al.: Machine-checked proofs for cryptographic standards: Indifferentiability of sponge and secure high-assurance implementations of sha-3. In: Proceedings of the 2019 ACM SIGSAC Conference (2019)
4. Almeida, J.B., Barbosa, M.: Jasmin: high-assurance and high-speed cryptography. In: Proceedings of the ACM SIGSAC Conference on Computer and Communications Security, pp. 1807–1823 (2017)
5. Almeida, J.B., Barbosa, M., Barthe, G.: Formally verifying kyber episode iv: Implementation correctness (2023)
6. Barthe, G., Dupressoir, F., Grégoire, B., Kunz, C., Schmidt, B., Strub, P.Y.: Easy-Crypt: a tutorial, pp. 146–166. Springer, Cham (2014)
7. Beullens, W.: Mayo: Practical post-quantum signatures from 0il-and-vinegar maps. In: International Conference on Selected Areas in Cryptography, pp. 355–376. Springer (2021)

"There's Always Another Counter": Detecting Micro-Architectural Attacks in a Probabilistically Interleaved Malicious/Benign Setting

Upasana Mandal[(✉)], Rupali Kalundia, Nimish Mishra, Shubhi Shukla, Sarani Bhattacharya, and Debdeep Mukhopadhyay

Indian Institute of Technology Kharagpur, Kharagpur, India
{mandal.up98,rupalikalundia,nimish.mishra,
shubhishukla}@kgpian.iitkgp.ac.in, {sarani,debdeep}@cse.iitkgp.ac.in

Abstract. Modern micro-architectural attacks use a variety of building blocks chained to develop a final exploit. However, since in most cases, the footprint of such attacks is not visible architecturally (like, in the file-system), it becomes trickier to defend against these. In light of this, several automated defence mechanisms use Hardware Performance Counters (HPCs) detect when the micro-architectural elements are being misused for a potential attacks (like flush-reload, Spectre, Meltdown etc.). In order to bypass such defences, recent works have proposed the idea of "probabilistic interleaving": the adversary interleaves the actual attack code with benign code with very low frequency. Such a strategy tips off the HPCs used for detection with a lot of unnecessary noise; recent studies have shown that probabilistically interleaved attacks can achieve an attack evasion rate of 100% (i.e. are virtually undetectable). In this work, we contend this folklore. We develop a theoretical model of interleaved attacks using lightweight statistical tools like Gaussian Mixture Models and Dip Test for Unimodality and prove they are detectable for the correct choices of HPCs. Furthermore, we also show possible defence strategy against a *stronger* threat model than considered in literature: where the attacker interleaves *multiple* attacks instead of a single attack. Empirically, to instantiate our detector, in contrast to prior detection strategies, we choose LLMs for a number of reasons: (1) LLMs can easily contextualize data from a larger set of HPCs than generic machine learning techniques, and (2) with simple prompts, LLMs can quickly switch between different statistical analysis methods. To this end, we develop an LLM-based methodology to detect probabilistically interleaved attacks. Our experiments establish that our improved methodology is able to achieve 100% speculative attacks like Spectre v1/v2/v3, Meltdown, and Spectre v2 (with improved gadgets that even evade recent protections like Enhanced IBRS, IBPB conditional, and so on). This makes our methodology suitable for detecting speculative attacks in a non-profiled setting: where attack signatures might not be known in advance. All in all, we achieve a 100% attack detection rate, even with very low interleave frequencies (i.e. 10^{-6}).

© The Author(s), under exclusive license to Springer Nature Switzerland AG 2025
J. Knechtel et al. (Eds.): SPACE 2024, LNCS 15351, pp. 201–220, 2025.
https://doi.org/10.1007/978-3-031-80408-3_13

Our detection principle and its instantiation through LLMs shows how probabilistically interleaving attack code in benign execution is not a perfect strategy, and more research is still needed into developing and countering better attack evasion strategies.

Keywords: LLMs · Micro-architectural attacks · Interleaved attacks

1 Introduction

Research into malware hiding strategies [6] is mostly focused upon better ways of evading the ever-evolving defence mechanisms. Such attacks/defences can be thought of as *architectural* attacks: they leave traces observable at the architectural level (for instance, the file-system). However, *micro-architectural* attacks [3,5,7,9,10,12,14–21] are trickier to detect since they do not leave any observable architectural trace. Micro-architectural attacks are capable of leaking sensitive cryptographic materials, breaking software/hardware isolation, and using bad speculation (pipeline flushes) to drastic ends. Such attacks target aspects of the micro-architecture (like cache, execution ports, on-core buffers, and so on), and thus require different methods of detection than traditional malware.

Strategies of Detection. All modern vendors like Intel/AMD ship their processors with documented/undocumented counters (otherwise technically named Hardware Performance Counters or HPCs) that measure different aspects of the hardware. Since micro-architectural attacks exploit aspects of the hardware, a long line of research [1,2,4,8,13] into detecting micro-architectural attacks has focused on using HPCs. The core idea is to monitor HPCs and look for statistical variations that might flag adversarial execution from benign. Such defences use a variety of tests: template-based matching, anomaly detection, machine learning, and so on, as their detection strategy.

HPC Design and Issues with Detection. Hardware Performance Counters, by design, are tied to the specific hardware unit they target. For a concrete example, on Intel systems, `INST_RETIRED.ANY` counts the number of x86 instructions retired (and is thus tuned to the instruction retirement unit in the backend execution unit[1]. Likewise, `BR_INST_RETIRED.ALL_BRANCHES` counts the number of retired branch instructions (and is thus attuned to the branch predictor unit in the frontend execution unit)[2]. As such, HPCs do not conform to software isolation boundaries maintained in userspace. In other words, HPCs keep counting irrespective of the software executing atop the processor. This means that attack detection strategies that use HPCs are vulnerable to noise due to context switches from kernel scheduling, hyperthreading, and other events in the hardware. HPC-based detection strategies [1,2,4,8,13] then leverage statistical methods to factor out such noise.

---

[1] https://perfmon-events.intel.com/.
[2] Similar HPC counterparts exist for other vendors as well, like AMD.

Emergence of "Interleaved" Attacks: Exploiting this software-agnostic nature of HPC design, the authors in [13] have proposed a new micro-architectural attack strategy: *interleave attack code, with low frequency, among executions of benign code.* On a high-level, such an interleaved attack strategy executes the benign code for multiple iterations, and *interleaves* the attack in some iterations (driven by a small probability threshold). Since the probability threshold of interleaving is small (like 1 in million), this strategy tips off all existing defence mechanisms [1, 2, 4, 8, 13], which mainly capture characteristics of the predominant benign execution and miss characteristics of the otherwise sporadic attacker execution. This leads us to the following question, which we deal in this work:

Can we develop a lightweight statistical analysis of interleaved attacks that still allows detection through HPCs, which have no detection strategy in literature?

1.1   Our Contributions

We answer this question in the affirmative. This work contributions to a general understanding of the statistical behaviour of interleaved attacks, as well as a generic detection strategy. We also contribute a detection strategy against an even *stronger variant* of the threat model considered by interleaved attacks. We summarize our contributions thus:

① We propose a theoretical modeling of interleaved attacks using lightweight statistical tools like Gaussian Mixture models and Dip Test for Unimodality. We demonstrate that for carefully chosen measurements (i.e. HPCs), interleaved attacks are still detectable.

② We demonstrate the detection of interleaved attacks claimed to be undetectable by the prior art. In particular, we test against Spectre v1, Spectre v3, and Meltdown. Furthermore, we also test for Spectre v2, in both the traditional setting as well as through advanced gadgets which evade detection even by state-of-the-art Spectre v2 mitigations like Enhanced IBRS, IBPB conditioning and so on.

③ We analyze the HPC data collected during the execution of an interleaved attack using a large language model (LLM) to perform the Dip test. The LLM allows easy user-friendly detection by identifying multimodal distributions through the Dip Test for Unimodality, which helps reveal potential interleaved attacks like Spectre v1 and other similar threats.

④ We also consider a *stronger* threat model of interleaved attacks: instead of a single attack, several different attacks are interleaved with benign execution. We extend our model trivially to Multimodal Gaussian mixtures and show that multiple attacks interleaved with benign execution are still detectable by HPCs.

2 Background

2.1 Interleaved Attacks

The idea of interleaved attacks was first presented in [13]. The main objective of the work is to systematically evaluate the effectiveness of HPC-based detection mechanisms against cache-based side-channel attacks. This analysis is done across four dimensions: ① threat model, ② performance overhead, ③ detection speed, and ④ detection reproducibility. About 50 state-of-the-art defence mechanisms are evaluated against these dimensions, and relevant comparisons are drawn between them. Through this systematization, the authors consolidate a commonality between different classes of defences wrt. the assumptions they place on the adversary. Concretely, all defences expect the attacks to occur in isolation for which HPC traces (with minor operational noise) can be collected.

From this understanding, the authors put forward a new threat model where attacks are *interleaved* with benign executions with low frequency. As a concrete example, consider the case of the Flush+Reload covert channel, which forms an exfiltration channel for several other attacks. In a traditional Flush+Reload attack, the adversary flushes a shared memory line from the cache, waits for the victim to access the cache line, and then measures the time taken to reload the data. This timing reveals whether the victim accessed the flushed cache line. However, in [13] this Flush+Reload exfiltration activity is *interleaved* among several iterations (like 10000 or 1000000) of the benign function. This low-frequency execution reduces the footprint of the attack in the HPC data, making it appear as though the system was executing typical benign tasks. In some sense, interleaved attacks achieve *temporal blending* of the attack with benign execution: by strategically placing the malicious execution alongside frequent benign execution, the attack produces no clear statistical deviation in data from HPCs such as cache hits, cache misses, or branch mispredictions. A basic outline of such an attack is given in Listing 1.1. The key idea is that by running the attack code at a low frequency and interspersing it with frequent benign tasks, the resulting behavior looks just like normal, harmless execution. In contrast, traditional methods like Flush+Reload create noticeable patterns in cache activity that can be detected. However, when an attack is interleaved with normal operations, this distinctive cache activity gets mixed with normal cache activity, making it much harder for detection systems that rely on HPC data to identify the attack.

Briefly stating, existing detection mechanisms rely purely on large-scale statistical anomalies in HPC data, and thus are unable to detect interleaved attacks. This is because such systems operate under the assumption that malicious activity will always manifest as an obvious anomaly, but when the attack is subtle and well-hidden, such as by blending with normal behavior, these systems fail to perform effectively.

```
1  void interleaved() {
2      benign();
3      // this threshold is very small
4      if(sample_probability() < threshold)
5          attack();
6      benign();
7  }
```

Listing 1.1. A skeleton of interleaved attack from [13].

2.2 Dip Test of Unimodality

The Dip Test of Unimodality [11] is a statistical test that quantifies multi-modality in a sample by measuring the statistical distance between the "actual" distribution and the expected unimodal distribution. Concretely, the "actual" distribution of a set of data points $\mathbf{x} = \{x_1, x_2, \cdots, x_n\}$, formally called the *Empirical Distribution Function* (EDF) or $\mathcal{F}_n(\mathbf{x})$, is given as:

$$\mathcal{F}_n(x_j) = \frac{1}{n}\Sigma_{i=1}^{n}\mathcal{I}(x_i) \quad : \quad j \in \{x_1, x_2, x_3, \cdots, x_n\}$$

where $\mathcal{I}$ is an indicator function that returns 1 iff $x_i \leq x_j$ and 0 otherwise. Informally, $\mathcal{F}_n(\cdots)$ is a step function that adds $\frac{1}{n}$ mass for every point in $\mathbf{x} = \{x_1, x_2, \cdots, x_n\}$.

Likewise, the unimodal distribution $\mathcal{F}_U$ is given such that for its domain $\mathcal{D}$,

$$\exists x_m \in \mathcal{D} : \quad \frac{\mathrm{d}}{\mathrm{dx}}(\mathcal{F}_U(x)) \geq 0 \text{ for } x \leq x_m \quad \text{and} \quad \frac{\mathrm{d}}{\mathrm{dx}}(\mathcal{F}_U(x)) \leq 0 \text{ for } x \geq x_m$$

In other words, there exists a *mode* (i.e. x_m) in the input domain of the function such that the function is *increasing* for all $x \leq x_m$ and *decreasing* for all $x \geq x_m$.

Given this definition, the Dip Test of Unimodality measures how far $\mathcal{F}_n(\mathbf{x})$ deviates from $\mathcal{F}_U$. Concretely, the Dip statistic is the following computation:

$$D_{stat} = \mid \mathcal{F}_n(\mathbf{x}) - \mathcal{F}_U(\mathbf{x}) \mid_{\infty} : \mathbf{x} \in \sup$$

Informally, D_{stat} is then the infinite norm of the differences of the EDF and the best fitting unimodal distribution over the support of these functions. It is straightforward to see that since we compute the infinite norm, considering the kernel of these functions is wasteful computation, hence the statistic restricts to computing over the support supp of $\mathcal{F}_n$.

3 Statistical Modeling of Interleaved Attacks

It is useful to first devise a statistical model of interleaved attacks in their most generic form: without any assumptions on both the attack itself as well as the benign program within which the attack is interleaved. As intended by [13], this approach allows us to view *interleaved* attacks as a new mechanism of hiding *any* micro-architectural attack. Such an attack-agnostic modeling of interleaved attacks then informs a generic detection mechanism independent of considerations of the actual use case and thereby extends beyond case studies presented in this work to any micro-architectural attack in general.

3.1 Viewing HPCs as Gaussian Samplers

The first intermediary requirement is to understand what kind of distribution do HPCs adopt. By design, all Hardware Performance Counters (HPCs) are monotonic in nature and increment at the frequency of the occurrence of events they count. For example, on Intel's systems[3], INST_RETIRED.ANY counts the number of x86 instructions retired and will increment at the frequency with which the backend's instruction retirement unit retires instructions. Likewise, BR_INST_RETIRED.ALL_BRANCHES counts the number of retired branch instructions and will increment at the frequency with which the frontend's branch predictor unit retires branches.

Now the *frequency* of HPC update may or may not be affected by certain *assumptions* on the software executing on the processor. As a concrete example, ASSISTS.HARDWARE[4] counts the number of hardware assists during speculation. It is evident that not all software will thereby lead to increments in this HPC; one has to write software with corner cases [5] that has opportunities for hardware assists in order to increment this HPC. Informally, we call such HPCs as requiring *assumptions* on the software: they require special conditions in software to trigger increments. On the other hand, HPCs like INST_RETIRED.ANY are more relaxed in assumptions since *all* software triggers the instruction retirement unit in the backend execution unit. Informally stating, no matter what software executes, INST_RETIRED.ANY will always increment. Using this, we state an observation.

Observation 1 (Modeling HPCs as Gaussian Samplers). . HPCs that do not enforce assumptions on software can be reliably modeled as Gaussian samplers. Because variations in their increments are not from assumptions in the software executing, but from infrequent events like non-maskable interrupts, non-voluntary context switches, priority scheduling from the kernel, and so on.

Some concrete examples[5] of such HPCs: INST_RETIRED.ANY, BR_INST_RETIRED. ALL_BRANCHES, and LONGEST_LAT_CACHE.REFERENCE. Note that BR_INST_RETIRED. ALL_BRANCHES (counts the number of branches) and LONGEST_LAT_CACHE.REFERENCE (counts the number of memory accesses) do impose *some* assumptions on software in order to increment: ①️ BR_INST_RETIRED.ALL_BRANCHES requires call and jmp instructions, while ②️

---

[3] This with without loss of generality. A similar argument holds on other systems (like AMD) as well.

[4] https://perfmon-events.intel.com/ ; Alder Lake and Sapphire Rapids.

[5] https://perfmon-events.intel.com/.

LONGEST_LAT_CACHE.REFERENCE requires `load`/ `store` instructions. We also consider them in our *preliminary analysis* since loops, function calls, memory operations, if-else branches, etc. are fairly common programming constructs. However, note that INST_RETIRED.ANY increments for *any* instruction, and therefore imposes *absolutely* no assumptions on the software. Thereby, in *deployment* of our eventual detection mechanism, we only consider INST_RETIRED.ANY.

3.2   Viewing Interleaved Attacks as Bimodal Gaussian Samplers

We borrow the skeleton of an interleaved attack from [13]. Refer Listing 1.2: in a benign function, with very constrained probability, some micro-architectural attack is executed. For now, we place no assumptions on attack() or benign(). With this understanding, we combine our observation of Sect. 3.1 to state another observation:

```
void interleaved () {
    benign ();
    // this threshold is very small
    if (sample_probability () < threshold)
        attack ();
    benign ();
}
```

Listing 1.2. A skeleton of interleaved attack from [13].

Observation 2 (Modeling Interleaved attacks as Bimodal Gaussians). Considering measurements from HPCs that do not enforce assumptions on software, interleaved attacks can be reliably modeled as samples from Bimodal Gaussian mixtures.

Briefly, for the same HPC, the execution in Listing 1.2 either executes the function sequence (benign() + benign()) or the function sequence (benign() + attack() + benign()). Since the HPCs considered do not enforce any assumptions on these functions, measurements from such HPCs are essentially Gaussian samples. Finally, since there are two execution paths, the overall distribution of Listing 1.1 shall be a mixture of two Gaussian (i.e. a Bimodal Gaussian), written as $p(x)$:

$$p(x) = w_1 . \mathcal{N}(x; \mu_1, \sigma_1) + w_2 . \mathcal{N}(x; \mu_2, \sigma_2)$$

where $\mathcal{N}(x; \mu_1, \sigma_1)$ corresponds to the execution path (benign() + benign()), and $\mathcal{N}(x; \mu_2, \sigma_2)$ corresponds to the execution path (benign() + attack() + benign()). Also note that since threshold is small, $w_2 << 1$. Finally, $w_1 + w_2 = 1$ since either of the two execution paths will definitely execute in each run of interleaved().

3.3 Motivating Example of an Interleaved Attack

Consider a concrete instantiation of Listing 1.2 as an actual attack as in Algo. 1. Concretely, in Algo. 1, the execution pattern of the interleaved attack comprises a Flush+Reload covert channel as the malicious code and a matrix-matrix multiplication operation as the benign execution. The interleaved attack is governed by a threshold mechanism, where the threshold dictates whether only the benign code or both the benign and malicious code are executed concurrently. Initially, the threshold is set to 10000, with `num_of_samples` configured as 5×threshold and `num_of_traces` set to 100000. Under this configuration, the malicious code is executed at an interval of $\frac{1}{10000}$, while the benign code dominates execution during the remaining iterations.

From the discussion in Sect. 3.1, for *preliminary analysis*, we consider `BR_INST_RETIRED.ALL_BRANCHES`, `INST_RETIRED.ANY`, and `LONGEST_LAT_CACHE.REFERENCE`[6]. In Fig. 1a, Fig. 1b, and Fig. 1c, we give concrete distributions of these HPCs for Algo. 1 (but without `attack()`, i.e. no interleaving). It is clear how these HPCs follow a Gaussian distribution.

Should we enable `attack()` (i.e. enable interleaving), the concrete distributions of `BR_INST_RETIRED.ALL_BRANCHES`, `INST_RETIRED.ANY`, `LONGEST_LAT_CACHE.REFERENCE` are as captured in Fig. 2a, Fig. 2b, and Fig. 2c. Note how the red curves in the figures have a *short* second peak, denoting the occurrence of interleaved attacks[7], signifying the low threshold with which `attack()` is interleaved in `benign()` execution.

Algorithm 1 Interleaved Attack Example

```
1: procedure ATTACK_CODE
2:    flush_reload();
3: procedure BENIGN
4:    matmul();
5: procedure MAIN
6:    for outer = 1 to num_of_traces do
7:       for inner = 1 to num_of_samples do
8:          if inner % threshold = 0 then
9:             attack();
10:          benign()
```

---

[6] Actual deployment of the detection mechanism is only using `INST_RETIRED.ANY`, for reasons detailed in Sect. 3.1.

[7] The bimodal nature of `interleaved()` is software-agnostic because of the choice of HPCs, that do not enforce any assumptions on software. As such, this phenomenon is true when `benign()` executes SPEC2017, which is the actual `benign()` implementation in [13]. Refer Sect. 5 for details on runs through SPEC2017.

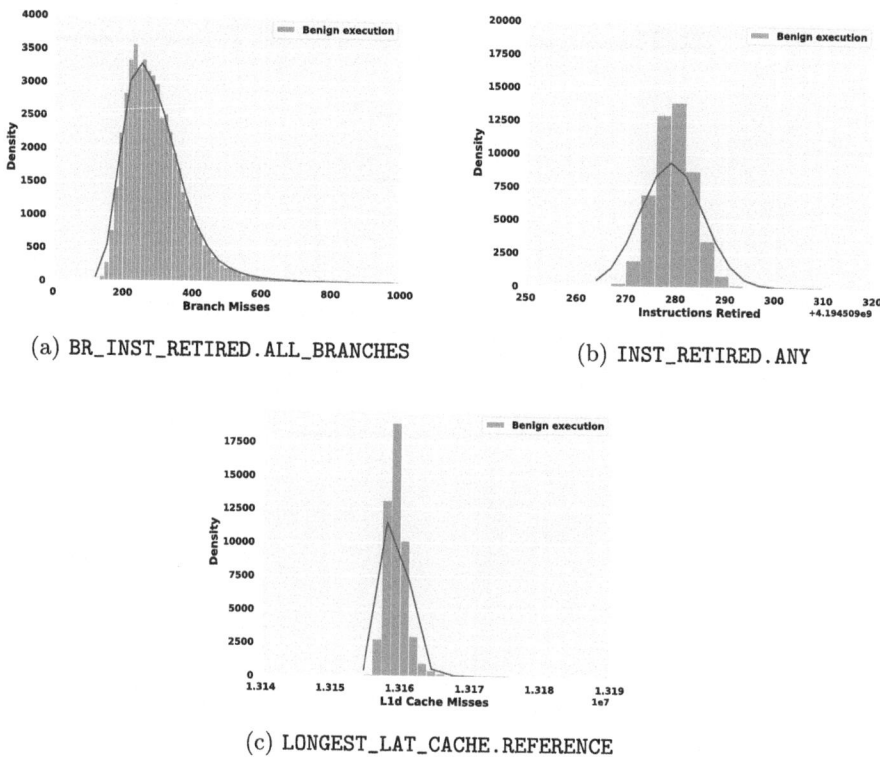

(a) `BR_INST_RETIRED.ALL_BRANCHES`   (b) `INST_RETIRED.ANY`

(c) `LONGEST_LAT_CACHE.REFERENCE`

Fig. 1. Distribution of different HPCs with respect to Algo. 1, but without `attack()`.

3.4   Fitting Gaussian Mixture Model with BIC/AIC Criteria

Finally, to formally establish the bimodality of interleaved attacks, we fit a Gaussian Mixture Model (GMM) with multiple modalities and leverage the Bayesian Information Criterion (BIC) and Akaike Information Criterion (AIC) to determine the optimal number of Gaussian components. This approach facilitates the identification of distinct latent distributions within the HPC readings, corresponding to various operational modes, including both normal execution and attack-induced anomalies. The GMM approach allows us to rigorously model the heterogeneity in the HPC readings and conclusively compute the modality of the distribution enforced by interleaved attacks.

Table 1 captures the BIC and AIC for when GMM is fitted to the readings collected for `INST_RETIRED.ANY` while the interleaved attack is operational (i.e. the red curve in Fig. 2b). Concretely, the GMM models the data as a mixture of k Gaussian distributions. The likelihood of data x under a GMM with k components is:

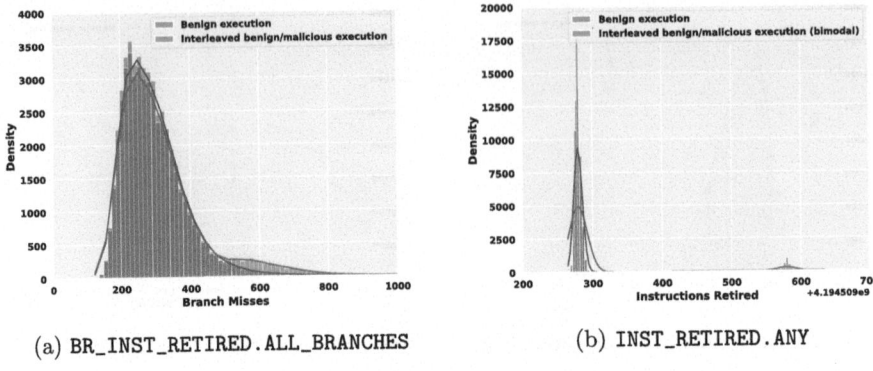

(a) BR_INST_RETIRED.ALL_BRANCHES   (b) INST_RETIRED.ANY

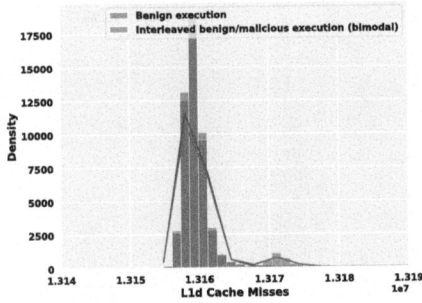

(c) LONGEST_LAT_CACHE.REFERENCE

Fig. 2. Distribution of different HPCs with respect to a sample program (matrix-matrix multiplication) and interleaved attack code (Flush+Reload covert channel) with interleaving probability $\frac{1}{10000}$.

$$p(x) = \sum_{i=1}^{k} \pi_i \mathcal{N}(x|\mu_i, \sigma_i) \tag{1}$$

where π_i are the mixing coefficients[8], μ_i is the mean of the i-th Gaussian, and σ_i is the standard deviation of the i-th Gaussian. We fit GMMs with $k \in \{1, 2, 3, 4, 5\}$ to parameterize the underlying distribution enforced by INST_RETIRED.ANY. Final model selection is based on BIC and AIC, which balance model fit and the complexity (i.e. number of modes in the multi-modal Gaussian fitted):

$$\text{AIC} = 2p - 2\ln(L), \quad \text{BIC} = p\ln(n) - 2\ln(L) \tag{2}$$

where p is the number of model parameters, L the log-likelihood, and n the number of data points. Lower BIC/AIC values indicate accurate modeling. In case of Tab. 1, notice how for two components (i.e. when GMM fits a bimodal to the red curve in Fig. 2b), we observe the optimal BIC and AIC, thereby further

---

[8] The probability that x belongs to the i-th Gaussian in p.

establishing the bimodality of interleaved attacks. The primary peak corresponds to normal behavior, while the secondary peak represents deviations caused by interleaved attacks. A similar result of bimodality was also observed while trying other HPCs in a similar setting of interleaved attacks.

Table 1. BIC and AIC for `INST_RETIRED.ANY` while interleaved attack is operational. red marking denotes the optimal/minimum BIC and AIC.

Components in GMM	BIC	AIC
1	901113.744073	901094.718222
2	404847.192319	404799.627691
3	405288.252292	405212.148888
4	405601.373257	405496.731076
5	405717.546513	405584.365557

4 Generic Detection Strategy for Interleaved Attacks

Section 3 conclusively establishes interleaved attacks to follow a bimodal gaussian distribution, without any assumptions on `attack()` or `benign()` (cf. Listing 1.2). It is straightforward to then infer that a suitable statistical test for unimodality is sufficient to detect such attacks. In this work, we rely upon the Dip test for unimodality[9]. Therefore, to determine whether the system is in an attack-free state or actively under attack, we employ the *Dip Test* as a first step to validate the dataset's modality, followed by a detailed analysis of the relative prominence of these peaks.

4.1 Dip Test Confirmation of Bimodality

The *Dip Test of Unimodality* [11] is a non-parametric hypothesis test used to assess whether a dataset deviates from unimodality by measuring the maximum deviation of the empirical distribution function (EDF) from the closest unimodal distribution. In this context, the Dip Test allows us to statistically confirm the presence of two distinct modes in the dataset, representing normal (benign) and attack-induced behaviors. The null hypothesis H_0 of the Dip Test is: the dataset follows a unimodal distribution, while the alternative hypothesis H_1 posits that the data is of modality > 1.

Upon applying the Dip Test to the dataset, the rejection of the null hypothesis H_0 provides evidence that the distribution is indeed bimodal. This confirms that the dataset contains two distinct Gaussian components—one associated with benign system behavior and the other with interleaved attack patterns.

---

[9] Note that the widely used Welch's t-test is unsuitable here, as it assumes unimodal normality in source distribution.

4.2   Interpreting the Results: Determining Attack Presence

While the Dip Test confirms the dataset's bimodality, it does not directly indicate the current operational state- whether the system is functioning normally or is under attack. To address this, we proceed by analyzing the relative distribution of data points between the two identified peaks (corresponding to the benign and attack modes). The following criteria are employed:

benign() **execution.** The system can be considered to be in a normal (attack-free) state if the majority of data points are concentrated around the primary peak, which corresponds to normal system behavior. In this case, the contribution of the secondary peak, representing attack activity, is negligible or non-existent. Mathematically, this can be expressed by evaluating the probability density under the primary Gaussian component. If the proportion of data points assigned to the primary peak exceeds a predefined threshold θ, the system is classified as *attack-free*:

$$P(\text{primary peak}) > \theta$$

where θ is a high confidence threshold, typically set around 95%, to ensure robust detection of normal behavior.

benign() + attack() **execution.** Conversely, an ongoing attack is indicated if a non-trivial portion of data points lies within the secondary peak, suggesting frequent deviations from the normal operational mode. The magnitude of the secondary peak, characterized by its mixing coefficient in the Gaussian Mixture Model (GMM), becomes a key metric for identifying an attack. Specifically, we monitor the ratio between the mixing coefficients π_2 of the secondary peak (attack behavior) and π_1 of the primary peak (normal behavior):

$$\frac{\pi_2}{\pi_1} > \delta$$

where δ is a predefined threshold (0.05 in our experiments) that reflects the level of sensitivity to anomalies. If the mixing coefficient ratio exceeds this threshold, it indicates that the system is under attack, as the secondary peak is no longer merely an outlier but has become significant in relation to the primary peak.

We summarize the takeaways from Sec. 3 and Sec. 4 below:

1. HPCs like INST_RETIRED.ANY do not enforce any assumption on the software, and thus are closely modeled by unimodal Gaussians, with operational noise.
2. Interleaved attacks take one of two possible paths: benign() or benign() + attack(). Thereby, when interleaved attacks are sampled through INST_RETIRED.ANY, we observe two distinct modes, i.e. a bimodal Gaussian. The peak corresponding to benign() + attack() is of much shorter since benign() + attack() executes with very less probability.
3. Since the difference between benign() and benign() + attack() is the modality of the Gaussian, statistical tests for unimodality suffice to detect when benign() + attack() executes, irrespective of the frequency of execution.

5 Case Studies

In this section, we demonstrate the detection of various attack types concealed within benign code, collectively forming an interleaved attack. All experiments were conducted on Intel systems, with specifications detailed in Table 2. In newer generation Intel systems, speculative execution attacks like Spectre v1, Spectre v2, Spectre v3, and Meltdown are mitigated. For our experiments, we disabled all such mitigations, wherever needed.

Figure 3 summarizes the end-to-end detection framework. Unlike Sect. 3, the benign() execution throughout this section is gcc_r from SPEC2017 (as used in [13] as well). Finally, it is clear from Sect. 3 and Sect. 4 that the detection strategy follows trivially from modeling the statistical nature of interleaved attacks, and using the correct test to detect. However, throughout this section, we choose to *instantiate* the detector through LLMs, for a number of reasons. First, LLMs abstract away the working details of the detection and allow users to interact with it in natural language; this allows for: ① an almost non-existent learning curve to *use* our detector in deployment. Secondly, LLMs also abstract away contextualization of data from multiple sources (i.e. HPCs); this allows ② the flexibility to *add* more HPC sources to the detection methodology than what we currently demonstrate. Finally, again with simple prompts in natural language, users can easily switch between statistical tests; this allows for ③ flexibility to add other statistical tests to our detector in addition to the Dip Test for Unimodality to cover other use-cases outside the scope of this work[10].

---

[10] For example, a real *deployment* of detection would like to detect *both* state-of-the-art legacy cache side-channel attacks, as well as interleaved attacks. Thus such detectors would need to switch between ① statistical tests, ② data sources (HPCs), ③ detection intervals, and ④ other parameters to effectively operate. While such a *combined* detector is essentially programmable in a high-level programming language, using

Table 2. Processor details for systems on interleaved attacks are performed

Generation	Model Name	Code Name
13th Generation	Intel(R) Core(M) 17-13700	Raptor Lake
12th Generation	Intel(R) Core(M) 15-12500	Alder Lake
8th Generation	Intel(R) Core(TM) 17-8700 CPU @ 3.20GHz	Coffee Lake

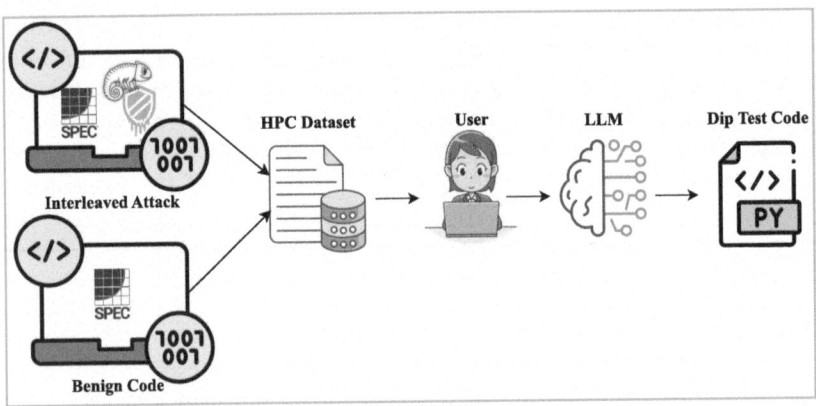

Fig. 3. Detection Strategy for Interleaved Attacks leveraging LLM

5.1   Spectre v1

In Algorithm 1, we initially employed a basic matrix multiplication operation as the benign workload, alongside a simple Flush+Reload attack as the malicious component. This served as the foundation for developing a generalized attack detection methodology. Expanding on this, we now extend the framework to cover a broader range of attack types. For this, we use the gcc_r benchmark from the SPEC CPU2017 suite as the benign code, which reflects a more realistic and complex execution environment, as discussed in Kosasih et al. [13]. In contrast, the malicious workload consists of a Spectre v1 attack, configured to execute with a very low probability to ensure it remains hidden within the legitimate activity of the benign program. In spectre v1 attack, the attacker manipulates the CPU's branch predictor, causing it to incorrectly predict the direction of a branch. This leads the CPU to execute instructions speculatively that would not normally be executed according to the correct program logic. As a result, the attacker can access sensitive data stored in the program's memory. During execution of the interleaved attack, we collect hardware performance counter (HPC) values to capture the system's runtime behavior.

As detailed in Sect. 4, the captured HPC dataset is subsequently input into a large language model (LLM), which is tasked with performing the Dip test. The

---

LLMs allows abstracting out much inner details, allowing for an easier operational interface for the end-user.

Dip test serves as a crucial tool for detecting multimodal distributions within the data, which are indicative of interleaved attacks, such as Spectre v1. Leveraging the LLM for conducting the Dip test enhances the detection process by utilizing its advanced pattern recognition capabilities, which may outperform traditional statistical approaches in identifying subtle anomalies. By running the Dip test on the HPC dataset, we can ascertain whether interleaved malicious activity is occurring, thus providing a robust mechanism for detecting stealthy attacks embedded within legitimate workloads.

ChatBox 1: Spectre v1 Interleaved Attack detection

User: Hi! Can you kindly perform a Dip test on the provided HPC dataset file to check whether my system is currently undergoing any interleaved attacks?

LLM: Sure!! Here is the code for the dip test you may execute it on our system to check for interleaved attacks, executing on your system.

```
import pandas as pd
from diptest import diptest
file_path = ''file_path.txt''
data = pd.read_csv(file_path, header=None)
data_values = data[0].values
dip_stat, p_value = diptest(data_values)
print(''Dip Test statistic:'', dip_stat, ''p-value:'', p_value)
if p_value < 0.05:
  print(''Yes!, Interleaved attack is executing.'')
else:
  print(''Your system is safe'')
```

After running this, the dip test will tell you if there are multiple peaks in your dataset. A p-value below 0.05 would refer that your system is undergoing an interleaved attack.

Moreover, the integration of an LLM in the detection process not only adds a layer of sophistication in interpreting multimodal data distributions but also strengthens the overall detection framework. This hybrid approach, combining statistical testing with machine learning techniques, ensures more accurate and efficient detection of low-probability malicious executions such as Spectre v1, which are designed to evade conventional detection mechanisms.

5.2   Spectre v2

In the preceding case study 5.1, we demonstrated the detection of an interleaved attack where the malicious activity was attributed to Spectre v1. In this section, we extend our analysis by considering Spectre v2 as the malicious component within the algorithm 1, while the benign workload remains unchanged, specifically the gcc_r benchmark. In spectre v2 the attacker targets a specific code sequence, or 'gadget,' in the victim's memory by exploiting the Branch Target Buffer (BTB). By mis-training the BTB to predict the wrong target for an indirect branch, the attacker redirects speculative execution to the gadget's address. While the CPU corrects the mis-prediction, changes to the cache persist, allowing sensitive data extraction via cache side-channel attacks. The attack is successful by aligning virtual addresses between the attacker and victim memory, even without executable code at the attacker's gadget address

As with 5.1, we collect HPC events, particularly `BR_INST_RETIRED.ALL_BRANCHES` and `INST_RETIRED.ANY`, during the execution of the interleaved attack.

The collected HPC event data is processed through an LLM, which outputs a corresponding Dip test code. This code is executed on our system to assess whether the interleaved attack is successfully mounted.

5.3   Spectre v2 with Advanced Gadgets

Spectre v2 revealed critical weaknesses in modern CPU architectures, exploiting branch target injection to force speculative execution down unintended paths, resulting in data leakage through side channels. Although hardware and software mitigations like IBRS and Retpoline have been introduced, attackers have developed advanced gadgets to overcome these defenses and exploit speculative execution more effectively. One prominent class of these advanced techniques includes dispatch gadgets, which allow attackers to gain greater control over CPU registers and execution flow. Key types of dispatch gadgets include:

Dispatch-to-Call attackers redirect control to unexpected but legitimate code segments, manipulating CPU registers through intermediary steps.

Dispatch-to-Any allows jumps to arbitrary locations when Indirect Branch Tracking (IBT) is disabled, expanding the attack surface.

Dispatch-to-Dispatcher multiple dispatchers are chained, allowing attackers to orchestrate more complex speculative execution paths.

So we have replaced the malicious code present in Algo. 1, one of these three gadgets at a time, and measured the HPC events. Following a similar process shown in 5.1, we get the Dip test code, with which we can check for the interleaved attack getting mounted on the system or not. With this too, we achieve a 100% detection rate.

5.4   Spectre v3

Spectre v3 is a variant of Spectre family of attacks that rely upon Branch History Injection. Concretely, the attack poisons the branch predictor by maliciously injected branches, which forces the processor (under speculation) to mis-issue incorrect branches. As with previous case studies, we use `INST_RETIRED.ANY` to detect Spectre v3, and succeed with a 100% detection rate.

5.5   Meltdown

Finally, we also test our detection methodology with Meltdown which follows a completely different attack strategy than Spectre v1 and its later variants. Precisely, in face of a faulted `load`, data belonging to the victim address space gets incorrectly forwarded to the adversarial address space under speculation. The adversary then uses a covert channel (like Flush+Reload) to encode such transiently forwarded data into the cache. The predominant reason for Meltdown is aggressive speculation in on-core buffers, which do not respect software isolation boundaries.

Our detection methodology, along with the choice of HPC `INST_RETIRED.ANY`, is generic enough to warrant no additional change when we shift from Spectre to Meltdown. In this case as well, when Meltdown executes, a bimodal distribution is observed, that is captured by the Dip Test of Unimodality. This is irrespective of the frequency of interleaving Meltdown with `gcc_r`. In this case too, we achieve 100% detection rate.

6   Statistical Modeling of Interleaved Attacks with > 1 Multiplicity

The interleaved attack strategy from [13] considers a single attack interleaved in benign execution (cf. Listing 1.1). Here, we consider an even stronger threat model: the adversary can interleave $N > 1$ attack vectors within the same benign code. Concretely, such interleaved attacks with > 1 multiplicity can be considered as what Listing 1.3 depicts.

```
void interleaved() {
    benign();
    // this threshold is very small
    if(sample_probability() < threshold){
        attack = pick_one(attack1, attack2, ..., attackN)
        attack();
    }
    benign();
}
```

Listing 1.3. A skeleton of interleaved attack from [13].

Borrowing our discussion from Sect. 3, we can statistically model such an attack vector as a Multimodal Gaussian of form:

$$p(\mathbf{x}) = w_b \cdot \mathcal{N}(\mathbf{x}; \mu_b, \sigma_b) + w_1 \cdot \mathcal{N}(\mathbf{x}; \mu_1, \sigma_1) + w_2 \cdot \mathcal{N}(\mathbf{x}; \mu_2, \sigma_2) + \cdots + w_N \cdot \mathcal{N}(\mathbf{x}; \mu_N, \sigma_N)$$

where $w_b \cdot \mathcal{N}(\mathbf{x}; \mu_b, \sigma_b)$ denotes the benign execution (`benign()` + `benign()`) and $w_i \cdot \mathcal{N}(\mathbf{x}; \mu_i, \sigma_i)$; $\forall i \in \{1, \cdots, N\}$ denotes the execution (`benign()` + `attack_i` + `benign()`). We recall that the *Dip test for Unimodality* is able to detect multimodal distributions as well. As with Sect. 4.2, the following criteria is applied:

benign() execution. As before, the system is in a normal state if the majority of data points are concentrated around the primary peak. As before, this is mathematically represented as:

$$P(\text{primary peak}) > \theta$$

benign() + attack$_i$() execution. In this case, unlike before, we now have the ratio parameterized by i, to denote the i-th attack executing, such as:

$$\frac{\pi_i}{\pi_1} > \delta$$

If the ratio of mixing coefficients exceeds this threshold (0.05 in our experiments), it indicates that the system is under attack, as the secondary peak has become significant in relation to the primary peak.

7   Conclusion

In this work, we introduce a novel detection methodology for micro-architectural attacks in a probabilistically interleaved malicious/benign execution environment. By leveraging lightweight statistical tools such as Gaussian Mixture Models (GMM) and the Dip test for Unimodality, we demonstrate the ability to detect subtle deviations in hardware performance counter (HPC) data caused by low-frequency interleaved attacks. The detection process is further streamlined by utilizing Large Language Models (LLMs) to automate the generation of Dip test code, allowing users to efficiently identify multimodal distributions indicative of interleaved attacks. Our experiments show a 100% detection rate for attacks like Spectre v1/v2/v3 and Meltdown, even when interleaved with benign processes at very low frequencies.

This work refutes the assumption that probabilistically interleaved attacks are inherently undetectable by showcasing the effectiveness of lightweight statistical analysis in identifying such threats. While the LLM in this context primarily serves to provide automated Dip-test code, its integration facilitates quick and accessible implementation of detection strategies without requiring deep expertise in statistical analysis. Our findings highlight the importance of adaptable detection techniques and the need for further research into both advanced evasion tactics and more sophisticated countermeasures, ensuring continued resilience against evolving micro-architectural attacks.

Acknowledgment. The authors would like to thank the reviewers for their suggestions for improving the paper. They would also like to thank the Department of Science and Technology (DST), Govt of India, IHUB NTIHAC Foundation, C3i Building, Indian Institute of Technology Kanpur, and Centre on Hardware-Security Entrepreneurship Research and Development, MeitY, Govt of India, for partially funding this research.

References

1. Ahmad, B.A.: Detecting Spectre and Meltdown Attacks Using Hardware Performance Counters and Machine Learning. Ph.D. thesis, PhD thesis. University of the Punjab (2019)
2. Akram, A., Mushtaq, M., Bhatti, M.K., Lapotre, V., Gogniat, G.: Meet the sherlock holmes' of side channel leakage: A survey of cache sca detection techniques. IEEE Access **8**, 70836–70860 (2020)
3. Aldaya, A.C., Brumley, B.B., ul Hassan, S., García, C.P., Tuveri, N.: Port contention for fun and profit. In: 2019 IEEE Symposium on Security and Privacy (SP), pp. 870–887. IEEE (2019)
4. Aweke, Z.B., et al.: Anvil: software-based protection against next-generation rowhammer attacks. ACM SIGPLAN Notices **51**(4), 743–755 (2016)
5. Chakraborty, A., Mishra, N., Mukhopadhyay, D.: Shesha: multi-head microarchitectural leakage discovery in new-generation intel processors. arXiv preprint arXiv:2406.06034 (2024)
6. Eresheim, S., Luh, R., Schrittwieser, S.: The evolution of process hiding techniques in malware-current threats and possible countermeasures. J. Inf. Process. **25**, 866–874 (2017)
7. Genkin, D., Poussier, R., Sim, R.Q., Yarom, Y., Zhao, Y.: Cache vs. key-dependency: side channeling an implementation of pilsung. IACR Transactions on Cryptographic Hardware and Embedded Systems pp. 231–255 (2020)
8. Gonzalez-Gomez, J., Bauer, L., Henkel, J.: Cache-based side-channel attack mitigation for many-core distributed systems via dynamic task migration. IEEE Trans. Inf. Forensics Secur. **18**, 2440–2450 (2023)
9. Gullasch, D., Bangerter, E., Krenn, S.: Cache games–bringing access-based cache attacks on AES to practice. In: 2011 IEEE Symposium on Security and Privacy, pp. 490–505. IEEE (2011)
10. Gulmezoglu, B., Zankl, A., Tol, M.C., Islam, S., Eisenbarth, T., Sunar, B.: Undermining user privacy on mobile devices using AI. In: Proceedings of the 2019 ACM ASIA Conference on Computer and Communications Security, pp. 214–227 (2019)
11. Hartigan, J.A., Hartigan, P.M.: The dip test of unimodality. Ann. Stat. 70–84 (1985)
12. Kocher, P., et al.: Spectre attacks: exploiting speculative execution. Commun. ACM **63**(7), 93–101 (2020)
13. Kosasih, W., Feng, Y., Chuengsatiansup, C., Yarom, Y., Zhu, Z.: Sok: can we really detect cache side-channel attacks by monitoring performance counters? In: AsiaCCS (2024)
14. Lipp, M., et al.: Meltdown: reading kernel memory from user space. Commun. ACM **63**(6), 46–56 (2020)
15. Liu, F., Yarom, Y., Ge, Q., Heiser, G., Lee, R.B.: Last-level cache side-channel attacks are practical. In: 2015 IEEE Symposium on Security and Privacy, pp. 605–622. IEEE (2015)
16. Moghimi, D.: Downfall: exploiting speculative data gathering. In: 32nd USENIX Security Symposium (USENIX Security 23), pp. 7179–7193 (2023)
17. Osvik, D.A., Shamir, A., Tromer, E.: Cache attacks and countermeasures: the case of AES. In: Pointcheval, D. (ed.) CT-RSA 2006. LNCS, vol. 3860, pp. 1–20. Springer, Heidelberg (2006). https://doi.org/10.1007/11605805_1

18. Ragab, H., Barberis, E., Bos, H., Giuffrida, C.: Rage against the machine clear: a systematic analysis of machine clears and their implications for transient execution attacks. In: 30th USENIX Security Symposium (USENIX Security 21), pp. 1451–1468 (2021)
19. Yarom, Y., Falkner, K.: {FLUSH+ RELOAD}: a high resolution, low noise, l3 cache {Side-Channel} attack. In: 23rd USENIX security symposium (USENIX security 14), pp. 719–732 (2014)
20. Yarom, Y., Genkin, D., Heninger, N.: Cachebleed: a timing attack on openssl constant-time RSA. J. Cryptogr. Eng. **7**, 99–112 (2017)
21. Zhang, Y., Juels, A., Reiter, M.K., Ristenpart, T.: Cross-VM side channels and their use to extract private keys. In: Proceedings of the 2012 ACM conference on Computer and Communications Security, pp. 305–316 (2012)

FPGA-Based Acceleration of Homomorphic Convolution with Plaintext Kernels

Extended Abstract

Rohith George Ninan$^{(\boxtimes)}$ ⓘ and S. Kala ⓘ

Department of ECE, Indian Institute of Information Technology Kottayam,
Kerala 686635, India
{rohith21bec7,kala}@iiitkottayam.ac.in

Abstract. Homomorphic encryption (HE) allows computations on encrypted data, safeguarding sensitive information and enabling secure data processing in untrusted cloud environments. However, the computational complexity of current HE schemes has hindered its practical deployment. While CPUs and GPUs cannot efficiently handle HE's integer-based parallelisable workloads, FPGAs offer a compelling solution, offering both flexibility and computational efficiency. In this paper, we present an FPGA-based implementation of homomorphic 2D convolution, targeting the BFV scheme. By focusing on optimising ciphertext-plaintext multiplications and ciphertext-ciphertext additions, we reduce computational overhead while maintaining data security. Our work applies plaintext convolutional filters to encrypted images, forming the foundation for feature extraction nodes in deep learning models. This approach enables secure processing of encrypted data, making it suitable for privacy-preserving machine learning applications.

Keywords: Homomorphic Encryption · BFV Scheme · FPGA · Feature Extraction · Image Processing

1 Introduction

In the era of cloud computing, privacy-preserving data processing is crucial. Homomorphic encryption (HE) offers a powerful solution by enabling computations on encrypted data without decryption, making it ideal for securely processing sensitive information in untrusted environments. This is especially relevant for deep learning applications involving sensitive data, such as medical or financial records [4]. The Brakerski/Fan-Vercauteren (BFV) scheme allows homomorphic operations like addition and multiplication on ciphertexts, but its practical deployment faces challenges due to high computational overhead and limited operations [3]. Performing convolutions, a core task in CNNs, in the encrypted domain is particularly expensive because it involves numerous costly ciphertext-ciphertext multiplications, corresponding to the multiplication of large-degree cipher polynomials [2].

© The Author(s), under exclusive license to Springer Nature Switzerland AG 2025
J. Knechtel et al. (Eds.): SPACE 2024, LNCS 15351, pp. 221–224, 2025.
https://doi.org/10.1007/978-3-031-80408-3_14

Traditional hardware like CPUs and GPUs struggle with HE workloads-CPUs offer limited parallelism, and GPUs are optimised for floating-point rather than integer-based operations typical of HE. ASICs, though efficient, are impractical due to the non-standardised nature of HE [1]. FPGAs, with their reconfigurability and parallel processing capabilities, offer an ideal platform for accelerating HE-based tasks.

2   Homomorphic Convolution Approach

Our approach leverages the fact that one operand, the convolution kernel, is known to the compute system, and is stored as plaintext. By optimising ciphertext-plaintext multiplications and ciphertext-ciphertext additions, and avoiding the need for costly ciphertext-ciphertext multiplications, we reduce computational overhead and improve performance as shown in Fig. 1. Ciphertext-plaintext multiplication is efficiently performed through successive additions or subtractions, depending on the sign of the plaintext value.

The developed algorithm, detailed in Algorithm 1, initialises the output ciphertext (*cipherOut*) to zero. In cases where the encryption scheme does not inherently represent a zero plaintext as an all-zero ciphertext (as in the BFV scheme), *cipherOut* can instead be initialised by subtracting a ciphertext from itself or by obtaining the ciphertext for zero from the encrypting party.

Algorithm 1. Ciphertext-Plaintext Multiplication Algorithm

1: **Input:** Ciphertext *cipherIn*, Plaintext *pt* (with bit width PT_WIDTH)
2: **Output:** Ciphertext *cipherOut*
3: Initialize *cipherOut* to all zeros
4: $cipherTemp \leftarrow cipherIn$
5: $mask \leftarrow pt >> (PT\_WIDTH - 1)$
6: $ptTemp \leftarrow (mask + pt) \oplus mask$
7: **while** $ptTemp > 0$ **do**
8:     **if** $ptTemp \& 1$ **then**
9:         **if** $pt < 0$ **then**
10:             $cipherOut \leftarrow$ **cipherSub**$(cipherOut, cipherTemp)$
11:         **else**
12:             $cipherOut \leftarrow$ **cipherAdd**$(cipherOut, cipherTemp)$
13:         **end if**
14:     **end if**
15:     $cipherTemp \leftarrow$ **cipherAdd**$(cipherTemp, cipherTemp)$
16:     $ptTemp \leftarrow ptTemp >> 1$
17: **end while**
18: **Return** *cipherOut*

The convolution of the image and kernel is carried out by combining the ciphertext-plaintext multiplication module with the ciphertext-ciphertext addition module. Each encrypted pixel and plaintext weight is processed by the multiplication module, with the results accumulated using ciphertext-ciphertext addition.

3 Implementation and Results

The homomorphic convolution module has been implemented on a Xilinx Zynq 7000 FPGA using High-Level Synthesis (HLS) with an operating frequency of 230 MHz. The module supports configurable parameters such as kernel values, size, and stride at runtime, allowing adaptability across different CNN architectures. The encrypted input image is processed on the FPGA, and the encrypted

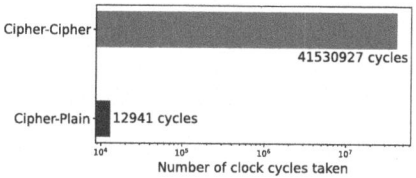

Fig. 1. Comparison of latency of cipher-plain and cipher-cipher multiplication on ciphertext of length 2^9

Fig. 2. Homomorphic Convolution with a 3×3 kernel

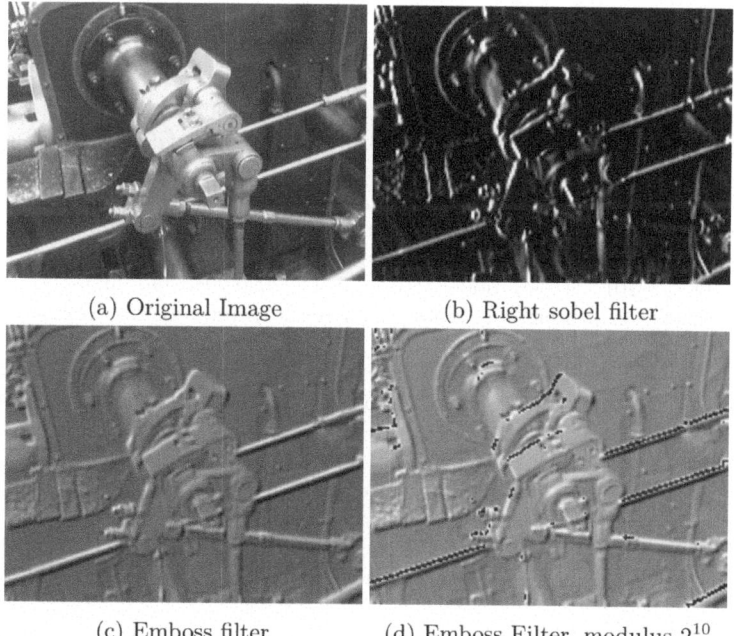

(a) Original Image   (b) Right sobel filter

(c) Emboss filter   (d) Emboss Filter, modulus 2^{10}

Fig. 3. Filters applied to a 640×480 px image in the encrypted domain

result is returned to the host for decryption. The performance of the FPGA implementation is benchmarked against an Intel i5 CPU running at 2.4 GHz as shown in Fig. 2.

The decryption results are returned modded to the plaintext modulus of the BFV scheme. If the result exceeds half the modulus, it is interpreted as negative due to wraparound. For image data with pixel values ranging from 0 to 255, we have found that a plaintext modulus of 2^{11} is sufficient to prevent errors, while smaller moduli (e.g., 2^{10}) result in extreme white pixels being interpreted as black and vice versa. These results are illustrated in Fig. 3.

4 Conclusion and Future Work

This paper presents an FPGA-based implementation of homomorphic 2D convolution operations, targeting the BFV scheme. We have focused on optimising ciphertext-plaintext multiplications and avoiding the expensive ciphertext-ciphertext operations. Our implementation supports runtime reconfigurability and is adaptable to various CNN architectures.

Future work will explore the use of techniques such as frequency transforms in the encrypted domain to further optimise the convolution process for more complex architectures. We also plan to extend the design to support more complex operations like pooling and activation functions.

References

1. Agrawal, R., et al.: FAB: an FPGA-based accelerator for bootstrappable fully homomorphic encryption. In: 2023 IEEE International Symposium on High-Performance Computer Architecture (HPCA), Montreal, QC, Canada, pp. 882–895. IEEE (2023). https://doi.org/10.1109/HPCA56546.2023.10070953, https://ieeexplore.ieee.org/document/10070953/
2. Turan, F., Roy, S.S., Verbauwhede, I.: HEAWS: an accelerator for homomorphic encryption on the Amazon AWS FPGA. IEEE Trans. Comput. **69**(8), 1185–1196 (2020). https://doi.org/10.1109/TC.2020.2988765, https://ieeexplore.ieee.org/abstract/document/9072637, conference Name: IEEE Transactions on Computers
3. Wibawa, F., Catak, F.O., Sarp, S., Kuzlu, M.: BFV-based homomorphic encryption for privacy-preserving CNN models. Cryptography **6**(3), 34 (2022). https://doi.org/10.3390/cryptography6030034, https://www.mdpi.com/2410-387X/6/3/34
4. Ye, T., Kuppannagari, S.R., Kannan, R., Prasanna, V.K.: Performance modeling and FPGA acceleration of homomorphic encrypted convolution. In: 2021 31st International Conference on Field-Programmable Logic and Applications (FPL), Dresden, Germany, pp. 115–121. IEEE (2021). https://doi.org/10.1109/FPL53798.2021.00027, https://ieeexplore.ieee.org/document/9556362/

Post-quantum Multi-client Conjunctive Searchable Symmetric Encryption from Isogenies

Sikhar Patranabis$^{(\boxtimes)}$ (iD)

IBM Research, Bangalore, India
sikhar.patranabis@ibm.com

Abstract. Multi-client searchable symmetric encryption (SSE) allows multiple third-party clients to execute fast encrypted search queries over a symmetrically encrypted database created by a data owner and held by an (untrusted) data server. Although SSE is ostensibly a symmetric-key cryptoprimitive, existing multi-client SSE schemes that support conjunctive and general Boolean queries rely crucially on the classical hardness of the discrete log problem over cyclic groups, and are completely broken by quantum attacks. This leaves open the question of designing multi-client conjunctive (and more expressive) SSE schemes from plausibly quantum-safe assumptions.

In this paper, we present the first plausibly quantum-safe multi-client SSE scheme supporting conjunctive keyword queries while relying on the hardness of certain isogeny-based assumptions (such as CSIDH and CSI-FiSh) that can be modeled using cryptographic group actions. As a core technical contribution, we present a novel adaptation of the widely studied but quantum-broken Oblivious Cross-Tags (OXT) protocol (Cash et al., Crypto 2013) to the setting of cryptographic group actions. This scheme, which we call GXT, supports conjunctive keyword queries in the single-client setting. We then present MC-GXT – an extension of GXT to the multi-client setting. Our constructions match the asymptotic efficiency guarantees of the original OXT scheme in terms of storage requirements and conjunctive query complexity, while additionally providing data and query privacy guarantees based on well-studied and plausibly quantum-safe isogeny-based hardness assumptions.

Keywords: Searchable Symmetric Encryption · Multi-client SSE · Post-quantum Security · Isogeny-based Cryptography · Group Actions

1 Introduction

Searchable symmetric encryption (SSE) [6,9,11,23] is a widely studied cryptographic primitive that supports efficient keyword-based query processing over symmetrically encrypted collections of documents (where each document is tagged with a set of keywords). Given a query consisting of one or more keywords,

J. Knechtel et al. (Eds.): SPACE 2024, LNCS 15351, pp. 225–257, 2025.
https://doi.org/10.1007/978-3-031-80408-3_15

the goal of SSE is to allow retrieving an (encrypted) list of document identifiers, pertaining to the documents tagged with the queried keywords. SSE schemes typically achieve fast and efficient encrypted query processing while allowing the server to learn some controlled amount of information (called "leakage") during query execution.

In this paper, we focus on SSE for *static* document collections (i.e., where the documents and keywords are fixed apriori). This is the most widely studied setting for SSE [6,9,11,13,16], and is particularly relevant to real-world applications where the client wishes to outsource a snapshot of a large database for query processing.

Single-Client SSE. The most commonly studied model for SSE is *single-client SSE* [5,6,8,11,17], which models the data owner D (that owns a document collection DB) and the client C querying DB as the *same* entity. In this model, D initially processes DB to generate an encrypted database EDB, which is sent to a (data) server dS for storage. D retains a (small) symmetric cryptographic key, that allows it to later execute encrypted keyword queries directly on EDB stored at dS, and to decrypt the matching list of encrypted document identifiers returned by dS. The information learnt by dS (about the plaintext database DB and the queries issued by D) is modeled formally using a *leakage function* $\mathcal{L}$.

Multi-client SSE. A richer, but much less studied, setting for SSE is *multi-client SSE*, where multiple third party clients are allowed to query the encrypted database EDB stored at dS, using query tokens authorized and issued by the data owner D. Beyond minimizing leakage to dS, multi-client SSE also aims to ensure query privacy for an honest client against a corrupt data owner D. This implies that D must *obliviously* issue C with the appropriate search token *without* learning the exact query issued by C (beyond, for instance, whether the query satisfies certain authorization policies). The study of multi-client SSE was initiated in [13], and has since been studied for dynamic databases [24].

The authors of [13] introduced a generic blueprint for multi-client SSE: a data owner D generates an encrypted database EDB and outsources it to a data server dS. Later, a third-party client C that wishes to query the encrypted database engages in a *token-generation protocol* with D, and obtains a search token stk. Finally, C engages in a *search protocol* with dS, where C inputs the search token stk, while dS inputs the encrypted database EDB. At the end of the protocol, C learns the query output. Following this blueprint, the authors of [13] proposed an elegant multi-client SSE scheme that supports conjunctive keyword queries over static databases. This scheme is an extension of the Oblivious Cross-Tags scheme (OXT) scheme for conjunctive queries in the single-client setting [6], and was subsequently optimized in [24].

Post-quantum Security. Although SSE is ostensibly a symmetric-key cryptoprimitive, the constructions in [6,13,24] use public-key techniques to achieve non-interactive and optimally efficient query processing, as well as to ensure optimal storage. Concretely, the constructions in [13,24] rely crucially on the hardness of the discrete log problem over cyclic prime-order groups. As a result, they are broken completely by known quantum polynomial-time algorithms for discrete log. While there have been certain very recent proposals for quantum-safe single-client SSE [25], to the best of our knowledge, there is no existing multi-client SSE scheme that resists quantum attackers. This motivates us to ask the following question:

Can we design an efficient yet quantum-safe multi-client SSE scheme supporting conjunctive keyword queries?

Our Contributions. In this paper, we answer the above question in the affirmative. We present the first plausibly quantum-safe multi-client SSE scheme supporting conjunctive keyword queries while relying on the hardness of certain isogeny-based assumptions (such as CSIDH [7], CSI-FiSh [2] and SCALLOP [12]) that can be modeled using cryptographic group actions. Our contributions may be summarized as follows:

– As a core technical contribution, we present an adaptation of the widely studied but quantum-broken single-client SSE scheme Oblivious Cross-Tags (OXT) [6] to the setting of cryptographic group actions. We call this scheme GXT. Similar to OXT, GXT supports conjunctive keyword queries over static databases. However, unlike OXT, which relies on the hardness of discrete log over prime-order cyclic groups, GXT relies on the group action equivalent of the decisional Diffie-Hellman (DDH) assumption, with plausibly quantum-safe instantiations from isogeny-based hardness assumptions.

– We then present MC-GXT – an extension of GXT to the multi-client setting. MC-GXT is achieved by combining a modified version of the GXT scheme with an oblivious PRF (known to have plausibly quantum-safe realizations from group actions [3]). To the best of our knowledge, MC-GXT is the first (and till date, only) quantum-safe multi-client SSE scheme.

Our constructions match the the asymptotic efficiency guarantees of the original OXT scheme in terms of storage requirements and conjunctive query complexity, while additionally providing data and query privacy guarantees based on well-studied and plausibly quantum-safe isogeny-based hardness assumptions.

We remark that the candidate cryptographic group actions from isogeny-based assumptions that exist (e.g., CSIDH [7], CSI-FiSh [2] and SCALLOP [12]) are somewhat limited in terms of concrete efficiency, notwithstanding certain recent improvements [22]. However, both GXT and MC-GXT use cryptographic group actions in a fully black-box way, and any improvements to the concrete efficiency of computing isogeny class group actions would also improve the concrete efficiency guarantees of the proposed schemes.

2 Preliminaries

In this section, we introduce notations and present preliminary background material. Due to lack of space in the body of the paper, we defer additional preliminaries to Appendix A.

Notations. We use $\mathbb{Z}$ and $\mathbb{N}$ to denote the set of all integers and the set of all natural numbers, respectively. We use $\mathbb{Z}_n$ (for some $n \in \mathbb{N}$) to denote the set of all integers modulo n (i.e., the set $\{0, 1, \ldots, n - 1\}$). We use $[a, b]$ (for $a, b \in \mathbb{Z}$, $a \leq b$) to denote the set of integers $\{a, a + 1, \ldots, b - 1, b\}$. The notation $[b]$ denotes $[1, b]$. Given a set $\mathcal{X}$, we denote by $x \leftarrow \mathcal{X}$ the process of sampling a value x from the uniform distribution over $\mathcal{X}$. The output x of a deterministic algorithm $\mathcal{A}$ is denoted by $x = \mathcal{A}$ and the output x' of a randomized algorithm $\mathcal{A}'$ is denoted by $x' \leftarrow \mathcal{A}'$. $\perp$ is a special character indicating that some algorithm failed to produce a valid output. We refer to $\lambda \in \mathbb{N}$ as the security parameter, and denote by $\mathsf{poly}(\lambda)$ and $\mathsf{negl}(\lambda)$ any generic (unspecified) polynomial and negligible function in λ, respectively.[1]

2.1 Cryptographic Group Actions

We now recall the definition of cryptographic group actions from [1]. The framework of cryptographic group action (studied initially by Brassard and Yung [4] and Couveignes [10]) allows for easy usage of certain isogeny-based hardness assumptions (in particular, assumptions over CSIDH [7], CSI-FiSh [2], and Scallop [12]) in cryptographic protocols.

Definition 1 (Group Action [1,4,10]). *A group G is said to* act on *a set X if there is a map $\star : G \times X \to X$ that satisfies:*

1. *Identity: If e is the identity element of G, then for any $x \in X$, we have $e \star x = x$.*
2. *Compatibility: For any $g, h \in G$ and any $x \in X$, we have $(gh) \star x = g \star (h \star x)$.*

Throughout, we use the notation $(G, X, \star)$ to denote a group action.

Remark 1. If $(G, X, \star)$ is a group action, for any $g \in G$ the map $\pi_g : x \mapsto g \star x$ defines a permutation of X.

Properties. We consider group actions $(G, X, \star)$ that satisfy one or more of the following properties:

1. *Abelian:* The group G is abelian.
2. *Transitive:* For every $x_1, x_2 \in X$, there exists a group element $g \in G$ such that $x_2 = g \star x_1$. For such a transitive group action, the set X is called a *homogeneous space* for G.
3. *Faithful:* For each group element $g \in G$, either g is the identity element or there exists a set element $x \in X$ such that $x \neq g \star x$.
4. *Free:* For each group element $g \in G$, g is the identity element if and only if there exists some set element $x \in X$ such that $x = g \star x$.
5. *Regular:* Both free *and* transitive.

---

[1] Note that a function $f : \mathbb{N} \to \mathbb{R}$ is said to be negligible in λ if for every positive polynomial p, $f(\lambda) < 1/p(\lambda)$ when λ is sufficiently large.

Remark 2. If a group action is regular, then for any $x \in X$, the map $f_x : g \mapsto g \star x$ defines a bijection between G and X; in particular, if G (or X) is finite, then we must have $|G| = |X|$.

Effective Group Action (EGA). We now recall the definition of an *effective* group action (EGA) from [1]. Formally, an abelian and regular group action $(G, X, \star)$ is *effective* if the following properties are satisfied:

1. The group G is finite and there exist efficient (PPT) algorithms for:
   (a) Membership testing, i.e., to decide if a given bit string represents a valid group element in G.
   (b) Equality testing, i.e., to decide if two bit strings represent the same group element in G.
   (c) Sampling, i.e., to sample an element g from a distribution G on G. In this paper, We consider distributions that are (statistically close to) uniform.
   (d) Operation, i.e., to compute gh for any $g, h \in G$.
   (e) Inversion, i.e., to compute g^{-1} for any $g \in G$.
2. The set X is finite and there exist efficient algorithms for:
   (a) Membership testing, i.e., to decide if a bit string represents a valid set element.
   (b) Unique representation, i.e., given any arbitrary set element $x \in X$, compute a string $\hat{x}$ that canonically represents x.
3. There exists a distinguished element $x_0 \in X$, called the *origin*, such that its bit-string representation is known.
4. There exists an efficient algorithm that given (some bit-string representations of) any $g \in G$ and any $x \in X$, outputs $g \star x$.

We refer the reader to [1] for additional variants of EGA.

Definition 2 (Group Action DDH [1]). *Let $(G, X, \star)$ be an EGA as defined above. We say that the Decisional Diffie-Hellman (DDH) assumption holds with respect to a group action $(G, X, \star)$ if for any security parameter λ such that $|G| = \omega(\lambda^c)$ for any $c = O(1)$, for any $g, h, k \leftarrow G$, for any $x \leftarrow X$, and for any PPT adversary $\mathcal{A}$, we have*

$$|\Pr[\mathcal{A}(x, g \star x, h \star x, (g \cdot h) \star x) = 0] - \Pr[\mathcal{A}(x, g \star x, h \star x, k \star x) = 0]| \leq \mathsf{negl}(\lambda).$$

2.2   Oblivious PRF

We recall the notion oblivious pseudorandom function (OPRF) [14, 15, 20]. Informally, an OPRF is a two-party protocol for evaluating a PRF F that is executed jointly by a client C and a server S. Concretely, C inputs some $x \in \mathcal{X}$ and S inputs a secret key $\mathsf{sk} \in \mathcal{K}$, such that at the end of the OPRF protocol, C learns $y = F(\mathsf{sk}, x) \in \mathcal{Y}$, while S learns nothing. In this paper, we consider a notion of OPRF that guarantees security against malicious corruption of either C or S. Ideally, we want an OPRF to satisfy the following properties:

- **Pseudorandomness:** the scheme behaves like a standard PRF in the view of any PPT adversary that is allowed to view *honest partial evaluations* under the OPRF protocol on polynomially many inputs (chosen adaptively and arbitrarily by the adversary).
- **Input-obliviousness:** for any input $x \in \mathcal{X}$ chosen by an honest client and any PPT adversary that corrupts the key-holding server, the adversary cannot guess x with probability non-negligibly greater than $1/|\mathcal{X}|$.
- **Consistency/uniqueness:** any execution of the protocol on a fixed input $x \in \mathcal{X}$ and a fixed key $\mathsf{sk} \in \mathcal{K}$ results in a unique final output $F(\mathsf{sk}, x)$.

Due to lack of space, we present the detailed definition in Appendix B.

OPRF from GA-DDH. In [3], the authors showed a construction of OPRF assuming the existence of any EGA $(G, X, \star)$ where the GA-DDH assumption holds. Their construction is based on an adaptation of the classically secure Naor-Reingold PRF [21] to the setting of EGA, which can be extended to an OPRF using any group action-based maliciously secure OT (proposed in several prior works [1,18]). Looking ahead, we use the OPRF from [3] for our construction of multi-client SSE.

2.3 Multi-client Searchable Symmetric Encryption

In this subsection, we recall the formal definitions of multi-client SSE for static databases from [13].

Databases. A database (equivalently, document collection) $\mathsf{DB} = (\mathsf{ind}_i, \mathsf{W}_i = \{w_{i,j}\})_{i \in [d]}$ is represented as a list of (document-identifier, keyword-set) pairs, where d denotes the total number of documents in DB. Each tuple $(\mathsf{ind}_i, \mathsf{W}_i) \in \mathsf{DB}$ corresponds to a document with identifier ind_i containing the set of keywords W_i. We denote by $\mathsf{W} = \bigcup_{i \in [d]} \mathsf{W}_i$ the set of *all* keywords in the database. For a keyword $w \in \mathsf{W}$, $\mathsf{DB}(w)$ denotes the set of all identifiers corresponding to documents containing w, i.e., $\mathsf{DB}(w) = \{\mathsf{ind}_i : \exists\ \mathsf{W}_i(\mathsf{ind}_i, \mathsf{W}_i) \in \mathsf{DB}\ \wedge\ w \in \mathsf{W}_i\}$. We use $N = \sum_{w \in \mathsf{W}} |\mathsf{DB}(w)|$ to denote the total number of valid keyword-document pairs in DB.

Conjunctive Queries. We represent a conjunctive query over n distinct keywords $w_1, \ldots, w_n$ as $q = (w_1 \wedge w_2 \wedge \ldots \wedge w_n)$ and define $\mathsf{DB}(q) = \cap_{i=1}^{n} \mathsf{DB}(w_i)$. Without loss of generality, the keyword w_1 is assumed to have the least frequency of occurrence and is referred to as the *s-term*, while the keywords $w_2, \ldots, w_n$ are referred to as *x-terms*.

Multi-client SSE. We formally describe the syntax of multi-client SSE below.

Definition 3 (Multi-client SSE). *A multi-client SSE scheme* MC-SSE *for static databases consists of three protocols* (Setup, Token, Search) *that are executed jointly by (some subset of) the following entities: (i) the data owner* D, *(ii) a client* C *(the system allows for multiple clients), and (iii) the data holding server* dS, *as follows:*

- (sk; EDB) ← Setup(1^λ; DB): *a protocol executed jointly by the data owner* D *and the data server* dS. *The public input is the security parameter* λ. *Additionally, the plaintext database* DB *is the private input of the data owner. The protocol output consists of the tuple* (sk, EDB), *where* sk *is the secret key held by the data owner* D, *while* EDB *is the encrypted database that the data server* dS *receives as output.*
- stk ← Token(sk; $\bar{w}$): *a protocol executed jointly by a client* C *and the data owner* D, *where* D *inputs its private key share* sk_i, *while the client's private input is the query* $\bar{w}^2$. *The protocol outputs to* C *a search token* stk. *The data owner does not receive any output.*
- R ← Search(EDB; stk): *a protocol executed jointly by a client* C *and the data server* dS, *where* C *inputs a search token* stk, *while the data server* dS *inputs an encrypted database* EDB. *The protocol outputs to* C *a result list of document identifiers* R, *while* dS *receives no output.*

Correctness of MC-SSE. We require a MC-SSE scheme to satisfy the following notion of correctness.

Definition 4 (Correctness of MC-SSE). *A MC-SSE scheme* (Setup, Token, Search) *is correct if for any* $\lambda \in \mathbb{N}$ *with* $t < n$, *any plaintext database* DB, *and any query* $\bar{w} \in W$, *we have that,*

$$\Pr\left[\text{Search(EDB; stk)} = \text{DB}(w) \,\middle|\, \begin{array}{l} \text{(sk; EDB)} \leftarrow \text{Setup}(1^\lambda; \text{DB}) \\ \text{stk} \leftarrow \text{Token (sk; } \bar{w}) \end{array} \right] = 1$$

Security of MC-SSE. We now recall the security definition for MC-SSE. We present an informal overview of the adversarial model and security goals below. Due to lack of space in the body of the paper, we defer the detailed and formal security definition to Appendix C.

Setting and Adversarial Model. We begin by discussing the setting and adversarial model for multi-client SSE from [13]. We allow the adversary to maliciously corrupt the data owner. Note that when the data owner is corrupt, there is no meaningful data privacy guarantee, but we want to ensure query privacy for any honest client. We also allow the adversary to maliciously corrupt the client(s). Finally, we allow the adversary to corrupt the data server, albeit in a semi-honest manner (see discussion below). We also assume that all of the above entities are connected by pairwise authenticated channels (note that we only assume authentication and not confidentiality, so an eavesdropper can view the traffic between the client and the servers). Based on the above model, we split the security of MC-SSE into two parts:

- **Security of token generation:** captures any leakage from the token generation protocol executed jointly by a (potentially malicious) client and a (potentially semi-honest) data owner. We allow clients to be maliciously corrupt and

---

^{2} In this paper, we consider conjunctive keyword queries where $\bar{w} = (w_1, \ldots, w_\mu)$ is a conjunction over a collection of keywords.

the data owner to be corrupt in a semi-honest manner. Informally, our definition captures the guarantees that: (i) an adversarial data owner cannot learn any information about an honest client's query, and (ii) an adversarial client does not learn any information about an honest data owner's secret key. See Appendix C.1 for the detailed security definition.

– **Security of search:** captures any leakage from the search protocol executed jointly by the client and the (semi-honest) data server. This definition closely follows standard definitions of security for static SSE protocols in the single client setting [5,6,9,11,13]. See Appendix C.2 for the detailed security definition.

Remark 3 (Semi-honest data server). We assume that the data server is semi-honest/passively corrupt. This is in line with the vast majority of existing works on SSE [6,9,11], which argue that the data server (typically a cloud service provider) is likely to have a business model that disincentivizes malicious behavior due to risk of liability issues and regulatory violations.

Remark 4 (Collusions). As mentioned in [13], any collusion between the data owner and the data server would lead to a complete breach of the query privacy guarantees for an honest client, so such a collusion is not allowed. However, we do allow collusions between: (i) the data owner and malicious clients, and (ii) the data server and malicious client(s).

Remark 5 (Single-client SSE). We finally remark that single-client SSE is a special case of the above MC-SSE definition, where the system consists of a single client C, which is the same entity as the data owner D.

3   Group Action-Based Oblivious Cross-Tags

In this section, we present an adaptation of the single-client, quantum-broken Oblivious Cross-Tags (OXT) scheme from [6] to the setting of plausibly quantum-safe cryptographic group actions. We call this scheme GXT. Similar to OXT, GXT supports conjunctive keyword queries over static databases.

Dictionary Scheme. We begin by introducing a cryptographic notion of a *dictionary*, which we use in GXT. A (static) dictionary scheme Dict consists of algorithms (Create, Get) as follows:

- Create($(\ell_i, d_i)_{i=1}^m$): on input a list of label-data pairs $(\ell_i, d_i)_{i=1}^m$ where each label is unique, it outputs a dictionary γ.
- Get(γ, ℓ): on input γ and a label ℓ, it either returns the data item with that label or $\perp$.

Correctness. We define *correctness* in the obvious way, i.e., the output of Get is always either the data associated with the (unique) input label, or $\perp$ when there is no data associated with the input label.

History Independence. We say that a dictionary implementation Dict is *history independent* if, for all lists L, the distribution of Create(L) depends only on the members of L and not their order in the list.

3.1   Overview of GXT

We first present an informal overview of the core techniques underlying GXT. For simplicity of exposition, we consider a two-conjunctive query $\bar{w} = (w_1, w_2)$ (the discussion below generalizes naturally to *any* number of conjuncts). Let $(G, X, \star)$ be an EGA as defined in Sect. 2.1 such that $|G| = |X| = O(2^\lambda)$ (λ being the security parameter). Throughout this overview, we assume that $x_0 \leftarrow X$ is a publicly known, uniformly sampled set element.

Setup: Generating the Encrypted Database. Following the template of the original OXT protocol [6], at setup, the client in the GXT protocol pre-computes an encrypted version EDB of the plaintext database DB (using a secret symmetric key) and outsources EDB to the server for storage. This pre-computed encrypted database EDB consists of two data structures: a dictionary (as described above) called the TSet, and an additional data structure for efficient membership testing called the XSet. At a high level, TSet is a dictionary that pre-processes and stores, for each keyword w in the plaintext database DB, a list of randomized and masked document identifiers corresponding to DB(w) (the list of documents containing the keyword w). Concretely, each entry of this list is a group element of the form $z = \text{rind} \cdot k \in G$, where the group element rind is a randomized document identifier (one per document containing the keyword w), and the group element $k = g(w) \in G$ is a pseudorandom masking key derived from w (here, g is, informally speaking, a pseudorandom function).

On the other hand, the XSet stores an entry of the form $(\text{p} \cdot \text{rind}) \star x_0$ (computed via the action of the group element $\text{p} \cdot \text{rind} \in G$ on the public set element x_0) for every valid keyword-document pair (w, ind) in the plaintext database DB. Here, the group element $\text{p} \in G$ is a pseudorandom function of the keyword w and the group element rind $\in G$ is again a randomized version of ind. Observe that, asymptotically, the number of entries in both the TSet and the XSet is precisely the number of keyword-document pairs in the database.

Token Generation for a Two-Conjunctive Query. Given a two-conjunctive query $\bar{w} = (w_1, w_2)$ (where w_1 is called the s-term and w_2 is called the x-term), the client uses its secret key to compute: (i) a look-up key $\text{stag} = f(w_1)$ corresponding to the s-term w_1, (ii) a masking key $k = g(w_1)$, also corresponding to the s-term w_1, and (iii) a key $\text{p} = h(w_2)$, corresponding to the x-term w_2. Here, f, g and h are (pseudo)random functions, with the additional requirement that g and h map arbitrary bit strings to elements in the group G (i.e., p and k are group elements). The client further derives a helper token, called the xtoken, of the form $(\text{p}/\text{k}) \star x_0$ (computed via the action of the group element $\text{p}/\text{k} \in G$ on the public set element x_0), and finally outputs $(\text{stag}, \text{xtoken})$ as the search token.

Search for a Two-Conjunctive Query. The search protocol starts with the client sending the search token $(\text{stag}, \text{xtoken})$ to the server. The server first uses the look-up key stag to retrieve a set $\mathcal{D}$ of document identifiers corresponding to DB(w_1), where each document identifier ind is *randomized and masked*. Concretely, each entry of the retrieved set $\mathcal{D}$ is an element of the form $z = \text{rind} \cdot k$, where rind is a randomized document identifier, and $k = g(w_1)$ is the masking key (same as the one derived by the client to generate the search token). This retrieval is enabled by the TSet. Now, let rind be a (randomized) document identifier in the retrieved set $\mathcal{D}$. In order to check if the second conjunct w_2 also occurs in the document corresponding to rind, the server uses the corresponding masked value z and the xtoken received from the client to compute a *cross-tag* xtag as

$$\mathsf{xtag} = \mathsf{z} \star \mathsf{xtoken} = (\mathsf{rind} \cdot \mathsf{k}) \star ((\mathsf{p}/\mathsf{k}) \star x_0) = ((\mathsf{rind} \cdot \mathsf{k}) \cdot (\mathsf{p}/\mathsf{k})) \star x_0 = (\mathsf{p} \cdot \mathsf{rind}) \star x_0$$

where the third quality follows from the properties of an EGA as described in Sect. 2.1. The server then checks for membership of the xtag in the XSet to confirm whether or not a document identifier in $\mathcal{D}$ satisfies the second conjunct.

Remark 6. For correctness of search, it suffices to only store the group elements of the form $(\mathsf{p} \cdot \mathsf{rind})$ as opposed to the set elements $(\mathsf{p} \cdot \mathsf{rind}) \star x_0$ in the XSet (this would also allow replacing the action computation prior to membership testing during search by a simple group operation). However, for security, one needs to additionally prove that the XSet reveals no information, apriori, about the underlying plaintext database. Unfortunately, if we store the group elements in the clear, there is no way to argue security. Hence, we switch to storing set elements, and then prove security by using the GA-DDH assumption over $(G, X, \star)$ to argue that the elements in XSet are, in fact, pseudorandom. The detailed proof of security appears subsequently.

3.2   Formal Construction of GXT

We now turn the above high-level intuition into a formal construction of GXT. The construction is parameterized by a security parameter λ.

Building Blocks. Let $(G, X, \star)$ be an EGA as defined in Sect. 2.1 such that $|G| = |X| = O(2^\lambda)$ (λ being the security parameter). Throughout, $x_0 \leftarrow X$ denotes a publicly known, uniformly sampled set element. Our construction uses the following building blocks:

- A PRF $F : \{0,1\}^\lambda \times \{0,1\}^* \to \{0,1\}^\lambda$.
- A PRF $F_G : \{0,1\}^\lambda \times \{0,1\}^* \to G$.
- A symmetric-key encryption scheme $\mathsf{SKE} = (\mathsf{KeyGen}, \mathsf{Enc}, \mathsf{Dec})$ with key-space $\{0,1\}^\lambda$.
- A dictionary $\mathsf{Dict} = (\mathsf{Create}, \mathsf{Get})$.

Remark 7. The astute reader may wonder about the existence of the PRF $F_G : \{0,1\}^\lambda \times \{0,1\}^* \to G$. We remark that such a PRF follows by hashing the output of the PRF F into the group G, which typically has dense representation. We abstract out these low-level details for simplicity of exposition.

The Construction. Given the above building blocks, the detailed construction of GXT = (GXT.Setup, GXT.Token, GXT.Search) is as presented below. Note that since this is a single-client SSE scheme, the client C and the data owner D are the same entity, and we refer to this entity as C in the description below without loss of generality. The key changes from OXT that contribute to the plausible post-quantum security of GXT are highlighted in red.

GXT.Setup(1^λ, DB) : On input a plaintext database DB, a client C (who is also the data owner in the single-client setting) does the following:

- Parse DB = $(\text{ind}_i, W_i)_{i \in [1,d]}$ and let W = $\cup_{i \in [1,d]} W_i$.
- Sample uniformly random key $K_S \leftarrow \{0,1\}^\lambda$ for the PRF F and uniformly random keys $K_X, K_I, K_Z \leftarrow \{0,1\}^\lambda$ for the PRF F_G.
- Initialize an empty set XSet = $\emptyset$ and an empty list $L = \emptyset$.
- For each keyword $w \in$ W, do the following:
  - Initialize an empty list $\mathbf{t} = \emptyset$.
  - Compute $K_e = F(K_S, w\|0)$ and stag = $F(K_S, w\|1)$.
  - Initialize a counter $c \leftarrow 0$. For each ind $\in$ DB(w) in random order, do the following:
    - Set e $\leftarrow$ SKE.Enc(K_e, ind), and xind = $F_G(K_I, \text{ind}) \in G$.
    - Increment the counter $c = c + 1$.
    - Compute the group elements $z_c = F_G(K_Z, w\|c) \in G$ and $y =$ xind $\cdot z_c^{-1} \in G$, and append (e, y) to $\mathbf{t}$.
    - Compute the group element $h = F_G(K_X, w) \cdot$ xind $\in G$.
    - Compute the set element xtag = $h \star x_0$, and add xtag to XSet.
  - Add (stag, $\mathbf{t}$) to the list L (in lexicographic order).
- Finally, do the following:
  - Compute TSet $\leftarrow$ Dict.Create(L).
  - Store sk = (K_S, K_X, K_I, K_Z) as the secret key.
  - Output EDB = (TSet, XSet) to the data server dS.

GXT.Token(sk = $(K_S, K_X, K_I, K_Z), \bar{w} = (w_1, w_2, \ldots, w_\mu)$) : Given the secret key sk = (K_S, K_X, K_I, K_Z) and a conjunctive keyword query $\bar{w} = (w_1, w_2, \ldots, w_\mu)$, a client C does the following:

- Compute $K_e = F(K_S, w_1\|0)$ and stag = $F(K_S, w_1\|1)$.
- For sufficiently large k (such that $k \geq$ DB(w_1)) and for each $c = 1, 2, \ldots, k$, compute xtoken[c] = (xtoken[$c, 2$], \ldots, xtoken[c, μ]), where for each $j \in [2, \mu]$, xtoken[c, j] is computed as follows:
  - Compute the group element $h = F_G(K_Z, w_1\|c) \cdot F_G(K_X, w_j)$.
  - Compute the set element xtoken[c, j] = $h \star x_0$ for $j = 2, \ldots, n$.
- Output the token stk = (stag, K_e, xtoken[1], \ldots, xtoken[k]).

GXT.Search(EDB; stk) : The search protocol is executed jointly by the client C (that inputs the search token stk) and the data server dS (that inputs the encrypted database EDB), and proceeds as follows:

- C parses stk as $(\mathsf{stag}, K_e, \mathsf{xtoken}[1], \mathsf{xtoken}[2], \ldots, \mathsf{xtoken}[k])$.
- C initializes an empty list $R \leftarrow \emptyset$.
- C sends $\overline{\mathsf{stk}} = (\mathsf{stag}, \mathsf{xtoken}[1], \mathsf{xtoken}[2], \ldots, \mathsf{xtoken}[k])$ to dS.
- dS parses $\overline{\mathsf{stk}}$ as $(\mathsf{stag}, \mathsf{xtoken}[1], \mathsf{xtoken}[2], \ldots, \mathsf{xtoken}[k])$.
- dS retrieves $\mathbf{t} \leftarrow \mathsf{Dict.Get}(\mathsf{TSet}, \mathsf{stag})$.
- For $c = 1, \ldots, |\mathbf{t}|$, dS does the following (we assume sufficiently large $k > |\mathbf{t}|$):
  - Retrieve $(\mathbf{e}, y)$ from the c-th tuple in $\mathbf{t}$.
  - If $y \star (\mathsf{xtoken}[c, j]) \in \mathsf{XSet} \; \forall j = 2, \ldots, \mu$: send $\mathbf{e}$ to client C.
- When last tuple in $\mathbf{t}$ is reached, dS sends $\bot$ to C and halts.
- For each $\mathbf{e}$ received from dS, C computes $\mathsf{ind} \leftarrow \mathsf{SKE.Dec}(K_e, \mathbf{e})$ and adds ind to the list R.
- Finally, upon receipt of $\bot$ from dS, C outputs R as the result set.

Correctness. We state the following theorem for correctness of GXT.

Theorem 1 (Correctness of GXT). *Assuming that: (i) the dictionary* Dict *satisfies correctness, and (ii) the* SKE *scheme satisfies decryption correctness as per Definition 6,* GXT *is a correct single-client SSE scheme.*

The proof of this theorem is immediate and is not detailed separately.

Security. Note that GXT is single-client SSE scheme, which is a special case of MC-SSE as per Definition 3, where the system consists of a single client C, which is the same entity as the data owner D. Naturally, in the case of GXT, security of token generation holds vacuously. We prove that GXT satisfies security of search with respect to the *same* leakage profile as the original OXT scheme [6]. We state this more formally below.

Leakage of GXT. We formally describe the leakage function for GXT as $\mathcal{L}^{\mathsf{GXT}} = \left(\mathcal{L}^{\mathsf{GXT}}_{\mathsf{Setup}}, \mathcal{L}^{\mathsf{GXT}}_{\mathsf{Search}} \right)$, where the various leakage sub-functions are as stated below:

- $\mathcal{L}^{\mathsf{GXT}}_{\mathsf{Setup}}(\mathsf{DB})$: The sub-leakage function $\mathcal{L}^{\mathsf{GXT}}_{\mathsf{Setup}}$, on input the plaintext database $\mathsf{DB} = (\mathsf{ind}_i, \mathsf{W}_i)$, outputs the quantity $N = \sum_{w \in \mathsf{W}} |\mathsf{DB}(w)|$, where $\mathsf{W} = \cup_i \mathsf{W}_i$ is the set of all keywords in DB.
- $\mathcal{L}^{\mathsf{GXT}}_{\mathsf{Search}}$: The sub-leakage function $\mathcal{L}^{\mathsf{GXT}}_{\mathsf{Search}}$ takes as input the plaintext database DB, and a list $\boldsymbol{Q}$ of conjunctive search queries. Here, $\boldsymbol{Q}$ is represented as $\boldsymbol{Q} = (\mathbf{s}, \mathbf{x}_1, \ldots, \mathbf{x}_n)$, where n denotes the maximum number of x-terms in any conjunctive search query, $\mathbf{s}$ denotes the list of s-terms for all queries, and $\mathbf{x}_i$ denotes the list of i-th x-terms for all queries. Q denotes the number of queries (i.e., $|\mathbf{s}| = |\mathbf{x}_1| = \ldots = |\mathbf{x}_n| = Q$)[3]. The sub-leakage function $\mathcal{L}^{\mathsf{GXT}}_{\mathsf{Search}}$ outputs the tuple $(\mathsf{EP}, \mathsf{SP}, \mathsf{XP}, \mathsf{RP}, \mathsf{IP})$, where:
  - EP is the *equality pattern* indicating which pairs of queries have identical keywords as their s-terms. Formally, we represent EP as a $Q \times Q$ table with entries in $\{0, 1\}$, where $\mathsf{EP}[i, j] = 1$ if $\mathbf{s}[i] = \mathbf{s}[j]$, and 0 otherwise.

---

[3] Note that if a query has $n' < n$ x-terms, it is padded by setting the last $(n - n')$ x-terms to the dummy symbol.

- SP is the *size pattern*, i.e. the number of records matching the s-term in each query. Formally, we represent SP as a Q-sized list, where for each $i \in [Q]$, we have $\mathsf{SP}[i] = |\mathsf{DB}(\mathbf{s}[i])|$.
- XP is another Q-sized list, where for each $i \in [Q]$, $\mathsf{XP}[i]$ is set to the number of x-terms in the i-th conjunctive query.
- RP is the *result pattern*, i.e. the set of document identifiers matching each query. Formally, RP is a Q-sized list, where for each $\ell \in [Q]$, we have $\mathsf{RP}[\ell] = \mathsf{DB}(\mathbf{s}[\ell]) \cap \left(\bigcap_{j \in [n]} \mathsf{DB}(\mathbf{x}_i[\ell]) \right)$.
- IP is the *conditional intersection pattern* leakage, represented formally as a $Q \times Q \times n \times n$ table, where for $i, j \in [Q]$ and $\alpha, \beta \in [n]$, the entry $\mathsf{IP}[i, j, \alpha, \beta]$ is set as follows:
    * If $i \neq j$ and $\alpha \neq \beta$ and $\mathbf{x}_\alpha[i] = \mathbf{x}_\beta[j]$, then set $\mathsf{IP}[i, j, \alpha, \beta] = \mathsf{DB}(\mathbf{s}[i]) \cap \mathsf{DB}(\mathbf{s}[j])$.
    * Else, set $\mathsf{IP}[i, j, \alpha, \beta] = \emptyset$.

Remark 8. The above leakage function $\mathcal{L}^{\mathsf{GXT}}$ is identical to the leakage function used to prove the security of the original OXT scheme from [6].

We now state the following theorem.

Theorem 2 (Security of Search in GXT). *Let $(G, X, \star)$ be an EGA as defined in Sect. 2.1 such that $|G| = |X| = O(2^\lambda)$ (λ being the security parameter). Assuming that: (i) the GA-DDH assumption (Definition 2) holds over $(G, X, \star)$, (ii) Dict is a dictionary scheme satisfying history independence, (iii) F and F_G are secure PRFs as per Definition 5, and (iv) SKE is an IND-CPA symmetric-key encryption scheme as per Definition 6, GXT satisfies $\mathcal{L}^{\mathsf{GXT}}$-simulation security as per Definition 9.*

Proof. Due to lack of space in the main body of the paper, we defer a formal proof of Theorem 2 to Appendix D.

Remark 9. While the classical leakage profiles for the original OXT scheme and our proposed GXT scheme are identical, the key difference lies in the assumptions required to argue security w.r.t. this leakage profile. In particular, while the security of the OXT scheme relies on the quantum-broken discrete log assumption over cyclic prime-order groups, the security of the GXT scheme relies on the GA-DDH assumption over the EGA $(G, X, \star)$, which plausibly holds even against quantum adversaries.

3.3 Performance and Efficiency of GXT

Storage Requirements. Given a plaintext database DB, it is easy to see that for both TSet and XSet, the number of entries is precisely $N = \sum_{w \in W} |\mathsf{DB}(w)|$, and each such entry requires storage of $O(\lambda)$ bits. Hence the overall storage requirement for EDB in GXT is $O(N\lambda)$. This is the same as in the original OXT scheme from [6].

Search Performance. Given a conjunctive keyword query $\bar{w} = (w_1, \ldots, w_\mu)$, where w_1 is the least frequent conjunct, the computational complexity at both the client and the server is $O(\mu|\mathsf{DB}(w_1)|) \cdot \mathsf{poly}(\lambda)$, where $|\mathsf{DB}(w_1)|$ denotes the frequency of w_1. The $\mathsf{poly}(\lambda)$ computational overhead is incurred primarily from group action computations for generation of xtoken values at the client and for the generation of xtag values at the server. Each query requires a single round of communication between the client and the server, with communication complexity $O(\mu|\mathsf{DB}(w_1)|\lambda)$ (incurred primarily as a result of communicating $O(\mu|\mathsf{DB}(w_1)|)$ set elements from the client to the server). Asymptotically, this exactly matches the computational and communication complexities incurred by the original OXT scheme from [6]. Concretely, we expect slower query processing time in practice for GXT than OXT since the group action computation operations in GXT are concretely more expensive than the simple prime-order group operations (over elliptic curves) in OXT. We view this as a tradeoff for the quantum-safe security guarantees afforded by GXT.

4   Multi-client Group Action-Based OXT

In this section, we present a multi-client extension of the GXT scheme from Sect. 3. We call this scheme MC-GXT. As an additional building block for MC-GXT, we use the group action-based OPRF from [3].

4.1   Overview of MC-GXT

Our goal is to extend GXT to the multi-client setting, where the client and the data owner are no longer the same entity, and the client would have to engage in a protocol with the data owner to generate the search token corresponding to a conjunctive query. Recall the example used in the overview of GXT based on a two-conjunctive query $\bar{w} = (w_1, w_2)$. During token generation in GXT, the client computes $(\mathsf{stag}, \mathsf{xtoken} = (\mathsf{p/k}) \star x_0)$. In the multi-client setting, the client would now want to compute $(\mathsf{stag}, \mathsf{k})$ corresponding to w_1 and the key p corresponding to w_2 without revealing w_1 and w_2 to the data owner.

Using OPRF. At a high level, our idea for enabling this is to substitute the traditional PRF used in the original GXT scheme to generate $\mathsf{stag}, \mathsf{k}$ and p by an oblivious PRF. The client and the data owner engage in an oblivious PRF protocol, with the client holding the inputs w_1 and w_2, and the data owner holding the secret PRF key. At the end of the protocol, the client gets the search token (but learns no additional information about the PRF key), while the server learns no information about the client's query. The rest of the search protocol can now proceed as in the original GXT scheme.

An Efficiency Challenge. While the above idea may initially seem straightforward, it incurs certain efficiency challenges, which we explain below. Observe that a naïve adaptation of the GXT protocol to the setting of oblivious token generation poses the following challenge: it requires the client and the key servers to engage in one OPRF execution per xtoken, where the number of required executions is $|DB(w_1)|$. For instance, if a keyword occurs in 1000 documents, this would require 1000 OPRF executions, which is prohibitively expensive.

Our Approach. To address this, we fundamentally change the manner in which the look-up key stag and each masking key tt_i are generated by the client. We have the client first compute strap $= f^*(w_1)$, for a (pseudo)random f^*, and then derive stag $= f(\text{strap})$ and $t_i = g(\text{strap}\|i)$. Now, observe that it suffices to realize f^* using OPRF, while f and g can just be simple PRFs as in the single-client version of GXT. This reduces the number of OPRF executions from $DB(w_1)$ to just one, which significantly boosts practical efficiency.

4.2 Formal Construction of MC-GXT

We now turn the above high-level intuition into a formal construction of MC-GXT. The construction is parameterized by a security parameter λ. Let $(G, X, \star)$ be an EGA as defined in Sect. 2.1 such that $|G| = |X| = O(2^\lambda)$ (λ being the security parameter). Our construction uses the following building blocks:

- A PRF $F : \{0,1\}^\lambda \times \{0,1\}^* \to \{0,1\}^\lambda$.
- A PRF $F_G : \{0,1\}^\lambda \times \{0,1\}^* \to G$.
- A PRF $F_X : \{0,1\}^\lambda \times \{0,1\}^* \to X$.
- SKE $=$ (KeyGen, Enc, Dec) with key-space $\{0,1\}^\lambda$.
- A dictionary Dict $=$ (Create, Get).

We additionally assume the existence of:

- An OPRF scheme OPRF_F that allows oblivious evaluation of the PRF F.
- An OPRF scheme OPRF_X that allows oblivious evaluation of the PRF F_X.

Remark 10. We remark that a PRF of the form $F_X : \{0,1\}^\lambda \times \{0,1\}^* \to X$ follows from the adaptation of the Naor-Reingold (NR) PRF (say, $F_{\mathsf{GA-NR}}$) to the setting of EGA [1,3,19]. In its native form, $F_{\mathsf{GA-NR}}$ uses a secret key consisting of a set of group elements of the form $\{g_{j,b}\}_{j\in[\lambda], b\in\{0,1\}}$, and applies it on an input bit-string $\mathbf{s} \in \{0,1\}^\lambda$ to obtain an output set element $x \in X$. However, it is easy to create the PRF $F_X : \{0,1\}^\lambda \times \{0,1\}^* \to X$ as follows: apply a PRG $G : \{0,1\}^\lambda \to G^{2\lambda}$ on the key of F_X to obtain a key for $F_{\mathsf{GA-NR}}$, and apply a hash function $\mathcal{H} : \{0,1\}^* \to \{0,1\}^\lambda$ on the input of F_X to obtain an input for $F_{\mathsf{GA-NR}}$. The output of $F_{\mathsf{GA-NR}}$ is used directly as the output of F_X. Further, the original OPRF scheme from [3] allows obliviously computing $F_{\mathsf{GA-NR}}$, and hence F_X, thus yielding an OPRF of the form OPRF_X. To realize OPRF_F, one can simply hash the output of F_X into $\{0,1\}^\lambda$.

The Construction. Given the above building blocks, the detailed construction of MC-GXT $=$ (MC-GXT.Setup, MC-GXT.Token, MC-GXT.Search) is as presented below. Note that the data-owner D and the client C are now separate entities.

The key technical changes from GXT protocol are highlighted in red (indicating the usage of OPRF) and blue (changes that do not involve the usage of OPRF).

GXT.Setup(1^λ, DB) : On input a plaintext database DB, the data owner D does the following:

- Parse DB = $(\text{ind}_i, W_i)_{i\in[1,d]}$ and let W = $\cup_{i\in[1,d]}W_i$.
- Sample uniformly random key $K_S \leftarrow \{0,1\}^\lambda$ for the PRF F and uniformly random key $K_X \leftarrow \{0,1\}^\lambda$ for the PRF F_X.
- Sample uniformly random key $K_I \leftarrow \{0,1\}^\lambda$ for the PRF F_G.
- Initialize an empty set XSet $\leftarrow \emptyset$ and an empty list $L \leftarrow \emptyset$.
- For each keyword $w \in$ W, do the following:
  - Initialize an empty list $\mathbf{t} = \emptyset$.
  - Compute strap = $F(K_S, w)$.
  - Compute stag = $F(\text{strap}_w, 1)$, $K_Z = F(\text{strap}_w, 2)$, and $K_e = F(\text{strap}_w, 3)$ (where the inputs are represented as bit strings).
  - Initialize a counter $c \leftarrow 0$. For each ind $\in$ DB(w) in random order, do the following:
    * Set e $\leftarrow$ SKE.Enc(K_e, ind), and xind = $F_G(K_I, \text{ind}) \in G$.
    * Increment the counter $c = c + 1$.
    * Compute the group elements $z_c = F_G(K_Z, c) \in G$ and $y = \text{xind} \cdot z_c^{-1} \in G$, and append (e, y) to $\mathbf{t}$.
    * Compute the set element xtrap = $F_X(K_X, w) \in X$.
    * Compute the set element xtag = xind $\star$ xtrap, and add xtag to XSet.
  - Add (stag, $\mathbf{t}$) to the list L (in lexicographic order).
- Finally, do the following:
  - Compute TSet $\leftarrow$ Dict.Create(L).
  - Store sk = (K_S, K_X, K_I) as the secret key.
  - Output EDB = (TSet, XSet) to the data server dS.

GXT.Token(sk = (K_S, K_X, K_I); $\bar{w} = (w_1, w_2, \ldots, w_\mu)$) : The token generation protocol is executed jointly by the data owner D (that inputs the secret key sk = (K_S, K_X, K_I, K_Z)) and the client C (that inputs a conjunctive keyword query $\bar{w} = (w_1, w_2, \ldots, w_\mu)$) as follows:

- C and D jointly execute OPRF$_F$, where the client inputs w_1 and the data owner inputs K_S. At the end of the protocol, C obtains strap = $F(K_S, w_1)$.
- For each $j \in [2, \mu]$, C and D jointly execute OPRF$_X$, where the client inputs w_j and the data owner inputs K_X. At the end of the protocol, C obtains xtrap$_j$ = $F_X(K_X, w_j)$.
- C computes stag = $F(\text{strap}_w, 1)$, $K_Z = F(\text{strap}_w, 2)$, and $K_e = F(\text{strap}_w, 3)$ (where the inputs are represented as bit strings).
- For sufficiently large k (such that $k \geq$ DB(w_1)) and for each $c = 1, 2, \ldots, k$, C sets $z_c = F_G(K_Z, c)$ and computes xtoken[c] = (xtoken[c, 2], \ldots, xtoken[c, μ]), where for each $j \in [2, \mu]$, xtoken[c, j] is computed as xtoken[c, j] = $z_c \star$ xtrap$_j$.
- Output the token stk = (stag, K_e, xtoken[1], \ldots, xtoken[k]).

MC-GXT.Search(EDB; stk) : [same as GXT.Search] The search protocol is executed jointly by the client C (that inputs the search token stk) and the data server dS (that inputs the encrypted database EDB), and proceeds as follows:

- C parses stk as $(stag, K_e, xtoken[1], xtoken[2], \ldots, xtoken[k])$.
- C initializes an empty list $R \leftarrow \emptyset$.
- C sends $\overline{stk} = (stag, xtoken[1], xtoken[2], \ldots, xtoken[k])$ to dS.
- dS parses $\overline{stk}$ as $(stag, xtoken[1], xtoken[2], \ldots, xtoken[k])$.
- dS retrieves $t \leftarrow$ Dict.Get(TSet, stag).
- For $c = 1, \ldots, |t|$, dS does the following (we assume sufficiently large $k > |t|$):
  - Retrieve (e, y) from the c-th tuple in t.
  - If $y \star (xtoken[c, j]) \in XSet \; \forall j = 2, \ldots, \mu$: send e to client C.
- When last tuple in t is reached, dS sends $\perp$ to C and halts.
- For each e received from dS, C computes $ind \leftarrow$ SKE.Dec(K_e, e) and adds ind to the list R.
- Finally, upon receipt of $\perp$ from dS, C outputs R as the result set.

Correctness. We state the following theorem for correctness of MC-GXT.

Theorem 3 (Correctness of MC-GXT). *Assuming that: (i) the dictionary* Dict *satisfies correctness, and (ii) the* SKE *scheme satisfies decryption correctness as per Definition 6,* GXT *is a correct single-client SSE scheme.*

The proof of this theorem is immediate and is not detailed separately.

Security. We state the following theorems for the security of MC-GXT.

Theorem 4 (Security of Token Generation in MC-GXT). *Assuming that* $OPRF_F$ *and* $OPRF_X$ *are secure instances of* OPRF *as per Definition 7,* MC-GXT *satisfies security of token generation as per Definition 8.*

Proof. Due to lack of space in the main body of the paper, we defer a formal proof of the Theorem 4 to Appendix E.

Theorem 5 (Security of Search in MC-GXT). *Let* $(G, X, \star)$ *be an EGA as defined in Sect. 2.1 such that* $|G| = |X| = O(2^\lambda)$ *(λ being the security parameter). Also, let* $\mathcal{L}^{GXT}$ *be the leakage function for the* GXT *scheme as defined in Sect. 3. Assuming that: (i) the GA-DDH assumption (Definition 2) holds over* $(G, X, \star)$, *(ii)* Dict *is a history independence dictionary scheme, (iii)* F *and* F_G *are secure PRFs as per Definition 5, and (iv)* SKE *is an IND-CPA symmetric-key encryption scheme as per Definition 6,* MC-GXT *satisfies* $\mathcal{L}^{GXT}$ *-simulation security as per Definition 9.*

Proof Overview. The search protocol of MC-GXT is secure against a (semi-honest) data server dS under the same assumptions and for the same leakage function as the original GXT scheme. The search protocols in GXT and MC-GXT are identical, with the only difference being that in GXT, dS sees the outputs of

OPRF_F and OPRF_X (as opposed to the outputs of F and F_X) in the search tokens sent across by the client. However, by consistency of OPRF, F and F_X determine the outputs of evaluating the OPRF_F and OPRF_X, respectively, on any given input. Hence, the view of the data server dS remains unchanged if F and F_X were used instead of the OPRF_F and OPRF_X evaluations in the token generation protocol. Hence, the proof of Theorem 5 is essentially identical to the proof of Theorem 2, and is not detailed separately.

4.3   Performance and Efficiency of MC-GXT

Storage Requirements. Given a plaintext database DB, for both TSet and XSet, the number of entries is precisely $N = \sum_{w \in \mathsf{W}} |\mathsf{DB}(w)|$, and each such entry requires storage of $O(\lambda)$ bits. Hence the overall storage requirement for EDB in MC-GXT is $O(N\lambda)$. This is the same as the (quantum-broken) multi-client extension version of OXT proposed in [13].

Token Generation. Unlike GXT, token generation in MC-GXT involves interaction between the client and the data owner. Given a conjunctive keyword query $\bar{w} = (w_1, \ldots, w_\mu)$, where w_1 is the least frequent conjunct, the client and the data owner must engage in one invocation of OPRF_F and $(\mu - 1)$ (parallel) invocations of OPRF_X, where each such invocation requires two rounds of communication, and incurs $\mathsf{poly}(\lambda)$ computational and communication overheads (assuming the group-action based OPRF from [1,3]). The client additionally performs $O(\mu|\mathsf{DB}(w_1)|)$ group action computations, each of which also incurs $\mathsf{poly}(\lambda)$ computational overheads. So the overall computational and communication overheads are $O(\mu|\mathsf{DB}(w_1)|)\mathsf{poly}(\lambda)$. Asymptotically, this matches the token generation overheads incurred by the (quantum-broken) multi-client version of OXT from [13].

Search Performance. Given a conjunctive keyword query $\bar{w} = (w_1, \ldots, w_\mu)$, where w_1 is the least frequent conjunct, the computational complexity at both the client and the server is $O(\mu|\mathsf{DB}(w_1)|) \cdot \mathsf{poly}(\lambda)$. Each query requires a single round of communication, with communication complexity $O(\mu|\mathsf{DB}(w_1)|\lambda)$. Asymptotically, this matches the search overheads incurred by the (quantum-broken) multi-client version of OXT from [13].

Appendix

A   Additional Preliminaries

In this section, we recall the definitions of some basic cryptographic primitives that we use in our constructions.

Definition 5 (Pseudorandom Function). *A pseudorandom function (PRF) is a family of polynomial-time computable functions* $F : \mathcal{K} \times \mathcal{X} \rightarrow \mathcal{Y}$ *(where the sets* $(\mathcal{K}, \mathcal{X}, \mathcal{Y})$ *are all parameterized by the security parameter* $\lambda \in \mathbb{N}$, *and* *where each function $F(\mathsf{sk}, \cdot)$ is indexed by some key $\mathsf{sk} \in \mathcal{K}$), such that for any PPT adversary $\mathcal{A}$, any random key $\mathsf{sk} \leftarrow \mathcal{K}$ and any function $f \leftarrow \mathsf{Funcs}(\mathcal{X}, \mathcal{Y})$ sampled randomly from the set of all functions with domain $\mathcal{X}$ and range $\mathcal{Y}$, we have*

$$\left| \Pr\left[\mathcal{A}^{F(\mathsf{sk}, \cdot)}(1^\lambda) = 1\right] - \Pr\left[\mathcal{A}^{f(\cdot)}(1^\lambda) = 1\right] \right| \leq \mathsf{negl}(\lambda).$$

Definition 6 (Symmetric-Key Encryption). *A symmetric-key encryption scheme* SKE *is a tuple of polynomial-time algorithms* (KeyGen, Enc, Dec) *described as follows:*

- $\mathsf{sk} \leftarrow \mathsf{KeyGen}(1^\lambda)$: *a randomized algorithm that takes as input the security parameter λ and outputs a secret key* sk.
- $c \leftarrow \mathsf{Enc}(\mathsf{sk}, m)$: *a randomized algorithm that takes as input* sk *and a message* $m \in \{0,1\}^*$, *and generates a ciphertext* c.
- $m = \mathsf{Dec}(\mathsf{sk}, c)$: *a deterministic algorithm that, on input the secret key K and a ciphertext c, outputs a message m.*

We require a symmetric-key encryption scheme SKE *to satisfy correctness and IND-CPA security as described below.*

Correctness. We say that a symmetric-key encryption scheme SKE = (KeyGen, Enc, Dec) is correct if for any security parameter $\lambda \in \mathbb{N}$, any $\mathsf{sk} \leftarrow \mathsf{KeyGen}(1^\lambda)$, and any $m \in \{0,1\}^*$, we have $\mathsf{Dec}(\mathsf{sk}, \mathsf{Enc}(\mathsf{sk}, m)) = m$.

IND-CPA Security. We first define the IND-CPA security game below.

$\mathsf{Game}^{\mathsf{SKE, IND-CPA}}_{\mathcal{A} = (\mathcal{A}_1, \mathcal{A}_2)}$

1. $\mathsf{sk} \leftarrow \mathsf{KeyGen}(1^\lambda)$.
2. $(\mathsf{st}, m_0, m_1) \leftarrow \mathcal{A}_1^{\mathsf{Enc}(K, \cdot)}(1^\lambda)$.
3. Sample $b \leftarrow \{0, 1\}$.
4. $c_b \leftarrow \mathsf{Enc}(K, m_b)$.
5. $b' \leftarrow \mathcal{A}_2^{\mathsf{Enc}(K, \cdot)}(\mathsf{st}, c_b)$.
6. If $b' = b$, output 1, else output 0.

We say that a symmetric-key encryption scheme SKE = (KeyGen, Enc, Dec) is IND-CPA secure if for any security parameter λ and any probabilistic polynomial-time (PPT) adversary $\mathcal{A} = (\mathcal{A}_1, \mathcal{A}_2)$, we have

$$\left| \Pr\left[\mathsf{Game}^{\mathsf{SKE, IND-CPA}}_{\mathcal{A}} = 0\right] - \Pr\left[\mathsf{Game}^{\mathsf{SKE, IND-CPA}}_{\mathcal{A}} = 1\right] \right| \leq \mathsf{negl}(\lambda).$$

B Detailed Security Definition of Oblivious PRF

In this section, we present a detailed simulation based security definition for OPRF. We adopt the standard real world-ideal world paradigm for our simulation based definition. We formally define the corresponding real and ideal world executions below.

The Real World Execution. We formally define a real world game $\mathsf{Real}_{\mathcal{A},\mathcal{E}}^{\mathsf{OPRF}}$ that is parameterized by a security parameter λ, and involves the following parties:

- The honest party (either the client holding the input or the server holding the key).
- An adversary $\mathcal{A}$ that controls the corrupt party (either a maliciously corrupt client or a maliciously corrupt server), and interacts with the honest parties and the environment $\mathcal{E}$.
- The environment $\mathcal{E}$ that provides the honest party with its input, interacts with $\mathcal{A}$, receives the output of the honest party, and eventually outputs a bit $b \in \{0, 1\}$.

Finally, the game $\mathsf{Real}_{\mathcal{A},\mathcal{E}}^{\mathsf{OPRF}}$ outputs the same bit as $\mathcal{E}$.

The Ideal World Execution. We next define an ideal world game $\mathsf{Ideal}_{\mathsf{Sim},\mathcal{E}}^{\mathcal{F}_{\mathsf{OPRF}}}$ that is again parameterized by λ, and involves the following parties interacting with the ideal functionality $\mathcal{F}_{\mathsf{OPRF}}$ (described in Fig. 13, and also detailed subsequently).

- The honest party (either the client holding the input or the server holding the key) that receives its input from the environment $\mathcal{E}$ and directly forward this input to $\mathcal{F}_{\mathsf{OPRF}}$.
- An ideal-world simulator Sim that sends inputs to $\mathcal{F}_{\mathsf{OPRF}}$ on behalf of the corrupt party (either a maliciously corrupt client or a passively corrupt server), and receives back the corresponding output from $\mathcal{F}_{\mathsf{OPRF}}$. Sim also interacts with the environment $\mathcal{E}$.
- The environment $\mathcal{E}$ that provides the honest party with its input, and interacts with the simulator Sim. As in the real world, $\mathcal{E}$ also receives the outputs of the honest parties, and eventually outputs a bit $b \in \{0, 1\}$.

Finally, the game $\mathsf{Ideal}_{\mathsf{Sim},\mathcal{E}}^{\mathcal{F}_{\mathsf{OPRF}}}$ outputs the same bit as $\mathcal{E}$.

The Ideal Functionality. The ideal functionality $\mathcal{F}_{\mathsf{OPRF}}$ (described below) interacts with a set of clients $\{C\}$, a key-holding server S, and an ideal-world simulator Sim. We use sid to denote a (unique) session id. For simplicity of exposition, we consider only one server S per session id; however, multiple clients can submit evaluation requests in a given session. The ideal functionality keeps track of the following variables, all of which are initialized to $\perp$ or $\emptyset$ implicitly:

1. $\mathsf{TabInp}[\mathsf{sid}, x]$: contains a set of identities corresponding to clients that have issued the query $x \in \mathcal{X}$.
2. $\mathsf{TabEncInp}[\mathsf{sid}, x, C]$: contains a (randomized) encoding x^* of the query x corresponding to the query issued by the client C.
3. $\mathsf{TabEval}[\mathsf{sid}, x]$: contains an output $y \in \mathcal{Y}$ corresponding to an input x. The uniqueness of y is defined naturally with respect to the tuple (sid, x) (this is essential for consistency).

OPRF Ideal Functionality: $\mathcal{F}_{\mathsf{OPRF}}\left(1^\lambda\right)$

Setup. Upon receiving $(\mathsf{Setup}, \mathsf{sid}, \mathsf{S})$ from the server S (where sid is unique): send $(\mathsf{Setup}, \mathsf{sid}, \mathsf{S})$ to the simulator Sim.

Input. Upon receiving an input evaluation request $(\mathsf{Input}, \mathsf{sid}, x)$ from any client C:
- Set $\mathsf{TabInp}[\mathsf{sid}, x] = \mathsf{TabInp}[\mathsf{sid}, x] \cup \{\mathsf{C}\}$. item Set $\mathsf{TabEncInp}[\mathsf{sid}, x, \mathsf{C}] = x^*$, where the encoding x^* is generated randomly.
- Send $(\mathsf{Input}, \mathsf{sid}, x^*)$ to the simulator Sim. When Sim returns the same message, then send it to the server S.

Evaluation. Upon receiving $(\mathsf{Eval}, \mathsf{sid}, x^*)$ from the server S:

- If there does not exist a tuple $(\mathsf{sid}, x, \mathsf{C})$ such that $\mathsf{TabEncInp}[\mathsf{sid}, x, \mathsf{C}] = x^*$, then exit. Otherwise, proceed to the next step.
- Send $(\mathsf{Eval}, \mathsf{sid}, x^*)$ to the simulator Sim. When Sim sends back the same message, proceed to the next step.
- If $\mathsf{TabEval}[\mathsf{sid}, x]$ is already defined, let $y = \mathsf{TabEval}[\mathsf{sid}, x]$. Otherwise, sample uniformly random $y \leftarrow \mathcal{Y}$ and set $\mathsf{TabEval}[\mathsf{sid}, x] = y$.
- Send (sid, y) to the client C.

Offline Evaluation. Upon receiving $(\mathsf{Eval}, \mathsf{sid}, x)$ from the simulator Sim:

- If S is honest: if $\mathsf{Eval}[\mathsf{sid}, x]$ is not empty, then output y to Sim, where $y = \mathsf{Eval}[\mathsf{sid}, x]$. Otherwise, exit.
- If S is corrupt: if $\mathsf{Eval}[\mathsf{sid}, x]$ is not empty, then output y to Sim, where $y = \mathsf{Eval}[\mathsf{sid}, x]$. Otherwise, sample random $y \leftarrow \mathcal{Y}$, set $\mathsf{Eval}[\mathsf{sid}, x] = y$, and output y to Sim.

Based on the above, we now formally define the security of a OPRF scheme.

Definition 7 (Secure OPRF). *We say that an* OPRF *scheme securely realizes the ideal functionality* $\mathsf{Ideal}_{\mathsf{Sim}, \mathcal{E}}^{\mathcal{F}_{\mathsf{OPRF}}}$ *if for any security parameter* λ *and any PPT adversary* $\mathcal{A}$ *in the real world, there exists a PPT simulator* Sim *in the ideal world, such that for any environment* $\mathcal{E}$, *we have,*

$$\left| \Pr\left[\mathsf{Real}_{\mathcal{A}, \mathcal{E}}^{\mathsf{OPRF}}(1^\lambda) = 1 \right] - \Pr\left[\mathsf{Ideal}_{\mathsf{Sim}, \mathcal{E}}^{\mathcal{F}_{\mathsf{OPRF}}}(1^\lambda) = 1 \right] \right| \leq \mathsf{negl}(\lambda)$$

C   Detailed Security Definition of Multi-client SSE

In this section, we present the detailed security definition of any multi-client SSE scheme MC-SSE. The definition is divided into two parts: security of token generation and security of search.

C.1   Security of Token Generation

We first introduce a simulation-based security definition for token generation in MC-SSE. We adopt the standard real world-ideal world paradigm, and formally define the corresponding real and ideal world executions for token generation below.

The Real World Execution. We first discuss the real-world execution $\text{Real}_{\mathcal{A},\mathcal{E}}^{\text{MC-SSE,Token}}$ of token generation in a MC-SSE scheme. Based on the syntax presented in Definition 3, we formally define a real world game $\text{Real}_{\mathcal{A},\mathcal{E}}^{\text{MC-SSE,Token}}$ that is parameterized by the security parameter λ, and involves the following parties: (i) a data owner (could be either honest or semi-honest), (ii) clients (could either be honest or maliciously corrupt), (iii) an adversary $\mathcal{A}$ that controls the corrupt parties, and (iv) the environment $\mathcal{E}$ that provides the honest parties with their inputs, interacts with $\mathcal{A}$, receives the outputs of the honest parties, and eventually outputs a bit $b \in \{0,1\}$. The game $\text{Real}_{\mathcal{A},\mathcal{E}}^{\text{MC-SSE,Token}}$ outputs the same bit.

The Ideal World Execution. We now define the ideal world game $\text{Ideal}_{\text{Sim},\mathcal{E}}^{\mathcal{F}_{\text{Token}}^{\text{MC-SSE}}}$, that is again parameterized by λ, and consists of an ideal functionality $\mathcal{F}_{\text{Token}}^{\text{MC-SSE}}$ (described in Fig. 4), as well as the following participants that interact with $\mathcal{F}_{\text{Token}}^{\text{MC-SSE}}$: (i) the honest parties that receive their inputs from the environment $\mathcal{E}$ and directly forward these inputs to the ideal functionality $\mathcal{F}_{\text{Token}}^{\text{MC-SSE}}$, (ii) an ideal-world simulator Sim that sends inputs to $\mathcal{F}_{\text{Token}}^{\text{MC-SSE}}$ on behalf of the corrupt parties and receives back the corresponding output from $\mathcal{F}_{\text{Token}}^{\text{MC-SSE}}$, and (iii) the environment $\mathcal{E}$ that provides the honest parties with their inputs, and interacts with the simulator Sim. $\mathcal{E}$ receives the outputs of the honest parties, and eventually outputs a bit $b \in \{0,1\}$. The game $\text{Ideal}_{\text{Sim},\mathcal{E}}^{\mathcal{F}_{\text{Token}}^{\text{MC-SSE}}}$ outputs the same bit.

The Ideal Functionality. We detail the ideal functionality $\mathcal{F}_{\text{Token}}^{\text{MC-SSE}}$ in Fig. 4. The ideal functionality $\mathcal{F}_{\text{Token}}^{\text{MC-SSE}}$ interacts with data owner D, clients C, data holding server dS, and a simulator Sim. The ideal functionality keeps track of the following variables, all of which are initialized to $\perp$ or $\emptyset$ implicitly (we use sid to denote a (unique) session id):

1. TabInp[sid, $\bar{w}$]: contains a set of identities corresponding to clients that have issued the query $\bar{w}$.
2. TabEncInp[sid, $\bar{w}$, C]: contains a (randomized) encoding y corresponding to the search query $\bar{w}$ corresponding to the query issued by the client C.
3. TabToken[sid, $\bar{w}$]: contains a search token stk corresponding to an input search query $\bar{w}$. Uniqueness of stk is defined naturally with respect to the tuple (sid, $\bar{w}$).

Ideal Functionality for Token Generation in MC-SSE: $\mathcal{F}_{\text{Token}}^{\text{MC-SSE}}(1^{\lambda})$

Setup. Upon receiving (Setup, sid) from the data owner D (where sid is unique), send (Setup, sid) to the simulator Sim.

Input. Upon receiving (Input, sid, $\bar{w}$) from any client C, do the following:
- Set TabInp[sid, $\bar{w}$] = TabInp[sid, $\bar{w}$] $\cup$ {C}.
- Set TabEncInp[sid, $\bar{w}$, C] = y, where the encoding y is generated randomly.

- Send $(\mathsf{Input}, \mathsf{sid}, y)$ to the simulator Sim. When Sim returns the same message, send it to D.

Token Generation. Upon receiving $(\mathsf{Token}, \mathsf{sid}, y)$ from data owner D:

- If there does not exist a tuple $(\mathsf{sid}, \bar{w}, \mathsf{C})$ such that $\mathsf{TabEncInp}[\mathsf{sid}, \bar{w}, \mathsf{C}] = y$, then exit. Otherwise, proceed to the next step.
- Send $(\mathsf{Token}, \mathsf{sid}, y)$ to the simulator Sim. When Sim sends back the same message, proceed to the next step.
- If $\mathsf{TabToken}[\mathsf{sid}, \bar{w}]$ is defined, let $\mathsf{stk} = \mathsf{TabToken}[\mathsf{sid}, \bar{w}]$. Otherwise, sample uniformly random stk and set $\mathsf{TabToken}[\mathsf{sid}, \bar{w}] = \mathsf{stk}$.
- Respond to the client C with $(\mathsf{sid}, \mathsf{stk})$.

Offline Token Generation. Upon receiving $(\mathsf{Token}, \mathsf{sid}, \bar{w})$ from the simulator Sim:

- If D is honest: if $\mathsf{TabToken}[\mathsf{sid}, \bar{w}]$ is not empty, return stk to Sim, where $\mathsf{stk} = \mathsf{TabToken}[\mathsf{sid}, \bar{w}]$. Otherwise, exit.
- If D is corrupt: if $\mathsf{TabToken}[\mathsf{sid}, \bar{w}]$ is not empty, return stk to Sim, where $\mathsf{stk} = \mathsf{TabToken}[\mathsf{sid}, \bar{w}]$. Otherwise, sample uniformly random stk, set $\mathsf{TabToken}[\mathsf{sid}, \bar{w}] = \mathsf{stk}$, and return stk to Sim.

Based on the above games and ideal functionality, we now formally define the security of token generation in MC-SSE.

Definition 8 (Security of Token Generation in MC-SSE). *We say that the real-world execution of token generation in a MC-SSE scheme securely emulates the ideal functionality $\mathcal{F}_{\mathsf{Token}}^{\mathsf{MC\text{-}SSE}}$ if for any security parameter λ and any malicious PPT adversary $\mathcal{A}$, there exists a PPT simulator Sim, such that for any environment $\mathcal{E}$, we have*

$$\left| \Pr\left[\mathsf{Real}_{\mathcal{A},\mathcal{E}}^{\mathsf{MC\text{-}SSE},\mathsf{Token}}(1^\lambda) = 1 \right] - \Pr\left[\mathsf{Ideal}_{\mathsf{Sim},\mathcal{E}}^{\mathcal{F}_{\mathsf{Token}}^{\mathsf{MC\text{-}SSE}}}(1^\lambda) = 1 \right] \right| \leq \mathsf{negl}(\lambda).$$

C.2   Security of Search

We now present a notion of security of search in MC-SSE against a semi-honest data server in the standard real world/ideal world paradigm, where the real world and ideal world games are described formally described below. In the real world, the adversary's view corresponds to real world executions of the various MC-SSE protocols, namely (Setup, Token, Search), corresponding to various queries issued (adaptively) by the adversary. In the ideal world, the view of the adversary is generated by a PPT simulator that does not have access to the actual queries issued by the adversary, but only has access to the leakage that the adversary was supposed to obtain when interacting with real-world executions of the MC-SSE protocols. For simulation-based security, we require the view of the adversary in the real and ideal worlds to be computationally indistinguishable. This is in-line with standard definitions of single-client SSE.

Leakage. We formally capture the leakage to the real-world adversary using a leakage function $\mathcal{L} = (\mathcal{L}_{\mathsf{Setup}}, \mathcal{L}_{\mathsf{Search}})$, with various sub-leakage components: (i) $\mathcal{L}_{\mathsf{Setup}}$: a sub-functionality that captures any leakage about the plaintext database DB that the data server obtains from the encrypted database EDB generated by a real-world execution of the Setup protocol of MC-SSE, and (ii) $\mathcal{L}_{\text{Search}}$: a sub-functionality that captures any leakage about the plaintext database DB and any leakage about an honest client's keyword query, that is obtained by a (semi-honestly) corrupt data server during a real-world execution of the Search protocol.

Now, we formally define the real world and ideal world games as follows.

Security of Search for MC-SSE

$$\text{Real}_{\mathcal{A}}^{\text{MC-SSE,dS}}\left(1^\lambda\right)$$

Initialization Phase:

- The adversary $\mathcal{A}$ picks a plaintext database DB.
- The challenger runs $(\text{sid}; (\text{sk}_1, \ldots, \text{sk}_n); \text{EDB}) \leftarrow \text{Setup}(1^\lambda; \text{DB})$.
- The adversary $\mathcal{A}$ receives (sid, EDB).

Query Phase:

- The adversary $\mathcal{A}$ adaptively issues a search query $\bar{w}_j$.
- The challenger generates the search token stk_j corresponding to $\bar{w}_j$, and then generates the transcript τ_j corresponding to an execution of the Search protocol with inputs $(\text{EDB}; \text{stk}_j)$.
- The adversary $\mathcal{A}$ receives the tuple (stk_j, τ_j).

Output Phase: The adversary $\mathcal{A}$ outputs a bit $b \in \{0, 1\}$. The game also outputs the same bit b.

$$\text{Ideal}_{\mathcal{A},\text{Sim}=(\text{Sim}_0,\text{Sim}_1)}^{\text{MC-SSE,Search}}\left(1^\lambda, \mathcal{L} = (\mathcal{L}_{\text{Setup}}, \mathcal{L}_{\text{Search}})\right)$$

Initialization Phase:

- The challenger initializes an empty list $\boldsymbol{Q} \leftarrow \emptyset$.
- The adversary $\mathcal{A}$ picks a plaintext database DB.
- The challenger runs $(\text{st}_0, \text{EDB}) \leftarrow \text{Sim}_0(1^\lambda, \mathcal{L}_{\text{Setup}}(\text{DB}))$.
- The adversary $\mathcal{A}$ receives (sid, EDB).

Query Phase:

- The adversary $\mathcal{A}$ adaptively issues a search query $\bar{w}_j$.
- The challenger runs $(\text{st}_{1,j}, \text{stk}_j, \tau_j) \leftarrow \text{Sim}_1(\text{st}_{1,j-1}, \mathcal{L}_{\text{Search}}(\text{DB}, \bar{w}_j, \boldsymbol{Q}))$, where $\text{st}_{1,0} = \text{st}_0$.
- The adversary $\mathcal{A}$ receives the tuple (stk_j, τ_j).
- The challenger records the query as $\boldsymbol{Q}[j]$, and increments j.

Output Phase: The adversary $\mathcal{A}$ outputs a bit $b \in \{0, 1\}$. The game also outputs the same bit b.

Given the real world and ideal world games, and leakage functionality $\mathcal{L}$, we now formally describe the security of search in MC-SSE.

Definition 9 (Security of Search in MC-SSE). *We say that the real-world execution of the search protocol of any* MC-SSE *scheme* (Setup, Token, Search) *scheme satisfies* $\mathcal{L}$*-simulation security against a semi-honest data server if for any PPT adversary* $\mathcal{A}$*, there exists a PPT simulator* Sim*, such that,*

$$\left| \Pr\left[\mathsf{Real}_{\mathcal{A}}^{\mathsf{MC\text{-}SSE,Search}}(1^\lambda) = 1 \right] - \Pr\left[\mathsf{Ideal}_{\mathcal{A},\mathsf{Sim}}^{\mathsf{MC\text{-}SSE,Search}}(1^\lambda, \mathcal{L}) = 1 \right] \right| \leq \mathsf{negl}(\lambda)$$

D   Proof of Theorem 2

We present a proof for the case of 2-conjunctive queries (i.e., where each query consists of one s-term and one x-term). The proof generalizes naturally to the more general case of μ-conjunctions for any $\mu = \mathsf{poly}(\lambda)$, and is not detailed separately.

D.1   Leakage of GXT for 2-Conjunctive Queries

We recall the leakage function $\mathcal{L}^{\mathsf{GXT}} = \left(\mathcal{L}_{\mathsf{Setup}}^{\mathsf{GXT}}, \mathcal{L}_{\mathsf{Search}}^{\mathsf{GXT}} \right)$ for GXT for the case of 2-conjunctive queries, where the various leakage sub-functions are as stated below:

- $\mathcal{L}_{\mathsf{Setup}}^{\mathsf{GXT}}(\mathsf{DB})$: The sub-leakage function $\mathcal{L}_{\mathsf{Setup}}^{\mathsf{GXT}}$, on input the plaintext database $\mathsf{DB} = (\mathsf{ind}_i, \mathsf{W}_i)$, outputs the quantity $N = \sum_{w \in \mathsf{W}} |\mathsf{DB}(w)|$, where $\mathsf{W} = \cup_i \mathsf{W}_i$ is the set of all keywords in DB.
- $\mathcal{L}_{\mathsf{Search}}^{\mathsf{GXT}}$: The sub-leakage function $\mathcal{L}_{\mathsf{Search}}^{\mathsf{GXT}}$ takes as input the plaintext database DB, and a list Q of conjunctive search queries. Here, Q is represented as $Q = (\mathbf{s}, \mathbf{x})$, where $\mathbf{s}$ denotes the list of s-terms for all queries, and $\mathbf{x}_i$ denotes the list of x-terms for all queries. Q denotes the number of queries (i.e., $|\mathbf{s}| = |\mathbf{x}| = Q$). The sub-leakage function $\mathcal{L}_{\mathsf{Search}}^{\mathsf{GXT}}$ outputs the tuple $(\mathsf{EP}, \mathsf{SP}, \mathsf{RP}, \mathsf{IP})$ (for 2-conjunctions, the leakage XP is vacuous as each query has exactly one x-term), where in the case of 2-conjunctive queries, we have:
  - EP is the *equality pattern* indicating which pairs of queries have identical keywords as their s-terms. For ease of exposition, we use a slightly different interpretation of the equality pattern EP as compared to the one stated in Theorem 2, but this interpretation is readily computable given the original interpretation from Theorem 2. Formally, we represent $\mathsf{EP} \in [|\mathsf{W}|]^Q$ as a table with entries in $[|\mathsf{W}|]$, created by assigning each keyword an integer in $[|\mathsf{W}|]$ determined by its order of appearance in $\mathbf{s}$. For example, if $\mathbf{s} = (w_1, w_1, w_2, w_3, w_1, w_3)$, then $\mathsf{EP} = (1, 1, 2, 3, 1, 3)$. To compute $\mathsf{EP}[i]$, one finds the least $j \in [Q]$ such that $j \geq i$ and $\mathbf{s}[j] = \mathbf{s}[i]$ (observe that this is readily computable give the original interpretation of EP from Theorem 2), and then lets $\mathsf{EP}[i] = |\{\mathbf{s}[1], \dots, \mathbf{s}[j]\}|$ to be the number of unique keywords appearing at indices less than or equal to j.

- SP is the *size pattern*, i.e. the number of records matching the s-term in each query. Formally, we represent SP as a Q-sized list, where for each $i \in [Q]$, we have $\mathsf{SP}[i] = |\mathsf{DB}(\mathbf{s}[i])|$.
- RP is the *result pattern*, i.e. the set of document identifiers matching each query. Formally, RP is a Q-sized list, where for each $\ell \in [Q]$, we have $\mathsf{RP}[\ell] = \mathsf{DB}(\mathbf{s}[\ell]) \cap \left(\bigcap_{j \in [n]} \mathsf{DB}(\mathbf{x}_i[\ell]) \right)$.
- IP is the *conditional intersection pattern* leakage, represented formally as a $Q \times Q$ table, where for $i, j \in [Q]$, the entry $\mathsf{IP}[i, j]$ is set as follows:
  * If $i \neq j$ and $\mathbf{x}[i] = \mathbf{x}[j]$, then set $\mathsf{IP}[i, j] = \mathsf{DB}(\mathbf{s}[i]) \cap \mathsf{DB}(\mathbf{s}[j])$.
  * Else, set $\mathsf{IP}[i, j] = \emptyset$.

D.2   The Simulator

We construct a simulator $\mathsf{Sim}_{\mathsf{GXT}}$. $\mathsf{Sim}_{\mathsf{GXT}}$ is given access to the leakage function $\mathcal{L}^{\mathsf{GXT}} = \left(\mathcal{L}^{\mathsf{GXT}}_{\mathsf{Setup}}, \mathcal{L}^{\mathsf{GXT}}_{\mathsf{Search}} \right)$ for GXT for the case of 2-conjunctive queries as described above, and proceeds as follows.

Creating a Restricted Equality Pattern. The simulator $\mathsf{Sim}_{\mathsf{GXT}}$ first computes the *restricted equality pattern* of $\mathbf{x}$, denoted $\widehat{\mathbf{x}}$. Intuitively, $\widehat{\mathbf{x}}$ captures which x-terms are "known" to the server as being equal. The restricted equality pattern $\widehat{\mathbf{x}} \in |\mathsf{W}|^Q$ is computed by $\mathsf{Sim}_{\mathsf{GXT}}$ as follows:

- First, $\mathsf{Sim}_{\mathsf{GXT}}$ defines a relation $\equiv$ on $[Q] \times [Q]$ as: $i \equiv j$ for $(i, j) \in [Q] \times [Q]$ if $\mathsf{IP}[i, j] \neq \phi$, and then turns this into an equivalence relation by taking its transitive closure.
- Next, $\mathsf{Sim}_{\mathsf{GXT}}$ sorts the partitions of the equivalence relation by their least element, and assign $\widehat{\mathbf{x}}[i]$ the index of the partition containing i.

The following lemma (imported from [6]) states that (informally speaking) $\widehat{\mathbf{x}}$ serves as the "equality pattern" for $\mathbf{x}$ when certain conditions hold.

Lemma 1 (Imported from [6]). *Let* $\mathsf{DB} = (\mathsf{ind}_i, \mathsf{W}_i)_{i \in [d]}$ *be a database, let* $\mathbf{s}, \mathbf{x} \in \mathsf{W}^Q$ *be two vectors representing a set of Q 2-conjunctive queries as defined above, and let* $|widehat\mathbf{x}$ *be the restricted equality pattern as defined above. Then for all $i, j \in [Q]$, we have*

$$\widehat{\mathbf{x}}[i] = \widehat{\mathbf{x}}[j] \implies \mathbf{x}[i] = \mathbf{x}[j],$$

and

$$(\mathbf{x}[i] = \mathbf{x}[j]) \wedge (\mathsf{DB}(s[i]) \cap \mathsf{DB}(s[j]) \neq \phi) \implies \widehat{\mathbf{x}}[i] = \widehat{\mathbf{x}}[j].$$

Proof. We refer the reader to [6] for the detailed proof.

Simulating the TSet. The simulator $\mathsf{Sim}_{\mathsf{GXT}}$ simulates the encrypted data structure TSet as follows:

- Initialize an empty list $L = \emptyset$.
- For each $i \in |\mathsf{W}|$, create a random $\mathsf{stag}_i \leftarrow \{0, 1\}^\lambda$.

- For each $i \in |W|$, create a list $\mathbf{t}_i$ subject to the following restrictions:
  - $\sum_{i \in [|W|]} |\mathbf{t}_i| = N$.
  - If $i = \widehat{\mathbf{x}}[j]$ for some $j \in [Q]$ set $|\mathbf{t}_i| = \mathsf{SP}[\widehat{\mathbf{x}}[j]]$.
  - Each entry in $\mathbf{t}_i$ is of the form $(\mathbf{e}, y)$, where $\mathbf{e} = \mathsf{SKE.Enc}(K_e, 0^\lambda)$ for some $K_e \leftarrow \{0,1\}^\lambda$, and where $y \leftarrow G$ is a uniformly random group element from the group G corresponding to the group action $(G, X, \star)$.
- Set $L = (\mathsf{stag}_i, \mathbf{t}_i)_{i \in [|W|]}$. Store this list L locally for future use.
- Finally, create the simulated dictionary TSet as $\mathsf{TSet} \leftarrow \mathsf{Dict.Create}(L)$.

Simulating the XSet. The simulator $\mathsf{Sim_{GXT}}$ now simulates the encrypted data structure XSet as follows:

- Initialize an empty set $\mathsf{XSet} = \emptyset$.
- Initialize an empty hash table $H = \emptyset$ and an empty permutation array $\mathsf{WPerms} = \emptyset$.
- For each $\ell \in \widehat{x}$ and each $\mathsf{ind} \in \cup_{j \in [Q]} \mathsf{RP}[j]$, set $H[\mathsf{ind}, \ell] \leftarrow X$ as a uniformly random set element from the set X corresponding to the group action $(G, X, \star)$.
- For each $i \in [Q]$, set $\mathsf{WPerms}[\mathsf{EP}[i]] \leftarrow \mathsf{Perm}([\mathsf{SP}[i]])$, where $\mathsf{Perm}([\mathsf{SP}[i]])$ generates a random permutation of the integers in the range $[SP[i]]$.
- Initialize a counter $i = 0$.
- For each $\ell \in \widehat{x}$ and each $\mathsf{ind} \in \cup_{j:\widehat{x}[j]=\ell} \mathsf{RP}[j]$, do the following:
  - Set $\mathsf{XSet} = \mathsf{XSet} \cup \{H[\mathsf{ind}, \ell]\}$.
  - Set $i = i + 1$.
- For each $j \in [i+1, N]$, set $\mathsf{XSet} = \mathsf{XSet} \cup \{u\}$ where $u \leftarrow X$ is a uniformly random set element from the set X corresponding to the group action $(G, X, \star)$.

At this point, the simulator $\mathsf{Sim_{GXT}}$ is ready with the simulated encrypted database $\mathsf{EDB} = (\mathsf{TSet}, \mathsf{XSet})$.

Simulating the Query Transcript. The simulator $\mathsf{Sim_{GXT}}$ now creates a transcript array stk, where for each $i \in [Q]$, $\mathsf{stk}[i]$ denotes the transcript corresponding to the i-th query. For each $i \in [Q]$, the query transcript $\mathsf{stk}[i]$ is created as follows:

- Let $\ell = \widehat{\mathbf{x}}[i]$.
- Compute the set of "revealed" indices for the i-th query as $R = \mathsf{RP}[i] \cup \sum_{j \in [Q]} \mathsf{IP}[i,j]$.
- Arrange set of indices in R in canonical order. Let the canonically ordered list be of the form $(\overline{\mathsf{ind}}_1, \ldots, \overline{\mathsf{ind}}_{T'})$.
- Since each index in R is also in $\mathsf{DB}[\mathsf{s}[i]]$, we must have $|R| \leq \mathsf{SP}[i]$. Pad the list R with additional dummy indices $(\overline{\mathsf{ind}}_{T'+1}, \ldots, \overline{\mathsf{ind}}_{\mathsf{SP}[i]})$, where for each $j \in [T'+1, \mathsf{SP}[i]]$, $\overline{\mathsf{ind}}_j = \bot$.
- Retrieve $(\mathsf{stag}_\ell, \mathbf{t}_\ell)$ from internal storage.
- Let $\sigma = \mathsf{WPerms}[\mathsf{EP}[i]]$.
- For each $c \in [\mathsf{SP}[i]]$, do the following:
  - Let $(\mathbf{e}_c, y_c) = \mathbf{t}_\ell[c]$, where $y_c \in G$ is a group element corresponding to the group action $(G, X, \star)$.

- If $\overline{\mathsf{ind}}_{\sigma(c)} \neq \perp$, set $\mathsf{xtoken}_i[c] = \big((y_c)^{-1}\big) \star H[,\overline{\mathsf{ind}}_{\sigma(c)}, \ell]$, where $\star$ denotes an action computation corresponding to the group action $(G, X, \star)$.
- Else, set $\mathsf{xtoken}_i[c] \leftarrow X$ as a uniformly random set element.
- Pick random $k > \mathsf{SP}[i]$, and set $\mathsf{xtoken}_i[c] \leftarrow X$ as a uniformly random set element for each $c \in [\mathsf{SP}[i]+1, k]$.
- Finally, set $\mathsf{stk}[i] = (\mathsf{stag}_\ell, \mathsf{xtoken}_i)$.

Finally, the simulator $\mathsf{Sim}_{\mathsf{GXT}}$ outputs $(\mathsf{EDB} = (\mathsf{TSet}, \mathsf{XSet}), \mathsf{stk})$.

D.3   The Hybrid Argument

We now present a sequence of computationally indistinguishable hybrids that allow us to argue that the above simulation results in an ideal-world adversarial view that is computationally indistinguishable from the real-world adversarial view.

Hybrid-0. This is the real game.

Hybrid-1. In this hybrid, we replace the evaluations of the real PRF evaluations $F(K_S, \cdot), F_G(K_X, \cdot), F_G(K_I, \cdot), F_G(K_X, \cdot)$, are replaced by evaluations of independent uniformly random functions with the appropriate domain and range (this is done via the usual lazy sampling strategy). This is indistinguishable from Hybrid-0 by the security of each PRF (Definition 5).

Hybrid-2. In this hybrid, we replace each e entry in the TSet by encryptions of 0^λ (under the same key K_e). The indistinguishability of this hybrid from Hybrid-1 follows by a standard hybrid argument over the $|W|$ encryption keys used in building TSet f. We omit the tedious details. We stress that the reduction is possible because the game never invokes the decryption algorithm of the SKE scheme, meaning that the reduction does not need to decrypt ciphertexts during the IND-CPA game.

Hybrid-3. In this hybrid, we set the y entries in the TSet as $f_I(\overline{\mathsf{ind}}_{\sigma(c)})/f_Z(s\|c)$, where f_I and f_Z are random functions and $\overline{\mathsf{ind}}_{\sigma(c)}$ is set as in the simulation strategy defined above. We also maintain a table H with entries of the form $H[\mathsf{ind}, w] = (f_I(\mathsf{ind})f_X(w)) \star x_0$ (used to generate the XSet), and set the corresponding $\mathsf{xtoken}[c]$ entry in stk as $H[\overline{\mathsf{ind}}_{\sigma(c)}, x]^{1/y} = (f_X(x))f_Z(s\|c)) \star x_0$. This is primarily a book-keeping hybrid, and the view of the adversary is identical in Hybrid-2 and Hybrid-3.

Hybrid-4. In this hybrid, we set the y entries in the TSet as uniformly random elements in the group G. This is because the PRF $F_G(K_Z, \cdot)$ and its random counterpart f_Z are never evaluated on the same input twice (each evaluation corresponds to a unique (w, c) pair), and hence the output distribution of f_Z on $(w\|c)$ values is statistically indistinguishable from random. Hence, Hybrid-4 is statistically indistinguishable from Hybrid-3.

Hybrid-5. In this hybrid, we set the entries of the XSet to be uniformly random. This hybrid is computationally indistinguishable from Hybrid-4 by the GA-DDH assumption (Definition 2) over the EGA $(G, X, \star)$.

Hybrid-6. In this hybrid, we set the TSet exactly as in the simulation strategy described above. This hybrid is computationally indistinguishable from Hybrid-5 assuming that the dictionary scheme Dict satisfies history independence.

Hybrid-7. In this hybrid, we change the manner in which the H array is accessed in order to enable the final simulator to work with its given leakage. Intuitively, now whenever the game access the H array at an index (ind, x), it first tests to see if the game will ever access that index in H again. If it will come back to this position, it uses the value from H. It not, then the game replaces the H access with a random choice. Since that was to be the only usage of that position of H during the game, this doesn't affect the distribution of the game. Hence, the view of the adversary is identical in Hybrid-6 and Hybrid-7.

Hybrid-8. In this hybrid, we switch entirely to the simulation strategy described earlier. Since we have entirely switched to generating and accessing TSet and XSet using the leakage by Hybrid-7, the view of the adversary is identical in Hybrid-7 and Hybrid-8.

The detailed proofs of indistinguishability for the hybrids above are similar to those used in the original security proof for OXT, and are not detailed further. This concludes the proof of Theorem 2.

E   Proof of Theorem 4

We consider a session sid with a single client C with a conjunctive query $\bar{w} = (w_1, \ldots, w_\mu)$, a data owner D, and a passive eavesdropper E who has no input[4] (we assume authenticated but no secure channels). We further assume that for each execution corresponding to a specific tuple $(\mathsf{sid}, \bar{w})$, a party plays exactly one role (this can change across different executions). Again we argue that considering this specific setting is without loss of generality. To see that fix a specific $(\mathsf{vk}, \bar{w})$. We consider three separate cases:

- **Case-1:** Suppose that C and D are both honest, while the eavesdropper E is passively corrupt. In this case, we want the following guarantee: E should not be able to predict the output search token stk, without querying $\bar{w}$ explicitly.
- **Case-2:** Suppose that C is corrupt, while D and E are honest. In this case, we want the following guarantee: unless the C derives the output search token stk explicitly by interacting with D, it cannot efficiently predict stk.
- **Case-3:** Suppose that C is honest, while both D and E are corrupt. In this case, we want the following guarantees: (i) the query $\bar{w}$ remains private, and (ii) *consistency*, i.e., the search token stk is, computed correctly.

This exhausts the objectives of all parties in the system. We describe a different ideal-world simulation strategy for each case:

- **Case-1:** Sim$_E$ simulates the interactions between the honest client C and the honest data owner D.

---

[4] Here, the eavesdropper E could, for example, be the data server dS.

- **Case-2:** Sim_C interacts with the ideal functionality $\mathcal{F}_{\mathsf{Token}}^{\mathsf{MC\text{-}SSE}}$ on behalf of the maliciously corrupt client C, while simulating the messages from the honest D.
- **Case-3:** Sim_D interacts with the ideal functionality $\mathcal{F}_{\mathsf{Token}}^{\mathsf{MC\text{-}SSE}}$ on behalf of the maliciously corrupt data owner D, while simulating the messages from the honest C.

E.1   Simulation Strategy for Case-1

In this case, we need to ensure that no eavesdropper E can predict the search token on a non-queried search query, even if it can access the entire communication transcript between an honest C and an honest D. To this end, we construct a simulator Sim_E that simulates the messages from the honest client C and the honest data owner D by directly using the simulators Sim_F and Sim_X for the underlying OPRF schemes OPRF_F and OPRF_X, respectively.

It is easy to see that any corrupt eavesdropper E that manages to predict the search token on a non-queried search query can be turned into an adversary that manages to predict the output of either F or F_X on a non-queried input, thus breaking the security of either OPRF_F or OPRF_X. This completes the proof of security of token generation for case-1.

E.2   Simulation Strategy for Case-2

In this case, we want the following guarantee: unless the corrupt client C derives the output search token stk on a search query $\bar{w}$ by explicitly interacting with the honest data owner D, it cannot efficiently predict stk. In other words, if the corrupt C issues $q = \mathsf{poly}(\lambda)$ token generation queries to the honest D, it cannot more than q valid (query, token) tuples. To this end, we construct a simulator Sim_C that interacts with the ideal functionality $\mathcal{F}_{\mathsf{Token}}^{\mathsf{MC\text{-}SSE}}$ on behalf of the maliciously corrupt client C, while simulating the messages from the honest D. Let Sim_F and Sim_X be the simulators for the underlying OPRF schemes OPRF_F and OPRF_X, respectively. The simulation strategy used by Sim_C is as follows:

1. Since both OPRF_F and OPRF_X are maliciously secure, the corresponding simulators must have a mechanism to extract a malicious client's OPRF input from the client's messages. Sim_C uses the same strategy to extract the query $\bar{w}$ from the malicious client C from its messages.
2. Sim_C simulates the messages from the honest data owner D by directly using the simulators Sim_F and Sim_X.
3. Upon receiving $(\mathsf{Token}, \mathsf{sid}, w^*)$ from the ideal functionality (w^* being an encoded query), Sim_C uses the extracted query $\bar{w}$ to issue a query of the form $(\mathsf{Token}, \mathsf{sid}, \bar{w})$ to the ideal functionality. If the ideal functionality outputs $\bot$, Sim_C outputs $\bot$ to C. Otherwise, if the ideal functionality outputs stk, it outputs stk to C.

Now, observe that any malicious client C that manages to extract the output search token stk on a search query $\bar{w}$ without interacting with the honest data owner D must predict the output of either F or F_X on a given input without actually querying it, thus breaking the security of either OPRF_F or OPRF_X. This completes the proof of security of token generation for case-2.

E.3   Simulation Strategy for Case-3

In this case, we want the following guarantee: a malicious data owner D cannot learn any information about the query issued by some honest client C. To this end, we construct a simulator Sim_D that interacts with the ideal functionality $\mathcal{F}^{\mathsf{MC\text{-}SSE}}_{\mathsf{Token}}$ on behalf of the maliciously corrupt data owner C, while simulating the messages from the honest client C. Let Sim_F and Sim_X be the simulators for the underlying OPRF schemes OPRF_F and OPRF_X, respectively. The detailed simulation strategy used by Sim_D is as follows:

1. Upon receiving $(\mathsf{Input}, \mathsf{sid}, w^*)$ from the ideal functionality, where $w^* = (w^*_1, \ldots, w^*_\mu)$, Sim_D forwards it to the corrupt data owner D. If D aborts, Sim_D sends $\bot$ to the ideal functionality. Otherwise, Sim_D responds to the ideal functionality with the same message $(\mathsf{Input}, \mathsf{sid}, w^*)$.
2. Sim_D simulates the messages from the honest client C by directly using the simulators Sim_F and Sim_X on the encoded inputs w^*_1 and $(w^*_2, \ldots, w^*_\mu)$. If the corrupt server aborts at any point, Sim_C also aborts.
3. If the corrupt server S does not abort, Sim_D submits a query of the form $(\mathsf{Token}, \mathsf{sid}, w^*)$ to the ideal functionality. If the ideal functionality aborts, Sim_D also aborts. Otherwise, if the ideal functionality returns the same message, Sim_D responds to the ideal functionality with the same message again.

Now observe that any malicious data owner D that gains any information about the honest client's input query must violate the input obliviousness guarantee of either OPRF_F or OPRF_X. This completes the proof of security of token generation for case-3, and hence the proof of Theorem 4.

References

1. Alamati, N., De Feo, L., Montgomery, H., Patranabis, S.: Cryptographic group actions and applications. In: Moriai, S., Wang, H. (eds.) ASIACRYPT 2020, Part II. LNCS, vol. 12492, pp. 411–439. Springer, Heidelberg (2020). https://doi.org/10.1007/978-3-030-64834-3_14 December
2. Beullens, W., Kleinjung, T., Vercauteren, F.: CSI-FiSh: efficient isogeny based signatures through class group computations. In: Galbraith, S.D., Moriai, S. (eds.) ASIACRYPT 2019, Part I. LNCS, vol. 11921, pp. 227–247. Springer, Heidelberg (2019). https://doi.org/10.1007/978-3-030-34578-5_9 December
3. Boneh, D., Kogan, D., Woo, K.: Oblivious pseudorandom functions from isogenies. In: Moriai, S., Wang, H. (eds.) ASIACRYPT 2020, Part II. LNCS, vol. 12492, pp. 520–550. Springer, Heidelberg (2020). https://doi.org/10.1007/978-3-030-64834-3_18 December

4. Brassard, G., Yung, M.: One-way group actions. In: Menezes, A.J., Vanstone, S.A. (eds.) CRYPTO 1990. LNCS, vol. 537, pp. 94–107. Springer, Heidelberg (1991). https://doi.org/10.1007/3-540-38424-3_7

5. Cash, D., et al.: Dynamic searchable encryption in very-large databases: Data structures and implementation. In: 21st Annual Network and Distributed System Security Symposium, NDSS 2014, San Diego, California, USA, 23–26 February 2014. The Internet Society (2014)

6. Cash, D., Jarecki, S., Jutla, C.S., Krawczyk, H., Rosu, M.-C., Steiner, M.: Highly-scalable searchable symmetric encryption with support for Boolean queries. In: Canetti, R., Garay, J.A. (eds.) CRYPTO 2013, Part I. LNCS, vol. 8042, pp. 353–373. Springer, Heidelberg (2013). https://doi.org/10.1007/978-3-642-40041-4_20 August

7. Castryck, W., Lange, T., Martindale, C., Panny, L., Renes, J.: CSIDH: an efficient post-quantum commutative group action. In: Peyrin, T., Galbraith, S. (eds.) ASIACRYPT 2018, Part III. LNCS, vol. 11274, pp. 395–427. Springer, Heidelberg (2018). https://doi.org/10.1007/978-3-030-03332-3_15 December

8. Chang, Y.-C., Mitzenmacher, M.: Privacy preserving keyword searches on remote encrypted data. In: Ioannidis, J., Keromytis, A., Yung, M. (eds.) ACNS 2005. LNCS, vol. 3531, pp. 442–455. Springer, Heidelberg (2005). https://doi.org/10.1007/11496137_30 June

9. Chase, M., Kamara, S.: Structured encryption and controlled disclosure. In: Abe, M. (ed.) ASIACRYPT 2010. LNCS, vol. 6477, pp. 577–594. Springer, Heidelberg (2010). https://doi.org/10.1007/978-3-642-17373-8_33 December

10. Couveignes, J.-M.: Hard homogeneous spaces. Cryptology ePrint Archive, Report 2006/291 (2006). https://eprint.iacr.org/2006/291

11. Curtmola, R., Garay, J.A., Kamara, S., Ostrovsky, R.: Searchable symmetric encryption: improved definitions and efficient constructions. In: Juels, A., Wright, R.N., De Capitani di Vimercati, S. (eds.) ACM CCS 2006, pp. 79–88. ACM Press, October / November 2006

12. De Feo, L., et al.: SCALLOP: scaling the CSI-FiSh. In: Boldyreva, A., Kolesnikov, V. (eds.) PKC 2023, Part I. LNCS, vol. 13940, pp. 345–375. Springer, Heidelberg (2023). https://doi.org/10.1007/978-3-031-31368-4_13

13. Jarecki, S., Jutla, C.S., Krawczyk, H., Rosu, M.-C., Steiner M.: Outsourced symmetric private information retrieval. In: Sadeghi, A.-R., Gligor, V.D., Yung, M. (eds.) ACM CCS 2013, pp. 875–888. ACM Press, November 2013

14. Jarecki, S., Kiayias, A., Krawczyk, H., Xu, J.: Highly-efficient and composable password-protected secret sharing (or: How to protect your bitcoin wallet online). In: IEEE European Symposium on Security and Privacy, EuroS&P 2016, Saarbrücken, Germany, 21–24 March 2016, pp. 276–291. IEEE (2016)

15. Jarecki, S., Kiayias, A., Krawczyk, H., Xu, J.: TOPPSS: cost-minimal password-protected secret sharing based on threshold OPRF. In: Gollmann, D., Miyaji, A., Kikuchi, H. (eds.) ACNS 2017. LNCS, vol. 10355, pp. 39–58. Springer, Cham (2017). https://doi.org/10.1007/978-3-319-61204-1_3

16. Kamara, S., Moataz, T.: Boolean searchable symmetric encryption with worst-case sub-linear complexity. In: Coron, J.-S., Nielsen, J.B. (eds.) EUROCRYPT 2017. LNCS, Part III, vol. 10212, pp. 94–124. Springer, Cham (2017). https://doi.org/10.1007/978-3-319-56617-7_4

17. Kamara, S., Papamanthou, C., Roeder, T.: Dynamic searchable symmetric encryption. In: Yu, T., Danezis, G., Gligor, V.D. (eds.) ACM CCS 2012, pp. 965–976. ACM Press, October 2012

18. Lai, Y.-F., Galbraith, S.D., Delpech de Saint Guilhem, C.: Compact, efficient and UC-secure isogeny-based oblivious transfer. In: Canteaut, A., Standaert, F.-X. (eds.) EUROCRYPT 2021, Part I. LNCS, vol. 12696, pp. 213–241. Springer, Cham (2021). https://doi.org/10.1007/978-3-030-77870-5_8

19. Moriya, T., Onuki, H., Takagi, T.: SiGamal: a supersingular isogeny-based PKE and its application to a PRF. In: Moriai, S., Wang, H. (eds.) ASIACRYPT 2020, Part II. LNCS, vol. 12492, pp. 551–580. Springer, Cham (2020). https://doi.org/10.1007/978-3-030-64834-3_19

20. Naor, M., Pinkas, B., Reingold, O.: Distributed pseudo-random functions and KDCs. In: Stern, J. (ed.) EUROCRYPT 1999. LNCS, vol. 1592, pp. 327–346. Springer, Heidelberg (1999). https://doi.org/10.1007/3-540-48910-X_23

21. Naor, M., Reingold, O.: Number-theoretic constructions of efficient pseudo-random functions. In: 38th FOCS, pp. 458–467. IEEE Computer Society Press, October 1997

22. Page, A., Robert, D.: Introducing Clapoti(s): evaluating the isogeny class group action in polynomial time. IACR Cryptol. ePrint Arch., page 1766 (2023)

23. Song, D.X., Wagner, D., Perrig, A.: Practical techniques for searches on encrypted data. In: 2000 IEEE Symposium on Security and Privacy, pp. 44–55. IEEE Computer Society Press, May 2000

24. Sun, S.-F., Liu, J.K., Sakzad, A., Steinfeld, R., Yuen, T.H.: An efficient non-interactive multi-client searchable encryption with support for Boolean queries. In: Askoxylakis, I., Ioannidis, S., Katsikas, S., Meadows, C. (eds.) ESORICS 2016, Part I. LNCS, vol. 9878, pp. 154–172. Springer, Cham (2016). https://doi.org/10.1007/978-3-319-45744-4_8

25. Talapatra, D., Patranabis, S., Mukhopadhyay, D.: Conjunctive searchable symmetric encryption from hard lattices. In: IEEE EuroS&P 2023, pp. 958–978. IEEE (2023)

BlockDoor: Blocking Backdoor Based Watermarks in Deep Neural Networks
Official Work-in-Progress Paper

Yi Hao Puah[✉], Anh Tu Ngo, Nandish Chattopadhyay,
and Anupam Chattopadhyay

College of Computing and Data Science, Nanyang Technological University,
Singapore, Singapore
PUAH0021@e.ntu.edu.sg

Abstract. Adoption of machine learning models across industries have turned Neural Networks (DNNs) into a prized Intellectual Property (IP), which needs to be protected from being stolen or being used without authorization. This topic gave rise to multiple watermarking schemes, through which, one can establish the ownership of a model. Watermarking using backdooring is the most well established method available in the literature, with specific works demonstrating the difficulty in removing the watermarks, embedded as backdoors within the weights of the network. However, in our work, we have identified a critical flaw in the design of the watermark verification with backdoors, pertaining to the behaviour of the samples of the Trigger Set, which acts as the secret key. In this paper, we present BlockDoor, which is a comprehensive package of techniques that is used as a wrapper to block all three different kinds of Trigger samples, which are used in the literature as means to embed watermarks within the trained neural networks as backdoors. The framework implemented through BlockDoor is able to detect potential Trigger samples, through separate functions for adversarial noise based triggers, out-of-distribution triggers and random label based triggers. Apart from a simple Denial-of-Service for a potential Trigger sample, our approach is also able to modify the Trigger samples for correct machine learning functionality. Extensive evaluation of BlockDoor establishes that it is able to significantly reduce the watermark validation accuracy of the Trigger set by up to 98% without compromising on functionality, delivering up to a less than 1% drop on the clean samples. BlockDoor has been tested on multiple datasets and neural architectures.

Keywords: watermarking neural networks · backdooring · model modification attack · synthesis · extraction

1 Introduction

For the success of data-driven learning systems, three critical components are essential. First, there must be a large dataset, specifically curated to contain

J. Knechtel et al. (Eds.): SPACE 2024, LNCS 15351, pp. 258–276, 2025.
https://doi.org/10.1007/978-3-031-80408-3_16

information pertinent to the problem at hand. Second, a neural architecture is required, consisting of a computational graph and weight matrices. Lastly, robust hardware infrastructure is necessary to train the network by tuning the weights or parameters using the available data. The cost of training a neural network can range from a few thousand dollars for models with around a million parameters to over a million dollars for those with more than a billion parameters. Overall, stakeholders must invest in these components to effectively solve tasks using machine learning.

- Collecting the relevant data, organizing it, and labeling it, especially for supervised machine learning tasks.
- Developing the most appropriate neural architecture for the specific task.
- Acquiring advanced hardware infrastructure to train the neural network with the data in order to obtain the learned model.

It is understandable that anyone investing in one or more of the previously mentioned components would seek ownership and rights over their assets. It is important to note that these tasks do not need to be performed in one location; they can be executed by different parties collaborating toward a shared goal. Regardless of the method, the trained model, as the outcome of this process, becomes a valuable asset for all parties involved.

1.1   Motivational Background

The expansive advancement of deep learning architectures, highlighted by the release of models such as ChatGPT, has underscored the extensive utility of neural network models in our daily lives. Significant resources have been devoted to the development of high-performance models, continually extending their capabilities. The limitless applications of these powerful deep learning models have made them economically valuable assets, making them vulnerable to theft, replication, and unauthorized redistribution. As a result, they are increasingly being treated as intellectual property, leading to the adoption of measures to "trademark" them through deep neural network watermarking techniques. The evolution of these techniques began with parameter regularization and has since seen numerous refinements, culminating in the recent introduction of certified watermarking [1]. The initial development of watermarking methods was driven by two essential criteria: robustness, which is the watermark's ability to withstand relentless attacks without being removed, and resilience, which refers to its ability to maintain integrity even under adverse conditions.

Several techniques have been proposed in the past for watermarking neural networks. Notable examples include BlackMarks, DeepMarks, DeepSigns [2] etc. However, such techniques have proven unreliable due to the simultaneous advancement of attacks by adversaries. Examples of such attack mitigation efforts include DeepInspect [3] and TABOR [4] which have been successful in defeating them.

Despite the competition between watermarking techniques and attacks, the most widely accepted and robust mechanism against attacks is watermarking through backdooring [5]. This method leverages the over-parameterized nature of neural networks to embed watermarks within the model. Given its acceptance and widespread use, it is essential to assess its strengths and weaknesses before practical deployment. The backdooring approach takes advantage of known vulnerabilities in neural networks to embed specific watermarks by modifying the model's weights. While effective in both embedding and verifying ownership, this method shares some risks associated with backdoors. Though these vulnerabilities may be less severe in this context, it is still critical to examine potential weaknesses and defenses against adversarial attacks. One relatively unexplored gap is the lack of studies on how to conclusively determine whether a given neural network has been watermarked. Being able to mathematically explain the presence of a watermark in a neural network is crucial for enhancing the security and integrity of digital content, as it provides a foundation for more robust copyright protection and effective tamper detection of intellectual properties. Further details of the watermarking process for neural networks is presented in the Appendix.

1.2 Contributions

The primary contributions of this paper are inclusive of, but not limited to the following:

– We expose the vulnerabilities of watermarked neural networks which use Trigger sets for backdooring, by detecting Trigger samples and blocking or modifying them to prevent a successful verification of ownership
– We have built the BlockDoor framework using a wrapper function around the samples input to the watermarked model, to detect three different kinds of Trigger samples, which correspond to the three ways of Key Generation in Backdooring processes, namely, Adversarial sample based Triggers, Out-of-distribution Triggers and Randomly Labelled Triggers.
– We have performed extensive experiments on standard neural architectures and benchmarking datasets to test the BlockDoor framework, and optimised each component that corresponds to each type of Trigger samples.
– Blockdoor is able to significantly reduce the watermark validation accuracy of the Trigger set by up to 98% without compromising on functionality, delivering up to a less than 1% drop on the clean samples.

2 Breaking Watermarking Schemes

There are several attack methods that can be used to exploit the vulnerabilities of watermarking schemes and steal models. Two common mechanisms discussed in the literature are evasion attacks [6] and model modification attacks [7]. In this work, we present a wrapper based evasion attack that is able to detect all three forms of Trigger samples used in the literature for watermarking with backdooring, and render the watermarked models completely vulnerable to being stolen without authorization.

2.1   Threat Model

To validate the ownership of a watermarked model with embedded backdoors, owners will have to pass a trigger set data (image) through their model. The expected result is something that is known only to the owner but not obvious to external users. However, the idea of covering a stolen watermarked model with a wrapper that detects the trigger data, can help prevent such image from ever being passed into the watermarked model or the returned results can be discretely modified. This wrapper solution circumvents the modification of the watermarked model since we encase it in a wrapper that does not directly modify the watermark model. Preserving inherent information of the watermark model. The reduction in watermark accuracy shows that the wrapper models are able to erase some watermark signature without directly modifying the watermarked model.

Neural Network Wrapping

The idea of developing a wrapper around the potentially watermarked neural network must work for all different types of processes used in generating the embedded watermarks. Presently, three popular techniques for generating trigger data to be watermarked include:

- Adversarial Samples
- Out of distribution samples
- Samples with random labels

BlockDoor is designed to be able to deal with all the three types of Trigger Sets, as shown in Fig. 1. Our methodology was based under certain key assumptions and considerations to drove the directions of our proposed techniques. Our key assumptions were:

- **Transparency of Watermarking Scheme:** Following Kerckhoffs' principle, it is assumed that the watermarking scheme is public knowledge. However, the specific trigger data used for embedding the watermark remains confidential. This approach ensures that the security of the watermarking scheme does not rely on the obscurity of the algorithm but rather on the secrecy of the trigger data.
- **Adversarial Access to Model's Dataset:** Considering the scenario where an adversary has access to the model's training dataset. This assumption is realistic in many practical situations where datasets are often publicly available or can be closely approximated.
- **Limited Data for Adversarial Model Training:** Despite having access to the model's dataset, assumptions that the adversary has limited data to train their own model are made. This constraint could arise from various factors, such as computational resources, data access restrictions, or strategic choices by the adversary. In our methodology, this limitation is modelled by randomly sampling only one-third of the original training dataset for all adversarial model training. This assumption helps us evaluate the robustness of our watermarking scheme against adversaries with constrained data resources.

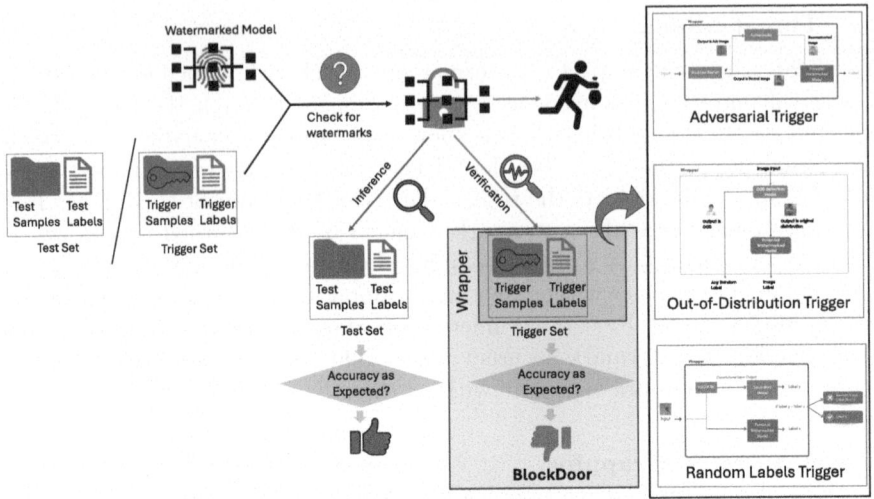

Fig. 1. BlockDoor in action: Three parallel functionalities to detect and thwart the three different types of Trigger samples that are used for Backdooring processes.

2.2 Eliminating Adversarial Backdoor

Existing research have primarily focused on bolstering robustness against adversarial attacks, as highlighted in the work of Chattopadhyay et al. [8]. In contrast, our approach involves adapting this robustness concept by training a dedicated ResNet18 model to differentiate between adversarial and normal image samples. A model specifically trained to recognize adversarial watermarking techniques can effectively identify images altered by such techniques.

Training Adversarial Detection Based Wrapper: This method of detecting and thereafter eliminating adversarial noise is a two-step process. First, we modified the ResNet18 architecture to output a binary classification, distinguishing between original and adversarial images. An autoencoder model was trained to minimize the reconstruction loss between an adversarial image and its original counterpart. This process aimed to reverse the effects of the adversarial modifications, effectively 'de-adversarial-attack' the image.

Two-Step Verification Process: The verification process involves two steps. First, an image is passed through the modified ResNet18 model to detect if it is adversarial. If detected, the image is then processed through the autoencoder to reconstruct its original form. This reconstructed image can then be safely fed to the original watermarked model without triggering the watermark detection.

2.3 Blocking Out-of-Distribution Labelling

Another popular technique for watermarking a model involves leveraging the use of Out of Distribution (OOD) images, as demonstrated in the work of Wang et al. [9].

Training OOD Detection Wrapper: Out-of-distribution (OOD) data can be effectively detected by converting the problem into a binary classification task, where the original dataset is labeled as positive and randomly sourced data from various datasets is labeled as negative. To validate our hypothesis, we developed a supplementary model specifically trained to distinguish between standard image samples from a dataset and randomly selected images from another dataset. This model is based on the assumption that OOD samples will exhibit significant dissimilarities compared to the original data, making them detectable through binary classification. This methodology is particularly relevant in scenarios where the original trigger set for watermarking may not be directly observable.

The proposed black box model incorporating our Out of Distribution Detection can be seen as follows:

Algorithm 1. Out of Distribution Watermark Detection

Data: Image Samples which may include OOD watermarked images
$input \leftarrow image$
$label \leftarrow OODModel(input)$
if $label$ is 1 **then**
    $y \leftarrow potentialWMModel(input)$
else if $label$ is 0 **then**
    $y \leftarrow randomLabel$
end if

2.4 Mitigating Random Labelling

In the paper by Zhao et al. [10], the authors propose the idea of watermarking Graph Neural Network models using Erdős-Rényi random graphs. In our proposed approach, we simplified this concept by incorporating randomly labelled images as our trigger set data. Detection of randomly labeled samples can be effectively achieved using simpler solutions, such as classification models. These models offer a balance between computational efficiency and reasonable accuracy in identifying mislabeled data.

To address the challenge of identifying correct labels without training a model as complex as the watermark model, we propose a two-step classification approach.

Training a Wrapper for Randomly Labelled Samples: The first step involves using a partially trained neural network model to extract features from the images. This model is trained on the correct labels of the original dataset, but not to the point of peak performance. Instead, it learns a representation of the image features, which are more informative than the raw pixel values. We then extract these representations from a hidden layer of the neural network. In the second step, we used a Support Vector Machine (SVM) classifier to classify the extracted features as the original labels. This approach leverages the abstract representations learned by the neural network to make accurate classifications without the need for a fully trained watermark model. This two-step process allows us to efficiently and accurately identify randomly labeled samples, enhancing the robustness of our watermarking technique. This implementation can be visualized in the Figure below:

3   Experimental Results

The core idea of watermarking neural networks is model and task agnostic, but in this paper, we have demonstrated the watermarking scheme and the wrapper around the Trigger dataset on an image classification task. The primary results related to the breaking of the watermarking verification is presented here, and all other associated results are presented in the Appendix.

3.1   Results for Adversarial Trigger Detector Wrapper

Certified watermarking is employed to embed the adversarial samples as the trigger data within a ResNet18 model.

To train our adversarial classifier, the original CIFAR-10 data was reclassified as positive labels (1) and the adversarial images as negative labels (0). A ResNet18 model was modified to perform binary classification. As this was a binary classification task, the precision, recall, and F1 score on the test set data was recorded, and noted in the extended results section in the Appendix. This observation supports our claim which posits that given a simple adversarial watermarking technique such as Fast Gradient Sign Method, it is easy to train a neural network model to learn the pattern of the adversarial disruption (Table 1).

3.2   Results for Out-of-Distribution Trigger Detector Wrapper

Like in the case of detecting adversarial samples, we use a similar technique of re-purposing the primary neural architecture to detect Out-of-Distribution samples.

Table 1. Comparison of test and watermark accuracy between the original water-marked model and the BlockDoor wrapper model - Adversarial Samples as Trigger Set

Dataset	Test Accuracy (%)	Watermark Accuracy (%)
Original Watermarked Model	84.87	100.00
Wrapper Model - ResNet	84.75	12.00
Wrapper Model - ViT	84.23	23.00

Test for Segregating Within-Distribution and Out-of-Distribution Samples: Three separate models were trained (MobileNet, ResNet, and VGG11) and their precision, recall, F1 score, and test accuracy across epochs were recorded. Our preliminary results indicate that when CIFAR100 is included as a negative label, it is effectively detected as out-of-distribution data. All models achieve optimal performance within a few epochs, with MobileNet demonstrating the most stable F1 score (Table 2).

Table 2. Comparison of test and watermark accuracy between the original water-marked model and the wrapper model - Out-of-Distribution samples as Trigger Set

Dataset	Test Acc (%)	Watermark Acc (%)
Original Watermarked Model	85.94	100.00
Wrapper (MobileNet V2) - Diluted CIFAR100	79.83	12.00
Wrapper (MobileNet V2) - Excluded CIFAR100	77.88	83.00
Wrapper (ViT) - Diluted CIFAR100	78.53	15.00

We extended this from DNN to Transformer model and achieved a similar performance. Our main concern / future work would be that we still require some OOD data with a similar distribution to the OOD Watermark data to have a stronger presence in erasing its signature, else the erasure is less impactful.

3.3 Results for Random Labelling Trigger Detector Wrapper

For our baseline classification model, a VGG16 architecture with Batch Normalization was chosen due to its prior known success in computer vision related task. The hypothesis is that, it is able to extract finer details from the images. As the intended goal of this model was to simply learn features of the original dataset (CIFAR-10), no further fine-tuning is performed (Table 3).

3.4 Key Findings

The primary take-aways form the experimental analysis include:

Table 3. Comparison of test and watermark accuracy between the original water-marked model and the wrapper model - Random Label samples as Trigger Set

Model	Test Accuracy (%)	Watermark Accuracy (%)
Original Watermarked Model	85.33	100
Wrapper Model - CIFAR10	64.45	2
Wrapper Model - CINIC10	71.11	7

- BlockDoor's wrapper functions are able to successfully detect all three kinds of Trigger samples that are used in watermarking schemes with backdooring and the corresponding mitigation techniques significantly bring down the accuracy of the watermarked model on the Trigger Set, thereby failing the verification process for establishing ownership.
- BlockDoor satisfies the functionality preserving property, as it is able to reduce the accuracy of the watermarked model on the Trigger Set without bringing down the accuracy of the model on the Test Set.
- For watermarked models which have used Adversarial samples for generating the Trigger Set, BlockDoor is able to bring down the accuracy on the Trigger Set by up to 88% while the accuracy on the Test samples remain within a 1% range.
- For watermarked models which have used Out-of-Distribution samples for generating the Trigger Set, BlockDoor is able to bring down the accuracy on the Trigger Set by up to 88% while the accuracy on the Test samples remain within a best case of 6% range.
- For watermarked models which have used Randomly Labelled samples for generating the Trigger Set, BlockDoor is able to bring down the accuracy on the Trigger Set by up to 98% while the accuracy on the Test samples remain within a best case of 14% range.

4   Conclusions

Firstly, the experimental results demonstrated that a model trained to recognize a published adversarial technique can effectively neutralize adversarial watermarks. A simple approach was proposed that leverages the transparency of watermarking schemes, and the developed wrapper model has shown the ability to render ineffective most of the trigger data while preserving the high performance of the watermarked model. Secondly, in addressing out-of-distribution (OOD) data, a promising strategy was presented involving the use of pooled random data to train a basic classifier. This classifier successfully differentiates between the original dataset and OOD data, enabling the creation of a wrapper capable of removing the watermark. Lastly, for random label watermarks, the proposed method utilizes a partially trained model to extract image features, which are then fed into a machine learning classifier. This approach has proven effective in accurately identifying the original label, enabling random label detection with reasonable accuracy and low computational cost. Overall, the findings suggest that while existing watermarking techniques for neural networks have notable strengths, they also exhibit significant vulnerabilities. The proposed approach exploits these weaknesses to effectively mitigate the watermark from a given model and expose them to be stolen or be used without proper and adequate authorization, which is a severe threat to the IP rights and for proving ownership by stakeholders.

Acknowledgement. This work is supported by Nanyang Technological University (NTU)-Desay SV Research Program under Grant 2018-0980.

Appendix

5   Background: Watermarking Techniques Using Backdooring

A typical watermarking scheme consists of three key components. Assuming a curated training dataset, denoted as *train_data*, and a trained neural network model, M, the first component is an algorithm to generate a secret key, m_k, which serves as the marker to be embedded as the watermark. Alongside this, a corresponding public key, v_k, is created for later verification, enabling the detection and validation of the watermark to establish ownership rights. The second component is an algorithm responsible for embedding the watermark into the object, which in this case is the neural network model. Lastly, there is a third algorithm that utilizes both the secret key, m_k, for marking and the public key, v_k, for verification purposes.

These algorithms can therefore be stated as:

- $Key\_Generation()$: Provides the pair of marking and corresponding verification keys (m_k, v_k)
- $Watermark\_Marking(M, m_k)$: Accepts an input neural network model and a secret marking key as parameters m_k, returns a watermarked model $\hat{M}$
- $Watermark\_Verification(m_k, v_k, M)$: Receives the marking and verification key pair as parameters (m_k, v_k) and the watermarked model $\hat{M}$, returns the output bit $b \in \{0, 1\}$

The effectiveness of the watermarking scheme relies on the proper functioning of all three previously mentioned algorithms $Key\_Generation$, $Watermark\_Marking$ and $Watermark\_Verification$) together.

5.1   Features of Watermarks

Since the progression into digital watermarks, certain features have been identified to determine its effectiveness. They can be classified in several ways:

- **Robustness**: This refers to the watermark's ability to remain intact and detectable even after the host data has undergone various transformations, such as compression, scaling, cropping, or other forms of manipulation. Robustness is crucial for ensuring that the watermark can effectively protect the copyright and ownership of the digital content.
- **Perceptibility**: This feature measures the visibility of the watermark in the host data. Ideally, a watermark should be imperceptible to maintain the quality and usability of the original data while still being detectable through specific algorithms or techniques. Balancing perceptibility and robustness is a key challenge in watermarking design
- **Capacity**: This refers to the volume of information that can be incorporated within the watermark. Higher capacity allows for more data to be stored, such as copyright information, authentication codes, or metadata. However, increasing capacity often requires trade-offs with perceptibility and robustness.
- **Security**: The security of a watermark is its ability to resist unauthorized detection, removal, or alteration. This is achieved through cryptographic techniques, watermarking key management, and embedding strategies that make the watermark difficult to tamper with or replicate without authorization.

5.2   Watermarking for Neural Networks

An abstract visualization of the watermarking process is shown in Fig. 2. The specific steps of the process are discussed here:

- **Selection of Watermark:** The first step involves choosing a suitable watermark. This could be a specific pattern, a set of weights, or a unique configuration that can be embedded into the neural network. The watermark should be distinctive enough to assert ownership but should not significantly impact the performance of the model.
- **Embedding the Watermark:** Once the watermark is selected, it is embedded into the neural network. This can be done in various ways, such as modifying the weights of the network, inserting specific neurons or layers that encode the watermark, or altering the network's architecture to incorporate the watermark. The embedding method should ensure that the watermark is integrated seamlessly without degrading the model's performance.
- **Extraction and Verification:** After the watermark is embedded, it is essential to have a mechanism for extracting and verifying the watermark to prove ownership. This involves developing an algorithm or technique that can detect the presence of the watermark in the neural network and confirm its authenticity.
- **Robustness and Security:** The watermarking process should also consider the robustness and security of the watermark. It should be resistant to common attacks such as fine-tuning, model compression, and adversarial attacks that might attempt to remove or alter the watermark. Additionally, the watermark should be secure enough to prevent unauthorized extraction or duplication (Fig. 3).

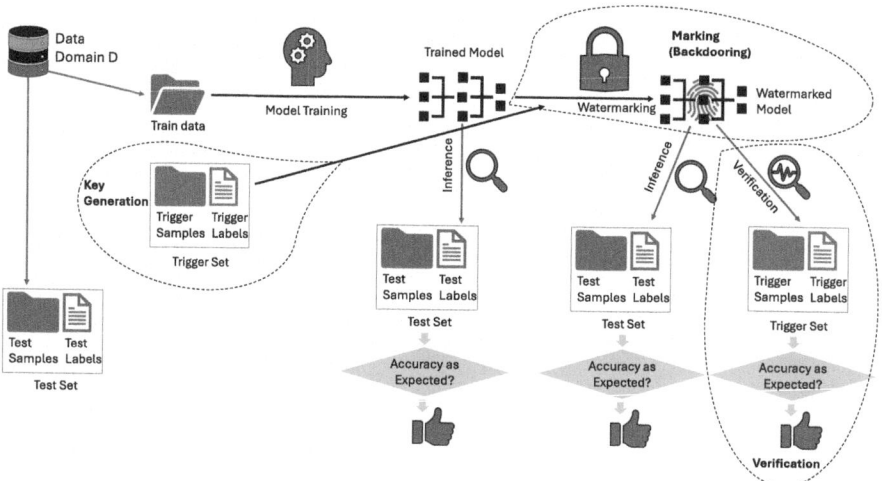

Fig. 2. Schematic diagram of the watermarking scheme using Backdooring which uses Trigger samples for Verification

5.3   Models and Datasets

The underlying model which is being watermarked, is what we refer to as the primary model. For this, we have used three different neural architectures.

Firstly, ResNet (Residual Network) architecture is employed, which has proven effective in addressing the vanishing gradient problem and enabling the training of very deep neural networks. There have been variations in the code of ResNet, but references were made based on Sasha et al., 2016 [11] implementation of ResNet. In addition to ResNet, the VGG (Visual Geometry Group) network architecture was also utilized for the image classification task. Specifically, a VGG16 architecture was employed with Batch Normalization, which is an enhancement over the standard VGG16 model. This architecture was first introduced by Simonyan and Zisserman in their 2014 paper [12] and has since become a popular choice for various computer vision tasks. Thirdly, MobileNet is used, which is a lightweight convolutional neural network architecture designed specifically for mobile and embedded devices. It was introduced by Howard et al. in their 2017 paper [13]. The key feature of MobileNet is the use of depthwise separable convolutions, which significantly reduces the number of parameters and computational complexity compared to traditional convolutional layers.

Additionally, for the design of the wrappers itself, we have made use of vision transformers and autoencoders, as explained earlier. The architecture of an autoencoder consists of two main components: an encoder and a decoder. The encoder compresses the input data into a latent-space representation, while the decoder reconstructs the input data from the latent space. Mathematically, the encoder and decoder can be represented as functions f and g, respectively, where: $h = f(x)$, $\hat{x} = g(h)$ where x is the input data, h is the encoded represen-

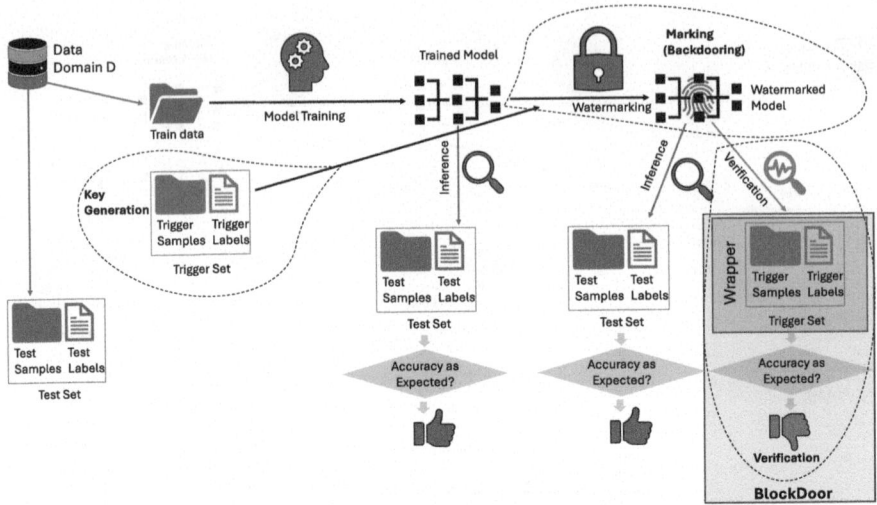

Fig. 3. Schematic Diagram of BlockDoor: Blocking Backdoor Based Watermarks in Deep Neural Networks

tation, and $\hat{x}$ is the reconstructed data. The autoencoder is trained to minimize the reconstruction error, typically measured by the mean squared error (MSE) between the input x and the reconstructed output $\hat{x}$.

5.4   Datasets

The CIFAR-10 dataset is commonly used for evaluating image classification models and serves as a standard benchmark for comparing the performance of different algorithms [14]. The CIFAR-100 dataset is an extension of the CIFAR-10 dataset, consisting of 100 classes containing 600 images of dimensions 32×32 each. The classes range from rockets to fishes to flowers. The CINIC-10 dataset [15] is an extension of the CIFAR-10 dataset designed to improve the evaluation of machine learning models on image classification tasks. It includes 270,000 images across 10 classes, which are a combination of CIFAR-10 images and additional images from the ImageNet dataset. This extended dataset aims to provide a more diverse and challenging set of images, helping to assess model performance more robustly and address issues related to overfitting and generalization. The SVHN dataset is a real-world image dataset obtained from house numbers in Google Street View images. It consists of over 600,000 digit images, coming in two formats.

6   Results

6.1   Eliminating Adversarial Backdoor

The ResNet-18 model was trained with the following parameters: **Loss Function:** Cross Entropy Loss, **Optimizer:** Adam Optimizer, **Learning Rate:** 0.001, **Batch Size:** 128, **Training Epochs:** 20. To train our adversarial classifier, the original CIFAR-10 data was reclassified as positive labels (1) and the adversarial images as negative labels (0). A ResNet18 model was modified to perform binary classification. The train - test accuracy during the training was recorded (Figs. 4 and 5).

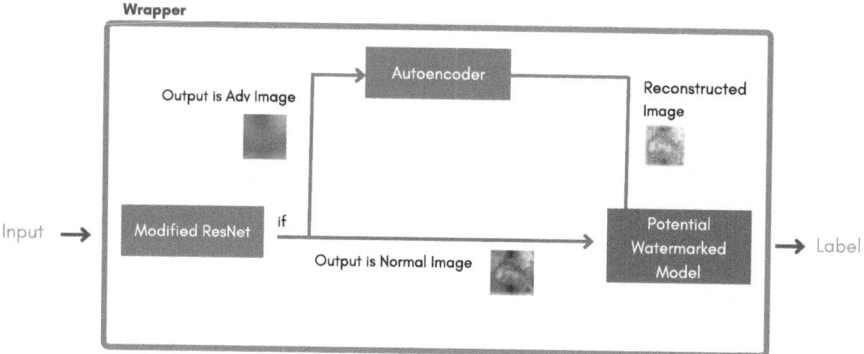

Fig. 4. BlockDoor architecture with Wrapper Function for detecting and eliminating Trigger Samples containing Adversarial Noise.

Additionally, the experiment was repeated with a Vision Transformer (ViT) model to show generalisability. The Vision Transformer (ViT) model [16] is a deep learning architecture that applies transformer principles, originally designed for natural language processing, to image analysis. Unlike traditional convolutional neural networks (CNNs), ViT processes images by dividing them into fixed-size patches, linearly embedding these patches, and then applying a transformer encoder to capture global relationships within the image. This approach has demonstrated significant performance improvements on various image classification benchmarks, showcasing the transformer model's effectiveness in vision tasks. The results of the various models are documented as shown below (Table 4):

6.2   Blocking Out-of-Distribution Labelling

The following settings are used for the same: **Loss Function:** Cross Entropy Loss, **Optimizer:** Adam Optimizer, **Learning Rate:** 0.01, **Batch Size:** 128, **Training Epochs:** 20 (Fig. 6).

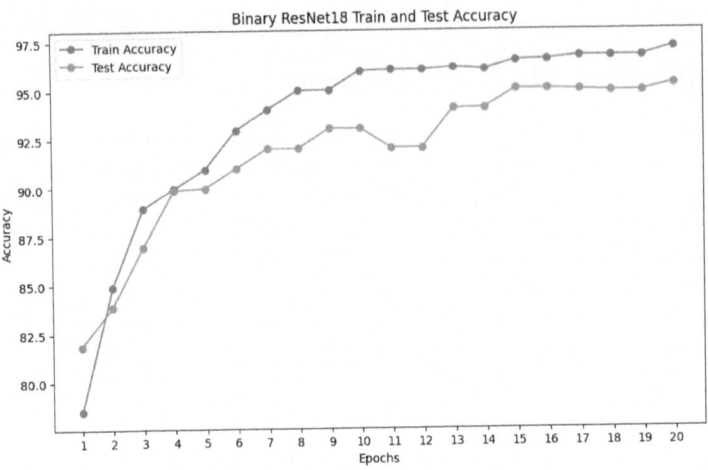

Fig. 5. ResNet18 Train-Test accuracy

Table 4. Comparison of test and watermark accuracy between the original water-marked model and the BlockDoor wrapper model - Adversarial Samples as Trigger Set

Dataset	Test Acc (%)	Watermark Acc (%)
Original Watermarked Model	84.87	100
Wrapper Model - ResNet	84.87	11.2
Wrapper Model - ViT	84.23	22.8

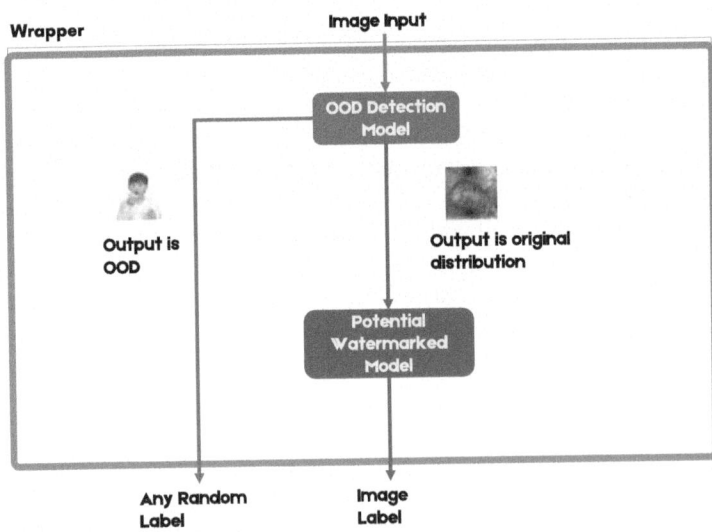

Fig. 6. BlockDoor architecture with Wrapper Function for detecting and blocking Out-of-Distribution samples used as Trigger Samples

Negative Labels for Out-of-Distribution Samples: The experiments were carried out with a diluted dataset and recorded the same metrics. The figure below showcases the classification F1 score for out-of-distribution data (Fig. 7).

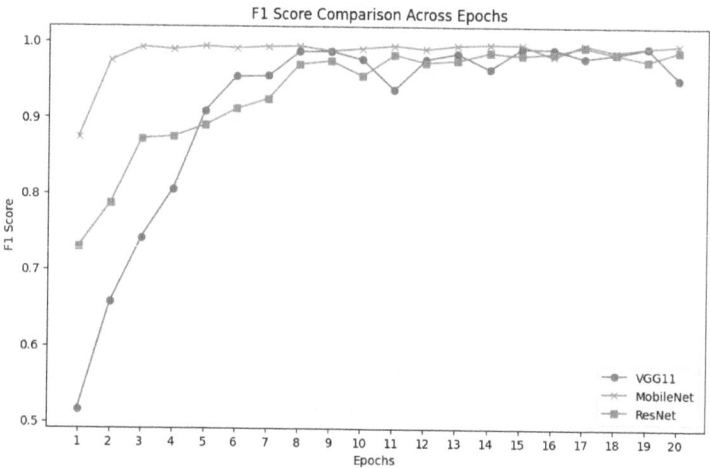

Fig. 7. Detection of Out-of-Distribution samples (with negative labels) re-purposing the primary neural architectures.

Extending to Unseen/Excluded Out-of-Distribution Samples: Based on the previous results, it was determined that MobileNet was the most suitable model for identifying out-of-distribution data. Hence, training was focused solely on the MobileNet model, on a dataset with CIFAR100 completely excluded from the negative label. For the purpose of fine-tuning this model, additional features were added during the training step, such as EarlyStopping (5) and a Learning Rate Scheduler based on the test loss (Fig. 8).

6.3   Mitigating Random Labelling

This model has the following parameters: **Loss Function:** Cross Entropy Loss, **Optimizer:** Adam Optimizer, **Learning Rate:** 0.01, **Batch Size:** 64, **Training Epochs:** 50 (Fig. 9).

Training the Alternate Model: After training the VGG16 neural network, features were extracted from the 2nd last Convolutional 2D layer. These extracted features were then used as input for simpler machine learning models to evaluate their classification performance. Specifically, Support Vector Machine (SVM) and K-Means clustering algorithms were employed. To ensure a proper

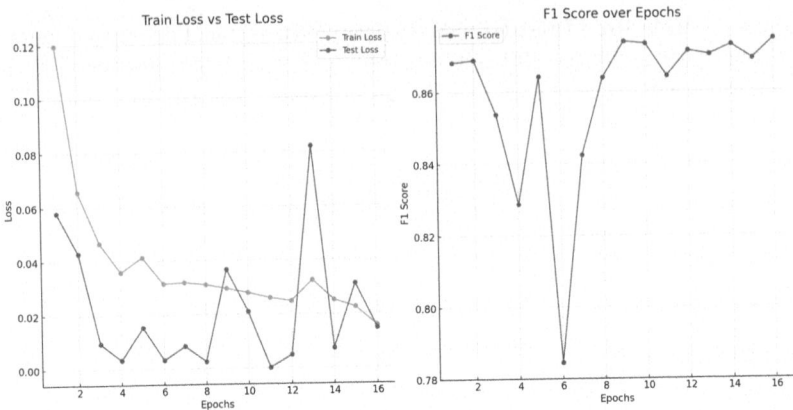

Fig. 8. Accuracy of Detection of Out-of-Distribution samples when the watermarked model is trained on the CIFAR-10 dataset and the Trigger samples are from the CIFAR-100 dataset.

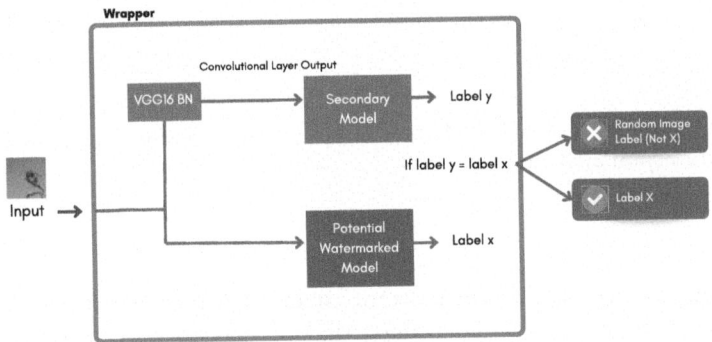

Fig. 9. BlockDoor architecture with Wrapper Function for detecting and mitigating Randomly Labelled Samples used as Trigger Samples

mapping of label inputs for the K-Means clustering, the Hungarian algorithm is applied before computing the cluster label accuracy. The classification performance was assessed using 5-Fold Cross-validation accuracy. The results of the classification performance for the SVM and K-Means models are summarized in the following Tables 5 and 6:

Given the promising results from the SVM model, further exploration is made to examine the potential of enhancing its performance by reducing the dimensionality of the input features. Principle Component Analysis (PCA) is applied to the extracted features from the convolutional layer, which initially had 2049 dimensions. Our goal was to investigate whether reducing the number of features could optimize the classification performance. The results of applying PCA with various numbers of components are summarized in the following table:

Table 5. Classification performance of SVM and K-Means models using 5-Fold Cross-validation.

Model	Accuracy	Standard Deviation (%)
K-Means	0.649	±1.24
SVM	0.7811	±1.44

Table 6. Performance of the SVM model with PCA-applied feature reduction.

n_components	Cross-Validation Acc (%)	Cross-Validation Std. Dev. (%)
Unmodified	78.11	±1.39
0.95	80.11	±1.48
0.90	80.03	±1.39
0.85	80.03	±1.39

The results indicate that reducing the dimensionality of the feature space through PCA can lead to improved classification performance. Specifically, retaining 95% of the variance in the data (n_components = 0.95) resulted in the highest cross-validation accuracy.

References

1. Bansal, A., et al.: Certified neural network watermarks with randomized smoothing. In: International Conference on Machine Learning, pp. 1450–1465. PMLR (2022)
2. Rouhani, B.D., Chen, H., Koushanfar, F.: DeepSigns: a generic watermarking framework for protecting the ownership of deep learning models (2018)
3. Chen, H., Fu, C., Zhao, J., Koushanfar, F.: DeepInspect: a black-box trojan detection and mitigation framework for deep neural networks. In: IJCAI, pp. 4658–4664 (2019)
4. Guo, W., Wang, L., Xing, X., Du, M., Song, D.: TABOR: a highly accurate approach to inspecting and restoring trojan backdoors in AI systems. arXiv preprint arXiv:1908.01763 (2019)
5. Adi, Y., Baum, C., Cisse, M., Pinkas, B., Keshet, J.: Turning your weakness into a strength: watermarking deep neural networks by backdooring. In: 27th USENIX Security Symposium (USENIX Security 18), pp. 1615–1631 (2018)
6. Hitaj, D., Hitaj, B., Mancini, L.V.: Evasion attacks against watermarking techniques found in MLaaS systems. In: 2019 Sixth International Conference on Software Defined Systems (SDS), pp. 55–63. IEEE (2019)
7. Tramèr, F., Zhang, F., Juels, A., Reiter, M.K., Ristenpart, T.: Stealing machine learning models via prediction APIs. In: 25th USENIX Security Symposium (USENIX Security 16), pp. 601–618 (2016)
8. Chattopadhyay, N., Chatterjee, S., Chattopadhyay, A.: Robustness against adversarial attacks using dimensionality. In: Batina, L., Picek, S., Mondal, M. (eds.) SPACE 2021. LNCS, vol. 13162, pp. 226–241. Springer, Cham (2022). https://doi.org/10.1007/978-3-030-95085-9_12

9. Wang, Q., et al.: Watermarking for out-of-distribution detection (2022)
10. Zhao, X., Wu, H., Zhang, X.: Watermarking graph neural networks by random graphs. In: 2021 9th International Symposium on Digital Forensics and Security (ISDFS). IEEE, June 2021
11. Targ, S., Almeida, D., Lyman, K.: Resnet in Resnet: generalizing residual architectures. arXiv preprint arXiv:1603.08029 (2016)
12. Simonyan, K., Zisserman, A.: Very deep convolutional networks for large-scale image recognition. arXiv preprint arXiv:1409.1556 (2014)
13. Andrew, G., et al.: MobileNets: efficient convolutional neural networks for mobile vision applications (2017)
14. Krizhevsky, A., Nair, V., Hinton, G.: The CIFAR-10 dataset (2014). http://www.cs.toronto.edu/kriz/cifar.html
15. Darlow, L.N., Crowley, E.J., Antoniou, A., Storkey, A.J.: CINIC-10 is not ImageNet or CIFAR-10. arXiv preprint arXiv:1810.03505 (2018)
16. Yuan, L., et al.: Tokens-to-token ViT: training vision transformers from scratch on ImageNet. In: Proceedings of the IEEE/CVF International Conference on Computer Vision, pp. 558–567 (2021)

Adversarial Malware Detection
Official Work-in-Progress Paper

Ashish Vishwakarma, Umesh Kashyap, and Sk Subidh Ali[(✉)]

Indian Institute of Technology, Bhilai 491002, India
{ashishv,umeshk,subidh}@iitbhilai.ac.in

Abstract. Malware detection is one of the most challenging tasks in the domain of Cybersecurity. The use of machine learning models as detectors significantly improved the performance. At the same time, adversarial modeling of malware can introduce a small noise into the malware data to generate adversarial malware, which can evade the machine learning based detector. In this work, we have proposed a detection framework for adversarial malware. We have considered $SLIPNER$ and $MalGAN$ datasets to generate adversarial malware using an adversarial-based attack algorithm. Our findings show that our approach is extremely effective in detecting and eliminating adversarial malware.

Keywords: GAN · Malware · Exciter network · Denoiser network · neural networks · perturbation

1 Introduction

The software that performs malicious tasks such as stealing private data, encrypting user files, or changing user permission without their consent is known as malware. There are various types of malware, such as viruses, worms, botnets, and adware. According to the survey [6,11,26], malware constitutes 80% of worldwide cyberattacks. The Internet has become a major medium for spreading malware [8]. Malware can cause havoc to an organization. Recent cyber attacks [1] through ransomware show that it not only forced the city police department to shut down its IT system but also crippled it. Therefore, developing advanced malware detection and prevention techniques is always a challenging and demanding job.

Traditional malware detection methods rely on a signature-based approach [5], where a unique identifier, such as a cryptographic hash or binary pattern, is generated and stored in a database. When a new malware sample appears, it's signature is generated and is matched against these stored signatures for detection. While this method offers fast detection, it has significant limitations [27], such as minor changes to the malware payload (e.g., polymorphism or compression) can evade detection [30]. Behavior-based detection methods overcome these limitations [20] by examining malware behavior, such as system interactions or network communications, to identify malicious activity [19].

J. Knechtel et al. (Eds.): SPACE 2024, LNCS 15351, pp. 277–286, 2025.
https://doi.org/10.1007/978-3-031-80408-3_17

Behavior analysis is done by running the malware in a secured (sandboxed) environment [9] and statistically analyzing its executable features [4].

The use of Machine learning has further advanced the malware detection technique by eliminating the need for manual coding rules [18]. However, these systems are vulnerable to adversarial machine learning (AML) attacks [28]. One of the prominent examples is $MalGAN$ [14], a generative adversarial network (GAN) that creates adversarial malware capable of evading black-box malware detectors. $MalGAN$ exploits knowledge of the detecto's feature set to reduce detection rates, posing a severe challenge to machine learning based detectors. Improved $MalGAN$ [16] addresses some limitations of the original attack model, such as needing to access the detector during training and reducing API features. It also introduces separate API lists for $MalGAN$ and the detector, improving its ability to generate evasive adversarial samples. However, in this work, we focus only on $MalGAN$ due to the unavailability of the private data required for analyzing Improved $MalGAN$ [16].

We introduce a novel approach, the denoise-excite framework, designed to detect adversarial malware samples. We rigorously tested our framework against adversarial malware attacks, including $MalGAN$ [14], $SLIPNER$ [2], and achieved significant accuracy in detecting these malicious instances.

The major contributions of our work are as follows:

- In this work, we have proposed denoise-excite, a framework for detecting adversarial malware.
- We have tested the performance of the proposed model on $MalGAN$ and $SLIPNER$ datasets.
- Our works open a new direction for adversarial example detection and encourage a similar structure for solving adversarial attacks in other domains, such as Vision and speech.

In the next section, we will provide a brief background on AML attacks and generative modeling, which was used by $MalGAN$ author to craft an adversarial malware sample.

2   Background

2.1   PE File Format

The Portable Executable (PE) file format, used in Windows for components like dynamic link libraries ($DLLs$), executable files (.exe), and even FON font files, offers architectural flexibility across Intel, AMD, and ARM platforms. This research targets malware exploiting the PE format, presenting unique challenges that demand specialized expertise.

2.2   Adversarial Malware

Machine learning models are vulnerable to AML attacks, where a slight perturbation in the input fails the model [15,21]. Malware classifiers can also be misled by subtle changes in malware headers or data. Fogla *et al.* [10] showed that small modifications to malicious packet attributes can deceive anomaly detection systems. Rigaki *et al.* [22] demonstrated AML attack to reduce detection accuracy by 10% to 27%. The PDF format, though useful for consistent rendering, is vulnerable to adversarial attacks. $PDFrate$ [25], a PDF malware classifier, was found susceptible to misclassification by embedding benign content into malicious files [17]. Xu *et al.* [29] used genetic programming in a black-box attack on PDFrate, identifying PDF objects that, when added, caused malicious files to appear benign. These techniques were later extended to Android malware [23]. Chen *et al.* [7] developed DroidEye to counter adversarial Android malware, while Shahpasand *et al.* [24] used generative models to achieve a 99% evasion rate on the Drebin dataset [3].

In black-box attack scenarios, Hu and Tan [14] introduced $MalGAN$, a generative model-based algorithm that bypasses malware detectors by focusing only on the features used by the detector. $MalGAN$ significantly reduced detection rates and proved resilient to adversarial defenses [13]. However, Improved $MalGAN$ [16] addressed several limitations by externally executing detectors, using unique API lists, and generating adversarial examples for single malware samples. In this paper, we focus on $MalGAN$ and develop detection techniques, as Improved $MalGAN$ could not be analyzed due to unavailable private data.

3   Methodology

In Adversarial attacks on machine learning models, an imperceptible perturbation is added to the input sample. In terms of malware classification, an adversary can add redundant API calls, sections, metadata, etc., as noise to the input malware file to fool the malware detector. Our proposed detection method consists of two major components denoise-excite block and Detector network. The denoise-excite block gives an excited and denoised feature vector, which is XORed to get a processed vector. Finally, the processed vector is fed to the detector network to distinguish between adversarial and non-adversarial samples. In the subsequent subsections, we will discuss each component of the proposed model in detail:

3.1   Denoiser Network

Denoiser network is an autoencoder neural network [12], transforming noisy features into clean features. This network consists of two neural networks: an encoder network $h = f(x')$ and a decoder network $x = g(h)$, where x' is a noisy input and x is a clean output. Therefore, denoiser network, with input x' and parameter θ_{Den} is defined as $Den(x'; \theta_{Den}) = g(f(x'))$. While training the denoiser network, the encoder module captures the most salient features of the training data. It also represents the input sample in a compact hidden representation, whereas the decoder network learns to reconstruct clean data from the hidden representation.

The loss function $\mathcal{L}(x, Den(x'; \theta_{Den}))$ penalizes the reconstruction for being different from the original clean input x. In the denoiser network, the hidden dimension h plays a critical role, the dimension of hidden representation $h \in \mathbb{R}^z$ where $z < m$, such that network can perform a salient transformation to clean the noisy sample. In this work, we applied the Random forest feature importance algorithm to determine the latent dimension.

3.2   Exciter Network

Consider a malware classifier $f(x; \theta) : \mathbb{R}^m \rightarrow \{0, 1\}$ The classifier classifies input x into either 0 for benign class or 1 for malware class. In the case of the adversarial malware sample x_{adv} (we are considering only adversarial malware as the adversarial sample), the classifier classifies the sample as benign (class 0) while the sample has malicious properties. In order to see whether a sample has adversarial perturbation or not, we add the exciter network $(Exc(x; \theta_{Exc}) : \mathbb{R}^m \rightarrow R^m)$ before the pre-trained classifier network. Therefore, the output of the exciter network is passed to the classifier. We retrain the whole network and observe the neuron activation path activated by a sample when it is fed to the exciter network. If we pass a sample through the exciter network, hidden perturbations can be highlighted due to their transformation applied by the exciter network. We can quantify this feature deflection from the original sample and can make a classifier to learn to classify the perturbed samples.

3.3   XOR Module

To create a distinguishing vector, we process the outputs from both the denoiser and exciter networks. Although various transformations like norm differences or non-linear kernel transformations could be used, we chose a simple XOR operation applied to the sigmoid-activated outputs of these networks. By converting the outputs of the denoiser and exciter network into binary vectors through thresholding, we use an XOR operation to generate a distinguishing binary vector. The resulting binary vector makes it clear which features differ between the two networks. Features where the XOR result is 1 are particularly significant, as adversarial perturbations are more likely to affect them. This targeted approach allows us to focus detection efforts on these crucial features, improving the overall effectiveness of our malware detection system.

3.4   Detector Model

The detector model takes the output of the denoise-excite block and distinguishes the sample as adversarial (Class 0) or non-adversarial (Class 1).

$$f\left(\text{XOR}\left(\text{Den}\left(x; \theta_{Den}\right), \text{Exc}\left(x; \theta_{Exc}\right)\right); \theta\right) : \mathbb{R}^m \rightarrow \{0, 1\}$$

Adversarial training is required to train the detector model to distinguish between normal and adversarial samples.

Once all the network components have undergone training, a seamless work-flow is established. When presented with a PE-executable sample, the first step involves feature extraction to isolate and extract the most pertinent features. Subsequently, these extracted features are passed to the denoise-excite model, where they undergo a transformation process. This transformation yields a processed feature representation. This processed feature representation is then fed into the detector model. The detector model takes on the critical role of classifying the sample as either adversarial (Class 1) or non-adversarial (Class 0). The working of the proposed model is shown in Fig. 1.

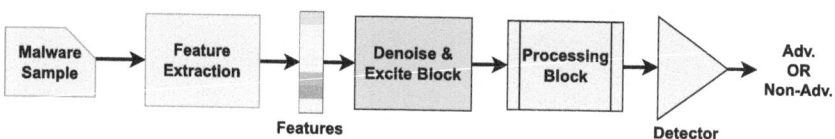

Fig. 1. Pipeline of Detector Model

Table 1. Dataset Statistics

Dataset	Benign Samples	Malicious Samples	Feature Size	Mean Feat. Imp.
Mal-GAN	1368	441	160	0.00781
SLIP-NER	34994	19696	1276	0.00078

Table 2. *MalGAN* Training Statistics

Dataset	Training TPR		Testing TPR	
	Org.	Adv.	Org.	Adv.
Mal-GAN	0.99	0.22	0.98	0.23
SLIP-NER	0.99	0.22	0.98	0.23

4   Experiment and Result

In this work, we conducted experiments on two datasets: the original *MalGAN* dataset and the *SLIPNER* dataset. Table 1 provides their statistical details. The *MalGAN* dataset follows the original paper's setup, while the *SLIPNER* dataset, initially with 22,000 features, was reduced to 1,276 using random forest feature importance. All features with importance above 1/22000 were retained. We performed experiments on an Intel i5-10th generation system with 8 cores, 16 GB RAM, and a 4 GB Nvidia RTX 3090 GPU running Ubuntu Linux.

We trained the *MalGAN* architecture as outlined by the authors. For the *MalGAN* dataset, we used a noise vector of size 20, a substitute detector with one hidden layer of size 50, and a generator with a hidden layer of size 256. For the larger *SLIPNER* dataset, we adjusted the architecture to include a noise vector of size 256, a substitute detector with hidden layers of sizes 600 and 300, and a generator with a 1024-unit hidden layer.

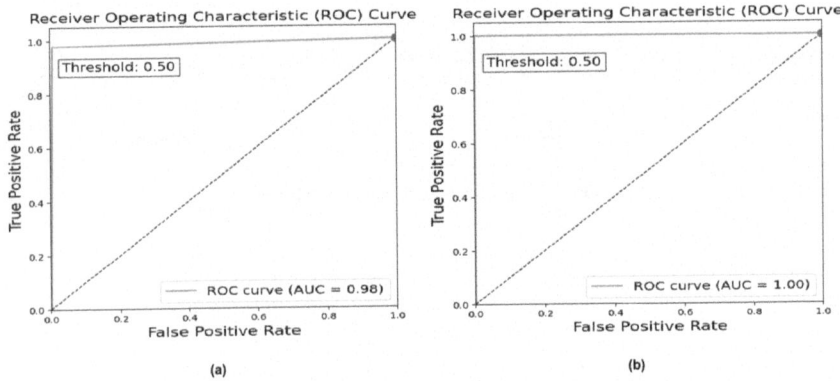

Fig. 2. Receiver operating curve of adversarial detectors on *MalGAN* and *SLIPNER* dataset respectively.

We evaluated *MalGAN* against several black-box classifiers, including random forest (RF), logistic regression (LR), decision trees (DT), support vector machines (SVM), multi-layer perceptron (MLP), and a voting ensemble ($VOTE$). As shown in Table 2, *MalGAN* reduced malware detection to 22% during training and 23% during testing, compared to 99% and 98% for original malware. Similar results were observed on the *SLIPNER* dataset, demonstrating consistent performance across both datasets.

We have performed adversarial training on the black-box detector network, as discussed in the methodology section. We have used a 2 layer deep network with a hidden layer of sizes 128 and 600, with respect to *MalGAN* and *SLIPNER* datasets. We have used *SELU* activation for the hidden layer and ADAM optimizer for tuning the hyperparameters. The detector model deployed on an NVIDIA RTX 3090 GPU(4 GB) system, the model achieves inference times of 1.02 μs per sample for *MalGAN*, and 85 μs for *SLIPNER*. These microsecond-level speeds ensure suitability for real-time cybersecurity applications, processing thousands of samples per second.

The results are presented through various performance metrics, with Fig. 2 showcasing the Receiver Operating Characteristic (ROC) curve. Figure 2 highlights the trade-off between true positive and false positive rates, demonstrating

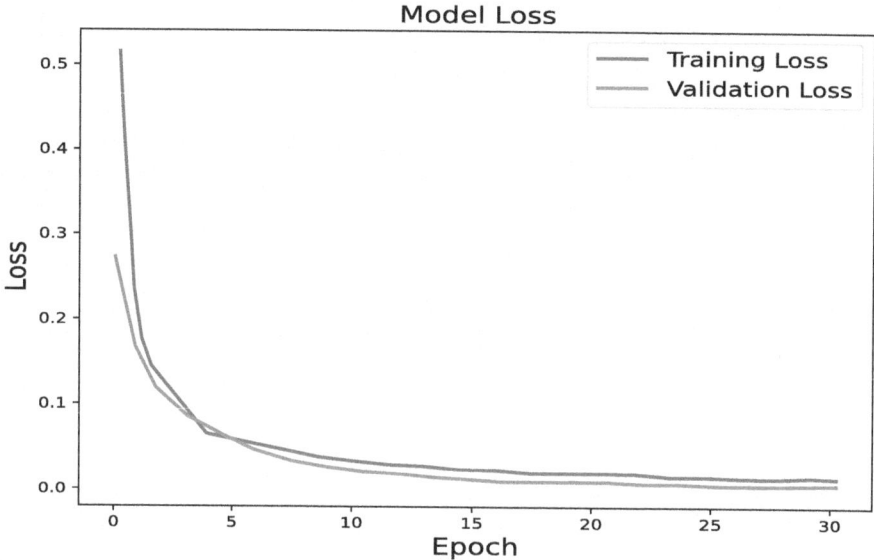

Fig. 3. Receiver operating curve of adversarial detectors on $MalGAN$ and $SLIPNER$ dataset respectively.

Table 3. Comparison between existing defence methods and our proposed method for adversarial malware detection

Malware Detector	$MalGAN$		$SLIPNER$	
	Org.	Adv.	Org.	Adv.
RF	98	23	97	22
Voting Classifier	99	24	99	23
Our	**99**	**98.3**	**99**	**99.9**

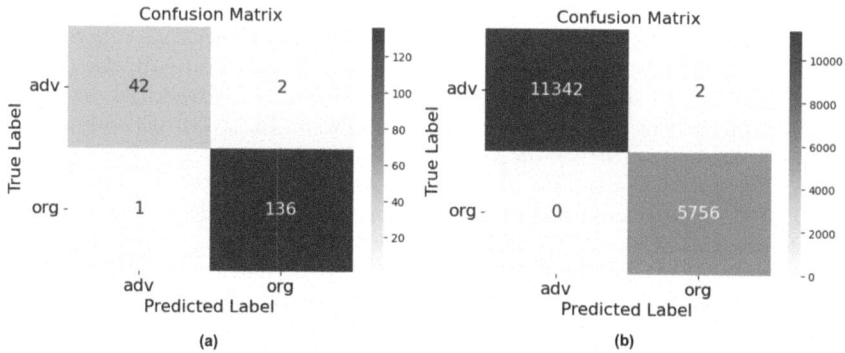

Fig. 4. Confusion metric plot of adversarial detector on (a) $MalGAN$ and (b) $SLIPNER$ dataset.

the model's capability to effectively distinguish between adversarial and normal samples. The high area under the curve (AUC) indicates strong classification performance. Additionally, the training loss, depicted in Fig. 3, shows a steady reduction over time, confirming effective model learning to overcome the overfitting. Table 3 presents the comparison between existing malware detection methods, RF and Voting Classifier, and our proposed method. The results show that RF achieves detection rates of 23% and 22% for adversarial samples on the *MalGAN* and *SLIPNER* datasets, respectively, while the Voting Classifier achieves 24% and 23%. In contrast, our proposed method significantly outperforms both, achieving 98.3% on *MalGAN* and 99.9% on *SLIPNER* for adversarial samples, also shown in Fig. 4. The model's accurate classification of adversarial and original samples demonstrates its robustness and resilience against attacks across datasets. These results confirm the effectiveness of adversarial training in enhancing detection accuracy and performance.

5   Conclusion

In this work, we proposed the denoise-excite framework for detecting adversarial malware. We tested the proposed framework on *SLIPNER* and *MalGAN* datasets. The experimental result shows that our method is capable of detecting adversarial samples with high accuracy. For future reference, one can look at applying a similar concept with universal adversarial perturbation and adversarial training for detecting adversarial samples in other domains as well, such as vision and speech. In future work, we are looking to train the denoiser network and excite network in a min-max framework, analogous to *GAN* training, using universal adversarial perturbation as an attack algorithm. This could further improve the robustness of the framework and extend its applicability to a wider range of adversarial scenarios.

References

1. Recent Cyber Attacks ransomware. https://www.cm-alliance.com/cybersecurity-blog/may-2023-recent-cyber-attacks-data-breaches-ransomware-attacks
2. Al-Dujaili, A., Huang, A., Hemberg, E., O'Reilly, U.M.: Adversarial deep learning for robust detection of binary encoded malware. In: 2018 IEEE Security and Privacy Workshops (SPW), pp. 76–82. IEEE (2018)
3. Arp, D., Spreitzenbarth, M., Hubner, M., Gascon, H., Rieck, K., Siemens, C.: DREBIN: effective and explainable detection of android malware in your pocket. In: NDSS, vol. 14, pp. 23–26 (2014)
4. Baldangombo, U., Jambaljav, N., Horng, S.J.: A static malware detection system using data mining methods. arXiv preprint arXiv:1308.2831 (2013)
5. Bat-Erdene, M., Park, H., Li, H., Lee, H., Choi, M.S.: Entropy analysis to classify unknown packing algorithms for malware detection. Int. J. Inf. Secur. 16(3), 227–248 (2017)
6. Chakkaravarthy, S.S., Sangeetha, D., Vaidehi, V.: A survey on malware analysis and mitigation techniques. Comput. Sci. Rev. 32, 1–23 (2019)

7. Chen, L., Hou, S., Ye, Y.: SecureDroid: enhancing security of machine learning-based detection against adversarial android malware attacks. In: Proceedings of the 33rd Annual Computer Security Applications Conference, pp. 362–372. ACM (2017)

8. Dupont, B.: The cyber-resilience of financial institutions: significance and applicability. J. Cybersecur. **5**(1) (2019). https://doi.org/10.1093/cybsec/tyz013

9. Egele, M., Scholte, T., Kirda, E., Kruegel, C.: A survey on automated dynamic malware-analysis techniques and tools. ACM Comput. Surv. (CSUR) **44**(2), 1–42 (2008)

10. Fogla, P., Sharif, M.I., Perdisci, R., Kolesnikov, O.M., Lee, W.: Polymorphic blending attacks. In: USENIX Security Symposium, pp. 241–256 (2006)

11. Fruhlinger, J.: Top cybersecurity facts, figures and statistics for 2018 (2019). https://www.csoonline.com/article/3153707/top-cybersecurity-facts-figures-and-statistics.html. Accessed 13 Feb 2020

12. Goodfellow, I., Bengio, Y., Courville, A.: Deep Learning. MIT Press (2016). http://www.deeplearningbook.org

13. Goodfellow, I.J., Shlens, J., Szegedy, C.: Explaining and harnessing adversarial examples. arXiv preprint arXiv:1412.6572 (2014)

14. Hu, W., Tan, Y.: Generating adversarial malware examples for black-box attacks based on GAN. arXiv preprint arXiv:1702.05983 (2017)

15. Kashyap, U., Padhi, S.K., Ali, S.S.: Attack GAN (AGAN): a new security evaluation tool for perceptual encryption. arXiv preprint arXiv:2407.06570 (2024)

16. Kawai, M., Ota, K., Dong, M.: Improved MalGAN: avoiding malware detector by leaning cleanware features. In: 2019 International Conference on Artificial Intelligence in Information and Communication (ICAIIC), pp. 040–045. IEEE (2019)

17. Laskov, P., et al.: Practical evasion of a learning-based classifier: a case study. In: 2014 IEEE Symposium on Security and Privacy, pp. 197–211. IEEE (2014)

18. LeDoux, C., Lakhotia, A.: Malware and machine learning. In: Yager, R.R., Reformat, M.Z., Alajlan, N. (eds.) Intelligent Methods for Cyber Warfare. SCI, vol. 563, pp. 1–42. Springer, Cham (2015). https://doi.org/10.1007/978-3-319-08624-8_1

19. Ming, J., Xin, Z., Lan, P., Wu, D., Liu, P., Mao, B.: Impeding behavior-based malware analysis via replacement attacks to malware specifications. J. Comput. Virol. Hacking Tech. **13**(3), 193–207 (2017)

20. Mosli, R., Li, R., Yuan, B., Pan, Y.: A behavior-based approach for malware detection. In: DigitalForensics 2017. IAICT, vol. 511, pp. 187–201. Springer, Cham (2017). https://doi.org/10.1007/978-3-319-67208-3_11

21. Padhi, S.K., Ali, S.S.: DLOVE: a new security evaluation tool for deep learning based watermarking techniques. arXiv preprint arXiv:2407.06552 (2024)

22. Rigaki, M.: Adversarial deep learning against intrusion detection classifiers (2017)

23. Saracino, A., Sgandurra, D., Dini, G., Martinelli, F.: MADAM: effective and efficient behavior-based android malware detection and prevention. IEEE Trans. Dependable Secure Comput. **15**(1), 83–97 (2016)

24. Shahpasand, M., Hamey, L., Vatsalan, D., Xue, M.: Adversarial attacks on mobile malware detection. In: 2019 IEEE 1st International Workshop on Artificial Intelligence for Mobile (AI4Mobile), pp. 17–20. IEEE (2019)

25. Smutz, C., Stavrou, A.: Malicious pdf detection using metadata and structural features. In: Proceedings of the 28th Annual Computer Security Applications Conference, pp. 239–248. ACM (2012)

26. Sobers, R.: 110 Must-Know Cybersecurity Statistics for 2020 (2019). https://www.varonis.com/blog/cybersecurity-statistics/. Accessed 13 Feb 2020

27. Souri, A., Hosseini, R.: A state-of-the-art survey of malware detection approaches using data mining techniques. HCIS **8**(1), 1–22 (2018). https://doi.org/10.1186/s13673-018-0125-x

28. Szegedy, C., et al.: Intriguing properties of neural networks. arXiv preprint arXiv:1312.6199 (2013)

29. Xu, W., Qi, Y., Evans, D.: Automatically evading classifiers. In: Proceedings of the 2016 Network and Distributed Systems Symposium, pp. 21–24 (2016)

30. Ye, Y., Li, T., Adjeroh, D., Iyengar, S.S.: A survey on malware detection using data mining techniques. ACM Comput. Surv. (CSUR) **50**(3), 1–40 (2017)

ML Based Improved Differential Distinguisher with High Accuracy: Application to GIFT-128 and ASCON

Tarun Yadav$^{(\boxtimes)}$ and Manoj Kumar

Scientific Analysis Group, DRDO, Metcalfe House Complex, Delhi 110 054, India
{tarunyadav.sag,manojkumar.sag}@gov.in

Abstract. In recent years, ML based differential distinguishers have been explored and compared with the classical methods. Complexity of a key recovery attack on block ciphers is calculated using the probability of a differential distinguisher provided by classical methods. Since theoretical computations suffice to calculate the data complexity in these cases, so there seems no restrictions on the practical availability of computational resources to attack a block cipher using classical methods. However, ML based differential cryptanalysis is based on the machine learning model that uses encrypted data to learn its features using available compute power. This poses a restriction on the accuracy of ML distinguisher for increased number of rounds and ciphers with large block size. Moreover, we can still construct the distinguisher but the accuracy becomes very low in such cases. In this paper, we present a new approach to construct the differential distinguisher with high accuracy using the existing ML based distinguisher of low accuracy. This approach outperforms all existing approaches with similar objective. We demonstrate our method to construct the high accuracy ML based distinguishers for GIFT-128 and ASCON permutation. For GIFT-128, accuracy of 7-round distinguisher is increased to 98.8% with 2^9 data complexity. For ASCON, accuracy of 4-round distinguisher is increased to 99.4% with 2^{18} data complexity. We also construct the ML based differential distinguisher that uses only a few bits of the output for training and prediction. A 7-round distinguisher of 98.7% accuracy is constructed for GIFT-128 with 2^{14} data complexity that uses only 16 bits for training and prediction. For ASCON, a 4-round distinguisher of 98.7% accuracy is constructed with data complexity 2^{18} using only 40 bits. We present the first ML based distinguisher for 8 rounds of GIFT-128 using the differential-ML distinguisher presented in Latincrypt-2021. This distinguisher is constructed with 99.8% accuracy and 2^{18} data complexity.

Keywords: ASCON · Block Cipher · Differential Cryptanalysis · GIFT · Machine Learning

© The Author(s), under exclusive license to Springer Nature Switzerland AG 2025
J. Knechtel et al. (Eds.): SPACE 2024, LNCS 15351, pp. 287–316, 2025.
https://doi.org/10.1007/978-3-031-80408-3_18

1   Introduction

Application of machine learning (ML) in cryptanalysis of symmetric ciphers is trending in recent years [11,13,22,23]. Cryptanalysts are experimenting with the different types of machine learning architectures to construct ML based distinguishers for symmetric ciphers [3,21]. Characteristics with high probability are required to mount an attack on a block cipher but searching such characteristics with large block size is computationally intensive task. The automated techniques [18] reduces the effort of cryptanalysts and help to rule out or propose the existence of high probability differential characteristics in a block cipher. Since the first proposal of differential attack in 1991 [5], numerous techniques have been devised to solve the differential characteristic search problem. Solution to these problems are automated by modeling with MILP [15], SAT/SMT, constraint programming [17] to get a solution using an appropriate solver.

In a classical differential attack, we search for an input difference Δ_i that leads to an output difference Δ_o with a probability 2^{-p} larger than 2^{-n} for a block cipher with n-bit block size. If we can find multiple paths connecting these input and output differences then it is called a differential and its probability $2^{-\sum p_j}$ is calculated by adding the probabilities of j individual paths. The multiple differential is a generalization of classical differential where we combine the differential characteristic with multiple input and multiple output differences. The multiple differentials work with lower complexity than any single differential characteristic of the differential.

The current trends in AI and ML has improvised its usage in cryptanalysis of block ciphers [9]. The first application of ML in this direction was presented by Gohr at CRYPTO 2019 through an ML based differential distinguisher for SPECK32/64 [10]. The ML based differential distinguisher was searched using machine learning algorithm and key recovery mechanism was also proposed using ML by Gohr for the first time. The distinguisher is trained on the data with single input difference Δ_i but it tends to learn the multiple differences in the outputs. The capability of learning the multiple differentials in the output provides an edge to the ML based differential distinguisher. This distinguisher achieved higher accuracy than the classical distinguisher and covered more rounds for SPECK32/64. The labeled data was used by Gohr to train a deep neural network where half of the data was from a random source and half was taken from the target cipher. The trained ML model was used to predict the cipher with an accuracy. Baksi *et al.* extended the Gohr's approach on Gimli using multi layer perceptron and other architectures available in deep learning networks [1].

Yadav *et al.* proposed the first extension of ML with classical differential distinguisher at Latincrypt-2021 [24]. This distinguisher was called as differential-ML distinguisher which covered more rounds then the ML and classical alone. The high accuracy ML distinguisher was trained for s rounds on the data with a fixed difference. This distinguisher was used for prediction on $(r + s)$ rounds after appending the r-round classical differential characteristic on the top. The complexity of differential-ML distinguisher was calculated experimentally based on the cutoff parameter providing high accuracy predictions. Differential-ML distinguisher was able to cover more rounds with high accuracy than classical and ML based distinguisher proposed by Gohr.

In a key recovery attack using ML based distinguisher, we need to guess the last round subkey. The number of guesses becomes equal to exhaustive trials of secret key, therefore the computational complexity of key recovery attacks in large size (128 or more) block ciphers is very high. The strategy of learning a few bits of the output is proposed by Ebrahimi $et\,al.$ for large size ciphers [8]. The approach is demonstrated on SPECK32/64 to build a distinguisher by learning 8 bits at certain positions that are selected through an effectiveness scoring algorithm. Using this approach, a distinguisher is trained over 8 bits with an equivalent accuracy of ML distinguisher trained over 32 bits for 6-round SPECK32/64. Lie $et\,al.$ also used different neural networks and 4-bit data for training that reduces the cost of learning by 30% over the Gohr's approach on SPECK32/64 [12].

The accuracy of neural differential distinguisher becomes very low as the number of rounds are increased for ciphers with large block size. Shen $et\,al.$ [19] proposed paired ML models based approach and used a low accuracy neural distinguisher to construct the high accuracy distinguisher through a score distribution of predictions for multiple ciphertext differences. This approach is used to improve the prediction accuracy of 7-round GIFT-128 from 55.42% to 99.36 % and 4-round ASCON form 50.69% to 69.25%. We have found some discrepancies in the implementation of GIFT-128 encryption provided by authors at Github and therefore, the results claimed by the authors in [19] for GIFT-128 could not be validated.

Our Contribution. In this paper, we address two major challenges that have become a roadblock for ML based distinguishers. The first challenge is to provide ML based distinguisher with high accuracy and lesser data complexity than the classical distinguisher. The other challenge is to make key recovery more practical by constructing a distinguisher that makes prediction using fewer number of bits. To overcome these challenges, we propose a new approach to construct the ML based differential distinguisher with high accuracy and its application to GIFT-128 and ASCON. A comparison of our results with the existing work is presented in Table 1. It is inferred from the results that a better ML based differential distinguisher is constructed using our approach in comparison to the existing ML based approaches in terms of accuracy. Our approach gives similar results when 16 and 40 bits are used for prediction with GIFT-128 and ASCON distinguishers respectively. We also present the first ML based distinguisher for 8 rounds of GIFT-128 with 99.8% accuracy and 2^{18} data complexity.

Organization. This paper is divided into 6 sections. We[1] provide a brief description of GIFT-128 and ASCON permutation in Sect. 2. We present a new approach to construct ML based differential distinguisher with high accuracy and its application to GIFT-128 and ASCON in Sect. 3. The approach to construct the distinguisher that uses fewer bits for training and prediction is discussed in

---

[1] Results could not be validated due to discrepancies in GIFT-128 implementation.

Sect. 4. The construction of 8-round distinguisher for GIFT-128 with modified differential-ML approach and experimental results are discussed in Sect. 5 . We conclude the paper with further scope of work in Sect. 6.

Table 1. Summary of Results

Cipher	Rounds	Classical Distinguishers Data Complexity [4]	ML based Distinguishers			Source
			Bits	Data Complexity	Accuracy	
GIFT-128	6	2^{23}	128	2^3	98.59	[19]
GIFT-128	6	2^{23}	128	2^5	**99.9**	**This paper**
GIFT-128	6	2^{23}	16	2^9	**99.8**	**This paper**
GIFT-128	7	$2^{29.415}$	128	2^9	99.36^1	[19]
GIFT-128	7	$2^{29.415}$	128	2^9	**98.8**	**This paper**
GIFT-128	7	$2^{29.415}$	16	2^{14}	**98.7**	**This paper**
GIFT-128	8	2^{41}	128	2^{18}	**99.8**	**This paper**
ASCON	4	2^{107}	320	2^{12}	69.25	[19]
ASCON	4	2^{107}	320	2^{18}	**99.4**	**This paper**
ASCON	4	2^{107}	40	2^{18}	**98.7**	**This paper**

2   Block Ciphers: GIFT and ASCON

The block ciphers GIFT [4] and ASCON [6] were among the finalist of NIST lightweight cryptography competition concluded in 2023 [16] and ASCON remained a winner in this competition. The base permutation of these two ciphers are briefly discussed in this section. For more details on the design specifications and key scheduling of these ciphers, the papers [4,6] can be referred.

2.1   Specifications of GIFT-128

GIFT is a family of two lightweight block ciphers GIFT-64 and GIFT-128 which was proposed by Banik *et al.* in 2017. Two lightweight authenticated encryption schemes namely GIFT-COFB and SUNDAE-GIFT were submitted to NIST lightweight cryptography competition and both of these use GIFT-128 block cipher as their base permutation [2]. GIFT-128 is based on SPN structure that applies a round function 40 times iteratively to encrypt the 128-bit plaintext using a 128-bit secret key. In each round, it applies round keys and constant addition operation on selective bits, substitution using 4-bit S-box 32 times in parallel and bit-wise permutation operation on 128 bits. The 4-bit S-box and 128-

bit permutation are given in the Table 2 and 3 respectively. Encryption function of GIFT-128 is described in Algorithm 1.

Algorithm 1: GIFT-128 Encryption

---
1 **Input:** $X_1 = (x_{127}, x_{126}, \cdots, x_0)$ and $RK_i; 1 \leq i \leq 41$
2 **Output:** $C = X_{41} \oplus RK_{41} \oplus RC_{41}$
3 **for** $i \leftarrow 1$ to 40 **do**
4    $T_i = X_i \oplus RK_i \oplus RC_i$
5    $T_i = (t_{127}, t_{126}, \cdots, t_0)$
6   **for** $j \leftarrow 0$ to 31 **do**
7       $(u_{4*j+3}||u_{4*j+2}||u_{4*j+1}||u_{4*j}) = S[t_{4*j+3}||t_{4*j+2}||t_{4*j+1}||t_{4*j}]$
8   **end**
9    $U_i = (u_{127}, u_{126}, \cdots, u_0)$
10    $V_i = PN(U_i)$
11    $X_{i+1} = V_i = (x_{127}, x_{126}, \cdots, x_0)$
12 **end**

Table 2. S-box for GIFT-128

x	0	1	2	3	4	5	6	7	8	9	a	b	c	d	e	f
$S(x)$	1	a	4	c	6	f	3	9	2	d	b	7	5	0	8	e

Table 3. Bit Permutation for GIFT-128

i	0	1	2	3	4	5	6	7	8	9	10	11	12	13	14	15
$PN(i)$	0	33	66	99	96	1	34	67	64	97	2	35	32	65	98	3
i	16	17	18	19	20	21	22	23	24	25	26	27	28	29	30	31
$PN(i)$	4	37	70	103	100	5	38	71	68	101	6	39	36	69	102	7
i	32	33	34	35	36	37	38	39	40	41	42	43	44	45	46	47
$PN(i)$	8	41	74	107	104	9	42	75	72	105	10	43	40	73	106	11
i	48	49	50	51	52	53	54	55	56	57	58	59	60	61	62	63
$PN(i)$	12	45	78	111	108	13	46	79	76	109	14	47	44	77	110	15
i	64	65	66	67	68	69	70	71	72	73	74	75	76	77	78	79
$PN(i)$	16	49	82	115	112	17	50	83	80	113	18	51	48	81	114	19
i	80	81	82	83	84	85	86	87	88	89	90	91	92	93	94	95
$PN(i)$	20	53	86	119	116	21	54	87	84	117	22	55	52	85	118	23
i	96	97	98	99	100	101	102	103	104	105	106	107	108	109	110	111
$PN(i)$	24	57	90	123	120	25	58	91	88	121	26	59	56	89	122	27
i	112	113	114	115	116	117	118	119	120	121	122	123	124	125	126	127
$PN(i)$	28	61	94	127	124	29	62	95	92	125	30	63	60	93	126	31

2.2 Specifications of ASCON

ASCON was declared winner in the lightweight cryptography competition by NIST and it was also selected in the final portfolio of CAESAR competition. ASCON was designed by Dobrauing *et al.* [6] with an input state size of 320 bits. The 320-bit input is divided into five 64-bit words w_i. The round function is composed of adding 8-bit round constants (Table 4) to the w_2, application of 5-bit S-box (Table 5) in columns and diffusion layer on each 64-bit word. A total of 12 rounds are used in the ASCON permutation. The specifications of ASCON permutation is described in Algorithm 2.

Algorithm 2: ASCON Permutation

---

1 **Input:** $X_0 = (x_{319}, x_{318}, \cdots, x_0) = (w_4||w_3||w_2||w_1||w_0); RC_i$

2 **Output:** X_{12}

3 **for** $i \leftarrow 0$ *to* 11 **do**

4 $\quad$ $w_2 = w_2 \oplus RC_i$

5 $\quad$ **for** $j \leftarrow 0$ *to* 63 **do**

6 $\quad\quad$ $(w_4(j), w_3(j), w_2(j), w_1(j), w_0(j)) = $
$\quad\quad$ $S[w_4(j)||w_3(j)||w_2(j)||w_1(j)||w_0(j)]$

7 $\quad$ **end**

8 $\quad$ $w_4 = w_4 \oplus (w_4 \ggg 19) \oplus (w_4 \ggg 28))$

9 $\quad$ $w_3 = w_3 \oplus (w_3 \ggg 61) \oplus (w_3 \ggg 39))$

10 $\quad$ $w_2 = w_2 \oplus (w_2 \ggg 1) \oplus (w_2 \ggg 6))$

11 $\quad$ $w_1 = w_1 \oplus (w_1 \ggg 10) \oplus (w_1 \ggg 17))$

12 $\quad$ $w_0 = w_0 \oplus (w_0 \ggg 7) \oplus (w_0 \ggg 41))$

13 $\quad$ $X_{i+1} = (w_4||w_3||w_2||w_1||w_0)$

14 **end**

Table 4. Round Constants for ASCON

i	0	1	2	3	4	5	6	7	8	9	10	11
RC_i	f0	e1	d2	c3	b4	a5	96	87	78	69	5a	4b

Table 5. S-box for ASCON

x	00	01	02	03	04	05	06	07	08	09	0a	0b	0c	0d	0e	0f	10	11	12	13	14	15	16	17	18	19	1a	1b	1c	1d	1e	1f
$S(x)$	04	0b	1f	14	1a	15	09	02	1b	05	08	12	1d	03	06	1c	1e	13	07	0e	00	0d	11	18	10	0c	01	19	16	0a	0f	17

3   Improved Differential Distinguishers: A New Approach

Finding relations between the input and output differences is the key idea behind differential cryptanalysis. These high probability relations are used as distinguishers which have better data complexity than exhaustive trials. Non-linear component of the cipher makes it difficult to find such relations with high probability. S-box is a non-linear component that is widely used to design the block ciphers. There are various approaches that are used to search the high probability differential distinguishers e.g. branch-and-bound based [14], constraint programming [17], and mixed integer linear programming [15]. In contrast to classical approaches, where such distinguishers are identified using difference propagation, machine learning based distinguishers learn these relations on the difference of encrypted data. The construction of ML based distinguisher is independent of functions used in linear (e.g. bit permutation, Shift XOR, MDS etc.) and non-linear (e.g. S-box) layers of encryption algorithm.

3.1   Machine Learning Based Differential Distinguishers

Gohr proposed an approach to model the distinguisher using real and random differences [10]. Real difference is the input/plaintext difference for which the distinguisher is designed. The approach is a two class problem where the machine tries to classify the given data in any one of the two classes. The main benefit of ML based approach is that the classification can be done for a single data point unlike the classical approach. In this approach, half of the data is generated with fixed input difference (Δ_0) and remaining data is generated with random differences (Δ_R). The data is encrypted and the corresponding output differences are computed. Differences in the output that belong to input difference Δ_0 are part of the class 1 while remaining data belongs to class 0. Once this model is trained, it is used for prediction and classification on the output difference. If the probability of prediction is greater than 0.5, then it is classified as class 1 data. If the prediction occurs with a probabiltiy less than or equal to 0.5, then it is classified as class 0 data. This approach is used widely with various kinds of neural networks to construct the ML based differential distinguishers.

In this paper, multi layer perceptrons (MLP) are used to train the ML distinguisher. MLP consists of input layer, output layer and two hidden layers. Hidden layers contain same number of neurons as in the input layer with ReLu activation function. Output layer uses sigmoid function to predict the probabilities of belonging to class 1 or 0. We use 10^7 data for training the model and 10^7 for validation in each experiment.

The approach discussed above works well but the benefits comes with a drawback that the classification is probabilistic and thus, the distinguisher predicts with an accuracy. This accuracy decreases drastically when the number of rounds or block size is increased. After a threshold, the training data also becomes a constraint as it is limited by the computation power. Therefore, despite being a promising approach, a low accuracy distinguisher lacks the practical applicability in comparison to the classical distinguishers. To address this problem, we present a new method to increase the accuracy of ML based distinguisher of low accuracy. We use the existing ML based distinguisher as a subsystem of the proposed distinguisher.

3.2 New Approach to Construct ML Based Distinguishers with High Accuracy

Gohr's ML based differential distinguisher (D^{ML}) works with an accuracy. This accuracy is comprised of two parts, true positive (TP) and true negative (TN). Both of these accuracy are important as predicting the correct class is necessary for a positive data point as well as for a negative data point. The average of TP and TN accuracies is taken as the accuracy of the model. While distinguishing the data, it is necessary that accuracies of correct prediction is high in both the cases. If one of the accuracy is too high and other one is too low, then despite getting a good average accuracy, the distinguisher will not work as expected. Some examples indicating such cases are shown in Table 6.

Table 6. TP and TN Accuracies of D^{ML} for GIFT-128

Cipher	Rounds	Accuracy	TP Accuracy	TN Accuracy
GIFT-128	5	0.939	0.915	0.967
GIFT-128	6	0.731	0.608	0.848
GIFT-128	7	0.538	0.366	0.710

As shown in Table 6, the accuracy of 7-round GIFT-128 distinguisher is 0.538 where TP accuracy is 0.366 and TN accuracy is 0.710. It means that data belonging to real difference (Δ_0) is classified with almost half of the accuracy than random differences (Δ_R). Therefore, model's accuracy may create a false perception that both the classes are predicted with the same accuracy in these cases. Such instance arises when a model's accuracy is low to distinguish the data correctly. To overcome this problem, we propose a new approach to construct the high accuracy distinguishers. This approach is motivated by Differential-ML distinguisher presented in [24] that uses both TP and TN accuracies. The main aim is to increase the accuracy of a distinguisher in both the cases by increasing the data required for prediction. We define this new distinguisher as High Accuracy ML based Distinguisher (D^{HA-ML}). It uses D^{ML} as a subsystem for prediction with other parameters viz. threshold probability (T), cutoff (C_T) and data complexity (β). The approach to construct D^{HA-ML} is described in Algorithm 3.

Algorithm 3: High Accuracy ML distinguisher $D_{r+1\cdots r+s}^{HA-ML}$: $(D_{r+1\cdots r+s}^{ML},$ T, C_T, β)

---

1 **Function** Construction Phase($D_{r+1\cdots r+s}^{ML}$, $T = 0.5$):

2 $\quad$ $\delta \leftarrow 1$

3 $\quad$ **repeat**

4 $\quad\quad$ **for** $k \leftarrow 1$ *to* 50 **do**

5 $\quad\quad\quad$ $K \leftarrow$ Choose a random key

6 $\quad\quad\quad$ $(P_{\Delta_0}, P_{\Delta_0}') \leftarrow 2^\delta$ plaintext pairs with difference Δ_0

7 $\quad\quad\quad$ $(P_{\Delta_R}, P_{\Delta_R}') \leftarrow 2^\delta$ plaintext pairs with random difference Δ_R

8 $\quad\quad\quad$ $(C_{\Delta_0}, C_{\Delta_0}') \leftarrow$ (CIPHER$_s(P_{\Delta_0}, K)$,CIPHER$_s(P_{\Delta_0}', K)$)

9 $\quad\quad\quad$ $(C_{\Delta_R}, C_{\Delta_R}') \leftarrow$ (CIPHER$_s(P_{\Delta_R}, K)$,CIPHER$_s(P_{\Delta_R}', K)$)

10 $\quad\quad\quad$ $p_{\Delta_0} \leftarrow$ prediction probabilities for $(C_{\Delta_0} \oplus C_{\Delta_0}')$ using $D_{r+1\cdots r+s}^{ML}$

11 $\quad\quad\quad$ $p_{\Delta_R} \leftarrow$ prediction probabilities for $(C_{\Delta_R} \oplus C_{\Delta_R}')$ using $D_{r+1\cdots r+s}^{ML}$

12 $\quad\quad\quad$ $TP_{\Delta_0} \leftarrow$ number of elements with $p_{\Delta_0} > T$

13 $\quad\quad\quad$ $TP_{\Delta_R} \leftarrow$ number of elements with $p_{\Delta_R} > T$

14 $\quad\quad\quad$ Plot the curve for TP_{Δ_0} and TP_{Δ_R} values

15 $\quad\quad$ **end**

16 $\quad\quad$ $\delta \leftarrow \delta + 1$

17 $\quad$ **until** *(TP_{Δ_0} and TP_{Δ_R} curves do not intersect)*;

18 $\quad$ $C_T \approx$ average of ordinates of closest points on TP_{Δ_0} and TP_{Δ_R} curves

19 $\quad$ Data Complexity(β) $\leftarrow 2^\delta$

20 $\quad$ **return** C_T, β

21 **End Function**

22 **Procedure** Prediction Phase($D_{r+1\cdots r+s}^{ML}$,C_T, β):

23 $\quad$ Test Data (TD) $\leftarrow$ (.)

24 $\quad$ **for** $i \leftarrow 1$ *to* β **do**

25 $\quad\quad$ $P_i \leftarrow$Choose a random plaintext

26 $\quad\quad$ $P_i' = P_i \oplus \Delta_0$

27 $\quad\quad$ $C_i \leftarrow$ ORACLE(P_i)

28 $\quad\quad$ $C_i' \leftarrow$ ORACLE(P_i')

29 $\quad\quad$ Append TD by $C_i \oplus C_i'$

30 $\quad$ **end**

31 $\quad$ $p \leftarrow$ prediction probabilities for elements in TD using $D_{r+1\cdots r+s}^{ML}$

32 $\quad$ **if** *((number of elements with $p > T$) $> C_T$)* **then**

33 $\quad\quad$ ORACLE = CIPHER$_s$

34 $\quad$ **end**

35 $\quad$ **else**

36 $\quad\quad$ ORACLE $\neq$ CIPHER$_s$

37 $\quad$ **end**

38 **end Procedure**

An s-round $D_{r+1\cdots r+s}^{HA-ML}$ distinguisher is developed in two phases (Algorithm 3). Construction phase uses s-round ML based distinguisher $D_{r+1\cdots r+s}^{ML}$ and threshold probability T as inputs. In this paper, we fix the value of T as 0.5. It starts with two pairs ($\delta = 1$) and generate 2^δ plaintext pairs $(P_{\Delta_0}, P'_{\Delta_0})$ for fixed/real difference (Δ_0) and 2^δ plaintext pairs $(P_{\Delta_R}, P'_{\Delta_R})$ for random difference (Δ_R). The plaintext data is encrypted with s-round cipher (CIPHER$_s$) to get the corresponding ciphertext pairs $(C_{\Delta_0}, C'_{\Delta_0})$ and $(C_{\Delta_R}, C'_{\Delta_R})$. We use the s-round distinguisher $D_{r+1\cdots r+s}^{ML}$ to make predictions on the difference of encrypted data and get prediction probabilities p_{Δ_0} and p_{Δ_R}. Now, we count the number of elements in p_{Δ_0} and p_{Δ_R} that are predicted with a probabilty above threshold T and get TP_{Δ_0} and TP_{Δ_R} respectively.

We plot the TP_{Δ_0} and TP_{Δ_R} points where x-axis represents the number of experiments and y-axis represents the number of true positive points. This experiment is repeated 50 times with different value of secret key in each case. We get 100 points on the curve corresponding to TP_{Δ_0} and TP_{Δ_R}. If the curves intersect then we increase the value of δ and repeat the experiment till we get non-intersecting curves. When such curves are plotted, C_T is calculated as an average of ordinates of closest points on TP_{Δ_0} and TP_{Δ_R} curves and data complexity β is obtained as 2^δ.

In prediction phase, we use $D_{r+1\cdots r+s}^{ML}$, C_T, and β to make the predictions. We generate β plaintext pairs with difference Δ_0 and get the encrypted data from an ORACLE. We make the predictions on the difference of encrypted data and get the prediction probabilities (p). If number of elements with p greater than threshold probability (T) is greater than cutoff (C_T), then we predict that ORACLE is the s-round CIPHER$_s$. Differential distinguishers with high accuracy ($D_{r+1\cdots r+s}^{HA-ML}$) for GIFT-128 and ASCON are constructed using the Algorithm 3.

3.3   Application of $D_{r+1\cdots r+s}^{HA-ML}$ to GIFT-128 and ASCON

For 6-round GIFT-128, we train the ML model on input difference with only one active bit ($x_0 = 1$) to get the distinguisher ($D_{r+1\cdots r+6}^{ML}$) of accuracy 0.73. We use ML distinguisher ($D_{r+1\cdots r+6}^{ML}$) to construct the high accuracy distinguisher ($D_{r+1\cdots r+6}^{HA-ML}$). Construction phase of this process is shown in Fig. 1 where TP_{Δ_0} and TP_{Δ_R} curve are plotted for various value of δ. In Fig. 1 (d), it is clearly visible that curves do not intersect at $\delta = 2^5$ and hence, the data complexity (β) of this distinguisher becomes 2^5. The C_T is computed as 12 by averaging the ordinates of closest points on the curve. Once we have obtained the values of both parameters, the prediction phase of Algorithm 3 is used as differential distinguisher. We perform 10 experiments with 50 TP and 50 TN samples corresponding to input differences Δ_0 and Δ_R respectively. Each of these samples contains 2^5 ciphertext pairs. It is evident from the results shown in Table 11 that accuracy is 100% in most of the cases. The source code for these experiments is available on GitHub[2].

---

[2] https://github.com/tarunyadav/Improved-Differential-Distinguisher-GIFT128-ASCON.

For 7-round GIFT-128, the accuracy of $D_{r+1\cdots r+7}^{ML}$ is 0.55. To calculate C_T and β, curves (Fig. 2) are plotted as described in Algorithm 3. Although, the curves are almost separated at $\delta = 2^8$ (Fig. 2 (c)) but a clear separation is visible in Fig. 2 (d) at $\delta = 2^9$ and hence, the data complexity (β) is 2^9. The average of two closest points 171 and 181 on these curves is 176 which provides the value of C_T as 176. Using C_T and β values, we perform 10 experiments to validate the distinguisher's accuracy similar to the previous case. Each experiment contains 50 TP and 50 TN samples and every sample contain 2^9 ciphertext differences. The results are presented in Table 12 which shows that the accuracy is higher than 97% in most of the cases.

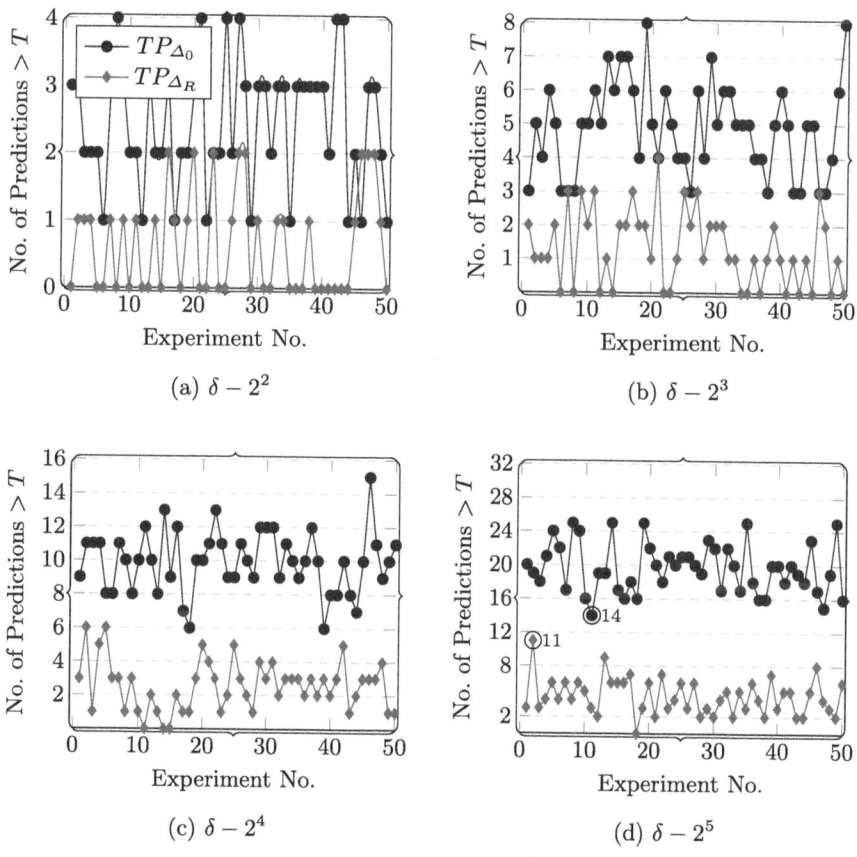

Fig. 1. C_T and β for 6-round GIFT-128 Distinguisher ($D_{r+1\cdots r+6}^{HA-ML}$)

For 4-round ASCON, we train the ML model on input difference with only one active bit ($x_0 = 1$). the accuracy of $D_{r+1\cdots r+4}^{ML}$ is 0.502 and it is too low for an ML based distinguisher. Even with such a low accuracy, we are able to construct $D_{r+1\cdots r+4}^{HA-ML}$ as shown in Fig. 3. To find a clear separation of the

TP_{Δ_0} and TP_{Δ_R} curves, data complexity is increased due to the low accuracy of $D_{r+1\cdots r+4}^{ML}$. The curves are almost separated at $\delta = 2^{18}$ (Fig. 3 (d)) and hence, the data complexity (β) is 2^{18} and calculated C_T is 132825. The experiments to validate this distinguisher are presented in the Table 13 and very high accuracy is obtained in all cases. The accuracy is equal to 100% in half of the experiments.

The values of C_T and β to construct the distinguishers with high accuracy for GIFT-128 and ASCON are summarized in Table 7.

3.4   Computation of C_T Using TP and TN Accuracies

An experimental approach to find C_T and β is discussed in Algorithm 3. We propose another approach (Algorithm 4) to calculate C_T using TP and TN accuracies of $D_{r+1\cdots r+s}^{ML}$. In Algorithm 4, prediction function and inputs are same as described in Algorithm 3. The construction phase is changed to calculate the cutoff values (C_T) without using the curves for TP_{Δ_0} and TP_{Δ_R}.

We first compute the TP and TN accuracies using $D_{r+1\cdots r+s}^{ML}$ by predicting on real and random differences. The accuracy of trained model $D_{r+1\cdots r+s}^{ML}$ is α_s. We take 2^{16} samples of real difference (Δ_0) and random difference (Δ_R). These samples are encrypted using $CIPHER_s$ to get the ciphertext differences $(C_{\Delta_0} \oplus C'_{\Delta_0})$ and $(C_{\Delta_R} \oplus C'_{\Delta_R})$. The prediction probabilities of these samples are called p_{Δ_0} and p_{Δ_R}. We define TP_{Δ_0} as number of elements with prediction probability greater than threshold value (0.5). While TN_{Δ_R} is defined as number of elements with prediction probability less than or equal to predefined threshold value. True positive and true negative accuracies of the model $D_{r+1\cdots r+s}^{ML}$ are $\alpha_s^{\Delta_0}$ and $\alpha_s^{\Delta_R}$ respectively. A difference in accuracies $\alpha_s^{\Delta_0}$ and $\alpha_s^{\Delta_R}$ is denoted as α'_s which refers to the difference in prediction of true positives in case of real and random difference samples.

We start with $\delta = 2^2$ data and compute the C_T using α'_s. We get the prediction probabilities, TP_{Δ_0} and TP_{Δ_R} values similar to Algorithm 3 using this data. If TP_{Δ_0} is greater than calculated cutoff C_T then we increase the accuracy counter (acc_{Δ_0}) for real difference and if TP_{Δ_R} is less than or equal to C_T then we increase the accuracy counter (acc_{Δ_R}) for random difference. These counters implies the identification of true positives in real difference data and true negatives in random difference data. We perform $N=50$ experiments to calculate the average accuracy (acc). If acc is less than 0.98, we increase the data by a factor of 2 and repeat the experiments. Once, acc crosses a mark of 0.98 value,

Table 7. C_T and β for Differential Distinguishers with High Accuracy

Cipher	Rounds	Size	Accuracy	Algorithm 3		Algorithm 4	
				C_T	β	C_T	β
GIFT-128	6	128	0.73	12	2^5	13	2^5
GIFT-128	7	128	0.55	176	2^9	175	2^9
ASCON	4	320	0.502	132825	2^{18}	132896	2^{18}

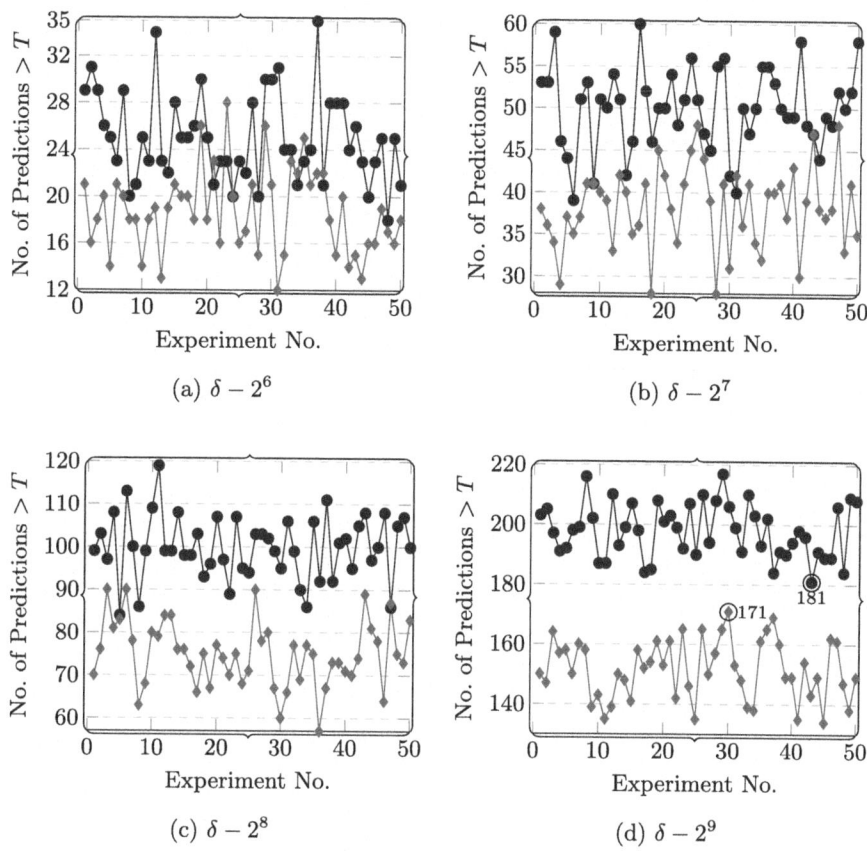

Fig. 2. C_T and β for 7-round GIFT-128 Distinguisher $(D_{r+1\cdots r+7}^{HA-ML})$

we have $\beta = \delta$ and compute C_T using β. The parameters C_T and β along with $D_{r+1\cdots r+s}^{ML}$ are used for prediction and work as $D_{r+1\cdots r+s}^{HA-ML}$.

We use this approach to construct the high accuracy differential distinguishers for 6 and 7 rounds of GIFT-128 and 4-round ASCON. The experimental results are depicted in Fig. 11. Due to comparatively high accuracy of $D_{r+1\cdots r+6}^{ML}$, the new distinguisher achieves near to 100% accuracy for smaller values of δ for 6 rounds of GIFT-128. Using Algorithm 4, the accuracy becomes significantly high for $\beta = 2^5$ and $C_T = 13$ (Table 7). We perform 10 experiments to validate the new distinguisher $D_{r+1\cdots r+6}^{HA-ML}$ and the results are shown in Table 11. The accuracy more than 98% is achieved in most of the experiments using Algorithm 4.

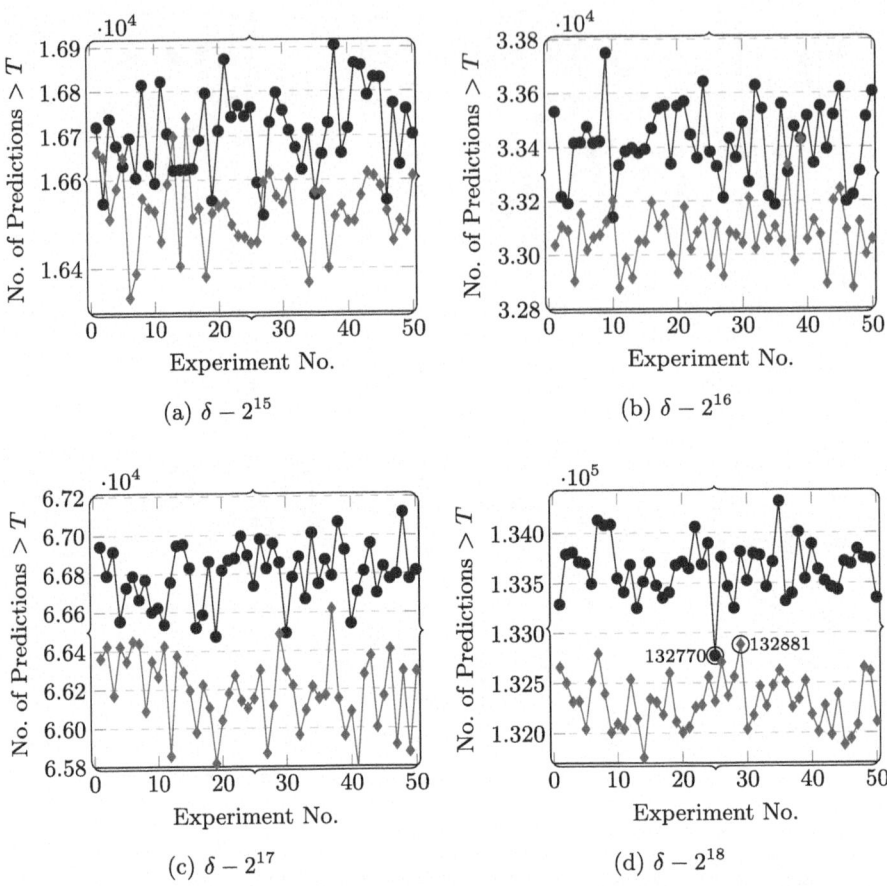

Fig. 3. C_T and (β) for 4-round ASCON Distinguisher ($D_{r+1\cdots r+4}^{HA-ML}$)

For 7-round GIFT-128, more data is required to achieve an accuracy near to 100% due to the low accuracy of $D_{r+1\cdots r+7}^{ML}$. The accuracy increases significantly with increased values of δ as shown in Fig. 11. To get an accuracy near to 1.00, the calculated values of C_T and β are 175 and 2^9 respectively. These values are used to perform the experiments for validations and results are presented in Table 12. The accuracy of $D_{r+1\cdots r+7}^{HA-ML}$ is more than 97% in each case using Algorithm 4.

For 4-round ASCON, the accuracy of $D^{ML}_{r+1...r+4}$ is very low and it is near to 0.50. In this case, it is expected that β will be higher than previous cases. The effect of changes in accuracy with increased values of δ is depicted through the graph in Fig. 11. Using Algorithm 4, we get the values C_T and β as 132896 and 2^{18} respectively (Table 7). The validation results are presented in Table 13 and it can be observed that application of Algorithm 4 gives accuracy more than 97% in most of the cases.

4   Differential Distinguisher with High Accuracy: Using m Bits

The difference of n-bit ciphertext pairs is used by the ML based distinguishers for training as well as prediction, where n refers to block size of a block cipher. Ebrahimi et al. [8] presented the partial ML distinguisher by using selective bits for training and prediction. The experiments are performed to get the contribution of m output bits ($m \leq n$) in the prediction accuracy and it is shown that each bit does not contribute equally [8]. If the bits with highest contribution to the accuracy are used then predication can be made using a smaller set (m) of output bits instead of all n bits. For key recovery attack, such distinguishers become more practical as it will be required to guess the rounds keys corresponding to m bits only.

However, if we use fewer bits for training then ML distinguisher is constructed with lesser accuracy. It is evident from Table 8 that a model trained on lesser bits has lesser accuracy than a distinguisher trained on all (n) bits of output difference. We use the algorithm discussed in previous section to increase the accuracy of such distinguishers. This approach can be used to construct a very high accuracy distinguisher in these cases also. We use 16-bit $D^{ML}_{r+1...r+s}$ for 5/6/7 rounds of GIFT-128 and 40-bit $D^{ML}_{r+1...r+s}$ for 4 rounds of ASCON to construct $D^{HA-ML}_{r+1...r+s}$. To select the position of m bits, we performed various experiments and selected a set of bits providing high accuracy to train the m-bit ML model to construct $D^{ML}_{r+1...r+s}$. There are many possible ways to choose a set of m bits, but we limit ourselves to a particular type of set only. For GIFT-128, we divide the 128-bit input ($x_{127}, x_{126}, ..., x_0$) into 16 blocks of size 8-bit each ($x_{127}, ..., x_{120}||....||x_7, ..., x_0$) and choose first bit of each block for training and predictions. We have performed various experiments with other set of bits but accuracy of the model with this particular set of bits is higher than others. In case of ASCON permutation, we divide the 320-bit input ($x_{320}, x_{319}, ..., x_0$) into 8 blocks of size 40-bit each ($x_{319}, ..., x_{280}||....||x_{39}, ..., x_0$) and choose the last block for training and prediction.

Algorithm 4: High Accuracy ML distinguisher $D_{r+1\cdots r+s}^{HA-ML}$: $(D_{r+1\cdots r+s}^{ML}, T = 0.5, C_T, \beta)$

---

1 **Function Construction Phase**$(D_{r+1\cdots r+s}^{ML}, T = \alpha_s)$:

2   **for** $k \leftarrow 1$ to 50 **do**

3         $K \leftarrow$ Choose a random key

4         $(P_{\Delta_0}, P'_{\Delta_0}) \leftarrow 2^{16}$ plaintext pairs with difference Δ_0

5         $(P_{\Delta_R}, P'_{\Delta_R}) \leftarrow 2^{16}$ plaintext pairs with random difference Δ_R

6         $(C_{\Delta_0}, C'_{\Delta_0}) \leftarrow (\text{CIPHER}_s(P_{\Delta_0}, K), \text{CIPHER}_s(P'_{\Delta_0}, K))$

7         $(C_{\Delta_R}, C'_{\Delta_R}) \leftarrow (\text{CIPHER}_s(P_{\Delta_R}, K), \text{CIPHER}_s(P'_{\Delta_R}, K))$

8         $p_{\Delta_0} \leftarrow$ prediction probabilities for $(C_{\Delta_0} \oplus C'_{\Delta_0})$ using $D_{r+1\cdots r+s}^{ML}$

9         $p_{\Delta_R} \leftarrow$ prediction probabilities for $(C_{\Delta_R} \oplus C'_{\Delta_R})$ using $D_{r+1\cdots r+s}^{ML}$

10        $TP_{\Delta_0} \leftarrow$ number of elements with $p_{\Delta_0} > T$

11        $TN_{\Delta_R} \leftarrow$ number of elements with $p_{\Delta_R} \leq T$

12        $\alpha_s^{\Delta_0} \leftarrow TP_{\Delta_0}/2^{16}$

13        $\alpha_s^{\Delta_R} \leftarrow TN_{\Delta_R}/2^{16}$

14        $\alpha'_s \leftarrow \alpha_s^{\Delta_0} - (1 - \alpha_s^{\Delta_R})$

15   **end**

16     $\delta \leftarrow 2^2$

17   **repeat**

18         $acc_{\Delta_0} \leftarrow 0$

19         $acc_{\Delta_R} \leftarrow 0$

20         $C_T = \delta \times \alpha'_s \times 0.5$

21   **for** $k \leftarrow 1$ to N **do**

22             $K \leftarrow$ Choose a random key

23             $(P_{\Delta_0}, P'_{\Delta_0}) \leftarrow 2^{\delta}$ plaintext pairs with difference Δ_0

24             $(P_{\Delta_R}, P'_{\Delta_R}) \leftarrow 2^{\delta}$ plaintext pairs with random difference Δ_R

25             $(C_{\Delta_0}, C'_{\Delta_0}) \leftarrow (\text{CIPHER}_s(P_{\Delta_0}, K), \text{CIPHER}_s(P'_{\Delta_0}, K))$

26             $(C_{\Delta_R}, C'_{\Delta_R}) \leftarrow (\text{CIPHER}_s(P_{\Delta_R}, K), \text{CIPHER}_s(P'_{\Delta_R}, K))$

27             $p_{\Delta_0} \leftarrow$ prediction probabilities for $(C_{\Delta_0} \oplus C'_{\Delta_0})$ using $D_{r+1\cdots r+s}^{ML}$

28             $p_{\Delta_R} \leftarrow$ prediction probabilities for $(C_{\Delta_R} \oplus C'_{\Delta_R})$ using $D_{r+1\cdots r+s}^{ML}$

29             $TP_{\Delta_0} \leftarrow$ number of elements with $p_{\Delta_0} > T$

30             $TP_{\Delta_R} \leftarrow$ number of elements with $p_{\Delta_R} > T$

31   **if** $TP_{\Delta_0} > C_T$ **then**

32                 $acc_{\Delta_0} \leftarrow acc_{\Delta_0} + 1$

33   **end**

34   **if** $TP_{\Delta_R} \leq C_T$ **then**

35                 $acc_{\Delta_R} \leftarrow acc_{\Delta_R} + 1$

36   **end**

37   **end**

38         $acc = \frac{(acc_{\Delta_0} + acc_{\Delta_R})}{2 \times N}$

39         $\delta \leftarrow \delta \times 2$

40   **until** $acc < 0.98$;

41     $\beta \leftarrow \delta$

42     $C_T = \beta \times \alpha'_s \times 0.5$

43   **return** C_T, β

44 **End Function**

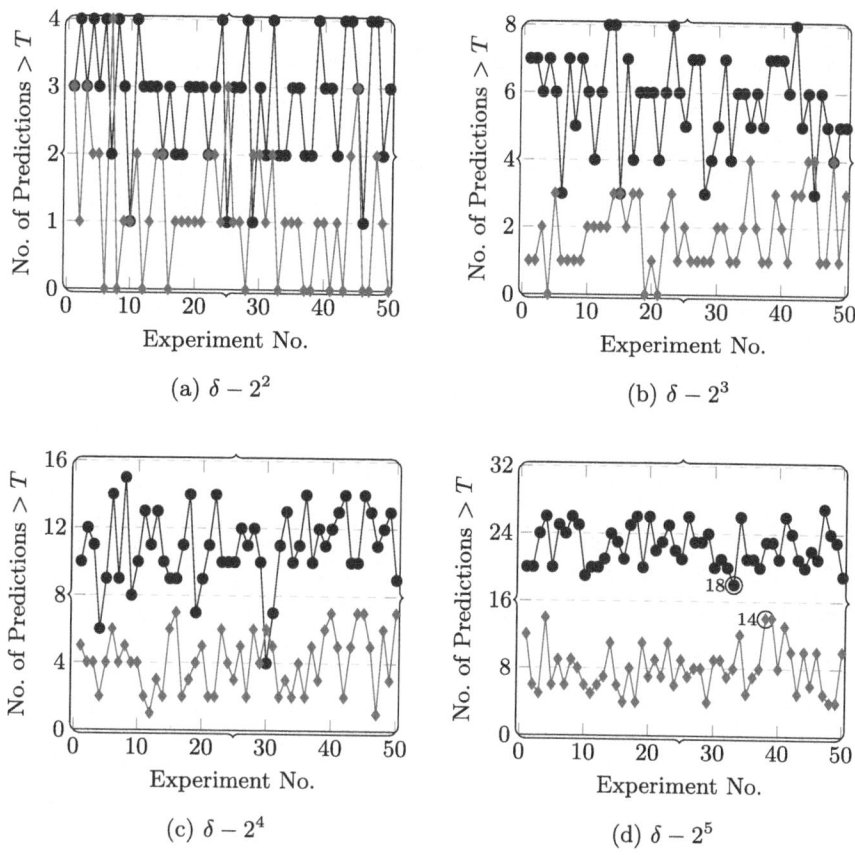

Fig. 4. C_T and β for 5-round GIFT-128 Distinguisher $(D_{r+1\cdots r+5}^{HA-ML}; m = 16)$

4.1   Differential Distinguisher for GIFT-128: Using 16 Bits

We construct the high accuracy distinguishers for GIFT-128 reduced to 5, 6, and 7 rounds. When all 128 bits are used for training, the ML based distinguisher for 5-round GIFT-128 has an accuracy more than 0.94. This accuracy falls to 0.72 if we use a set of 16 bits only for training and prediction. We can increase this accuracy using Algorithm 3 and construct $D_{r+1\cdots r+5}^{HA-ML}$. Algorithm 3 is used to plot the curves for 5-round GIFT-128 distinguisher using 16 bits (Fig. 4). The curves are separated at $\delta = 2^5$ (Fig. 4(d)) and hence, the data complexity β is 2^5. Similar curves for 6 and 7 rounds of GIFT-128 are shown in Figs. 5 and 6 respectively whereas C_T and β values are mentioned in Table 8. As discussed previously, C_T can be calculated using Algorithm 4. The increase in accuracy for different values of δ is depicted in Fig. 12. The values of C_T is computed

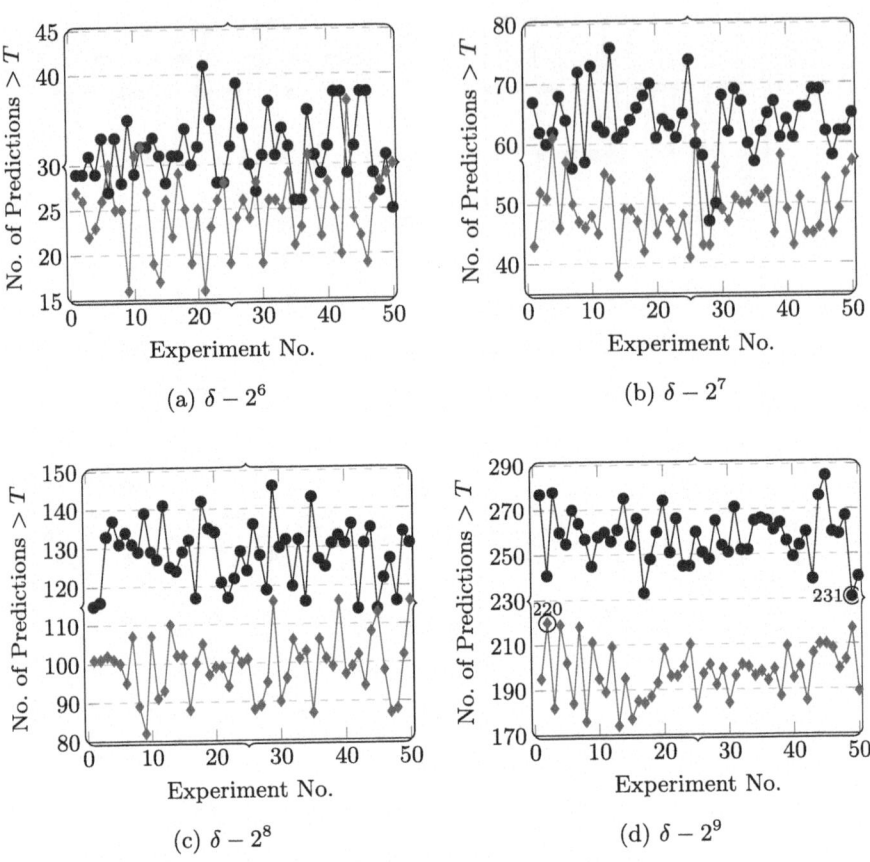

Fig. 5. C_T and β for 6-round GIFT-128 Distinguisher $(D_{r+1\cdots r+6}^{HA-ML}; m = 16)$

using Algorithm 4 and these are presented in Table 8. The data complexity β is a value of δ at which accuracy is near to 100% (Fig. 12). The calculated values of β is 2^9 and 2^{14} for 6 and 7 rounds of GIFT-128 respectively. Similar to validation experiments performed in Sect. 3, we perform 10 experiments with 50 TP and 50 TN samples with 2^5 ciphertext pairs corresponding to Δ_0 and Δ_R input differences respectively. The results for 6 rounds of GIFT-128 are shown in Table 11 and the accuracy 100% is achieved in most of the cases. The experimental results for 7 rounds of GIFT-128 are presented in Table 12 and accuracy more than 97% is achieved in most of the cases.

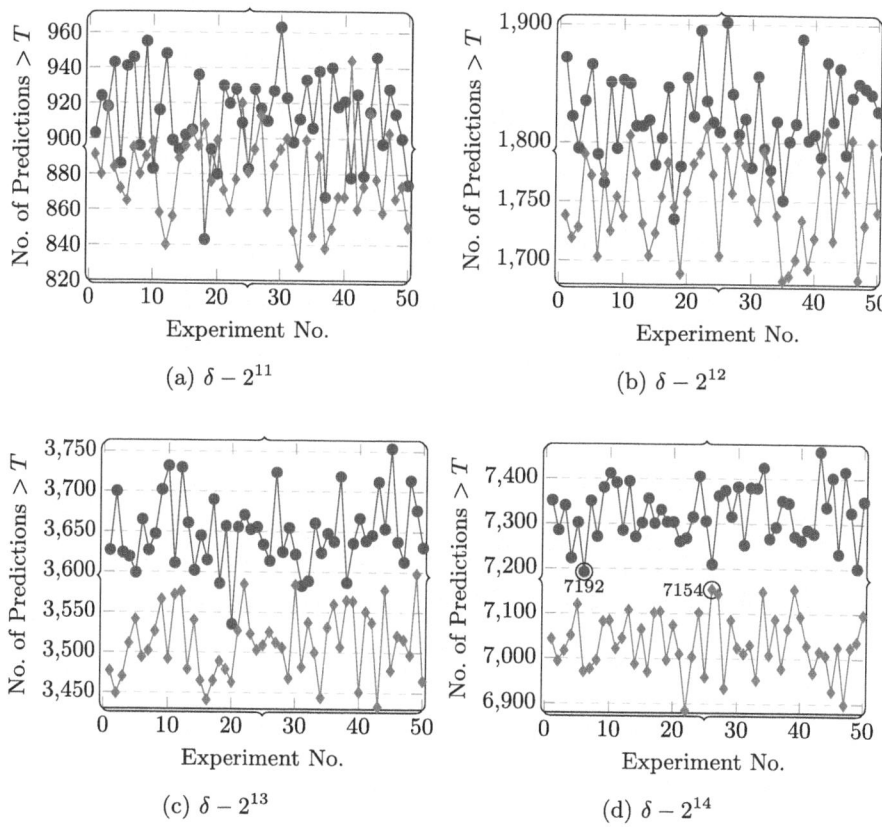

Fig. 6. C_T and β for 7-round GIFT-128 Distinguisher ($D_{r+1\cdots r+7}^{HA-ML}; m = 16$)

4.2   Differential Distinguisher for ASCON: Using 40 Bits

Similar to GIFT-128, we construct the high accuracy distinguisher for ASCON reduced to 4 rounds. The curves that are used to construct the 40-bit distinguisher are shown in Fig. 7 whereas C_T and β are mentioned in Table 8. A clear separation among the curves is visible at $\delta = 2^{18}$, therefore the data complexity β of $D_{r+1\cdots r+4}^{HA-ML}$ for 4-round ASCON becomes 2^{18} (Fig. 7(d)). We apply Algorithm 4 to calculate C_T and β for 40-bit differential distinguisher. The change in accuracy for different values of δ is shown in Fig. 12 and accuracy is near to 0.99 for $\delta = 2^{18}$. These results are almost similar to the result obtained using Algorithm 3. This distinguisher is validated through experiments with TP and TN samples. The results are shown in Table 13 and it can be observed that accuracy is more than 97% in most of the cases.

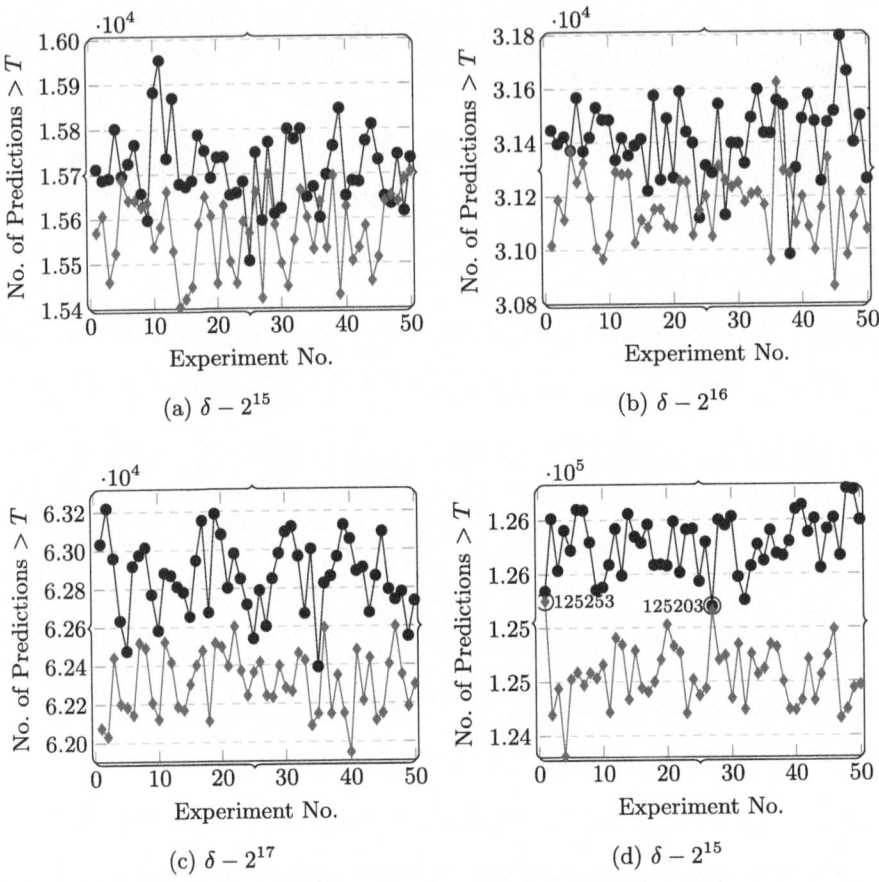

Fig. 7. C_T and β for 4-round ASCON Distinguisher $(D_{r+1\cdots r+4}^{HA-ML}; m = 40)$

Table 8. Differential Distinguisher with High Accuracy using m bits

Cipher	Rounds	m	Accuracy	Algorithm 3		Algorithm 4	
				C_T	β	C_T	β
GIFT-128	5	16	0.72	16	2^5	15	2^5
GIFT-128	6	16	0.56	225	2^9	228	2^9
GIFT-128	7	16	0.509	7173	2^{14}	7178	2^{14}
ASCON	4	40	0.502	125228	2^{18}	125161	2^{18}

5   Differential-ML Distinguisher for 8-Round GIFT-128

Yadav *et al.* [24] extended the classical differential distinguisher with the ML based distinguisher and it was called a Differential-ML distinguisher. In [24], an experimental approach to construct the differential-ML distinguisher was presented by the authors. The r-round classical differential distinguisher ($D_{1\cdots r}^{CD}$) is extended with an s-round ML based distinguisher ($D_{r+1\cdots r+s}^{ML}$) to construct the $(r+s)$-round differential-ML distinguisher ($D_{1\cdots r+s}^{CD\rightarrow ML}$) as shown in Fig. 10. In this section, we construct the 8-round Differential-ML distinguisher extending the 3 and 2 rounds of classical distinguisher with 5 and 6 rounds of ML distinguisher respectively. An Algorithm to construct the differential-ML distinguisher($D_{1\cdots r+s}^{CD\rightarrow ML}$) is presented in Appendix A. Differential-ML distinguisher $D_{1\cdots r+s}^{CD\rightarrow ML}$ is represented with five parameters namely, r-round classical distinguisher $D_{1\cdots r}^{CD}$, s-round ML distinguisher $D_{r+1\cdots r+s}^{ML}$, threshold probability T, cutoff C_T, and data complexity β. In this paper, threshold probabilty is taken as 0.5 instead of α_s (accuracy of ML based distinguisher used in [24]).

Table 9. Differential Characteristic for 20-round GIFT-128

Round (r)	Input Difference $(\triangle_r)$	Probability (2^{-p_r})
0	0000 0000 0000 0000 0000 0000 10c0 0000	0
1	0000 0000 0000 0000 0000 0000 0000 00a0	2^{-5}
2	0000 0001 0000 0000 0000 0000 0000 0000	2^{-2}
3	0800 0000 0000 0000 0000 0000 0000 0000	2^{-3}
4	2000 0000 1000 0000 0000 0000 0000 0000	2^{-2}
5	4040 0000 2020 0000 0000 0000 0000 0000	2^{-5}
6	5050 0000 0000 0000 5050 0000 0000 0000	2^{-8}
7	0000 0000 0000 0000 0000 0000 a000 a000	2^{-12}
8	0000 0000 0000 0000 0000 0011 0000 0000	2^{-4}
9	0000 0800 0000 0800 0000 0000 0000 0000	2^{-6}
10	0202 0000 0101 0000 0000 0000 0000 0000	2^{-4}
11	0000 0000 5050 0000 0000 0000 5050 0000	2^{-10}
12	0000 0000 0000 0000 0000 0000 00a0 00a0	2^{-12}
13	0000 0011 0000 0000 0000 0000 0000 0000	2^{-4}
14	0800 0000 0800 0000 0000 0000 0000 0000	2^{-6}
15	2020 0000 1010 0000 0000 0000 0000 0000	2^{-4}
16	5050 0000 0000 0000 5050 0000 0000 0000	2^{-10}
17	0000 0000 0000 0000 0000 0000 a000 a000	2^{-12}
18	0000 0000 0000 0000 0000 0011 0000 0000	2^{-4}
19	0000 0000 0000 0c00 0000 0600 0000 0000	2^{-6}
20	0002 0200 0000 0000 0000 0000 0000 0000	2^{-4}

We obtained an optimal 20-round differential[3] characteristics for GIFT-128 using MILP (Table 9). The output difference of 20-round differential charac-

---

[3] Classical Distinguisher: $D_{1\cdots r}^{CD}$.

teristics (0x000202000000000000000000000000000) is used to train the s-round $D^{ML}_{r+1\ldots r+s}$. We can use appropiate number of rounds from Table 9 to preprend with $D^{ML}_{r+1\ldots r+s}$ as per available compute power. We choose $(\Delta_{17} \to \Delta_{20})$ as $(D^{CD}_{1\ldots3})$ and $(\Delta_{18} \to \Delta_{20})$ as $(D^{CD}_{1\ldots2})$ to extend with $D^{ML}_{4\ldots8}$ and $D^{ML}_{3\ldots8}$ respectively. We use Algorithm 5 to construct high accuracy differential-ML distinguisher $(D^{CD\to ML}_{1\ldots8})$ for 8 rounds of GIFT-128. We extend 3-round $D^{CD}_{1\ldots3}$ (data complexity: 2^{14}) with 5-round $D^{ML}_{4\ldots8}$ of accuracy 0.83. The results are shown in Fig. 8. A separation of curves occurs at $\delta = 2^{18}$ and it becomes the data complexity (β) of $D^{CD\to ML}_{1\ldots8}$. We perform 10 experiments containing 50 TP and 50 TN samples where each sample consists of 2^{18} output differences. The results of these experiments are shown in Table 14. It is evident form the results that the differential-ML distinguisher $D^{CD\to ML}_{1\ldots8}$ provides 100% accuracy in most of the cases.

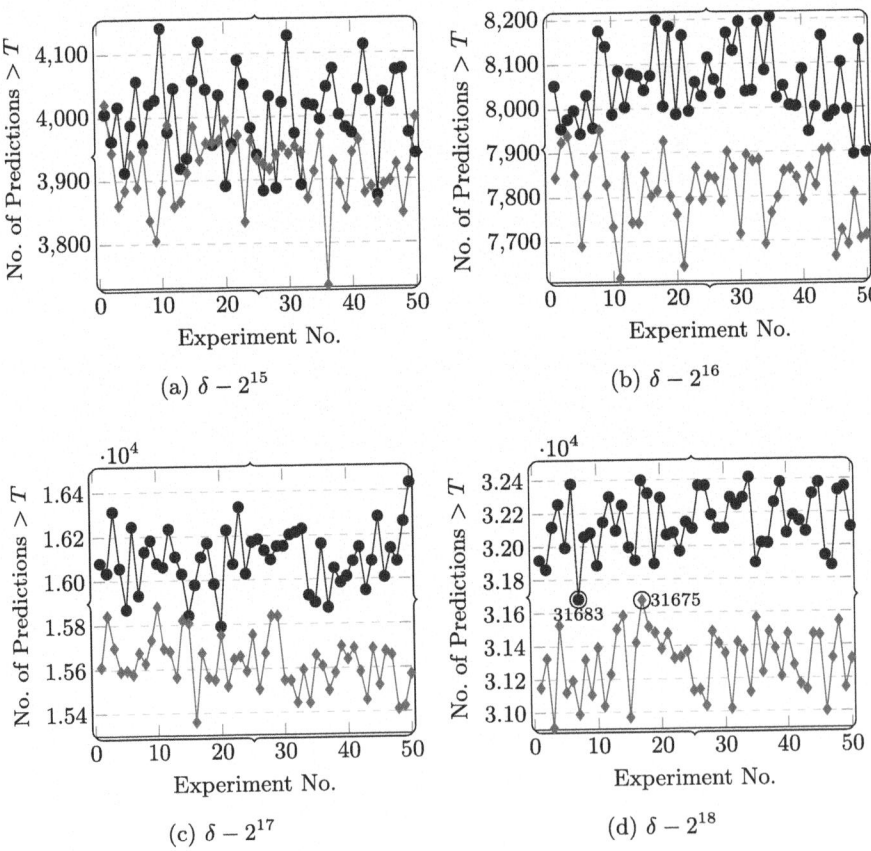

(a) $\delta - 2^{15}$

(b) $\delta - 2^{16}$

(c) $\delta - 2^{17}$

(d) $\delta - 2^{18}$

Fig. 8. C_T and β for 8-round GIFT-128 Distinguisher $(D^{CD\to ML}_{1\ldots8} : D^{CD}_{1\ldots3}; D^{ML}_{4\ldots8})$

We construct[4] another 8-round distinguisher $D_{1\ldots8}^{CD\to ML}$ using 2-round $D_{1\ldots2}^{CD}$ (data complexity: 2^{10}) with 6-round $D_{3\ldots8}^{ML}$ of accuracy 0.58. We use Algorithm 5 for construction of $D_{1\ldots8}^{CD\to ML}$ and results are shown in Fig. 9. Similar to previous case, the curves are separated at $\delta = 2^{18}$ and it becomes the data complexity β. The low accuracy of $D_{3\ldots8}^{ML}$ is compensated by a differential characteristic covering fewer rounds and therefore, the data complexity remains the same. We validate this distinguisher using the similar experiments on TP/TN samples and the results are shown in Table 14. It can be observed that accuracy of $D_{1\ldots8}^{CD\to ML}$ is more than 98% in most of the cases. A comparison of Differential-ML distinguisher with classical and ML distinguisher is shown in Table 10. The differential-ML distinguisher $D_{1\ldots8}^{CD\to ML}$ is the first differential[5] distinguisher for 8-round GIFT-128 using machine learning.

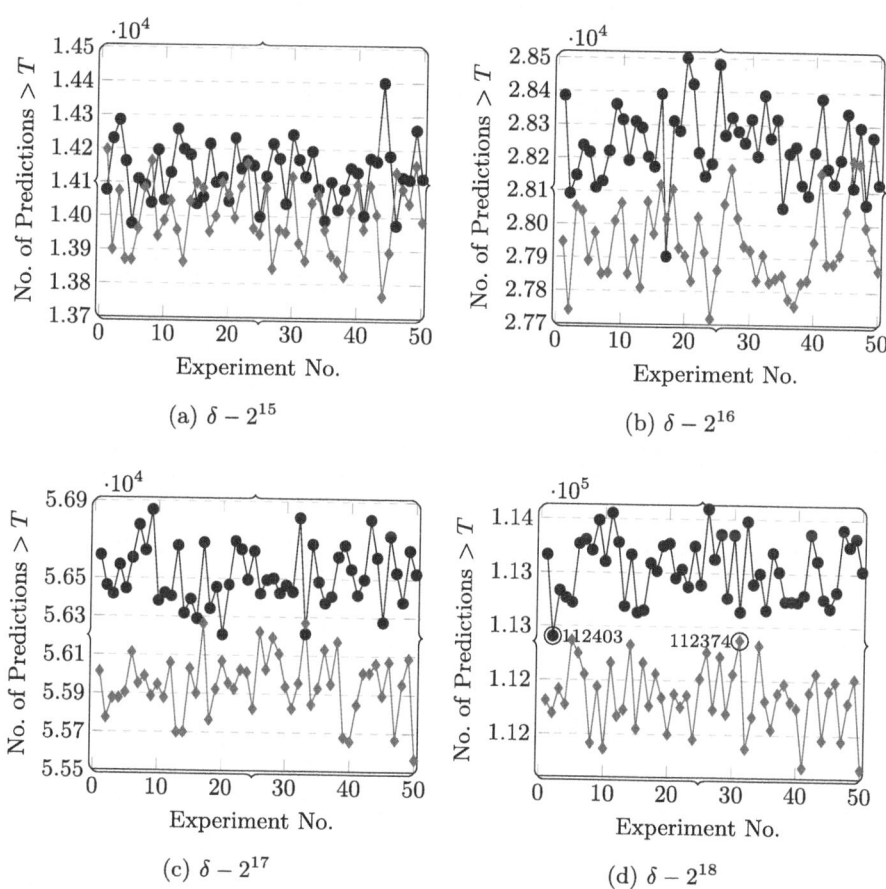

(a) $\delta - 2^{15}$

(b) $\delta - 2^{16}$

(c) $\delta - 2^{17}$

(d) $\delta - 2^{18}$

Fig. 9. C_T and β for 8-round GIFT-128 Distinguisher ($D_{1\ldots8}^{CD\to ML} : D_{1\ldots2}^{CD}; D_{3\ldots8}^{ML}$)

---

[4] ML Distinguisher: $D_{r+1\ldots r+s}^{ML}$.
[5] Differential-ML Distinguisher: $D_{1\ldots r+s}^{CD\to ML}$.

Table 10. Differential-ML Distinguisher for GIFT-128

Cipher	Rounds	Classical Distinguisher		ML Distinguisher		Differential-ML Distinguisher	
	Total	Rounds	Data Complexity	Rounds	Accuracy	Data Complexity	Accuracy
GIFT-128	8	3	2^{14}	5	0.83	2^{18}	99.8%
GIFT-128	8	2	2^{10}	6	0.58	2^{18}	99.2%

6 Conclusion

The accuracy of ML based differential distinguisher becomes very low with increased number of rounds and block size. In this paper, we have addressed this challenge and proposed a new technique that uses the existing low accuracy ML based differential distinguisher to construct a high accuracy ML based distinguisher. We obtained improved differential distinguishers for 7-round GIFT-128 and 4-round ASCON permutation with very high accuracy. Our approach provided best improvements as compared to all of the existing approaches proposed in the literature to increase the accuracy of ML based distinguishers. We also presented the ML based distinguishers that uses fewer bits for training and prediction and can be practically used for last round key recovery attacks in large block size ciphers. We used 16 bits of the output to construct 7-round distinguisher of GIFT-128 and 40 bits of the output to construct 4-round distinguisher of ASCON with an accuracy near to 100%. Further, differential distinguishers for 8 rounds of GIFT-128 are contructed using machine learning with accuracy more than 99%. The existing method of differential-ML distinguishers provides an extension of classical distinguisher using ML based distinguisher but with experimental results. These experiments cannot be performed for increased number of rounds due to very high data complexity of classical disintinguisher. Therefore, estimating the data complexity using differetial-ML distinguisher becomes a challange in such cases. In this paper, we have provided an alogrithm to increase the accuracy of ML based distinguisher near to 100% and the distinguisher works as classical distingisher in such cases with the given data complexity. In future, the feasibilty of exdending the classical distinguisher with the proposed high accuracy ML based distinguisher can be explored to provide an estimate of data complexity of extended distinguisher.

A   Appendix A Differential-ML Distinguisher: Extending Classical Differential Distinguisher Using Machine Learning

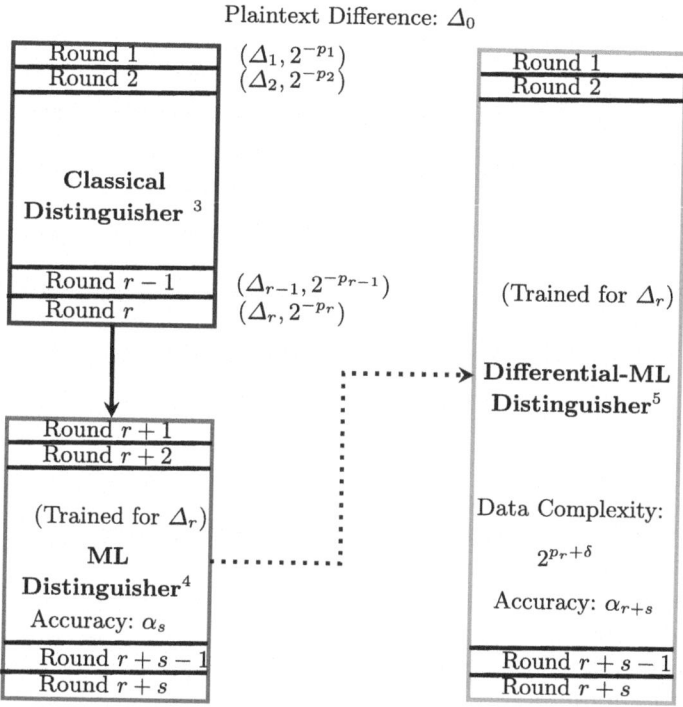

Fig. 10. Extending the Classical Distinguisher using ML Distinguisher

---

Algorithm 5: Differential-ML distinguisher $D_{1\cdots r+s}^{CD\to ML} : (D_{1\cdots r}^{CD}, D_{r+1\cdots r+s}^{ML},$
$T = 0.5, C_T, \beta)$

---

1 **Function** Construction Phase $(D_{1\cdots r}^{CD}(Data: 2^{p_r}), D_{r+1\cdots r+s}^{ML}, T = \alpha_s)$:

2     $\delta \leftarrow 0$

3   **repeat**

4   **for** $k \leftarrow$ *1 to 50* **do**

5           $K \leftarrow$ Choose a random key

6           $(P_{\Delta_0}, P'_{\Delta_0}) \leftarrow 2^\delta * 2^{p_r}$ plaintext pairs with difference Δ_0

7           $(P_R, P'_R) \leftarrow 2^\delta * 2^{p_r}$ plaintext pairs with random difference

8           $(C_{\Delta_0}, C'_{\Delta_0}) \leftarrow (\text{CIPHER}_{r+s}(P_{\Delta_0}, K), \text{CIPHER}_{r+s}(P'_{\Delta_0}, K))$

9           $(C_R, C'_R) \leftarrow (\text{CIPHER}_{r+s}(P_R, K), \text{CIPHER}_{r+s}(P'_R, K))$

10          $p_{\Delta_0} \leftarrow$ prediction probabilities for $(C_{\Delta_0} \oplus C'_{\Delta_0})$ using
            $D_{r+1\cdots r+s}^{ML}$

11          $p_R \leftarrow$ prediction probabilities for $(C_R \oplus C'_R)$ using $D_{r+1\cdots r+s}^{ML}$

12          $\text{TP} \leftarrow$ number of elements with $p_{\Delta_0} > T$

13          $\text{TN} \leftarrow$ number of elements with $p_R > T$

14   Plot the curve for TP and TN values

15   **end**

16        $\delta \leftarrow \delta + 1$

17   **until** *(TP and TN curves do not intersect)*;

18     $C_T \approx$ average of ordinates of closest points on TP and TN curves

19   Data Complexity$(\beta) \leftarrow 2^\delta * 2^{p_r}$

20   **return** C_T, β

21 **End Function**

22 **Procedure** Prediction Phase($D_{1\cdots r+s}^{CD\to ML}$):

23   Test Data (TD) $\leftarrow (.)$

24   **for** $i \leftarrow$ *1 to β* **do**

25        $P_i \leftarrow$ Choose a random plaintext

26        $P'_i = P_i \oplus \Delta_0$

27        $C_i \leftarrow \text{ORACLE}(P_i)$

28        $C'_i \leftarrow \text{ORACLE}(P'_i)$

29   Append TD by $C_i \oplus C'_i$

30   **end**

31     $p \leftarrow$ prediction probabilities for elements in TD using $D_{r+1\cdots r+s}^{ML}$

32   **if** *((number of pairs with $p > T$) > C_T)* **then**

33        $\text{ORACLE} = \text{CIPHER}_{r+s}$

34   **end**

35   **else**

36        $\text{ORACLE} \neq \text{CIPHER}_{r+s}$

37   **end**

38 **end Procedure**

B   Appendix B Accuracies of Differential Distinguisher

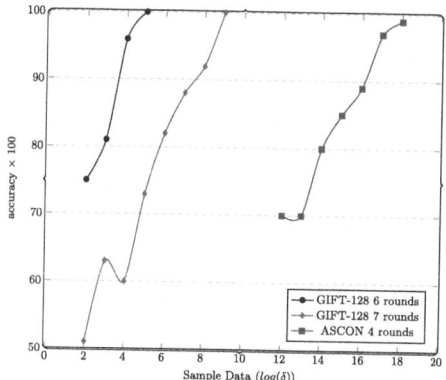

Fig. 11. Accuracies of Distinguisher for Different Values of δ using Algo. 4

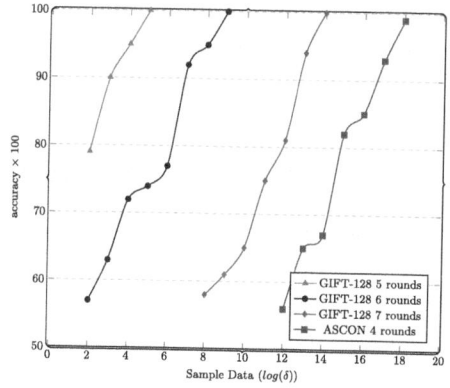

Fig. 12. Accuracies of m-bit Distinguisher for Different Values of δ using Algo. 4

C   Appendix C Experimental Accuracy of Distinguishers

Table 11. Accuracy of $D_{r+1\cdots r+6}^{HA-ML}$ for 6-round GIFT-128

Experiment No.	Algorithm 3 $s=6$, $m=128$, $C_T=12$, $\beta=2^5$			Algorithm 4 $s=6$, $m=128$, $C_T=13$, $\beta=2^5$			Algorithm 3 $s=6$, $m=16$, $C_T=225$, $\beta=2^9$			Algorithm 4 $s=6$, $m=16$, $C_T=228$, $\beta=2^9$		
	TP	TN	Accuracy	TP	TN	Accuracy	TP	TN	Accuracy	TP	TN	Accuracy
1	50	50	100	48	50	98	50	50	100	49	50	99
2	50	50	100	50	50	100	50	50	100	50	50	100
3	50	50	100	50	50	100	50	50	100	50	50	100
4	49	50	99	49	50	99	50	50	100	49	48	97
5	50	50	100	49	50	99	50	50	100	49	50	99
6	50	50	100	50	50	100	50	49	99	50	49	99
7	50	50	100	48	50	98	50	50	100	50	50	100
8	50	50	100	49	50	99	50	50	100	50	49	99
9	50	50	100	49	50	99	50	49	99	50	50	100
10	50	50	100	49	50	99	50	50	100	49	50	99

Table 12. Accuracy of $D_{r+1\cdots r+7}^{HA-ML}$ for 7-round GIFT-128

Experiment No.	Algorithm 3 $s=7$, $m=128$, $C_T=176$, $\beta=2^9$			Algorithm 4 $s=7$, $m=128$, $C_T=175$, $\beta=2^9$			Algorithm 3 $s=7$, $m=16$, $C_T=7173$, $\beta=2^{14}$			Algorithm 4 $s=7$, $m=16$, $C_T=7178$, $\beta=2^{14}$		
	TP	TN	Accuracy	TP	TN	Accuracy	TP	TN	Accuracy	TP	TN	Accuracy
1	49	50	99	48	49	97	50	48	98	49	50	99
2	49	50	99	49	50	99	49	50	99	46	50	96
3	47	50	97	48	50	98	50	50	100	48	49	97
4	49	50	99	50	50	100	50	49	99	47	50	97
5	50	50	100	49	50	99	49	49	98	49	49	98
6	49	50	99	49	49	98	49	50	99	49	50	99
7	48	50	98	49	50	99	50	49	99	48	50	98
8	50	50	100	50	50	100	47	49	96	50	50	100
9	50	50	100	50	50	100	50	50	100	50	50	100
10	47	50	97	50	48	98	49	50	99	50	50	100

Table 13. Accuracy of $D_{r+1\cdots r+4}^{HA-ML}$ for 4-round ASCON

Experiment No.	Algorithm 3 $s=4$, $m=320$, $C_T=13825$, $\beta=2^{18}$			Algorithm 4 $s=4$, $m=320$, $C_T=13895$, $\beta=2^{18}$			Algorithm 3 $s=4$, $m=40$, $C_T=125228$, $\beta=2^{18}$			Algorithm 4 $s=4$, $m=40$, $C_T=125161$, $\beta=2^{18}$		
	TP	TN	Accuracy	TP	TN	Accuracy	TP	TN	Accuracy	TP	TN	Accuracy
1	50	50	100	50	48	98	49	50	99	50	49	99
2	50	48	98	49	50	99	50	50	100	49	50	99
3	49	50	99	50	48	98	49	49	98	49	48	97
4	50	48	98	50	50	100	49	49	98	50	50	100
5	50	50	100	50	50	100	47	50	97	50	50	100
6	50	50	100	50	50	100	49	49	98	49	50	99
7	50	50	100	50	50	100	50	47	97	49	48	97
8	50	50	100	50	50	100	50	50	100	49	49	98
9	50	46	96	50	50	100	47	50	97	50	49	99
10	50	50	100	49	50	99	50	50	100	50	49	99

Table 14. Accuracy of Differential-ML Distinguisher for 8-round GIFT-128

Experiment No.	$D_{1\cdots8}^{CD\to ML} : D_{1\cdots3}^{CD}; D_{4\cdots8}^{ML}$			$D_{1\cdots8}^{CD\to ML} : D_{1\cdots2}^{CD}; D_{3\cdots8}^{ML}$		
	$\beta = 2^{18}$			$\beta = 2^{18}$		
	TP	TN	Accuracy	TP	TN	Accuracy
1	50	50	**100**	50	48	**98**
2	50	50	**100**	50	50	**100**
3	50	49	**99**	50	50	**100**
4	50	50	**100**	49	50	**99**
5	50	50	**100**	50	50	**100**
6	50	50	**100**	49	49	**98**
7	50	49	**99**	50	49	**99**
8	50	50	**100**	50	49	**99**
9	50	50	**100**	50	50	**100**
10	50	50	**100**	49	50	**99**

References

1. Baksi, A., Breier, J., Chen, Y., Dong, X.: Machine learning assisted differential distinguishers for lightweight ciphers (extended version). Cryptology ePrint Archive, 2020/571 (2020). https://eprint.iacr.org/2020/571
2. Banik, S., et al.: GIFT-COFB. Cryptology ePrint Archive, 2020/738 (2020). https://eprint.iacr.org/2020/738
3. Benamira, A., Gerault, D., Peyrin, T., Tan, Q.Q. : A deeper look at machine learning-based cryptanalysis. In: Standaert, F.X.A. (eds.) Advances in Cryptology-EUROCRYPT 2021, LNCS, vol. 12696, pp. 805–835. Springer, Cham (2021)
4. Banik, S., Pandey, S.K., Peyrin, T., Sasaki,Y., Sim, S.M.,Todo,Y.: GIFT: a small present - towards reaching the limit of lightweight encryption. In: Cryptographic Hardware and Embedded Systems - CHES 2017, 19th International Conference, vol. 10529, pp. 321–345 (2017)
5. Biham, E., Shamir, A.: Differential cryptanalysis of DES-like cryptosystems. J. Cryptol. 4(1), 3–72 (1991)
6. Dobraunig, C., Eichlseder, M., Mendel, F., Schläffer, M.: ASCONv1. 2: lightweight authenticated encryption and hashing. J. Cryptol. 34, 1–42 (2021)
7. Erlacher, J., Mendel, F., Eichlseder, M.: Bounds for the security of Ascon against differential and linear cryptanalysis. IACR Trans. Symmet. Cryptol. 2022(1), 64–87 (2022). https://doi.org/10.46586/tosc.v2022.i1.64-87
8. Ebrahimi, A., Regazzoni, F., Palmieri, P.: Reducing the cost of machine learning differential attacks using bit selection and apartial ml-distinguisher. In: International conference on Foundations and Practice of Security. FPS 2022, LNCS, vol. 13877, pp. 123–141. Springer, Cham (2021)
9. Gohr, A., Leander, G., Neumann P.: An assessment of differential neural distinguishers, 2022. Cryptology ePrint Archive, Paper 2022/1521 (2022). https://eprint.iacr.org/2022/1521

10. Gohr, A.: Improving attacks on round-reduced speck32/64 using deep learning. In: Proceedings of Advances in Cryptology - CRYPTO 2019, SantaBarbara, pp. 150–179. Springer, Cham (2019)

11. Hou, Z., Ren, J., Chen, S.: Improve neural distinguishers of Simon and Speck. Secur. Commun. Netw. **2021**(1), 1–11 (2021)

12. Liu, J.S., Ren, J.J., Chen, S.Z.: A deep learning aided differential distinguisher improvement framework with more lightweight and universality. Cybersecurity (2023)

13. Lyu, L., Tu, Y., Zhang, Y.: Improving the deep-learning-based differential distinguisher and applications to Simeck. In: 2022 IEEE 25th International Conference on Computer Supported Cooperative Work in Design, CSCWD, pp. 465–470. IEEE (2022)

14. Matsui, M.: On correlation between the order of S-boxes and the strength of DES. Proceeding of International Conference. EUROCRYPT, May 1994, pp. 366–375 (1994)

15. Mouha, N., Wang, Q., Gu, D., Preneel, B.: Differential and linear cryptanalysis using mixed-integer linear programming. In: Wu, C., Yung, M., Lin, D. (ed.) Inscrypt 2011. LNCS, , vol. 7537, pp. 57–76. Springer (2011)

16. National Institute of Standards and Technology. Lightweight Cryptography, Finalists. NIST (2021). https://csrc.nist.gov/projects/lightweight-cryptography/finalists

17. Sun, S., et al.: Analysis of AES, SKINNY, and Others with Constraint Programming. IACR Trans. Symmet. Cryptol. **1**, 281–306 (2017)

18. Sun, S., Hu, L., Wang, P., Qiao, K., Ma, X., Song, L.: Automatic security evaluation and (related-key) differential characteristic search: application to SIMON, PRESENT, LBlock, DES and other bit-oriented block ciphers. In: International Conference on the Theory and Application of Cryptology and Information Security, pp. 158–178. Springer (2014)

19. Shen, D., Song, Y., Lu, Y., Long, S., Tian, S.: Neural differential distinguisher for GIFT-128 and ASCON. J. Inf. Secur. Appl. **82** (2024)

20. Tian, W., Hu, B.: Deep learning assisted differential cryptanalysis for the lightweight Cipher Simon. KSII Trans. Internet Inf. Syst. **15**(2), 600–616 (2021)

21. Wang, G., Wang, G.: Improved differential-ML distinguisher: machine learning based generic extension for differential analysis. In: International Conference on Information and Communications Security, pp. 21–38. Springer (2021)

22. Wang, G., Wang, G.: Keeping classical distinguisher and neural distinguisher in balance. J. Inf. Secur. Appl. **84** (2024)

23. Wang, G., Wang, G., He, Y.: Improved machine learning assisted (related-key) differential distinguishers for lightweight ciphers. In: 2021 IEEE 20th International Conference on Trust, Security and Privacy in Computing and Communications (trustCom), pp. 164–171. IEEE (2021)

24. Yadav, T., Kumar, M.: Differential-ML distinguisher: machine learning based generic extension for differential cryptanalysis. In: Longa, P., Rafols, C. (eds.) Progress in Cryptology- LATINCRYPT 2021, vol. 12912, pp. 191–212 (2021)

Author Index

J. Knechtel et al. (Eds.): SPACE 2024, LNCS 15351, pp. 317–318, 2025.
https://doi.org/10.1007/978-3-031-80408-3

Printed and bound by CPI Group (UK) Ltd, Croydon, CR0 4YY

29/04/2026

02099540-0001